D1541583

Game Design Foundations

Second Edition

Roger E. Pedersen

Wordware Publishing, Inc.

Library of Congress Cataloging-in-Publication Data

Pedersen, Roger E.
  Game design foundations / by Roger E. Pedersen. — 2nd ed.
    p. cm.
  Includes index.
  ISBN 13: 978-1-59822-034-6
  ISBN 10: 1-59822-034-9 (paperback; CD-ROM)
  1. Computer games--Programming. I. Title.
  QA76.76.C672P43 2009
  794.8'1526--dc22   2009019189
                                                        CIP

Jones and Bartlett Publishers, LLC
40 Tall Pine Drive
Sudbury, MA 01776
978-443-5000
info@jbpub.com
www.jbpub.com

ISBN 13: 978-1-59822-034-6
ISBN 10: 1-59822-034-9

10 9 8 7 6 5 4 3 2 1
0905

This book is dedicated to my beautiful daughters
Michele, Brooke, Megan, and Meredith
and granddaughters Rileigh, Brianna, Sydney, and Lillian.

Contents

Contents

Contents

Contents

Contents

Contents

Acknowledgments

Special thanks to:

The book's technical reader and editor: Alan Dunkin

The chapter technical readers: Wayne Imlach, Devin Grayson, Nick Smolney, Joseph Hatcher, and Sean Scott

Photographers: Bessalel Yarjovski and Dorothy Cimo

The Wordware editorial staff: Tim McEvoy, Martha McCuller, and Beth Kohler

Chapter 1

The Game Designer

For the past two decades, people I've met in the streets proudly state it to me.

For over 20 years, people in planes, trains, buses, and automobiles have chatted about it with me.

In every computer superstore and every computer outlet, gaming fans have argued and bragged about it.

For numerous years at computer gaming conferences and conventions, game programmers, graphic artists, and even producers have secretly whispered it to me.

Even now, you the reader are thinking the exact same thoughts:

"I have a concept for the most amazing and revolutionary game."

"This game of mine will blow away every game that has ever been published."

"I played the 'hot game,' and with a few of my additions and real 'cool' puzzles or tricks it could be so much better."

We all have great gaming concepts that would have millions of gaming fanatics praising our genius and creativity. So why aren't there millions of game designers? What transpires from concept to a product on the shelf?

NJ IGDA game design challenge

Let's get started with some background information we need to understand before we begin designing this great game that exists in our minds.

Game Designers Are *Not* Programmers

You are a designer, a creator of game concepts. You need to be able to convey your ideas for others to carry out.

You do not need to be an expert in programming, programming languages, operating systems, or what 3D card is best for your game.

Your job is to tell the programmers, in a document, to design for you a "temple." It is the programmers' job to create your temple by using any material they wish — marble, brick, wood, or even straw. They must be able to make the structure stable and functional.

Game Designers Are *Not* Artists

You are the designer and not the artistic talent. You do not need to be an expert in graphic packages, various graphics file formats, or graphics libraries.

Your job is to tell the graphic artists, in a document, that your "temple" needs to be decorated. It is the artists' job to decide how to set the environment by creating marble statues, elaborate tapestries, ornate wooden wall carvings, and exquisite stained glass creations. There will be objects and characters in your design, but the artists will be given freedom to create them (see Pedersen Principle 3 in Chapter 2).

The designer must supply the artists with samples of environments, layouts of user interfaces, and maps of the terrain or world. Later, we talk about research that you, as the designer, must provide the staff regarding your game (see Chapter 6, "Game Research").

Game Designers Are *Not* Audio Engineers or Musicians

You are the designer and not a songwriter, composer, or sound effects person.

Your job is to tell the audio engineers and music people when and where there is to be music and sound effects in your game or world.

Through research you will be able to describe your thoughts and suggest possible audio examples of music styles (jazz, classical, or rock), music moods (excited, calming, or scary), voices for characters (e.g., famous voices or accents or dialects like British, Southern American, and Spanish), and sound effects (based on player input or gameplay reactions).

Game Designers Are Visionaries

You are the creator, the life giver, and the visionary of your game.

The game is a dream running inside your head that needs to be expressed to others. Publishers, producers, programmers, graphic artists, audio specialists, and even you yourself need to see written documentation describing your fantastic vision, your concept. You need to map out the playing field, describe the rules and features that make your concept unique and special, and resolve the potential unknown and empty areas (an area of unforeseen paths).

No one else can make these judgments and additions to your vision. Your decisions should be free from technology, free from any limitations of the developer's ability, and able to go outside the boundaries of today's thinking. This is your innovation, your vision, your genius. Let the technical and artistic people best implement your ideas and negotiate your design issues. Innovation is a possibility becoming a reality.

The Pedersen Advice to Those Who Are Not Yet Gaming Professionals

Often high school students and their parents ask me about "going to college to be a game designer" (or game programmer or game artist). I have been involved in designing curriculum and teaching game development at prestigious colleges such as NYU, Bloomfield College (http://campus.bloomfield.edu/cat/gamedev.asp), Gibbs College (a two-year college), and Globe Institute of Technology and been an advisor and curriculum organizer for Thinnox Design Academy (thinnox.com), a digital technology school in Mississauga, Canada. It is my firm belief that a student should get his or her degree in a discipline such as programming or graphic arts so if the gaming career doesn't work out, he or she has a solid education to fall back on. I have seen enthusiastic college graduates get burned out by the gaming industry. I have also seen major layoffs that had hundreds of gaming professionals collecting unemployment. A game programmer can easily land a programming job at a bank, brokerage firm, even at Microsoft or Apple. An artist can work at an advertising firm, an Internet firm, a magazine publisher, or develop websites for small businesses. I don't want to discourage anyone from entering the exciting game business, but I also don't want to see you on the sidewalk outside the GDC (Game Developers Conference) in San Francisco with a sign reading "Will Design Games for Food!"

Now back to the good stuff....

Can My "Idea" Make Millions?

In this book, I give away over 1,200 ideas (on the companion CD) that would make excellent games. If you learn anything from this chapter, it should be that your hard work and ability to communicate your ideas to others to make the finished game is what a game designer does. We all have "ideas" for games. I don't know how many want-to-be game designers can't tell me about their secret game because they think that I will hear it, run out, spend 6 to 12 months developing their game, and make millions without them. Believe me, I have many game ideas that I don't have time to develop, so why in the world would I steal your game idea? Unless you have the dedication to spend hundreds of hours working on a game idea, and unless you can effectively communicate in detail every corner of the world you're creating, the game will never be finished. Only you can champion your game concept and vision.

And boasts of having the "world's best game idea" are not unique. The film industry has heard similar boasts since it began back in the days of black and white silent films. Just take a look at a few articles on the Internet such as Tom Sloper's "Game Design 101: "I Have a Great Idea for a Video Game… How Do I Sell It and Get Rich and Famous?" (www.sloperama.com/advice/idea.htm), David Perry's (the Shiny founder and game industry legend) "Don't Send That Game Design!" (www.dperry.com/archives/articles/by_dp/dont_send_that_1/), and Alan Emrich's "The Real Value of a Great Game Idea: Will Your Brilliant Game Idea Make You Rich and Famous?"(www.alanemrich.com/Writing_Archive_pages/Game_idea_value.htm).

Why Make Game$?

Because the gaming industry makes billions!

Let's look at the salaries for programmers, artists, game designers, producers, audio engineers, and testers from 2006, 2007, and 2008 published by *Game Developer* magazine in its *Game Career Guide* "Game Industry Salary Survey" (http://gamedeveloper.texterity.com/gamedeveloper/2008careerguide/).

Programmers' Salaries

Average salary across all levels:
  2006: $82,107 2007: $80,886 2008: $83,383

Experience	Title	2006	2007	2008
< 3 years	Programmer	$52,989	$57,913	$57,665
	Lead Programmer	$76,848	$73,311	$75,761
	Technical Director	N/A	N/A	$80,833
3-6 years	Programmer	$73,618	$74,707	$75,070
	Lead Programmer	$81,591	$80,132	$77,418
	Technical Director	$107,738	$91,944	$111,250
> 6 years	Programmer	$90,658	$88,841	$94,525
	Lead Programmer	$100,528	$98,152	$103,409
	Technical Director	$121,071	$119,142	$128,676

2007: On average, women represented 3% and made $71,071 compared to the men's $81,186.

2008: On average, women represented 3% and made $78,184 compared to the men's $83,579.

Artists' and Animators' Salaries

Average salary across all levels:

    2006: $65,986   2007: $65,107   2008: $66,594

Experience	Title	2006	2007	2008
< 3 years	Artist/Animator	$45,675	$45,396	$43,657
	Lead Artist/Animator	N/A	$46,618	$40,417
3-6 years	Artist/Animator	$61,065	$61,661	$58,452
	Lead Artist/Animator	$68,112	$69,052	$68,041
	Art Director	$65,313	$69,000	$81,071
> 6 years	Artist/Animator	$69,457	$71,964	$74,335
	Lead Artist/Animator	$82,750	$86,250	$84,236
	Art Director	$98,696	$99,136	$102,806

2007: On average, women represented 9% and made $55,234 compared to the men's $66,104.

2008: On average, women represented 8% and made $61,250 compared to the men's $67,056.

Game Designers' Salaries

(We didn't forget about you!)

Average salary across all levels:

    2006: $63,986   2007: $61,538   2008: $63,649

Experience	Title	2006	2007	2008
< 3 years	Game Designer	$43,486	$44,342	$46,208
	Writer	$51,944	$45,313	$51,731
3-6 years	Game Designer	$54,777	$52,892	$54,716
	Writer	$61,000	$48,500	$59,167
	Lead Designer	$72,125	$66,944	$60,833
> 6 years	Game Designer	$69,813	$67,361	$74,688
	Writer	N/A	$80,147	$52,500
	Lead Designer	$88,734	$88,575	$98,370

2007: On average, women represented 7% and made $54,597 compared to the men's $62,031.

2008: On average, women represented 8% and made $55,156 compared to the men's $64,396.

Game Producers' Salaries

Average salary across all levels:

2006: N/A   2007: $77,131   2008: $79,970

Experience	Title	2007	2008
< 3 years	Associate Producer	N/A	$46,667
	Game Producer	$52,885	$62,500
3-6 years	Associate Producer	N/A	$55,833
	Game Producer	$62,150	$67,500
	Executive Producer	$92,206	$93,611
> 6 years	Associate Producer	N/A	$65,147
	Game Producer	$82,981	$89,184
	Executive Producer	$127,372	$125,000

2007: On average, women represented 18% and made $67,031 compared to the men's $79,375.

2008: On average, women represented 18% and made $72,398 compared to the men's $79,970.

QA (Quality Assurance) Testers' Salaries

(A foot in the door position.)
Average salary across all levels:

2006: $37,210   2007: $37,861   2008: $30,309

Experience	Title	2006	2007	2008
< 3 years	Game Tester	$24,797	$24,559	$25,142
	Q/A Lead	$33,125	$29,907	$38,611
3-6 years	Game Tester	$29,722	$28,750	$38,553
	Q/A Lead	$43,125	$45,786	$41,905
> 6 years	Game Tester	N/A	N/A	$43,056
	Q/A Lead	$61,310	$66,574	$70,658

2007: On average, women represented 5% and made an unknown salary (low sample size) compared to the men's $37,917.

2008: On average, women represented 6% and made $34,375 compared to the men's $39,309.

Audio/Sound Designers' and Musicians' Salaries

Average salary across all levels: 2008: $73,764

Experience	Title	2008
< 3 years	Sound/Audio Designer	$64,583
3-6 years	Sound/Audio Designer	$59,605
	Composer/Musician	$61,500
	Sound/Audio Director	$80,192
> 6 years	Sound/Audio Designer	$83,214
	Composer/Musician	$91,413

2008: On average, women represented 8% and made $69,375 compared to the men's $73,764.

Workshop

Assignments

Many future "game designers" read the first edition of this book and thought the concepts presented were relevant only to computer and console games. I believe that the concepts and practices that you will learn in this book extend to all games including board games, ARGs (alternate reality games), and electronic games.

Our first assignment is one that the members of the NJ IGDA (International Game Developer's Association) often enjoy participating and competing in. (The NJ chapter has weekly Internet chats on Sundays at 9 p.m. EST and can be contacted at NJChapter.com and through the IGDA website at www.IGDA.org.)

Assignment 1:

Every town has a dollar store or a pharmacy that sells inexpensive toys and office supplies. The first part of this assignment is to visit that store and spend $10 to $20 on graph paper and 10 to 15 randomly selected toy and office supply items. As an example (this is not a shopping list), some of these items could be play money, paper clips, toy plastic soldiers, a collection of erasers, and so on. Be creative! You're a game designer!

Take your collection of stuff and divide it in half. For more fun, place the items in a paper bag so they are hidden and randomly draw out half of the items. Using the graph paper and the selected items (the "stuff"), set a timer for 15 minutes and design a game.

At the NJ IGDA meetings, we break into four or more teams of four members and create our game based on the leader's scenario. Past scenarios have been to create a game for the Nintendo DS (Dual Screen), create a game for handicapped players, or create a sports game based on a reality show.

Assignment 2:

This assignment is based on an NJ IGDA meeting led by one of its coordinators, Mike Sweeney, and uses information from Wikipedia to describe Acclaim Entertainment and its game titles. (From http://en.wikipedia.org/wiki/Acclaim_Entertainment, April 20, 2009.)

Acclaim Entertainment was an American video game developer and publisher. It developed, published, marketed, and distributed interactive entertainment software for a variety of hardware platforms, including Sega's Mega Drive/Genesis, Saturn, Dreamcast, and Game Gear; Nintendo's NES, SNES, Nintendo 64, GameCube, Game Boy, Game Boy Color, and Game Boy Advance; Sony's PlayStation and PlayStation 2; Microsoft's Xbox; and, to a lesser extent, personal computer systems and arcade games. It also released video games for the Sega Master System in Europe.

The waning of the arcade game industry, coupled with some poor sales and public enthusiasm for several key titles, led to the eventual loss of many of their licenses. One result of this was their late refactoring of the Dave Mirra's Freestyle BMX series. To add to that, their arcade game Batman Forever had poor sales also due to poor gameplay.

A less significant aspect of Acclaim's business was the development and publication of strategy guides relating to their software products and the issuance of "special edition" comic magazines, via Acclaim Comics, to support the more lucrative brand names.

During Acclaim's decline toward bankruptcy, they made several infamous business and marketing decisions. One example was a promise to UK gamers that a £500 prize would be awarded to up to five winners who would name their baby "Turok" to promote the release of Turok Evolution. Another was an attempt to buy advertising space on actual tombstones for the Shadow Man game.

Acclaim also suffered multiple lawsuits, a portion of them with former partners. Mary-Kate and Ashley Olsen sued over unpaid royalties. In the last iteration of the BMX series, semi-nude, nude, and porn content (e.g., full motion video of strippers and nude female riders) was added in hopes of boosting sales. However, like most of their other contemporary titles, BMX XXX sold poorly and was derided for its trashy content and poor gameplay. Dave Mirra himself publicly disowned the game, stating that he was not involved in the decision to include nudity, and he sued Acclaim for fear of being associated with BMX XXX. Another was from Acclaim's own investors, claiming that Acclaim management had published misleading financial reports.

According to the same article in Wikipedia, Acclaim filed for Chapter 7 bankruptcy in September of 2004, which virtually annihilated the company by liquidating all assets to pay off the company's enormous debt of reportedly over $100 million.

Your Assignment Is…

You've been hired by wealthy investors and given $10 million to purchase the "fire sale" Acclaim properties in a secret bid. Read the game descriptions on the following pages and submit your bid to purchase one or more of these Acclaim titles. On your own or in a team (for more "fun") follow these instructions:

1. The total U.S. dollars bid on all game titles desired cannot exceed $10 million.

2. After 20 minutes of reading the supplied descriptions and deciding your bid on each available title, write on a blank sheet of paper the game's title, your name or team number, and your bid amount for that title.

3. Upon receiving the bids, the designated judge or teacher will sort each title by bid value and reveal who has won each title.

4. Each designer or team must design a premise for that license's sequel, describing the gameplay and unique selling point (USP) or proposition. (USP was once known as "unique selling point" but is now more commonly referred to as "unique selling proposition.")

5. Each team will present the game premise, and the other teams will by secret vote grade that team. The judge or teacher will collect the votes. The designer or team with the highest score wins, and is determined by adding up the points awarded for each game license purchased. Each game is scored with an A being 5 points, B being 4, C being 3, and D being 2.

   For example, if Team A purchased two games and game one is scored as an A (5 points) and game two gets a C (3 points), then Team A has earned 8 points. The strategy involves designing the best game(s) within the time limit.

The game titles and series up for sale are the following:

- All-Star Baseball
- Burnout
- XGRA: Extreme G-Racing Association
- Forsaken
- Shadow Man series
- Turok Dinosaur Hunter series game Turok: Evolution
- Mary-Kate and Ashley Olsen series

The following illustrations and descriptions may be used to help you with your decisions.

All-Star Baseball

(from http://en.wikipedia.org/wiki/All-Star_Baseball, April 20, 2009)

All-Star Baseball is a baseball video game series developed and published by Acclaim Entertainment. The series began in 1998 with the release of All-Star Baseball '99. The announcers John Sterling and Michael Kay have been added during the ballgame from 1998-2000 for N64. The final release in the series (due to the bankruptcy of Acclaim) is All-Star Baseball 2005.

Within the individual games, there are several different modes of play, such as exhibition, managing an existing Major League Baseball team, or creating a team. Many North American cities are available for "expansion" in addition to Mexico City and Puerto Rico.

The series usually features pro-athlete Derek Jeter on the cover.

Burnout

(from http://en.wikipedia.org/wiki/Burnout_(series), April 20, 2009)

Burnout (sometimes Burnout: Battle Racing Ignited) is a series of high-speed racing games for the PlayStation 2, PlayStation 3, PlayStation Portable, Xbox, Xbox 360, Nintendo DS, and Nintendo GameCube game consoles. Also, for the very first time, a PC version of the latest installment in the series, Burnout Paradise, has been released.

The game series was developed by Criterion Games and published by Acclaim and later EA Games. Burnout and Burnout 2: Point of Impact drew critical acclaim and a large fan base in Europe, as well as an underground following in the U.S. It was not until the release of Burnout 3: Takedown that the series would have mass appeal to U.S. players.

Burnout originally featured a small collection of cars, including the small Compact, the Saloon (as well as a sports-modified GT version), the Pickup, and the Muscle. This collection grew in Burnout 2 to include cars such as the Oval racer, the Cop Car, the Classic, the Gangster, and the Hot Rod. Once Burnout 3: Takedown was released, the original cars were no longer used, with the exception of the Custom Coupe Ultimate, a lime green coupe that was one of the "Custom" cars in Burnout 2 (this car also reappears in Burnout Legends and Burnout Dominator). The same happened in Burnout Revenge, where the car collection was entirely new. For the most part, Burnout Paradise's car collection is all new but there are some vehicles (such as the aforementioned "Custom Coupe Ultimate" and the Custom Roadster from Burnout 2 or the Revenge Racer from Burnout Revenge) that are models from previous Burnout games. Paradise is also the first Burnout game to designate manufacturers and real car model names for its vehicles (such as the "Carson Annihilator" or "Nakamura Ikusa GT").

XGRA: Extreme-G Racing Association

(from http://en.wikipedia.org/wiki/XGRA, April 20, 2009)

XGRA: Extreme G-Racing Association is a futuristic racing game and the follow-up to Extreme-G 3. This game features more tracks as well as a brand new weapon system.

At the turn of 2080, SINN (Sports Interactive News Network) announced XGRA (Extreme-G Racing Association) had declared the Global Season Tour of 2080 was going to take place, so riders from all over the world geared up and got ready to compete.

The game features a wide range of riders, tracks, and bikes. These bikes can accelerate incredibly rapidly, going from 0 mph to 300 mph in a matter of seconds. It is even possible to break the sound barrier during gameplay: breaking of the sound barrier occurs around 750 mph, at which point all sound effects except the item collection sound, other drivers' taunts, and the sounds of your own weapons firing cut out.

Forsaken

(from http://en.wikipedia.org/wiki/Forsaken_(game), April 20, 2009)

Forsaken is a 3D first-person shooter video game. The game was developed by Probe Entertainment (UK) and distributed by Acclaim Entertainment (USA). The PC version was released on April 30, 1998. Forsaken was also released on the PlayStation and Nintendo 64.

Similar to Descent, Forsaken had a strong following due to its "six degrees of freedom" gameplay, but suffered in popularity to the conventional ground-based 3D first-person shooter games because of its challenging nature.

In the distant future, the advancement of science has exceeded humanity's ability to control it. During a subatomic experiment, an accident causes an uncontrollable fusion reaction, utterly destroying the surface of the planet Earth.

One year later, Earth has been classified as "condemned" by the ruling imperial theocracy, meaning that it is now legal for anyone to salvage anything left on the planet. Mercenaries from all over come to raid the dead planet, forced to battle not only each other, but the robot sentinels that the government has left behind.

Forsaken is based on a 3D engine that allows unlimited 360-degree movements. This concept is similar to the Descent series. According to a *GameSpot* review, "Forsaken is, at its core, a Descent clone. But stunning graphics, a dazzling array of weapons, and above-average level design make the whole thing seem fresh."

The single-player mode has four difficulty levels: easy, normal, hard, and total mayhem. Each has progressively stronger enemies and less ammo to spare. Due to the near-impossible challenge presented by the latter mode, Acclaim provided the patch 1.00 that (among other things) decreased the difficulty of the game dramatically. There are 15 levels that have to be completed by the player — sometimes within a time limit — and occasionally include a huge end-boss against which the player must exhaust a fair amount of ammunition while dodging excessive retaliatory fire. In order to complete a mission, different efforts must be made by the player such as finding the exit or activating triggers to open locked doors. The primary objective is to destroy the enemies within a level. The enemies are static (turrets launching homing missiles, drones, other mercenaries, etc.), though not all will be spawned at the start of a level.

Each level includes a hidden crystal, and once all are collected a secret map is unlocked.

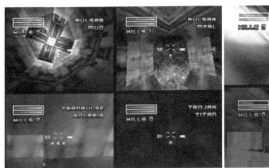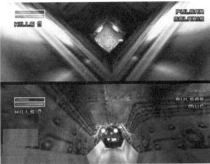

Shadow Man

(from http://en.wikipedia.org/wiki/Shadow_Man_(video_game), April 20, 2009)

Shadow Man is a video game developed by Acclaim Studios Teesside and published by Acclaim Entertainment. It was designed by Guy Miller and Simon Phipps. It is loosely based on the *Shadowman* comic book series published by Valiant Comics and was released in 1999 for the Nintendo 64, Sony PlayStation, Sega Dreamcast, and PC. A sequel, entitled Shadow Man: 2econd Coming, was released exclusively on Sony's PlayStation 2 three years later in 2002.

Shadow Man is an adventure game comparable to games like Tomb Raider or the Legend of Zelda series. Most gameplay takes place in a third-person perspective, though there is an option for first-person aiming. The player can run, jump, climb, swim, and perform various other actions. Combat is focused on the use of firearms, the most important of which is the Shadowgun, a pistol through which Mike can channel his shadow power and reap life energy from his enemies. Numerous other weapons also exist, such as voodoo implements, ordinary Earth weapons, and some oddly-designed Deadside firearms.

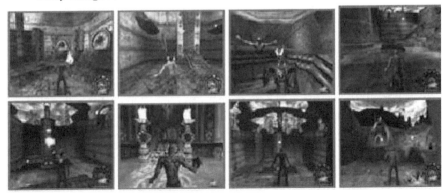

Shadow Man is also one of few games of its time to feature a 3D targeting feature (pioneered by The Legend of Zelda: Ocarina of Time a year earlier). This allowed for the player to lock on to an enemy and strafe around them as desired during combat. Also unique to a game of its time, Shadow Man has a dual-wielding system, allowing the player to equip two items controlled by two different buttons/keys and use them independently of each other yet at the same time.

Turok Dinosaur Hunter Series

(from http://en.wikipedia.org/wiki/Turok:_Evolution, April 20, 2009)

Turok: Evolution is a first-person shooter video game developed and published by Acclaim Entertainment. The game was originally released for the Game Boy Advance but then later released for the Nintendo GameCube, PlayStation 2, and Xbox in 2002. A port for the PC was released in 2003 for the European market. It is followed by a 2008 entry in the Turok video games series, simply called Turok.

The game follows Tal'Set, a Native American who is transported to the Lost Land while fighting Captain Tobias Bruckner of the United States Army; apparently this occurs in the late 19th century, around the time of the Indian Wars. He is rescued by the seer Tarkeen who says he is the legendary Son of Stone, known to them as Turok.

The story then introduces a new villain, the Sleg, who are a lot like the dinosoids and Purr-Linn from the previous games. The Sleg themselves largely seem to have no greater objective than enslaving humans. Eventually, however, their leader, the genocidal Lord Tyrannus, reveals his plan to destroy the human city of Galyana with an army led by a colossal beast called the Juggernaut, which resembles a Amphicoelias, but is much larger. He also allows Bruckner to join the Sleg army. When Tal'Set saves the River Village's "Wise Father" from a Sleg base, he re-encounters Bruckner and a team of Sleg. Both he and the "Wise Father" are quickly rescued by Djunn. Later, Tal'Set destroys the Suspended City that bridges the gap across a ravine that Lord Tyrannus' forces are attempting to cross to reach Galyana. Following this, he engages and disables the Juggernaut.

At the very end of the game, Bruckner appears riding a Tyrannosaurus and serves as the game's last boss (the first boss being a Styracosaurus). Tal'Set defeats Bruckner, but refuses to kill him: Tal'Set doesn't believe he deserves a warrior's death. He leaves him to be eaten by Compsognathus instead.

The game ends with Tal'Set accepting his role as Son of Stone and becoming Turok. Lord Tyrannus is also seen at a Sleg castle, mourning his defeat.

Mary-Kate and Ashley Olsen Series

The Olsen twins, Mary-Kate and Ashley, are turning 16, and they're celebrating with this collection of party games and,  you guessed it, driving lessons. The good news is that if you can help them get past the obstacles and pass the test, they'll take you out with their new driver's licenses to a variety of fun mini-game activities like rock climbing, riding Jet Skis, surfing, ATV quad racing, and shopping for clothes. Earn points in the party games and spend them to upgrade the car and unlock cool tunes and cooler outfits.

Remember, after purchasing this title you have to negotiate with the Olsen Twins on your game's contents.

Thoughts for Discussion

Based on the game industry's salary data, discuss diversity in the industry and how it can be improved.

Chapter 2

The "Pedersen Principles"

After going on several game company interviews where I told the same game work experience stories, I decided to write down these stories into principles to share with future employers and game industry friends. "The 'Pedersen Principles'" was first published on www.gamasutra.com in 1995.

The article has since been mandatory reading for students at the Art Institute of California, the University of Maryland, and the University of Utrecht (Netherlands) Masters program, translated into other languages on sites such as www.gpgstudy.com/gamasutra/19990305_pedersen.html, and referenced in www.ademar.org/texts/processo-desenv-games.pdf.

In 2005 during the Xtreme Game Developer's Xpo at the Computer History Museum in Mountainview, CA (www.computerhistory.org), I gave a lecture about the "Pedersen Principles." In it, I updated the original article with reader and student comments and added an 11th principle.

Since 1983, I have worked in the computer and video gaming industry in various roles, including executive producer, producer, game designer, technical director, and programmer.

Throughout my years of industry experience, I have learned many important principles. In keeping with my philosophy that game developers should freely share and exchange information relevant to our industry, I present 11 principles of game design and production that everyone in the industry should be acquainted with.

Principle 1: Understand the Roles of the Designer and Producer

It's vital to know what lines of responsibility are drawn within game development organizations. This knowledge gives you an understanding of which people are responsible for which game components, who makes design and production decisions, and so on.

The game designer. The game designer is the visionary, somewhat like a book's author. This person has outlined the scope and description of the product with sufficient detail so that others can understand and develop the product. Just as a book author sees his creation develop differently when made into a film, the game designer needs to accept and solicit modifications from the team members, the publisher, and the public during the development process. Often, one of the game designer's tasks is to create, update, and maintain the project bible — the game's lengthy design specification. This document details the gameplay, describes characters and settings (possibly including diagrams or drawings), includes level descriptions and possibly maps of areas to explore, positions, and actions for each character or class of character, and so on.

The producer. The producer is the project's manager, its champion. The producer must keep the entire team productive and the lines of communication open. This person is a diplomat, a politician, a troubleshooter, a force needed to keep the project on track. The producer must keep marketing, advertising, and public relations teams up to date with the progress of the game, and be honest about its features, performance, and other claims that will be made to consumers. These teams must understand the gameplay, its features, and story line to generate great ads, media hype, magazine previews, and so on. In return, these nontechnical team members, by virtue of their continuous contact with the public, provide the game developers with feedback from the public, magazines, and retail channels about what features are currently hot in games.

The producer needs to facilitate communication between the whole team and provide timely support for each developer, which includes ensuring that:

- Artists and animators provide artwork, animations, and temporary placeholders for art to the programmers on time.
- Programmers provide the artists with current versions of the game so they can see their artwork in a real-time gameplay mode. The producer must also make sure that the programmers provide a current version of the game to the sales, public relations, and marketing teams, along with supporting documentation and reports. These reports describe gameplay, special features, hardware requirements, and supported hardware and peripherals, and contain screen shots that best portray the product for ads, promotional sheets, previews, and reviews for magazines. The producer also needs to ensure that programmers work with the quality assurance (QA) testers and provide them with play instructions, special key combinations, hints, and details of undocumented features and actions.
- Audio engineers and composers provide voice-over, editing, sound effects (SFX) creation, and music scoring. These engineers and composers also need to view and play the current version to check and validate the timing, usage, and clarity of their work.

- The designer (if not a member of the day-to-day team) needs to see the current version to confirm that the product is in line with the current design specifications and the core concept of the game.

- The QA testers report problems to the producer. The problems must be categorized as major (crash, function or action not working), minor (text misspelling, character movement too fast or slow, response time feels wrong), glitches (sound or graphic problems), improvements (add a new feature, improve the character's interaction or behavior, clarify a confusing aspect of the design or gameplay), a video game standards issue (the triangle button does not perform as the standard function definition), or multiplatform inconsistency (PC version vs. console version).

Whether one person assumes the role of both producer and designer or several people handle these tasks, there must be one producer whose word is final, whose decisions are followed, and whose leadership is trusted and motivating.

- *Reader A comments: Having taken part in independent game development for nearly a year (without any pay) I find these principles to be solid and true. I have been doing work as a designer and a producer. It is very easy to get the two mixed up. It's good to separate the two aspects and designate individuals to their respective roles, and to make sure that each has a firm grasp on what their goals and responsibilities are.*

- *Reader B comments: The first principle talks about the different roles that are involved when developing a game. This delimits the role of the game designer as the creative mind of the team, whereas the producer is more focused on managing the team, and the financial and marketing sides of the project.*

- *Reader C comments: I found the first "Pedersen Principle" very informative. It gave me a better understanding of the role of a designer and producer, how much they are involved with the productivity of the team, and how much they depend on the team to actually get things done in order and on time.*

Principle 2: No Designer or Producer Is an Island

Gathering information throughout the product development cycle and knowing what to do with it is the trait of a great designer and producer.

Designers should research their subject matter and evaluate outside suggestions and opinions. The audience demands and expects films and books to seem realistic and accurate. The computer and video game audience should accept nothing less.

When undertaking the development of a sports game (e.g., baseball), a designer may feel that he knows the sport from playing it and viewing it on TV. However, much more research must be undertaken to create an immersive experience for consumers. Whether the game genre is sports, RPG, adventure, or simulation, the first step is to research similar titles in that genre. You can do this by surfing the Internet, purchasing competitive games, reading reviews of similar genre titles, collecting marketing materials and advertisements from other publishers' websites, and so on. This information is invaluable when you are designing a new product.

If you are the producer of an upcoming baseball game, you ought to know the common elements found in other baseball titles, as well as special features that differentiate each product from its competitors. You should read reviews of similar titles and the competing titles' list of features. From this freely collected information, a designer can understand which features and gameplay customers expect, special features that the competition offers, and the criteria upon which the reviewers will base their critiques.

As the designer and/or producer, you must ask yourself:

- Does your game suffer the same poor or awkward design flaw as a previously released title in the same or similar genre? The design of the game needs to address how to be better than its competitors. The design must be able to handle flaws, difficulties, and problems that reviewers and customers have complained about in previous versions of this product or in other similar genre titles. As the decision maker, you must listen to your development team, your marketing and sales team, retailers, and your game playing audience.

- Do the ideas of the game designer and the team outweigh those of the reviewer(s)? The ideas that are formed must have been based on a perceived problem. Most reviewers try to accurately explain and critique the product to the public. There's a significant difference between discarding a reviewer's opinion and listing the problems and how your design addresses each one.

- Does the design consider comments from previous or potential customers? Customers enjoy great products. My experience (in producing sports, gambling, and trivia/puzzle titles) indicates that customers (fans) will buy any product in the genre they enjoy. Their expectations are that your product will teach them something new about the activity, they will gain experience and be able to brag to their friends and associates, and/or that they'll be able to someday master the game. I've received a great deal of fan mail in which consumers have cited the aspects of my games that they enjoyed. These letters also tell me what additions to the game they would like to see in future releases. Magazines publish readers' letters that praise and criticize the products. Market research and beta test groups of potential and previous customers can be worthwhile in the final design stages to tweak the product before its release.

- Are the team's ideas and opinions seriously considered in the design of the product? See Principle 3 for more information about this.

- Can the addition of a feature expand the customer base and get more publicity? In the mid-1990s, I was the director of development, game producer, and game designer for Villa Crespo Software, a Highland Park, IL game company. Based on the popularity of buying and renting video tapes, we developed Flicks: Film Review Library, which was a database and trivia game that reviewed over 30,000 films and listed the cast, the director, the film's genre, and a synopsis of the film.

  Initially there was no field for "closed captioning" and after meeting with the NCI (National Captioning Institute) the CC (closed caption) field was added during the development, instantly adding four million members of the hearing-impaired and non-English speaking audiences to the product's customer base. Newsletters of the NCI that reached this consumer sector gave the product free, positive reviews because it included information vital to their readership. Although many films claim to have closed captioning, the NCI validates this and was able to provide Villa Crespo Software with its official CC film list.

The producer should collect information from team members about improvements that can be made to the product, and relay this information to the designer. The producer must be able to recognize a good idea when he hears it, and incorporate that idea in the game to make it a better product.

Designers should be adaptable and open to ideas that can make their games better. Producers need to be managers, leaders, and diplomats who can take information from all sources. They also need to be experts in getting good suggestions as well as communicating them to the decision makers.

- *Reader D comments: The second principle is something I find myself getting caught in constantly. I feel the need to micromanage, to constantly badger my team with questions, asking for updates, and offering assistance where I can.*

  I have had days where I see nothing being produced and I have had to just sit back and let them come to me at times. This ties into the third principle of letting them do their jobs. They know what they need to do and just need the space to do so.

- *Reader E comments: In Principle 2 I see the importance of cool ideas. On my first homework assignment, I found out that another student in my class had three similar ideas about the list of elements assignment. So I can see how the hundreds of people working in a gaming company would often have the same ideas.*

- *Reader F comments: The second principle provided the biggest insight for me, since it made me aware that a game designer has to do lots of research and reflect about the game design process too. This also means you have to assume the role of a critic toward your games in order to learn from them what worked and what didn't.*

Chapter 2

Principle 3: Let Professionals Do Their Jobs

Most projects have a team of talented professionals made up of designers, programmers, graphic artists, audio technicians, testers, marketing coordinators, and so on. Each of these team members brings his or her own unique, important talents to bear on the project. Producers and designers must rely on these professionals and their particular points of view to improve and facilitate the development process. Regardless of the product's genre, each member can make a product better.

For instance, the quality assurance (QA) and testing people can suggest gameplay improvements before the product is shipped. No member of the team plays the game for hours at a time like a QA person does, and therefore their initial experiences are similar to that of the potential customer. In fact, members of the QA team have probably played more games in a particular genre than the rest of the team combined. The QA tester will experience features of the same product dozens if not hundreds of times with tons of small variations (and sometimes a few big ones). This really skews their point of view of a product (typically toward cynicism). The best customer experience you can get is with an initial group of external testers or with focus groups.

The producer must not only trust the team members, but also rely on them for input to create the best product.

- *Reader G comments: Teamwork! Once again true for every leader in all companies. Leaders need to be able to work as a team member to get things done and to keep control of their team to get what needs to be done.*
- *Reader H comments: The third principle, "Let Professionals Do Their Job," sounds like a self-evident thing, but from my experience in the non-game software industry, I know that this principle is often violated.*

Principle 4: KISS (Keep It Simple, Stupid)

Every aspect of a product should be intuitive and easy to understand.

For instance, allowing players to access every option within two button clicks may be simpler than having 37 unique keys to press. Forcing a player to press Alt+Ctrl+Shift A to get his character to kick an opponent would be ridiculous. Likewise, having to press a sequence of keys A, B, C, and D to control the movements of an airplane in a flight simulator would drive the average player crazy. If a player has to repeatedly press four keys to perform a task, the game design should include a superkey or a one-key macro to simplify the operation.

Keep design interfaces simple. I once designed games for an arcade manufacturer, and the president of this company taught me a valuable lesson about design. He said if a player doesn't grasp the interface of a computer game or video game, that player will read the manual since $50 (or so) was invested in the game. With arcade games, however, the player has only invested a quarter or two, so if the game isn't understandable, addictive, and compelling, the player moves on to the next machine. Who cares about wasting pocket change? While this is especially critical for arcade games, I think it's important to remember when designing games for any platform.

■ *Reader I comments: KISS has been a mantra of mine during the entire time of working on this project. If the GUI isn't simple, it will drive away players. If the documentation isn't simple, it will confuse people. If the concept is not solid yet simple, it will just evolve into a big mess of feature creep.*

■ *Reader J comments: I believe that the fourth principle is very true!*

It is very important to keep a game simple enough to allow the player to get into the game. A game having a complicated button setup may discourage the player from playing further. The game might be great in terms of story, graphics, and special features, but with my own experiences, I have learned that once game controls are horribly implemented, it just ruins the game altogether. An example of this is the latest Tomb Raider for the PlayStation 2, Tomb Raider: The Angel of Darkness.

I am a serious, diehard Tomb Raider fan to the fullest and I have been very disappointed with the last four Tomb Raider titles. I have literally had to force myself to complete these games because of my loyalty to the series, but I must say that for me there were some frustrating times.

Principle 5: Schedules Are Like Rules

Schedules are like rules; they are created by those in charge and are meant to be obeyed, but they are also designed to allow exceptions if evidence warrants special circumstances.

Likewise, milestones that are created at the beginning of the project may need to be changed based on problems that occur during development. For instance, the decision to change the original game specification (e.g., to support a new computer or new 3D card, or alter preplanned artwork or audio clips) in order to make a better product is a situation that may warrant "breaking the rules" that the schedule spells out.

If another month of development time would greatly improve the gameplay, remove minor bugs, or allow for better visuals or audio effects, then circumstances justify deviating from the schedule.

To ship a game on a target day, month, or year, regardless of the state of the product at that time, can spell disaster for that product (not to mention the harm it does to the publisher's reputation). Missing seasonal dates like Christmas is bad, but shipping a buggy or poorly made product is worse.

When planning for milestones, slippage should always be counted as a possible scenario and should be factored in as much as realistically possible.

You should only modify a project schedule if there are valid reasons. The team and publisher must agree that the additional time will substantially benefit the product.

■ *Reader K comments: Scheduling is something that will hopefully be tackled, but since I have been working online and have only met two of the members of the team in person, it is very difficult to keep on schedule and keep the others motivated. The longer we work on this, the more of an uphill battle it becomes.*

Principle 6: The Yardstick: One Day's Pay for a Week's Worth of Fun

If a customer pays $50 (plus tax) for a game that I've worked on, that amounts to the average teenager's one-day net pay. (A teenager who works part time for five hours a day and earns $10 an hour brings home around $50 a day.) If the player reports enjoying the game for at least one week, then I am happy. If the player feels ripped off due to poor game design, numerous bugs, obstacles in playing the game (e.g., multi-CD swaps, memorizing numerous keystrokes, and so on), poor quality audio, or some other problem, then the game designer and any team members who knew of these problems beforehand are to blame.

Every member of the team should be proud of their product. They should consider the praise from consumers, reviewers, and the industry as part of their reward for the time and work they spent on the game.

■ *Reader L comments: The Yardstick is a good measure. I have spent countless hours on this project, focusing on all aspects of development, even doing e-mail and voice interviews for this product. (After hearing myself I have reached the conclusion that I need someone more personable to do the interviews.)*

■ *Reader M comments: Gamers these days are blown away by blockbuster online hits such as Battlefield Vietnam, Warcraft, and Everquest. These blockbuster games are still fun after months (even a year) of play. Because of the long shelf life of these games, my original notion for a successful game was: "One day's pay for several month's worth of fun." My expectations were too high. So this simple yardstick was actually a relief to hear. I would be content if my games entertained the consumer for at least a week.*

Principle 7: I Never Met a Genre I Didn't Like

A student who doesn't enjoy math can study hard and still earn an A in class. Similarly, a designer or producer does not have to have experience working on a particular genre to create a good game within that genre. In fact, a designer or producer doesn't have to even be an enthusiast of that genre in order to get good results. Putting together a team in which at least one member enjoys the genre (or studying competing products of the genre) is what is critical.

Often just one enthusiastic team member can show similar games that he has enjoyed, and thereby turn every team member into a knowledgeable player of the genre. Combining fanatical genre loyalists along with non-genre players on the development team can result in benefits you may not have considered. For instance, a non-genre player can suggest modifications to a game's design by pointing out aspects of the genre he finds unappealing, whereas a fanatic of the genre can lend his expertise and advice to keep a game faithful to the genre.

A knowledgeable developer or producer may ask the entire team to play similar games in that genre and ask each team member to critique the products. This technique can help the development of your product, and it's time well spent.

■ *Reader N (a male) comments: The seventh principle seems like probably the largest obstacle. Though I understand it, I'd really have a hard time working on a game such as Barbie: Sleeping Beauty. But then again, if I were being paid to work on it, I'm sure I'd find that passion for being a princess somewhere deep inside of me...*

■ *Reader O comments: I found interesting the concept of having team members who aren't well-versed in the genre as opposed to working with team members who are all veterans of the genre. I didn't consider that having people outside of the genre could actually benefit the quality of the game design as they contribute feedback from a different perspective.*

■ *Reader P (a female) comments: In general, I agree with most of the principles, but I'm not sure if I can follow principle seven in every case, since I usually don't like FPS games that much. I've recently played Painkiller and I was a bit turned off by the brutality and graphic display of the violence. I won't object to doing an FPS, but I'd probably not display the violence. I'd probably just make the enemies disappear in a cloud of smoke or something.*

Principle 8: Be True to Your License

Games based on licensed products often cause players to make certain assumptions about those titles. There are preconceptions about the gameplay, content, and target audience. In stores, it's the licensed titles that get noticed first, regardless of their marketing and advertising. Game designers must understand this customer mentality. The designer must understand everything about that license in order to provide the kind of entertainment that the target consumers have anticipated.

For instance, a baseball game that uses a particular baseball team's manager in its title suggests a strategy sports game. Players would probably assume that they would be responsible for making decisions about the players and batting order. On the other hand, a licensed product linked to a professional baseball player would suggest an emphasis on sports action, such as pitching and batting.

There's a reason why licenses cost big bucks. Designers and producers must use the license and the game's characters to leverage consumer preconceptions to the title's benefit.

Principle 9: Share Your Toys!

Throughout the years, many game developers have bounced ideas off me, asked me questions, and so on. I have, and will always, welcome these inquiries because I believe it's for the greater good of the industry. Since I have always been interested in creating and exploring ideas, I'll gladly help when someone wants information. Three occasions in particular are worth relating:

- In 1985, an auto mechanic who owned an Atari 520ST called me to pick my brain about game design and various game projects he was working on. For several months we talked, and he often sent me samples of his artwork as well as demos of the concepts we'd discussed. Sometime around 1987 he had an interview with a major publisher and discussed taking the demos and artwork with him. I encouraged him and wished him success.

  A few weeks later he announced that he was hired as a "platform level" designer. Within months, he became the top "platform level" game designer for this company, and he worked on the most well-known titles in the industry. He eventually left this publisher to join another equally large publisher as the head of game design. He appeared in several magazines displaying his platform level designs. To this day, I've never met him and have only seen the magazine articles that he sent me, but I feel happy that I was a small influence in his life and in the industry.

  Today, he writes a column for gaming sites like Gignews.com, helping other aspiring game designers.

- When I was working on All Dogs Go to Heaven, a game for the PC and Amiga based on the Don Bluth film, I met a young man who worked at an arcade. On several occasions, I gave him $10 in tokens to show me the latest video games. As he played, I observed him and asked questions like, "How did you know to do that?" After we got to know each other better, he showed me several comic book sketches that he had drawn, which were great.

  When I was contracted to produce and develop All Dogs Go to Heaven, I asked him to do all the artwork. Since he was new to computer graphics and animation, I taught him the mechanics of using a Summagraphics tablet and the functions and features of various graphics packages. He learned quickly and produced some of the finest artwork that CGA (four-color palette) and EGA (16-color palette) would allow.

After the release of this title, he went to work for a Florida publisher as a computer and video game graphic artist. When the company moved to California, he moved with them. The last I heard, he was moving on to one of the big publishers as a senior graphics person.

■ A high school student sent me a concept for a game show game. The description read well, but the demo he sent me was terrible. Over several months on the phone, we fixed many of the game's rules and aspects of the gameplay, which greatly improved the game. I programmed the game, and hired an artist to provide the graphics.

When I went to Villa Crespo Software outside of Chicago, we published the game and called it Combination Lock. The game was fun to play and it was the first product to feature on-screen players of all races. The high school student and I shared in the profits for several years.

The reason I relate these stories is that I want to emphasize the benefit to those who help budding game developers. When the opportunity to help someone comes knocking on the door, offer that person hospitality and kindness. The results will benefit the "seeker of knowledge," will honor you, "the master," and will benefit the industry as more creative thinkers join in.

■ *Reader Q comments: One of my passions is helping others. I used to be an evangelist for WildTangent and I'm still active in helping people with Dark Basic Pro programming and using DoGA CGA (a free graphics and modeling studio). I enjoy creating models and custom parts and sharing programming tips. I find that helping the community creates a shared knowledge base, which promotes better game development.*

■ *Reader R comments: Principle nine is the most important one to me because it is great to help others achieve their goals and dreams. Along with that, it also gives you a sense of self pride and accomplishment to help others.*

Principle 10: There's No Magic Formula for Success

Keep in mind that no one individual or company of any size has discovered the formula for "what makes a successful product." Like film, art, and music, games appeal to a variety of consumer tastes, and of course taste is subjective.

Some developers of past hits have credited their success to the underlying technology that their game used. Other developers claim that their game transports the player into a surreal and immersive universe. Yet others feel that their game's success is due to the way it engrosses the player in a realistic simulation, challenging them with its compelling design. Behind each successful title is a unique list of traits that made it popular with consumers.

The bottom line is simple: A well-designed product based on a team effort with a simple, user-friendly interface developed within a reasonable time frame will be successful.

- *Reader S comments: On the final two principles, I completely agree. I think the more we are willing to work with one another, the more rewards we will reap in the long run. I'd give my left leg to break into this business. I have been playing and designing games since I was a kid, only I didn't realize that I was designing games. I saw it as just a hobby. I remember getting a TRS 80 when I was like 10 and I taught myself to program. I even made a Berserker clone on it. I have since stopped being interested in programming though, and would prefer designing. Coding is just too tedious! But were I to be in the biz, I'd totally want to be open and helpful toward those who also wanted to do so. That would be like the coolest thing ever. To take a new upcoming kid or even a 30-year-old, and show him that it is possible, that you too can be an utter geek who loves games and gamers.*

- *Reader T comments: I'm relieved that there is no magic formula for success, because then I don't need to spend my time worrying about doing something exactly like Game Company X or Game Developer Y. As an avid game player, I keep notes of what things I liked and disliked about the games I've purchased and played. Many of my online game buddies and I discuss the hits and misses of games we've played. Instead of studying formulas and statistics, I feel that time is better spent playing the games, talking to the player community, and developing some good sense about what elements make a successful game.*

- *Reader U comments: I'm a terrible businessman. I know that. I measure success by a different ruler than other people. I create programs for projects and hobbies that I want to support. I enjoy seeing people use my utilities and games or learning from what I taught them. Financial success is nice, but it is not the only goal that you should measure success by. Nice. Keep up the passion of helping others.*

Principle 11: The Importance of Networking

Over the years, networking with other people interested in the gaming industry and those who are working in the industry has been important to me. The reader should visit sites such as igda.org, Gamasutra.com, and GameDev.net on at least a weekly basis, read *Game Developer* every month, and attend the local IGDA and game meet-up groups. Searching Facebook, MySpace, and Moby Games for network friends as well as joining LinkedIn and corresponding with the gaming industry's top designers, producers, programmers, artists, and executives are all great ways to keep in touch. I would suggest that any aspiring game professional attend the annual Game Developers Conference (www.gdconf.com), the Austin Game

Developers Conference (www.austingdc.net), and VGXPO
(www.videogame.net/vgxpo), which has the "old school" arcade and video
console games plus a weekend seminar called "Breaking In."

Here is a wonderful letter that one of the promising "Full Sail" students sent me after the Game Developers Conference:

> *Hi Mr. Pedersen,*
>
> *This is David B, I hung out with you at this year's GDC (the tall blond
> Full Sail guy). I just wanted to thank you again for introducing me to peo-
> ple like Tommy Tallarico, Andre La Mothe, and taking me to parties like
> the Course Technologies' Book party. That really meant a lot, I won't forget
> what you've done for me.*
>
> *You'll always be a hero of mine and if I can ever do anything for you, let
> me know.*
>
> *I just wanted to keep in touch and catch up with you. I also wanted to let
> you know, I got a job! :) I'm going to be working at Genuine Games, Inc.
> in Los Angeles, CA!! They wanted me to start work there on Sept. 13th, so
> I've got to pack up quick and jump across the country in a couple of weeks.*

For a few years, I taught an online course called "Game Design" to
Gameversity students who lived all over the world, including the United
States, Mexico, and Serbia.

The first thing I wanted to know from my students was what exactly
they wanted to learn about being a "game designer" in the course (I'm
GameProducer):

<GameProducer>   *What expectations and anticipations do you have for the
                  Game Design course?*

<Somnath>   *First of all, I want to be able to understand the writing
             concepts.*

<Nifty>   *I'm hoping to come out of this better able to shape my ideas
           into GDDs.*

<Somnath>   *Putting your thoughts in game design, having the patience,
             perseverance, and passion to create your vision.*

<zircher>   *To motivate and guide me to complete the game design and
             documentation for my next project.*

<D_Rock>   *To learn how to make a good game design document.*

<Nifty>   *Knowing how to pitch myself and my ideas would be a high
           priority as well.*

<Somnath>   *Be able to market your ideas to the world. To understand what
             the customer would appreciate. To design a game that will sell
             to the gaming masses irrespective of fanatical genres.*

<zircher>   *My scope is a little smaller, self publishing to a niche market,
             but mainstream success would be nice.*

Chapter 2

Workshop

Assignments

Assignment 1: Select one of the "Pedersen Principles" and comment about how it relates to your thinking and experience.

Assignment 2: Discuss (a) a genre that you would want to develop a new game in, (b) a licensed game in a genre that you'd want to design a game in, and (c) a genre that would be the most difficult to develop a game in and how you would accomplish its design.

Assignment 3: Discuss a game with a complex interface and how you would redesign it for easier play.

Assignment 4: Find at least three job postings on the Internet for "game designers" and write your own cover letter that addresses every requirement and why you should get this job.

Exercises

Exercise 1: Now that you understand the roles of the game designer and the producer, answer the following questions about the roles with either "game designer" or "producer."

1. Who is the "communication facilitator"?
2. Who is the game's "visionary"?
3. Who is the author of the GDD?
4. Who is the game's champion?
5. Who does the QA team report problems and bugs to?
6. Who should accept and solicit game modifications?
7. Who is the game's "project manager"?
8. Who must act as a diplomat and politician?

Exercise 2: Explain the concept of KISS in your own words.

Exercise 3: Further explain the roles of the game designer and producer.

1. Should the producer test the game? Explain your answer.
2. Should the game designer manage the programmers and artists? Explain your answer.

Unguided Exercises

Unguided Exercise 1: Name some gaming websites that a serious game designer should visit weekly.

Unguided Exercise 2: Internet Search

1. What is the name of the game industry's annual convention?
2. When will it be held next?

3. Where will it be held?

4. What options are available for students to attend?

Thoughts for Discussion

1. What legitimate events could cause the game's planned schedule to be adjusted?

2. Discuss a game that suffered from "premature shipping," where the game shipped on schedule with obvious problems and bugs that might have decreased possible sales.

3. In "Pedersen Principle" terms, what does the "yardstick" measure?

4. Discuss the following for a game based on a license:

    a. What benefits does a licensed game provide?

    b. As a game designer, how do you take advantage of the license?

    c. What issues may arise in the license's boundaries?

Chapter 2

Chapter 3

Game Genres

Choosing a Game Genre to Design

When describing a game to others, you must express its genre or type. Genres can fall into categories like action, adventure, casual, educational, role-playing game (RPG), simulations, sports (including fighting games), strategy, and other (puzzle games and toys). Many games cross genre boundaries ("hybrids") or are truly several genres in one.

Some games, like action-shooters, RPGs, or adventure games, can be labeled by the game's point of view (POV). A "first-person" POV is one that approximates viewing your environment through the lens of a video camera. A "third-person" POV has the player's character or persona in view as though a video camera is following their movement. In the "third-person" POV (often called "3PS"), the video camera may be stationary (like on a tripod) or free moving, showing various angles of the player. A "first-person shooter" (FPS) is another way to describe the POV for a combat-shooter game like Doom or Quake. Other popular FPS game series include Call of Duty, BioShock, Descent, and Half-Life. Some 3PS games and series include Tomb Raider, Bully, MDK, Resident Evil (also referred to as a "survival horror" game), Gears of War, and Uncharted: Drake's Fortune.

Some action-shooters are categorized as both FPS and 3PS, such as Deus Ex, Frontlines: Fuel of War, and Metal Gear Solid. One of the design aspects of these games (FPS and 3PS) are "mods" or "modding," which means the games can be retailored in terms of graphics and scripting to create a brand new game. Mods can be developed from FPS, 3PS, role-playing games (RPGs), and real-time strategy games (RTSs). "Partial conversions" use many of the game's assets with some new design or graphic elements. "Total conversions" have new gameplay and assets, but use the underlying 3D engine and AI capabilities. These mods have led to a new cinematic art form called "machinima," where filmmakers use the 3D games and their assets to create inexpensive films. Some of the best machinima examples are *Red vs. Blue* based on Halo (http://rvb.roosterteeth.com/home.php) and *What Is Machinima?* based on Grand Theft Auto (www.flingfilms.com/production_notes.php?film=wim and www.bitfilm.com/network/member.php?page=fd&fid=1157&id=111099).

In the following sections we describe each genre. At the end of each section is a list of the best-selling games of that genre for the years 2006 to 2008 from websites such as IGN.com, Gamespot.com, Gamezone.com, and GameSpy.com for various platforms such as Windows PC, video game consoles (GameCube, PlayStation2, PlayStation 3, Wii, Xbox, and Xbox 360), handhelds (Nintendo Dual Screen, PlayStation Portable, Nintendo Gameboy Advanced), and wireless (mobile/cell phones).

Action Games

Action games are non-stop, finger flying ("twitch") games. In the early games (such as Asteroids, Pac-Man, and Space Invaders), arcade-style action games involved shooting vector spaceships or dot-munching balls. Later came "platform," "rail," or "side scrollers" that dominated the action game genre (such as Sonic, Mario, and Mega Man). Now, first-person shooter (FPS), third-person shooter (3PS), and massively multiplayer online first-person shooter (MMOFPS) games are the trend in action gaming.

Action games are those in which you move, attack, move, react, and move again. They revolve around the gamer who is always central to the play and in control. During an action game, action is the emphasis, not storytelling. Action games will use pregame "splash" screens and animation as well as interlevel screens to tell their story. Even in an FPS, the main emphasis is action, whether that is fighting or gathering weapons and ammunition, shields, and objects like health and experience points.

PlanetSide was one of the first MMOFPS games. In it, thousands of players wage a persistent war of unprecedented scale. PlanetSide has 26 weapons, 20 vehicles and aircraft, 10 implants, 7 armor configurations, and 5 types of facilities where 200+ players and vehicles can fight on a single battlefield. Players connect through the Internet to Sony's Online Entertainment servers, which requires a subscription fee. Other early MMOFPS games include Project Visitor (2000), World War II Online (2001), and Neocron (2002).

Top-Selling Action Games

2006

PC: LEGO Star Wars II: The Original Trilogy, Condemned: Criminal Origins, Scarface: The World Is Yours

FPS: Half-Life 2: Episode One, Battlefield 2142, Red Orchestra: Ostfront 41-45, Prey

Game Cube: Chibi-Robo!, The Legend of Spyro: A New Beginning

Nintendo DS: Platform: New Super Mario Bros., Yoshi's Island DS, Kirby: Squeak Squad, Metroid Prime: Hunters, Star Fox Command

Nintendo GBA: Scurge: Hive, Drill Dozer

PSP: Platform: Ready at Dawn, Mega Man Powered Up,
                 Syphon Filter: Dark Mirror, Daxter
                 FPS: Medal of Honor Heroes
PS2:   Okami, Bully, Kingdom Hearts II
                 FPS: Black
PS3:   FPS: Resistance: Fall of Man
Wii: Elebits, Super Monkey Ball: Banana Blitz
                 FPS: Call of Duty 3
                 Platform: Rayman Raving Rabbids
Wireless: Mafia Wars Yakuza, Mission: Impossible II, Alpha Wing 2,
                 Brothers in Arms 3D
                 Platform: Rayman Raving Rabbids, Tropical Madness,
                 Bonk's Return
Xbox: Tom Clancy's Splinter Cell Double Agent, Call of Duty 3
Xbox 360:   FPS: Dead Rising, Saints Row, Gears of War, Tom
                 Clancy's Rainbow Six: Vegas, Call of Duty 3, Prey, Tom
                 Clancy's Ghost Recon Advanced Warfighter

2007

PC: FPS: Unreal Tournament 3, Crysis, BioShock
Nintendo DS: Quendan 2
                 Platform: Sonic Rush Adventure, Drawn to Life
PSP: Syphon Filter: Logan's Shadow, Disgaea: Afternoon of
                 Darkness, Ratchet & Clank: Size Matters
PS2:   God of War II, Syphon Filter: Dark Mirror
PS3:   Uncharted: Drake's Fortune, Ninja Gaiden Sigma
                 Platform: Ratchet & Clank Future: Tools of Destruction
                 FPS: Call of Duty 4: Modern Warfare, The Orange Box:
                 Half-Life 2: Episode Two, Team Fortress 2, Portal
Wii: Resident Evil 4: Wii Edition, Resident Evil: The
                 Umbrella Chronicles, Battalion Wars 2, Scarface: The
                 World Is Yours, WarioWare: Smooth Moves
                 Platform: Super Mario Galaxy
Wireless: FPS: Prey Mobile
XBox 360:   Lost Planet: Extreme Condition, Assassin's Creed,
                 Crackdown, Ace Combat 6: Fires of Liberation
                 FPS: Tom Clancy's Ghost Recon Advanced Warfighter 2,
                 BioShock, Halo 3, Call of Duty 4: Modern Warfare, The
                 Orange Box: Half-Life 2: Episode Two, Team Fortress 2,
                 Portal

Chapter 3

2008

Some of the action games released in 2008 include Harry Potter & the Half-Blood Prince (action-adventure – PC, DS, PSP, PS2, PS3, Wii, Xbox 360), Ninja Gaiden II (Xbox 360), Hellboy: The Science of Evil (PSP, PS3, Xbox 360), Turok (action-FPS – PC, PS3, Xbox 360), Unreal Tournament (action-FPS – PC, PS3, Xbox 360), The Legend of Spyro: Dawn of the Dragon (DS, PS2, PS3, Wii, Xbox 360), Star Wars: The Force Unleashed (PC, DS, PSP, PS2, PS3, Wii, Xbox 360), Tomb Raider: Underworld (platform – PC, DS, PSP, PS2, PS3, Wii, Xbox 360), LEGO Indiana Jones: The Original Adventure (action-adventure – PC, DS, PSP, PS2, PS3, Wii, Xbox 360), and Iron Man (PC, DS, PSP, PS2, PS3, Wii, Xbox 360).

PC:	Dead Space
	3PS: Devil May Cry 4
	FPS: Left 4 Dead, Far Cry 2
Nintendo DS:	Ghostbusters, Incredible Hulk, The Spiderwick Chronicles, Castlevania: Order of Ecclesia
PSP:	Incredible Hulk, God of War: Chains of Olympus
PS2:	Incredible Hulk
	3PS: Grand Theft Auto: San Andreas
PS3:	Incredible Hulk, Dead Space
	FPS: Metal Gear Solid 4: Guns of the Patriots, Devil May Cry 4
	3PS: Grand Theft Auto IV, Resident Evil 5
Wii:	Worms: A Space Oddity, Incredible Hulk, deBlob, No More Heroes
Wireless:	Crazy Taxi
Xbox 360:	Incredible Hulk, The Spiderwick Chronicles, Geometry Wars: Retro Evolved 2
	FPS: Battlefield: Bad Company
	3PS: Grand Theft Auto IV, Devil May Cry 4

Adventure Games and Puzzles

Adventure games are quests where puzzles are presented along the journey.

In the early days of interactive gaming, adventure games ruled. They were easily ported from the mainframe computer days to the low-resolution monitors on the 1980s microcomputers.

Gamers (in those days, computer "geeks" and "nerds") loved Tolkien (author of *The Hobbit* and *The Lord of the Rings*) and *Star Trek*, which were a prominent part of the first text adventure games from the mainframe era.

Soon many companies were formed and products hit the shelves based on text adventure games (no graphics, just text and your imagination). The stories were compelling and the games were addictive.

As computers advanced with more memory and better graphics, graphic adventure games appeared and became popular. Computer gaming fanatics loved solving the designers' tricky puzzles. Eventually though, the other genres began to win the consumers' popularity contest. In the late 1990s, publishers and distributors had an "adventure games are *dead*" attitude.

Hybrid adventure games soon appeared, and out of the ashes, several successful "action-adventure" games entered the realm of major hits and mega-sellers.

In an adventure game, you (the player) start with a limited inventory of supplies, weapons, and food. You are sent on a quest (to save the princess, to free the slaves being held captive by an evil emperor, or to find and return the Golden Fleece). Along the journey you are presented with puzzles to solve. The designer can make it an obvious puzzle or hide the puzzle within the story (but nevertheless it's still a puzzle to solve). Usually all gameplay, storytelling, or advancement is paused until the puzzle is solved. A puzzle can be a physical puzzle (maneuver objects in a precise order, move an object, acquire an object, or build an object), a verbal puzzle (solve a riddle, discover the secret password, learn a phrase to say), a timing puzzle (perform tasks in a precise order or within a specific amount of time), a labyrinth (maze) traversal, or a cavern exploration.

Adventure Puzzles

Most puzzles in action-adventure games have one correct solution. I prefer to design puzzles with at least three correct solutions, which I call "physical," "logical/intellectual," and "reasonable" challenges.

Let's examine these challenges as though we were Ulysses in Homer's *Odyssey*. At one point, Ulysses is confronted by a Cyclops (a one-eyed giant), and cannot pass until he completes a challenge.

The physical challenge would involve fighting the Cyclops, which is 15 feet tall and carries a huge wooden club. One possible outcome would be that Ulysses beats the Cyclops with a few injuries and then passes. Another outcome would be that Ulysses gets pummeled and survives (with injury ranging from barely survives to moderately injured), then he awakens in a cage. The "captured" scenario would set up an escape puzzle for Ulysses to solve and escape from the cage and the Cyclops' domain.

The logical/intellectual challenge would involve a battle of the wits such as challenging the Cyclops to a drinking game. Perhaps Ulysses plays a "rock-paper-scissors" style game where the loser must drink an entire flask of ale. Eventually, either Ulysses or the Cyclops will succumb to the drink and pass out. If the Cyclops passes out after drinking an enormous amount of ale, Ulysses may pass unharmed with a little "happy" effect. If Ulysses passes out, he'll awake imprisoned with an awful hangover. The "captured" scenario would set up an escape puzzle for Ulysses to solve and escape from the cage and the Cyclops' domain.

The reasonable challenge would have Ulysses ignoring the Cyclops' blocked passage and detouring through miles of treacherous mountain passages free of monsters and Cyclops. This challenge wastes a lot of time and energy but causes little physical damage.

Eventually, all three of these challenges have Ulysses ending up at the next destination.

Top-Selling Adventure Games

2006

PC:	Sam & Max Season One, Episode 101: Culture Shock
Nintendo DS:	Dragon Quest Heroes: Rocket Slime, Castlevania: Portrait of Ruin
Game Cube:	Legend of Zelda: Twilight Princess, Harvest Moon: Magical Melody
PS2:	Okami, Yakuza
Wii:	Legend of Zelda: Twilight Princess
Wireless:	Stranded, Darkest Fear

2007

PC:	Sam & Max Season One, Episode 101: Culture Shock, Sherlock Holmes: The Awakened, Destination: Treasure Island
Nintendo DS:	The Legend of Zelda: Phantom Hourglass, Heroes of Mana, Lunar Knights, Final Fantasy Fables: Chocobo Tales, Hotel Dusk: Room 215, Phoenix Wright: Ace Attorney Trials and Tribulations
PSP:	Sid Meier's Pirates!, Lara Croft Tomb Raider: Anniversary
Wii:	Metroid Prime 3: Corruption, Harry Potter and the Order of the Phoenix, Zack & Wiki: Quest for Barbaros' Treasure
Xbox 360:	Castlevania: Symphony of the Night

2008

Some of the adventure games released in 2008 include Prince of Persia (PC, PS3, Xbox 360), Saints Row 2 (PC, PS3, Xbox 360), The Mummy: Tomb of the Dragon Emperor (DS, PS2, Wii), and Ghostbusters: The Video Game (PC, PSP, PS2, PS3, Wii, Xbox 360).

PC:	Deadliest Catch: Alaskan Storm, Alone in the Dark, The Chronicles of Narnia: Prince Caspian
Nintendo DS:	Time Hollow, Gauntlet, Broken Sword, Lock's Quest
PSP:	Wall-E

PS2:	The Chronicles of Narnia: Prince Caspian
PS3:	Final Fantasy Versus XIII
Wii:	Nancy Drew: The White Wolf of Icicle Creek
Wireless:	Hello Kitty London, Katamari Damacy Mobile
Xbox 360:	Indiana Jones, Too Human

Casual Games

Casual games include board games, card games (gambling games included), and game shows.

Board games can include classic games like chess, checkers, Othello, and Go, as well as versions of retail board games. Board games are popular and addictive, as well as commonly known by a wide (mass market) audience. For instance, gamers may buy a chess program even if they don't play chess just because they'd like to own a chess program (especially one that everyone is talking about).

A chess enthusiast may buy several chess programs because of the varying playing strengths, game features (Internet, various time controls, and analysis features), or game gimmicks (a Civil War set where the pieces shoot and engage in combat).

In the 1980s I developed several computer versions of popular children and young adult board games. The executives at these companies worried that the computer versions of their games would cannibalize the retail toy sales. In a phone conversation, I discussed several key advantages of having both the retail toy board game version and the computer version of their games.

- The retail toy board game has sold in stores for many years and will continue to sell as predicted.
- The computer version of the game...
  - Will add additional revenue — a new market of customers who own computers and most likely already own the toy board game version.
  - Will ensure that the game board and pieces will not get lost, which often happens to the retail toy version.
  - Will ensure that players follow the rules and cheating cannot happen.
  - Will address each player by name and reward the player for successful interactions and through animation and sounds get/train the player to successfully complete his or her turn.
  - Can be saved and continued at any time without setting up the board and pieces.
  - Can be played by a solo player, perhaps a child who is home from school.

Game shows are addictive and popular. Everyone wants to be a contestant on his or her favorite show! Gamers can experience through sound and animation the thrill of being on a game show without leaving their office or home. They can play against "real" opponents (via networks or the Internet) or against the program's AI (artificial intelligence). Experienced gamers can feel successful by doing well and winning the game show's prizes, cash, or whatever. Other gamers can practice and perform better without the embarrassment of performing poorly in the real world.

Licensing game shows is expensive because of the high costs for the rights of a successful show. The success of the game's sales often depends on the success of the TV show and not how well the game is designed.

The benefits of a licensed game show are that the audience understands the game and how to play it. The game's producer has play content such as questions and their answers, the game show's logo, its theme music, stage props, photos and recordings of the game show host and contestant(s) playing the game, and additional on-air staff such as sexy ladies holding metal briefcases. The game show may allow the designer to work with the show's writers and set and costume designers and record the voice of the show's announcer and host.

Villa Crespo Software's Combination Lock (left) and Gametek's Press Your Luck (right).

Card games include trading card games, solitaire, cribbage, hearts, rummy, Old Maid, bridge, and all gambling games (poker, blackjack, keno, slot machines, roulette, craps, and baccarat). Like computer versions of classic board games, gamers want to own quality computer versions (good skill level or interesting features) of card games.

Gambling games have a unique attribute in that gambling gamers are always seeking an edge against the casinos and their poker night buddies. They believe that if one gambling game teaches you one expert strategy, then buying another isn't repetitive but may teach you another much needed lesson.

Besides entertaining gamers, casual games can train, educate, and improve the gamer's knowledge and skill level. Casual games have a mass-market audience that knows and understands the product based on its name and package graphics. They have a longer shelf life than this month's popular game. Publishers and developers can easily understand the game's concept and concentrate on the game's features and graphics.

The best-selling casual games (listed by popularity) can be categorized as:

- Match three (Big Kahuna Reef 2, 10 Talismans, Amazonia, Bejeweled 2 Deluxe, Burger Rush)
- Time management (Diner Dash, Cake Mania, Alice Greenfinger, Fashion Boutique)
- Hidden object (Mystery Case Files: Prime Suspects, Hide and Secret)
- Card and board (Monopoly: Here & Now, Governor of Poker, Risk, Slingo Quest)
- Simulation (Virtual Villagers, Fish Tycoon) and strategy (Clue Classic, Build-a-lot)
- Shoot three or marble popper (Luxor 2, Sparkle, Inca Ball)
- Adventure (Super Granny 3, Tradewinds Caravan, Agatha Christie: Peril at End House)
- Object inlay or brain teaser (Hidden Wonders of the Depths) and word (Scrabble)

Top-Selling Casual Games

2006

PC:	Egyptian Addition, Scrubbles, Blast Miner, TubeTwist, Eets: Hunger. It's Emotional
Nintendo DS:	Clubhouse Games
Wireless:	Bomb Jack, Elfin Forest, Ice Age 2: Arctic Slide, Magnetic Joe

2007

PC:	Pathstorm, Words Kingdom, Sally's Salon, Chocolate Castle, Peggle, Diner Dash: Flo on the Go, Professor Fizzwiggle and the Molten Mystery, Secret of Bird Island, Mystery Case Files: Ravenhearst, Prism: Light the Way, Bookworm Adventures
Nintendo DS:	Cake Mania, New York Times Crosswords, Prism: Light the Way, Planet Puzzle League, Nervous Brickdown, WarioWare: Smooth Moves
Wireless:	Prism: Light the Way

2008

PC:	Fashion Solitaire, Sling-Do-Ku, Jojo's Fashion Show, Peggle Nights, Bejeweled Twist, Chocolatier 2: Secret Ingredients
Mac:	Chocolatier 2: Secret Ingredients

Chapter 3

Nintendo DS: USA Today Crossword Challenge
Wireless: Mephisto Chess Mobile Edition

Educational Games

Educational games emphasize learning. They are designed to teach or reinforce a learned concept. Educational games look like games of other genres, but they are their own genre because they emphasize education.

The most basic (and to me boring) educationally designed game would be text exercises like fill-in-the-blank, multiple-choice, or essay. With a little imagination, you could turn the multiple-choice text exercise into a fun game show where the host asks the student an education-oriented question and correct answers earn points or virtual cash.

History lessons could be turned into adventure games or RPGs, where the student plays the key character and must answer relevant historical questions or resolve a historical situation properly. Games based on literature could be graphic stories with relevant questions that when answered correctly let the student proceed to the next chapter.

Educational Game as an Adventure Game

In 1983 a major book publisher had me design and program several games that were to accompany their new school textbooks.

World-Wide Reporter was a game where the player, as a top-notch reporter, was sent around the world to get the scoop on headline stories. Based on 50 cities covered in the accompanying textbook, over 20 facts about each city were saved as clues. The student would receive one to two clues about a city and a clue about the story to cover, such as "the Mona Lisa was stolen from the Louvre Museum." Then at the airport, the student would see a display of five cities and have to select a city to fly to. If the student understood the clue(s) and flew to the right city, he or she would get another clue for the next city. If a mistake was made, additional clues would be given, directing the student to the right city. After the student had traveled to five cities, he or she would receive one of several citations and make front-page news (with the student's name in huge, bold letters).

Let's say you're interested in chemistry and would like to create a fun and educational chemistry game. In your travels adventuring throughout the human body, you need to find "nitrogen." In your inventory you have a container of carbon dioxide. The player would have to figure out or know that carbon dioxide is comprised of one atom of carbon (atomic weight 6) and two atoms of oxygen (atomic weight 8), and that the sought-after nitrogen has an atomic weight of 7. The player would examine each element found and weigh it against the carbon and the oxygen. Nitrogen is the only element heavier than carbon and lighter than oxygen. This design could make learning chemistry (the atomic weights and names) interesting and fun.

Educational Game as a Sports Game

In 1984, I designed and copyrighted two math titles: Mathathon and Geomnastics.

In Mathathon, the student was a marathon runner competing with a dozen computer opponents in a race. The goal was to finish in first place by quickly and correctly answering algebraic math questions (addition, subtraction, multiplication, division, and quadratic equations). Every quarter mile of the marathon's 26.2-mile distance, the student was presented with an algebraic question as the player's runner ran in place or drank some water. The student was given 10 seconds to answer the problem. If the correct answer was entered, the runner would continue to race. Otherwise, the problem would be partially solved and the student would have 10 more seconds to answer it. This would continue until the correct answer was entered by the student or solved by the game. When the race ended, the winner was placed on a pedestal with his or her name prominently featured as music played. A list of missed problems could be reviewed or printed.

In Geomnastics, the student was to choreograph a balance beam routine by selecting beam maneuvers and answering geometry questions. Each balance beam maneuver had a difficulty level and a geometry question of equal difficulty. After an entire routine was created and the geometry questions answered, the student would see his or her choreographed routine performed. After the routine, the five judges would give the gymnast a score from 0 to 10 based on the correctness of the student's answers, the difficulty of the problems, and the amount of time it took to answer the questions. The student could replay his or her routine, checking each problem with the correct answer. A student who received high marks from the five judges (45 points or better) would receive a gold medal. Silver and bronze medals were awarded to lesser scores.

Educational games have become more interactive over the last few years. They now have graphics, sound, and gameplay on par with the other genres. Many educational titles have linked themselves to licensed properties like TV shows, cartoons, and films.

Top-Selling Educational Games

2006

PC:	Sponge Bob Square Pants: Nighty Nightmare, Nancy Drew: Danger by Design, Miss Spider Scavenger Hunt, Bookworm Adventures, flOw, Mindscape's Brain Trainer
Nintendo DS:	Brain Age: Train Your Brain in Minutes a Day, Big Brain Academy, Nintendogs
PSP:	Mind Quiz, Passport to London

Chapter 3

2007

Nintendo DS:	Brain Age 2: More Training in Minutes a Day, My Spanish Coach, Cooking Guide: Can't Decide What to Eat?
PS2:	EyeToy: Play Sports, EyeToy: Play Astro Zoo
Wii:	Big Brain Academy: Wii Degree, My Word Coach, Donkey Kong Jr. Math

2008

PC:	MindHabits
Nintendo DS:	Professor Brainium's Games, Quick Yoga Training, Margot's Word Brain, Gourmet Chef, Professor Layton and the Curious Village, Asterix Brain Trainer
PSP:	flOw
PS2:	Buzz! Junior: Robo Jam, EyeToy: Play Hero
PS3:	LittleBigPlanet, Hell's Kitchen
Wii:	Wii Fit, Hell's Kitchen, My Spanish Coach
Xbox 360:	Brain Challenge, Hell's Kitchen

Role-Playing Games (RPGs)

Role-playing games (RPGs) have vast worlds to explore where parties of players roam the terrain seeking treasures, objects of desire, and ways to increase their experience and health status and destroy monsters and obstacles that get in their way.

RPGs started as dungeon crawls through paper labyrinths created by "masters" (dungeon designers). A master would create an elaborate labyrinth filled with traps, monsters, and evil magic. The party would enter the maze armed with individual skills, magical abilities, and weapons. On each turn the party would try to outwit, outspell with magic, and outfight the master's creation.

The world of the Internet has enabled millions of RPG fans to explore larger terrains and more exotic quests. The acronym MMORPG stands for massively multiplayer online RPG, a game in which parties of friends or groups from around the world form to explore, collect, and fight other parties and monsters. MMORPGs can have numerous parties, each on various quests and with their own goals.

An RPG has a specific goal, and after many hours of play there is an ending. MMORPGs may have no specific ending and can be played until you've completed all the quests or until another MMORPG or Internet game requires your time and attention.

RPGs are not limited to Tolkien-type storylines. Space stations, the Ice Age, fifteenth-century European exploration, the discovery of the Americas, and futuristic scenarios can all be viable venues for an RPG. Even life today could be used, such as life in a foreign country, life on an Indian reservation, or life in an Amish community.

Some of the best known MMORPGs are games such as Age of Conan: Hyborian Adventures, Anarchy Online, Asheron's Call, City of Heroes, City of Villains, Dark Age of Camelot, EverQuest, Final Fantasy XI, The Matrix Online, Second Life, Ultima Online, and World of Warcraft.

Top-Selling Role-Playing Games

2006

PC:	The Elder Scrolls IV: Oblivion, Neverwinter Nights 2
Nintendo DS:	Final Fantasy III, Magical Starsign, Pokemon Mystery Dungeon: Blue Rescue Team
Nintendo GBA:	Final Fantasy V Advance, Super Robot Taisen: Original Generation
Game Cube:	Baten Kaitos Origins
PSP:	Valkyrie Profile: Lenneth, Dungeon Siege: Throne of Agony
PS2:	Final Fantasy XII, Suikoden V, Xenosaga Episode III
Wireless:	The Elder Scrolls IV: Oblivion, Orcs & Elves
Xbox 360:	The Elder Scrolls IV: Oblivion

2007

PC:	The Witcher, Jade Empire Special Edition
Nintendo DS:	Pokemon Diamond/Pearl, Dragon Quest Monster: Joker, Orcs & Elves
PSP:	Jeanne d'Arc
PS2:	Odin Sphere, Rogue Galaxy, Shin Megami Tensei: Persona 3
PS3:	The Elder Scrolls IV: Oblivion, Folklore
Wii:	Super Paper Mario, Fire Emblem: Radiant Dawn
Wireless:	Orcs & Elves
Xbox 360:	Mass Effect, Elder Scrolls IV: The Shivering Isles, Eternal Sonata

2008

PC:	Neverwinter Nights 2: Mysteries of Westgate, Diablo III, Age of Conan: Hyborian Adventures, Fallout 3
	MMORPG:Warhammer Online: Age of Reckoning, World of Warcraft: Wrath of the Lich King
Nintendo DS:	Chrono Trigger DS, The World Ends With You, Mega Man Star Force 2, Final Fantasy Tactics A2: Grimoire of the Rift
PSP:	Crisis Core: Final Fantasy VII, Kingdom Hearts: Birth by Sleep, The Elder Scrolls Travels: Oblivion
PS2:	Shin Megami Tensei: Persona 3 FES, Dokapon Kingdom

PS3: Final Fantasy XIII, Rise of the Argonauts, Fallout 3, White Knight Story

Wii: Final Fantasy Fables: Chocobo's Dungeon, Dokapon Kingdom, Tales of Symphonia: Dawn of the New World

Wireless: Before Crisis: Final Fantasy VII, Kingdom Hearts: Coded

Xbox 360: Fable II, Lost Odyssey, Fallout 3, Tales of Vesperia, Rise of the Argonauts

Simulation Games

Simulation games (or sims) let gamers experience real-world situations from a safe practice area. Since the 1950s, the Department of Defense has trained the military with computerized simulators like flight sims, tank sims, and wargaming sims (such as missile launching and combat).

Simulations are exciting and have a real-world feeling to them. Most of the real-world applications we are trying to simulate would be extremely dangerous and very expensive outside of the computer. Navigating and reproducing practice scenarios are more practical and easier to set up inside a simulator.

Simulations can be classified as either "vehicle simulations" or "managing simulations." Vehicle sims include driving or piloting trucks, cars (stock, Formula-1, high-performance), motorcycles, boats, submarines, airplanes, helicopters, spaceships, space stations, and so on.

Managing sims include managing a nuclear power plant, running a brokerage company trying to predict the stock market, being mayor of a city or president of the United States, owning a golf course, managing the city zoo, being the emperor of Rome, owning an amusement park (roller coasters and rides), and even managing the lives of families or ant colonies.

Many gamers dream of sitting in a Formula-1 race car with the engine purring as the green light signals the start of the race and then driving at speeds of over 200 mph around the track until the checkered flag waves them in as the winner.

What about the car crashes that we often see or the high-speed turns that sometimes slam cars into the wall? How can a driver safely practice maneuvering and avoiding obstacles? Drivers can't really practice driving expensive Formula-1s at all the different tracks in every weather condition. This is where a good simulation becomes valuable. Even novice drivers can access racing simulations and live out their dreams. Scenarios can be set up for weather conditions like rain, fog, snow, or extreme heat. Car conditions could be set up like tire, radiator, or engine problems. The drivers can practice turns and curves at various speeds without the fear of injury to the car or themselves.

Even those who are not professional drivers or members of the military can try out simulators in person. Visitors to Florida's DisneyQuest can experience the CyberSpace Mountain roller coaster simulator. The AllEars website (http://allears.net/btp/dqfaq.htm) describes the simulator as a touch-screen computer you use to design your own roller coaster with the help of Bill Nye the science guy. "Physics are no object — this is a roller coaster in space. When you're done, you can jump into a simulator and actually ride your creation in full 360-degree motion." The people waiting in line for the simulator can watch on a screen as players ride their created roller coaster rides.

The key to vehicle simulations is realism — quick and accurate responses to the gamer's input and the situation being simulated.

There's an old, comical story that goes...

Aboard a commercial flight from New York to Miami, the pilot passes out. The flight attendant enters the passenger cabin and announces, "The captain has passed out. Is there any passenger on board who has any experience in flying a jet? Possibly someone who flew jets in the Air Force?"

No one answers.

The flight attendant again appeals to the passengers, "Does anyone have a pilot's license, either commercial or private?"

Still no one answers.

Hopelessly, the flight attendant again pleads, "Has any passenger scored above 300 points in Microsoft's Flight Simulator?"

Yes, simulators have gotten that good. In fact, many flight simulators running on PCs can be used to log flight hours for private licenses.

Gamers can learn how to use the airplane's controls and instruments, lift off and land an airplane, and navigate it in the simulation. They can make mistakes and test normally dangerous situations like stalling, flying upside down, or spiraling downward without the fear of injury and costly damage. Scenarios can be safely tried and retried. Reading from a manual about the "how-tos" and "whys" is fine, but trying an action and failing is a better reinforcement of the concepts. Simulator pilots can crash and live to tell about it.

In a simulation, we can fly anything from a Cessna to an F-18 jet. The first PC F-18 jet simulation was so accurate and realistic that (the story goes) the military advisors forced the developers to reverse the controls.

The Apollo 13 astronauts practiced their procedures using a simulator for weeks before the launch. When Apollo 13 experienced trouble, it was the backup team and the onground simulator that solved the problems and advised the crew in space how to get back to Earth.

Managing simulations have gamers acting as the U.S. president, making executive decisions that affect the entire country, reviewing congressional bills, meeting with senators to encourage votes for desired bills, interviewing with the press, and chatting with voters.

One of the most popular sims has the gamer acting as the mayor of a large city. As mayor, you decide on issues like building and road construction and public safety issues like police and fire personnel. Other sims are

Chapter 3

more concerned with overseeing a neighborhood and dealing with the daily activities of families and neighbors.

Regardless of the type of simulation you want to design, accurate research, realism, and fun gameplay are the critical issues to address.

Top-Selling Simulation Games

2006

PC:	1701 A.D., City Life, Sid Meier's Railroads!
Nintendo DS:	Cooking Mama: Cook-Off
PSP:	The Sims 2: Pets
PS2:	Tourist Trophy: The Real Riding Simulator, The Sims 2: Pets
Wireless:	Nightclub Empire, My Dog, Dogz

2007

PC:	School Tycoon, Game Tycoon, RollerCoaster Tycoon 3, Luxury Liner Tycoon
Nintendo DS:	Luminous Arc, Front Mission
PSP:	Sid Meier's Pirates!, Dungeons & Dragons Tactics
PS2:	Soul Nomad & the World Eaters, Romance of the Three Kingdoms XI, Star Trek: Conquest
PS3:	Blazing Angels 2
Wii:	Fire Emblem: Radiant Dawn, Pokemon Battle Revolution, Metal Marines
Wireless:	Rise of the Lost Empires, Company of Heroes, Age of Empires III Mobile
Xbox 360:	Battlestations: Midway

2008

PC:	Spore, Virtual Villagers 3: The Secret City
Nintendo DS:	Animal Paradise, Sim City, Zoo Tycoon 2, Sid Meier's Civilization Revolution, Final Fantasy Tactics A2: Grimoire of the Rift, Drone Tactics
PSP:	The History Channel: Great Battles of Rome, Wild ARMs XF
PS2:	Chaos Wars
PS3:	PixelJunk Monsters, World in Conflict: Soviet Assault
Wii:	Worms: A Space Oddity, Neo Nectaris
Wireless:	Empire Earth, War Diary: Burma
Xbox 360:	Viva PiZata: Trouble in Paradise, Operation Darkness, Halo Wars, Tom Clancy's EndWar

Sports Games (Including Fighting Games)

Sports games typically fall into two varieties: the player POV (point of view) also called "twitch games," and the manager POV (strategy game). Usually the player POV version is designed for a younger audience (under 20 years old) where quick finger dexterity is more critical to gameplay. The manager POV audience is more concerned with planning, realism, statistics, and strategy.

Let's look at several sports and learn how to use these POVs in each case.

In golf, the player POV game would have the gamer controlling the club selection, the club's swing arc and velocity, and the contact with the ball. Various gamer interactions would be used to compute the outcome of the golfer's swing or putt. The manager POV game would allow the gamer to select a proper club, have the ability to check the wind condition and terrain (banks and obstacles like sand traps, water, and trees), suggest the proper swing and velocity from a list of common settings, and determine the outcome of the golfer's swing based on the selected criteria and real-world statistics.

In a baseball game, the player POV would allow the gamer to decide on several conditions. While in the field, the gamer would select a pitch type (curveball, slider, or fastball), interact to set the pitch speed, and aim the ball at a specific location in the batter's strike zone. On a hit pitch, the gamer would have to maneuver the outfielders and decide who to throw the ball to as the play is in action. While at bat, the gamer would select the intended hit (desired power from a long high drive, hard hit grounder, or bunt) and through interaction respond to an incoming pitch. The gamer would also interact to force players to run to a base after a ball is hit and steal a base when desired. The manager POV game would be more concerned with setting up the starting lineup, determining substitutions and pinch hitters when needed, instructing batters when to hit away, play it smart, or bunt, and acting as a base coach by advising on leading, stealing, or advancing to the next base when the ball has been hit. The manager would select a starting pitcher based on his pitching cycles (a season view, not a one-game view), select closing (relief) pitchers, and determine when to retire a pitcher. The manager gamer makes strategic decisions and lets the game handle the individual ballplayer's responses based on these decisions.

In football, the player POV game would have the gamer maneuvering each of his team's players on offense and defense. A play's outcome would be the result of the player's interaction. The manager POV game would have the gamer deciding on the offensive plays from a playbook and the defensive formations selected from a list. The play's outcome would be decided by calculating the two sides statistically based on the offensive play, the defensive formation, and each team's current lineup of players.

Chapter 3

Fighting games are usually from the fighter POV (eye of the fighter) or third-person POV. Fighting games would include martial arts, boxing, wrestling, and weapons combat.

Top-Selling Sports Games

2006

PC:	FIFA Soccer 07, Madden NFL 07
	Racing: GTR 2, TOCA Race Driver 3, FlatOut 2
Nintendo DS:	FIFA Soccer 07, True Swing Golf, Mario Hoops 3-on-3
	Racing: Tony Hawk's Downhill Jam, Need for Speed Carbon: Own the City
Game Cube:	FIFA Soccer 07, Madden NFL 07
	Fighter: Naruto: Clash of Ninja 2
	Racing: Need for Speed Carbon: Own the City
PSP:	Madden NFL 07, MLB 06: The Show, NBA 07
	Fighter: Tekken: Dark Resurrection, Def Jam Fight for NY: The Takeover
	Racing: Need for Speed Carbon: Own the City, Race Driver 2006
PS2:	Madden NFL 07, NCAA Football 07, World Soccer Winning Eleven 9, Tony Hawk's Project 8, NFL Street 3, NBA Ballers: Phenom
	Fighter: Mortal Kombat: Armageddon, Dragon Ball Z: Budokai Tenkaichi 2, Street Fighter Alpha Anthology, The King of Fighters 3
	Racing: FlatOut 2, Need for Speed Carbon: Own the City, TOCA Race Driver 3
PS3:	NBA 2K7, NHL 2K7, Fight Night Round 3
	Racing: Need for Speed Carbon: Own the City, Ridge Racer 7
Wii:	Wii Sports, Madden NFL 07
	Racing: Excite Truck, Need for Speed Carbon: Own the City
Wireless:	Madden NFL 07, JAMDAT Sports MLB 2006, Derek Jeter Pro Baseball 2006, Tony Hawk's American Wasteland, Mini Golf Magic, Beach Ping Pong
	Fighter: Super K.O. Boxing, Fight Night Round 3, Street Fighter II
	Racing: Asphalt 3: Street Rules, Moto Racing Fever
Xbox:	FIFA Soccer 07, Madden NFL 07, NCAA Football 07
	Racing: Need for Speed Carbon: Own the City, FlatOut 2, TOCA Race Driver 3
Xbox 360:	Rockstar Games Presents Table Tennis, NHL 2K7

Fighter: Fight Night Round 3, Dead or Alive 4, Ultimate Mortal Kombat 3

Racing: Burnout Revenge, Test Drive Unlimited

2007

PC: Out of the Park Baseball 2008

Racing: DiRT, RACE 07: The WTCC Game, TrackMania United

Nintendo DS: Tiger Woods PGA Tour 08, Tony Hawk's Proving Ground, FIFA Soccer 08, Madden NFL 08

Fighting: Bleach: The Blade of Fate, Ultimate Mortal Kombat, WWE SmackDown! vs. Raw 2008

Racing: Race Driver: Create & Race, Diddy Kong Racing DS, Need for Speed: ProStreet, Juiced 2: Hot Import Nights

PSP: Winning Eleven: Pro Evolution Soccer 2007, Virtual Soccer 2007, The BIGS

Racing: Burnout Dominator

PS2: MBL 07: The Show, Winning Eleven: Pro Evolution Soccer 2007, FIFA Soccer 08

Fighting: Guilty Gear XX Accent Core, Dragon Ball Z: Budokai Tenkaichi 3, The King of Fighters XI

Racing: Burnout Dominator

PS3: Skate, The BIGS, NBA Street Homecourt, NHL 08, Tiger Woods PGA Tour 08

Fighting: Virtua Fighter 5, Tekken 5: Dark Resurrection, Def Jam: Icon

Racing: MotorStorm, DiRT

Wii: SSX Blur, Mario Strikers Charged, Madden NFL 08, MLB Power Pros, Mario & Sonic at the Olympic Games

Wireless: Fighter: Pillowfight

Racing: The Fast and the Furious: Fugitive 3D

Xbox 360: Skate, College Hoops 2K6, Madden NFL 08, NHL 08, The BIGS

Fighting: Virtua Fighter 5 Online, Def Jam: Icon

Racing: Forza Motorsport 2, DiRT, FlatOut Ultimate Carnage, Project Gotham Racing 4

2008

Some of the more recent sports games (including fighting and racing) include FIFA 09 (PC, DS, PSP, PS2, PS3, Wii, Wireless, Xbox 360), Pro Evolution Soccer 2008 (PC, DS, PSP, PS2, PS3, Wii, Xbox 360), NBA 2K9 (PC, PS2, PS3, Xbox 360), Don King Presents Prizefighter (DS, Wii, Xbox 360), Sega Superstars Tennis (PSP, PS2, PS3), NHL 09 (PC, PS2, PS3,

Chapter 3

Wireless, XBox 360), NASCAR 09 (PS2, PS3, Xbox 360), Madden NFL 09 (DS, PSP, PS2, PS3, Wii, Xbox 360), Shaun White Snowboarding (PC, DS, PSP, PS2, PS3, Wii, Xbox 360), Tiger Woods PGA Tour (PSP, PS2, PS3, Wii, Xbox 360), and WWE SmackDown! vs. Raw 2009 (DS, PSP, PS2, PS3, Wii, Wireless, Xbox 360).

PC:	Baseball Mogul 2009
	Racing: GRID, Pure
Nintendo DS:	AMF Bowling: Pinbusters
	Racing: Yamaha Supercross, GRID
PSP:	Hot Shots Golf: Open Tee 2, MLB '08: The Show
	Racing: WipEout Pulse
PS2:	MLB Power Pros 2008 Hands-On, MLB '08: The Show
PS3:	Hot Shots Golf: Out of Bounds, Beijing 2008: Olympic Games, MLB '08: The Show
	Fighting: Pirates vs. Ninjas Dodgeball, Dynasty Warriors 6
	Racing: Burnout Paradise, GRID, Pure, Midnight Club: Los Angeles, WipEout HD, Gran Turismo 5 Prologue
Wii:	Sega Superstars Tennis
	Fighting: Super Smash Bros. Brawl
	Racing: Sonic Riders: Zero Gravity, Mario Kart Wii, Yamaha Supercross
Wireless:	Mario & Sonic at the Olympic Games
Xbox 360:	Beijing 2008: Olympic Games, Golf: Tee It Up!
	Fighting: Pirates vs. Ninjas Dodgeball, Dynasty Warriors 6, Soulcalibur IV
	Racing: Burnout Paradise, GRID, Pure, Midnight Club: Los Angeles

Strategy Games

Strategy games are games that require thought and planning. The game's winner is determined through a "battle of the minds."

What makes strategy games different from other genres is that the designer creates rules and goals, but it is the gamer who decides what strategy to use to achieve those goals and outwit his opponent(s).

War games are strategy games although they are simulations of actual or fictitious events.

Strategy games can be played as real-time or turn-based games. In real time, all players including the computer-controlled (AI) players are competing nonstop, simultaneously. In turn based, each player completes his turn before the next player begins.

A typical POV or perspective of strategy games is an overhead view, which allows all players to see the entire playing area.

Top-Selling Strategy Games

2006

PC:	Company of Heroes, Medieval II: Total War, DEFCON, Warhammer 40,000: Dawn of War: Dark Crusade, Star Wars: Empire at War, Galactic Civilization II: Dread Lords
Nintendo DS:	Age of Empires: The Age of Kings, Mage Knight: Destiny's Soldier
PSP:	Field Commander, Metal Gear Acid 2
PS2:	Disgaea 2: Cursed Memories, Full Spectrum Warrior: Ten Hammers
Wireless:	Tornado Mania, Naval Battle: Mission Commander, Civilization III

2007

PC:	World in Conflict, Company of Heroes: Opposing Forces, Supreme Commander, Europa Universalis III
Nintendo DS:	Final Fantasy XII: Revenant Wings, Worms: Open Warfare 2, Theme Park, Rune Factory: A Fantasy Harvest Moon, Front Mission
PSP:	Final Fantasy Tactics: The War of the Lions
PS2:	GrimGrimoire
Wii:	Fire Emblem: Radiant Dawn
Xbox 360:	Rise of the Lost Empires

2008

PC:	Command & Conquer: Red Alert 3, Galactic Civilizations II: Twilight of the Arnor, Chocolatier 2: Secret Ingredients, Sins of a Solar Empire
Nintendo DS:	Sid Meier's Civilization Revolution
PSP:	R-Type Command, My Stylist
PS2:	Innocent Life: A Futuristic Harvest Moon
PS3:	Command & Conquer: Red Alert 3, Valkyria Chronicles, Sid Meier's Civilization Revolution, PixelJunk Monsters
Wii:	Battalion Wars 2, Pokemon Battle Revolution
Wireless:	Medieval: Total War
Xbox 360:	Halo Wars, Sid Meier's Civilization Revolution, Operation Darkness, Command & Conquer 3: Kane's Wrath, Supreme Commander

Chapter 3

Other Games (Puzzles, Music, and Toys)

The "other games" genre includes games that are puzzles, music, and toys that have remained popular and do not easily fit into any other genres.

Puzzle games have a simple goal: to solve the puzzle. Gamers may have to unscramble a picture, keep dropping blocks until time runs out, complete a level, or maneuver pieces until they are placed into their correct location.

Music games have recently become popular and have a place on the best seller and innovation list. Due to their uniqueness, the latest technology such as wireless and infrared communication, and user/player-friendly input devices such as a guitars and drums, music games have sold well and have had successful sequels.

Toy games let the gamer construct objects such as a virtual robot to command, a remote-control car to drive, or an airplane to fly. Other toy games can be like a Rube Goldberg contraption where you construct an activity structure that uses energy to start the flow and ends with a static state. Think of an enormous layout of dominoes standing upright. When the gamer knocks over the first domino, they all fall down in sequence until the entire array of blocks is laying static.

Gamers enjoy puzzle and toy games. Historically they are difficult to market since they are usually unique and publishers must find new and unique ways to pitch them correctly.

Top-Selling Puzzle, Music, and Toy Games

2006

Nintendo DS:	Tetris DS, Magnetica, Mario vs. Donkey Kong 2: March of the Minis
	Music: Elite Beat Agents
PSP:	Mercury Meltdown, Lumines II, Gunpey, Exit
	Music: Gitaroo Man Lives!
PS2:	Music: Guitar Hero II, Lumines Live!, SingStar Rocks!
Wii:	Trauma Center: Second Opinion
Wireless:	Diner Dash, Brain Challenge, Lumines, Gunpey EX, WordKing Spelltris

2007

PC:	Portal, Puzzle Quest: Challenge of the Warlords, Switchball
	Music: Guitar Hero III: Legends of Rock
Nintendo DS:	Picross DS, Puzzle Quest: Challenge of the Warlords, Planet Puzzle League
	Music: Jam Sessions, Hannah Montana: Music Jam, Ontamarama

PSP: Crush, Puzzle Quest: Challenge of the Warlords

PS2:   Puzzle Quest: Challenge of the Warlords

                Music: Guitar Hero III: Legends of Rock, Karaoke Revolution Presents: American Idol

PS3:   Super Puzzle Fighter II Turbo HD Remix

                Music: Guitar Hero III: Legends of Rock, Rock Band

Wii: Music: Guitar Hero III: Legends of Rock, Dance Dance Revolution: Hottest Party

Wireless: Critter Crunch

                Music: Guitar Hero Mobile

Xbox 360:   Puzzle Quest: Challenge of the Warlords, Switchball, Super Puzzle Fighter II Turbo HD Remix

                Music: Guitar Hero III: Legends of Rock, Rock Band

2008

Some of the music games released in 2008 include Guitar Hero: World Tour (PC, PS2, PS3, Wii, Xbox 360) and Rock Band 2 (PS2, PS3, Wii, Xbox 360).

PC: Crazy Machines 2, Line Rider 2: Unbound, Neopets Puzzle Adventure, World of Goo

                Music: Audiosurf

Nintendo DS: Wordmaster, Line Rider 2: Unbound, Neopets Puzzle Adventure, Professor Layton and the Curious Village

                Music: High School Musical 2: Work This Out

PSP: DownStream Panic!, Fading Shadows, Echochrome, Patapon

PS3:   Echochrome

Wii: deBlob, Line Rider 2: Unbound, Neopets Puzzle Adventure, Pop, Boom Blox, Magnetica Twist

Wireless: Paris Hilton's Diamond Quest

                Music: Tap Tap Dance

Xbox 360:   Puzzle Quest: Galactrix

Online Games

Online games take gaming from the solo player to a community of players in a virtual world or playground. Online games can be compared to Disney World or Universal Studios, whereas a video game is a single, entertaining ride. In solo games, the player competes against NPCs (nonplayer characters) and their AI (artificial intelligence). In online games, the world is filled with NPCs and other human players. Online gaming is larger but similar to network and LAN (local area network) gaming. The online games that have corresponding solo versions have more quests, objects to search for, and multiplayer game options.

Multiplayer games have several types of play such as deathmatch, capture the flag (CTF), cooperative play, and king of the hill (KOTH).

In deathmatch play, all players compete against each other to eliminate the most opponents. In capture the flag play, players must seek out and capture the opposing side's team flag and take that flag back to their own home base to win. In cooperative play, all players are on the same team and control one of the team's members. In king of the hill play, the player who occupies a specific marked area for the longest cumulative time wins the game.

Online games allow people to communicate with each other by text, voice, or through their avatars (the player's on-screen persona).

Top-Selling Online Games

2006

PC:	Company of Heroes, Battlefield 2142, DEFCON
Nintendo DS:	Metroid Prime: Hunters, Tony Hawk's Downhill Jam
PSP:	Syphon Filter: Dark Mirror, Metal Gear Solid: Portable Ops, Medal of Honor Heroes
PS2:	Metal Gear Solid 3: Subsistence, SOCOM: U.S. Navy SEALs Combined Assault
PS3:	Resistance: Fall of Man, Call of Duty 3, NBA 2K7
Xbox:	Tom Clancy's Splinter Cell Double Agent, Call of Duty 3
Xbox 360:	Assault Heroes, Small Arms, Tom Clancy's Rainbow Six: Vegas, Gears of War

2007

PC:	World in Conflict, Call of Duty 4: Modern Warfare, Unreal Tournament 3, The Orange Box: Team Fortress 2
Nintendo DS:	Pokemon Diamond/Pearl, FIFA Soccer 08, Race Driver: Create & Race, Ultimate Mortal Kombat, Worms: Open Warfare 2
PSP:	Syphon Filter: Combat Ops, Star Wars Battlefront: Renegade Squadron, Ratchet & Clank: Size Matters
PS3:	Call of Duty 4: Modern Warfare, Calling All Cars, Warhawk, Tom Clancy's Rainbow Six: Vegas
Wii:	Medal of Honor: Heroes 3, Guitar Hero III: Legends of Rock
Wireless:	Tetris Multiplayer
Xbox 360:	Halo 3, Call of Duty 4: Modern Warfare

2008

PC: Left 4 Dead, Call of Duty: World at War, Tom Clancy's Rainbow Six: Vegas 2

Nintendo DS: Advance Wars: Days of Ruin, Call of Duty: World at War, Skate It, Tecmo Bowl: Kickoff

PSP: Buzz! Master Quiz, WipEout Pulse

PS3: Rock Band 2, Call of Duty: World at War, Soulcalibur IV, Resistance 2, Tom Clancy's Rainbow Six: Vegas 2, Burnout Paradise

Wii: Mario Kart Wii, Super Smash Bros. Brawl

Wireless: Guitar Hero World Tour

Xbox 360: Left 4 Dead, Gears of War 2, Rock Band 2, Call of Duty: World at War, Soulcalibur IV, Tom Clancy's Rainbow Six: Vegas 2, Burnout Paradise, Gears of War 2

Last Thoughts

As game designers it is vital that we analyze, recognize, and play the best-selling, innovative, and award-winning games of the past. The games listed in this section have unique gameplay and game mechanics, are innovative, and have won the distinguishing accolade of "Game of the Year." These titles should be on your "to-play" list.

The following are grouped by platform for the years 2006 to 2008 and collected from websites such as IGN.com, Gamespot.com, Gamezone.com, and GameSpy.com.

Game of the Year (By Platform)

PC:

2006 The Elder Scrolls IV: Oblivion, Company of Heroes

2007 BioShock, Call of Duty 4: Modern Warfare, Crysis, World in Conflict, The Orange Box: Half-Life 2: Episode Two, Team Fortress 2, Portal

2008 Fallout 3, Warhammer Online: Age of Reckoning, Left 4 Dead, World of Warcraft: Wrath of the Lich King, Grand Theft Auto IV, World of Goo, Galactic Civilizations II: Twilight of the Arnor, Mass Effect, Sins of a Solar Empire, Spore, Crysis Warhead

Nintendo DS:

2006 New Super Mario Bros., Elite Beat Agents

2007 The Legend of Zelda: Phantom Hourglass, Picross DS, Planet Puzzle League, Puzzle Quest: Challenge of the Warlords, Pokemon Diamond, Hotel Dusk: Room 215, Contra 4

Chapter 3

2008	Professor Layton and the Curious Village, Space Invaders Extreme, Final Fantasy Tactics A2: Grimoire of the Rift, Trauma Center: Under the Knife 2, Castlevania: Order of Ecclesia, The World Ends With You, Ninja Gaiden: Dragon Sword

Game Cube:

2006	The Legend of Zelda: Twilight Princess

PSP:

2006	Syphon Filter: Dark Mirror, Daxter, Killzone: Liberation
2007	Syphon Filter: Logan's Shadow, Disgaea: Afternoon of Darkness, Jeanne d'Arc, Puzzle Quest: Challenge of the Warlords, Ratchet & Clank: Size Matters, Sid Meier's Pirates!, Crush
2008	God of War: Chains of Olympus, WipEout Pulse, Patapon, N+, Space Invaders Extreme, Crisis Core: Final Fantasy VII

PS2:

2006	Final Fantasy XII, Okami, Bully
2007	God of War, Guitar Hero III: Legends of Rock, Rogue Galaxy, Shin Megami Tensei: Persona 3, Tomb Raider: Anniversary, GrimGrimoire

PS3:

2006	Resistance: Fall of Man
2007	The Elder Scrolls IV: Oblivion, Uncharted: Drake's Fortune, Ninja Gaiden Sigma, Ratchet & Clank Future: Tools of Destruction, Call of Duty 4: Modern Warfare, Assassin's Creed, Warhawk, Rock Band
2008	Fallout 3, LittleBigPlanet, Metal Gear Solid 4: Guns of the Patriots, Grand Theft Auto IV, Rock Band 2, Valkyria Chronicles, Resistance 2, Dead Space, Burnout Paradise

Wii:

2006	The Legend of Zelda: Twilight Princess, Elebits
2007	Super Mario Galaxy, Metroid Prime 3: Corruption, Zack & Wiki: Quest for Barbaros' Treasure, Super Paper Mario, Resident Evil 4: Wii Edition, WarioWare: Smooth Moves
2008	Mario Kart Wii, Boom Blox, Super Smash Bros. Brawl, World of Goo, deBlob, Wii Fit, No More Heroes, Mega Man 9, Tetris Party, Wario Land: Shake It!

Wireless:

2006	Tornado Mania, Mafia Wars Yakuza, Super K.O. Boxing
2007	Digital Chocolate Café
2008	Spore, I-play Bowling, Ego

XBox:

> 2006   Tom Clancy's Splinter Cell Double Agent, Scarface: The World Is Yours

XBox 360:

> 2006   Gears of War, The Elder Scrolls IV: Oblivion, Tom Clancy's Rainbow Six: Vegas
>
> 2007   BioShock, Call of Duty 4: Modern Warfare, Halo 3, Mass Effect, The Orange Box: Half-Life 2: Episode Two, Team Fortress 2, Portal, Rock Band, Forza Motorsport 2
>
> 2008   Fallout 3, Gears of War 2, Grand Theft Auto IV, Left 4 Dead, Dead Space, Fable II, Prince of Persia, Rock Band 2, Burnout Paradise, Soulcalibur IV

Workshop

Assignments

Assignment 1: Create a game for the action, sports, simulation, and strategy genres using at least five of the following elements:

- Ball
- Balloon
- Bicycle
- Car
- Cookies
- Dog
- Fish
- Monkey
- Pizza
- Water

Assignment 2: Create a game from one of the following classic television shows. Describe the genre, gameplay, and USP for your game.

- *Friends*
- *Gilligan's Island*
- *The Sopranos*
- *ER*
- *The Honeymooners*
- *The Love Boat*
- *West Wing*
- *Boston Legal*

Exercises

Exercise 1: Describe a game that could be designed from an unpublished license and the genre the game would fall into.

Exercise 2: Describe the difference between a first-person shooter and a third-person shooter.

Exercise 3: List 10 current games that can be categorized as an FPS and 10 that can be categorized as a 3PS.

Exercise 4: List 10 recent games, including the genre, publisher, price, and platform.

Chapter 3

Exercise 5: List the current top 10 games for one platform and describe their popularity.

Exercise 6: Describe two top hybrid type games, and for each game analyze how the designer merged the types to make a great game.

Unguided Exercises

Unguided Exercise 1: List and describe a few games and licenses that can be categorized as linear, nonlinear, and emergent play.

Unguided Exercise 2: Analyze and describe an action-shooter game or war game that has multiplayer features and categorize the features.

Unguided Exercise 3: List some classic games such as board games that would make good game concepts and describe one in terms of its game mechanics.

Unguided Exercise 4: Compare the differences in a title that's both a console game and a computer game.

Unguided Exercise 5: Describe the benefits and constraints that a licensed property brings to the game design.

Thoughts for Discussion

1. Discuss favorite classic and current games.
2. Discuss why certain games have become favorites (e.g., great stories, addictive, great interaction, beautiful graphics).
3. Discuss the history of games in relation to faster hardware and better storage mediums that hold more data.
4. Discuss innovations that could improve the game experience.
5. Discuss favorite shows and films that would make great games.
6. Discuss favorite licensed property games.
7. Discuss the POV vs. the intended audience.
8. Discuss potential writers and actors who would benefit the game.
9. Looking at successful franchises such as Mario, Pokemon, The Sims, Final Fantasy, Need for Speed, Grand Theft Auto, Madden NFL, or FIFA, what new and innovative features could be added for the next sequel?

Chapter 4

Game Concepts and Ideas

Games Are *Not* Linear

Books and movies are linear forms of storytelling. They have a straight path from the beginning to the end.

Although there have been numerous attempts in both mediums to allow the reader or viewer to select the next path leading to one of several endings, I consider these to be attempts to make them more "game-like" (nonlinear).

Games Have a Goal

The goal in chess is for one player to force a winning situation by "checkmate" or having the opponent resign (quit). The goal in many sports games is to outscore the opponent. The goal in Othello is to occupy the most spaces on the board. The goal in a game where you oversee a city or a planet may be to restore balance to a chaotic environment.

Other noteworthy goals for games might be based on "losing for a greater good," like in the film *Brewster's Millions* where Richard Pryor must become penniless to inherit the family fortune. In a game based on this movie, each turn the player receives a set amount of money to invest unwisely and after a set number of turns, the player must be broke.

Or more altruistic goals could be the game's goal, such as "self sacrifice," "helping the less fortunate," or "giving up all worldly possessions for a cause."

Games such as The Sims and SimCity are called "sandbox games" since they have no goals or objectives.

Games Must Be Winnable

Only a fool would agree to play the "Heads I win, tails you lose" game. Almost as bad would be a game where you need to roll the dice three times and get a 12 (two 6s) each time to win. Winnable? Yes. Worth playing this game? No. (The winning odds are 1 in 46,656.)

You should design the game to be winnable, or at least possibly winnable through multiple paths.

In a multiplayer game, give each player equal strengths and weaknesses at the start. A good game lets each player have an equal chance and ability to win. You should spend time and pay attention to designing balance in your game. Let random events and the player's decisions and actions determine the new game situation (such as the player's current position).

Start of the Game

All games have the players in some initial position or setup.

In chess, it's the opening position of the 16 white and 16 black pieces. In a world domination or strategy game, it's each player's currently occupied terrain. In a role-playing game (RPG), it's the adventuring party consisting of various races, skills (magic, fighting, learned skills like locksmithing), and occupations (soldier, priest, blacksmith) preparing to start a quest. In a sports game, it's the team's or player's starting formation or position. In an adventure game, it might be a puzzle to solve or a direction to initially explore.

In a puzzle game, it's the initial setup of the puzzle's challenge. Perhaps the game could be designed to have a random start position.

Some games can be unbalanced, allowing the more skillful player to have a handicap in the initial position.

Middle/Ending of the Game

Whatever the game type, there should be numerous paths for the player to take or random events to occur to move the player along and finally determine the winner.

Many games (for example, adventure games) give the player a score at the end of the game. The game's main goal is to finish the assigned quest. The game's secondary goal is to better the previous score and eventually earn the perfect score. Puzzle games could reward the player with a password that would allow access to higher levels.

In games, the goal is to win, but in many games tying (drawing) or losing a well-played game against a much stronger and skillful opponent is a rewarding and satisfactory outcome.

When designing your game, think about your audience and the challenges and hoops you've put them through to reach the final plateau where they now stand awaiting their reward.

Design an ending worthy of a winner and acceptable to the non-winner who has just finished your game. Think fireworks, a ticker-tape parade, or the cheers of millions. These may seem overboard and silly, but to a traveler who has spent time journeying across the game you've designed, the spectacular ending is a marvelous reward and justly warranted. Think of your gamer as the conquering hero who is entering the city to pay homage to you the designer, or the parade for the sports team that has won the national championship, or the audience's excitement and atmosphere before an encore at a concert.

Interactive Games

The games that we play and design for PCs, video game consoles, handhelds, arcades, wireless devices, and the Internet are interactive. The player uses an input device to give the game feedback or an action.

Some traditional input devices include keyboards, joysticks, trackballs or other mouse-type objects, game controllers, touch screens, light pens, and voice recognized input. Newer technology input devices for games utilize eye movement, facial expressions, brainwave input, and the "sip/puff controller" that was designed for the disabled.

The following is a quote from the Entertainment Software Association's website page at http://www.theesa.com/facts/salesandgenre.asp:

According to data compiled by the NPD Group, a global market research company, and released by the ESA in January 2008, computer and video game companies posted record sales in 2007. The industry sold 267.8 million units, leading to an astounding $9.5 billion in revenue.

Of these sales:

- Game console software sales totaled $6.6 billion with 153.9 million units sold;

- Computer games sales were $910.7 million with 36.4 million units sold; and,

- There was a record $2.0 billion in portable software sales with 77.5 million units sold.

NPD's research also showed:

- On average, nine games were sold every second of every day of 2007;

- Halo 3, the best-selling title of 2007, took in more revenue in its first day of sales than the biggest opening weekend ever for a movie (*Spider-Man 3*) and the final *Harry Potter* book's first day sales; and,

■ The entertainment software industry sold over 13.4 million portable game units in 2007, easily trumping the much-hyped Apple iPhone, which sold just 4 million units.

Game Ideas

At this stage, you understand the gaming genres and are probably eager to become a game designer. What you need next is a clear vision of a game concept.

If you don't already have an idea in mind, you can always "creatively borrow" ideas from other sources and tailor them to your liking. Some sources that are great to "borrow" from are books, movies, history, science, art, music, sports, card and board games, and everyday life itself.

If ideas are truly worth a dime a dozen, then here's over $10 worth of ideas for you to use as the basis for a game design concept. An expanded version of the following is available on the book's companion CD.

Here is a sampling:

Sports

1. Archery
2. Arm wrestling
3. Badminton
4. Baseball
5. Basketball
6. Biathlon
7. BMX biking
8. Bobsled (and Skeleton)
9. Boogie boarding or bodyboarding
10. Bowling
    a. Standard 10 pin
    b. Candle pin
    c. Duck pin
    d. Bowls, Bowling on the green, Lawn bowling
    e. Bocce
    f. Skittles
    g. Canadian five pin
11. Boxing
12. Cricket
13. Croquet
14. Cross-country skiing
15. Curling
16. Cycling
    a. The match sprint
    b. The Olympic sprint
    c. The individual pursuit
    d. The team pursuit
    e. The points race
    f. The keirin
    g. The Madison
    h. Sprint race
    i. Messenger race
    j. Freight bike race
    k. Unicycling
17. Darts
18. Demolition derby
19. Diving
20. Dodgeball
21. Dog racing
22. Dog sledding
23. Equestrian
    a. Dressage
    b. Show jumping
    c. Eventing
    d. Combined driving
    e. Endurance riding
    f. Reining
24. Extreme fighting
25. Fencing
26. Field hockey
27. Fishing
28. Football

29. Formula-1 racing
30. Golf
31. Gymnastics
32. Hockey (ice or roller)
33. Horse racing
34. Horseshoe pitching
35. Hunting
36. Ice skating
37. Jai Alai
38. Jet Skiing
39. Jousting
40. Judo
41. Karate
42. Kayaking
43. Kendo
44. Kung Fu
45. Lacrosse
46. Luge
    a. Timed luge races
    b. Dual luge races
    c. Mass luge races
    d. Super mass luge races
    e. Street luge
    f. Classic luge (buttboard)
47. Miniature golf
48. Monster truck rally
49. Motorcycling
50. NASCAR racing
51. Paintball
52. Pentathlon
53. Polo (horse)
54. Pool
    a. Straight
    b. Rotation pool
    c. Snooker
    d. Billiards
    e. Bumper pool
    f. Eight ball
    g. Nine ball
55. Quoits
56. Racquetball
57. Rodeo
58. Roller derby
59. Roller skating
60. Rowing
61. Rugby
62. Sailing
63. Shuffleboard
64. Skateboarding
65. Skeet shooting
66. Skiing
67. Snowboarding
68. Snowmobiling
69. Soccer
70. Softball
71. Speed skating
72. Squash
73. Sumo wrestling
74. Surfing
75. Swimming
76. Table tennis
77. Tennis
78. Tobogganing
79. Track and field
    a. The decathlon
    b. The heptathlon
    c. The high jump
    d. The long jump
    e. The triple jump
    f. The pole vault
    g. The shot put
    h. The discus
    i. The javelin
    j. The hammer throw
80. Trampoline
81. Trapshooting
82. Triathlon
83. Volleyball
84. Wakeboarding
85. Water polo
86. Water skiing
87. Wrestling

Chapter 4

Board Games

1. Backgammon
2. Go
3. Checkers
4. Hangman (like Wheel of Fortune)
5. Chess
6. Mahjong
7. Dominoes
8. Othello

Card and Gambling Games

1. Baccarat
2. Blackjack
3. Bridge
4. Caribbean Stud poker
5. Craps
6. Cribbage
7. Gin rummy
8. Go fish
9. Hearts
10. Keno
11. Old maid
12. Paigow poker
13. Poker: Draw, Five-Card Stud, Seven-Card Stud, Texas Hold 'Em, Omaha
14. Red dog
15. Roulette
16. Sic bo
17. Slots
18. Solitaire
19. Spades
20. Video poker
21. War

Simulations

1. Become a rock star
2. Operate a semi-truck for cross-country delivery
3. Be a train engineer
4. Drive a motorcycle across the country
5. Pilot a helicopter
6. Pilot an airplane: Cessna, 727, 747, F-16, F-18
7. Be an automotive repair technician
8. Be a brain surgeon
9. Be a dentist
10. Be a doctor: diagnose patients
11. Race a 4x4 truck
12. Run a car rental company
13. Build and operate a casino
14. Manage a cinema chain
15. Run a corporation
16. Manage a cruise line
17. Manage a gaming company
18. Operate a golf resort
19. Manage a hospital
20. Manage a major newspaper
21. Manage a movie studio
22. Manage a pizza delivery restaurant
23. Manage a railroad
24. Manage a resort island
25. Manage a restaurant chain
26. Manage a zoo
27. Manage an amusement park
28. Manage an overnight delivery carrier
29. Manage a university
30. Run for president
31. Run for senator
32. Simulate a human internal disease
33. Operate a nuclear power plant
34. Simulate an ant colony
35. Simulate the stock market
36. Operate a brokerage company

Science

Astronomy   Earth science
Biology   Ecology
Chemistry   Physics

History

Events   Inventions
Explorers   Wars
Famous people

Literature

The Bible
Classical literature
Modern literature
Mythology

Art

How can artwork be made into a game?

We could design a game in which we need to locate various artworks of famous painters. The beginning goal could be "The museum would like you to acquire a Renoir" and you adventure into the world seeking "Luncheon of the Boating Party." Another scenario could be like in the film *The Thomas Crown Affair*, where you desire to steal famous works of art and replace them with perfect forgeries.

You can even look at a masterpiece and create a story from it. Imagine what actions and situations preceded the painting as though it was a photograph.

Georges Seurat, French, 1859-1891. A Sunday Afternoon on La Grande Jatte, 1884-86. Oil on canvas, 207.6 x 308 cm. Helen Birch Bartlett Memorial Collection, 1926.224. Image used with permission, Copyright © 2001, The Art Institute of Chicago.

Chapter 4

A Pulitzer Prize-Winning Play Based on a Painting

For example, the play *Sunday in the Park with George* was inspired by Georges Seurat's painting entitled "A Sunday Afternoon on the Island of La Grande Jatte."

Georges Seurat was the founder of the 19th-century French school of Neo-Impressionism whose technique for portraying the play of light using tiny brushstrokes of contrasting colors became known as "Pointillism." Director and author James Lapine's collaboration with Stephen Sondheim, based on Georges Seurat's masterpiece, won the 1985 Pulitzer Prize for Drama.

Sunday in the Park with George takes place on an island somewhere in the Seine where an artist, George, and Dot, his model and mistress, are involved in an elaborate painting session. Later, Dot decides to leave George for a pastry baker and travels to America. She secretly is carrying George's child. The play continues years later (1984) following Dot's family and the painting, which is being celebrated at its 100th anniversary.

Wow! All this from a single masterpiece.

The expanded version of this chapter's list of game ideas, included on the companion CD, contains an extensive list of artists and descriptions of their works you can use to design stories from.

Music

How can music be made into a game?

We could go back in time and aid each composer in creating his or her masterpiece.

We could use the music as the basis for a game design, such as Tchaikovsky's "Peter and the Wolf" or Rossini's "William Tell Overture" (also known as the "Lone Ranger Theme").

We could educate ourselves on the different types of music, and in an RPG where we have several towns and cities, we could have a different type or style of music being played in each town.

The Tom Hanks film *That Thing You Do* was based entirely on a band that really only played one song for the entire film.

The sales figures for music games such as the Guitar Hero series and Nintendo DS's Electroplankton demonstrate how much players enjoy games of this nature.

In January 2008, Activision and the NPD Group announced that the Guitar Hero franchise had set an industry record by surpassing $1 billion in North American retail sales in just 26 months.

Dance and Musical Instruments

Dancing and playing various instruments are educational but can also be fun if the game is designed that way. Playing an instrument while adventuring through a fantasy land or playing chords or notes to interact with the world or to compete in a sport are interesting and fun ways to learn. Some of these instruments can be merged together in a game, like learning the piano and organ at the same time in one well-designed game concept.

Here are a few specific game ideas for this topic:
1. Dancing
   a. Country-western
   b. Competition ballroom
2. Play the strings:
   a. Violin
   b. Viola
   c. Cello
   d. Bass
   e. Banjo
   f. Guitar
3. Play the piano
4. Play the organ
5. Play the carillon
6. Play the woodwinds: flute
7. Play the brass: trumpet
8. Play percussion: drums (snare and bass)
9. Play the accordion
10. Play the harmonica

In 1999 Konami released in North America and Europe their game Dance Dance Revolution (also called DDR), where players step on a special floor marked with colored arrows matching the symbols displayed on the screen as pulsating music accompanies their "dance movements." Players can play DDR alone or in competition with other players. Originally, DDR was released for the arcade platform, and then with a dance pad as an input device for the Sony PlayStation and later the PlayStation 2, Microsoft's Xbox, Xbox 360, Nintendo Wii, N64, PC, Gamecube, and Dreamcast.

In December 2003, Konami announced DDR sales surpassing 6.5 million units worldwide with 1.5 million copies sold in Europe, 1 million copies sold in the U.S., and 4 million units sold in Japan.

Chapter 4

Movies and Film

When obtaining game ideas from a film (or movie) we want to utilize the film's premise (plot, theme, and action) and not its character names, costumes, creature design and look, or names of places and objects.

The film *Alien* has a unique character (the alien), a specific spaceship design, and a famous cast and character names. If we want to mimic *Alien* in our game design, first we would call our game something interesting and descriptive like Space Predator or Space Cannibal to get the audience, publishers, and stores interested and to give a preconceived notion about the game.

If we decided that our alien creature was to look like a carnivorous dinosaur, we might title the game Space Raptor to bring in the *Jurassic Park* audience. We would design our own alien, perhaps describing it or using an artist's sketch of our scary alien vision. We may use the crew dynamics of the film *Alien*, such as each member's rank, sex, age, and race and then change the character names and faces to differ from the film.

In our pitch to publishers and in future sales and marketing material, we would utilize the *Alien* basis to correlate potential sales, audience interest, and a marketing strategy. We would obviously claim that our game is scarier and better than the film that spawned two sequels (*Aliens* and *Alien 3*) as well as several lesser rip-off films. Our pitch would include the facts that in 1979 *Alien* was the top-grossing film and in 1997 *Alien 3* was that year's top-grossing film. Also based on the film data, we could list the demographics of our audience like age, sex, and income level as well as international appeal.

As in life and in books, films, and games, "there is nothing new under the sun."

Workshop

Assignments

Assignment 1:
1. List five games and describe their gameplay and strategy to win.
2. List five platforms and the input devices that they support.

Assignment 2: Select an input device and describe how the player uses it and technically how it works.

An example would be a mouse that has two or three buttons that can be pressed, where the player moves the mouse to change the X and Y positions. The program receives the current mouse position in relation to the screen resolution. Each mouse button updates that button's status, such as up, down, single-click, or double-click.

Assignment 3: Select a film from the list of films and a sport from the list of sports included in the expanded version of this chapter on the companion CD.

From these selected items, describe the selected sports game using the premise from the chosen film. An example would be a baseball game between teams composed of characters from *The Pirates of the Caribbean* and those from *The Lord of the Rings* (Golem is the umpire with a double dose of Orlando Bloom).

Exercises

Exercise 1: Select five of the following game designers:

Chris Crawford	Richard Garriott
David Perry	Roberta Williams
Hideo Kojima	Shigeru Miyamoto
Hironobu Sakaguchi	Shinji Mikami
Jason Rubin	Sid Meier
Jordan Mechner	Warren Spector
Kazunori Yamauchi	Will Wright
Peter Molyneux	Yuji Naka

1. Where does the designer live?
2. What games has he/she designed?
3. What company has published the designer's games?
4. Why is this designer suited to work on games of this genre or theme?

Exercise 2: Select five of these top game publishers:

Nintendo	Namco Bandai
Electronic Arts	Vivendi Games
Ubisoft	Capcom
THQ	Konami
Take-Two Interactive	NCSoft
Sega of America	Buena Vista Games
Sony Computer Entertainment	Atlus Games
Microsoft Game Studios	LucasArts
Eidos Interactive	Midway Games
Square Enix	

1. List the address or country of the publisher's main office.
2. What are their best game titles?
3. What platforms does the publisher sell games for?
4. What was this company's latest revenue?
5. How many employees does this company currently employ?

Chapter 4

Unguided Exercises

Unguided Exercise 1: Why are "sandbox games" not considered interactive games and what do players enjoy about these games?

Unguided Exercise 2: Every player has a favorite game. Briefly discuss that game's beginning premise or background story, the initial gameplay setting, the middle of the game's variation, and the winning conditions.

Thoughts for Discussion

1. What game idea would you like to work on?
2. Discuss how a film or book would make a great interactive game and some unique ways in which the player interacts with the story.
3. Describe the difference between a film and an interactive game.
4. How can games add more emotions and make players laugh or cry?

Chapter 5

The Game Design Process

In the game development process there are two major styles: "carefully planned/schedule-driven development" and "organic design."

In this book we teach the "carefully planned" style, which emphasizes written documentation such as the one pager, game proposal, executive summary, and finally the Game Design Document (or GDD). The Game Design Document is also referred to as the game's bible, and the carefully planned style of development follows the GDD to the letter. The GDD is based on the game designer's vision, research, and license or storyline, plus additional input by other team members during the preliminary design phase. Sometimes a game designer may have a general concept, and an artist or programmer suggests an innovative technique to achieve that concept through code or animation.

The word "organic" in the phrase "organic game design" means a living, growing entity of life; therefore the organic design style of development is an ongoing process that tries to implement new, original, and innovative ideas by trial and error.

The "One Pager" Concept Document

The first document that a game designer creates is called a "One Pager." The One Pager explains and sells your game's concept to publishers and developers and puts your ideas and vision into a concise document. A One Pager can be one or two pages (double-spaced preferred but single-spaced in lieu of a partial third page).

The One Pager always begins with your game's title. You are selling the game's name as well as its design.

The first sentence of the document is the most important and often the hardest one to write. In one sentence you must describe your game concept. Let me repeat this rule: You must explain the entire game in *one sentence*. Usually, the sentence repeats the game's title and includes the game's genre and a basic description or overview of the concept.

Describing a product with once sentence is often referred to as the "elevator pitch" because it highlights the games features and allows you to explain your game in a short amount of time, usually within one minute. Some examples are:

■ Gangster is an FPS (first-person shooter) where the player is a gangster like Jesse James, Clyde Parker, or John Dillinger and the player is placed in the gangster scenarios and must successfully complete each mission.

■ P-Man is an arcade-style action game where you maneuver a dot-munching, animated circle through a labyrinth, trying to destroy flashing bases as six enemy squares eagerly roam the maze seeking to capture you.

■ Couch Potato Baseball is a 3D sports game (baseball), where the player selects his All-Star team and manages the team through a season of play to the World Series by selecting his All-Star team players, assigning each game's lineup, selecting the pitchers, trading players, and bringing up triple-A players.

The One Pager also includes other gaming issues. You need to list your game's features (cover the basic, standard features as well as special features that make your concept different or better than the current, competing games), the hardware and software needed (required) and suggested (recommended) to properly play your game, and similar and competing games (their title, publisher, retail price, and platforms such as Windows Vista, PlayStation 3, PlayStation Portable, Nintendo Wii, Nintendo DS, and Microsoft's Xbox and Xbox 360). You may also include any marketing and sales issues that will help sell your concept and increase interest in your game such as a license, anticipated audience (gender, age ranges of players), and pertinent data (for a sports game the number of players and worldwide audience numbers).

After you write the One Pager to your liking, show it to avid game players and fans as well as nonplayers. The One Pager is important and should be understandable and interesting to everyone from business people to hardcore gamers.

The purpose of a concept document is to sell the idea for your game to your team, company, or funding source.

"One Pager" Overview

The One Pager must contain the following items.

- Title: The title must be brief, descriptive, and "catchy." Try to come up with a name that will attract players to your game.

- Genre: Use one of the genres or a hybrid genre such as "action-adventure."

- Platform: What platforms will you target and why? Which platform will the development start with and which platforms would the game be ported to?

- Premise (or high concept): Up to two sentences describing the unique "hook" of the game. Think of the premise as words that will be used on an advertisement or on the front of the game's packaging.

- Backstory: How did we get here? What happens before the game begins?

- Target rating: Indicate what the expected ESRB rating for your game will be and why (content reasons and your reasons as a selling point).

- Target market: The target market is the portion of the game-playing audience that will be most likely to play your game, including a specific age range and gender. How does the target market tie into the game's genre?

- Player motivation: How does the player win? What will drive the player to actually play the game to the end? For example, the player could be motivated by a desire to beat the enemy, successfully solve puzzles, collect treasures, or explore worlds.

- USP (unique selling proposition/point): What makes your game stand out? Why will game players buy your game over the competitors' titles? Why should your game be developed? What is special about this game?

- Competitive analysis: Select three game titles currently on the market that are similar and could be considered competitors of your game. Describe each of these titles (one sentence per title) including its platform, price, and sales figures. Discuss why your game can attract the same audience and establish a competitive edge over the other titles.

- Goals: What are your expectations for this game as an experience? Besides the "fun factor," will the game provide excitement, tension, suspense, challenge, humor, or emotions such as sadness, fear, amusement, or a good feeling? Can players create their own stories and characters? Discuss how the game is designed to fulfill these goals.

Sample One Pager Documents

Note that in the following example the name in parentheses is a placeholder.

(Megan Pedersen)'s International Wakeboarding Open

[the opening sentence]

(Megan Pedersen)'s International Wakeboarding Open is a 3D, third-person wakeboarding sports competition that lets the player(s) (single and multiplayer) compete in up to seven international venues and choreograph their acrobatic maneuvers through each course's obstacles and wakes.

[game marketing and sales pitch]

(Megan Pedersen)'s International Wakeboarding Open will appeal to all extreme sports enthusiasts and features the top women's wakeboarding champion (Megan Pedersen). Wakeboarding has been featured on ESPN, ESPN2, and OLN, reaching over 70 million households. (Megan Pedersen) has won numerous wakeboarding championships, including the Van Triple Crown of Wakeboarding Championship, the Wakeboarding National Championship, the World Championship, and the X Games Championship.

Wakeboarding is the fastest-growing watersport in the world — increasing over 100 percent in participation over the past three years. Wakeboarding is a combination of surfing, skateboarding, snowboarding, and water skiing. A wakeboard looks like a snowboard with a pair of bindings attached to it. The wakeboarder carves turns with body leans and by rocking the board.

[game concept overview (premise)]

(Megan Pedersen)'s International Wakeboarding Open has each player competing in from one to seven countries in the circuit. The participating locations will be Orlando, U.S.; Sydney, Australia; Johannesburg, South Africa; Tokyo, Japan; Paris, France; Venice, Italy; and Buenos Aires, Argentina. In the single-player mode, the player will practice his or her maneuvers and learn new ones. Based on the player's learned skill level, he or she will be able to compete for the championships. Players need to master the basic skills before attempting the expert tricks and maneuvers. In the multiplayer mode (via the Internet or network), players will take turns competing in one or more countries for individual championships or for the Grand Prix Circuit Championship of (Megan Pedersen)'s International Wakeboarding Open.

[target audience/demographics/market]

The intended audience will be males between the ages of 8 and 20 who enjoy extreme sports. Also, since a famed female wakeboarder (Megan Pedersen) is featured, an anticipated female audience of ages 8 to 17 is projected.

[intended platform]

The platform for this game will be Windows Vista and XP as the first release, with Microsoft's Xbox/Xbox 360, Sony's PlayStation 2 and 3, and the Nintendo DS to follow.

[similar and competitive games]

Similar, successful games have been Tony Hawk's Proving Ground (Nintendo Wii version is $29.95, Nintendo DS version is $19.95, PlayStation 2 version is $19.95, PlayStation 3 version is $39.95, Xbox 360 version is $39.95), Tony Hawk's Project 8 (Sony PSP version is $39.95), EA's Skate (Xbox 360 version is $39.95 and PlayStation 3 version is $39.95), Tony Hawk's Motion (Nintendo DS version is $29.99), EA's Skate It (Nintendo Wii version is $49.95), Ubisoft's Sunny Garcia Surfing (PlayStation 2 version is $28.85), Ubisoft's Shaun White Snowboarding (Nintendo DS version is $29.99, PlayStation 2 version is $39.99, PlayStation 3 and PSP versions are $39.99, Xbox 360 version is $59.99), Ubisoft's Shaun White Snowboarding Road Trip (Nintendo Wii version is $49.99), and Activision's Kelly Slater's Pro Surfer (Gameboy Advance version is $19.95).

[game specifics]

(Megan Pedersen)'s International Wakeboarding Open has a 3D behind-the-wakeboarder POV (point of view) where the player controls the boarder's lateral movement, speed and forward movement (by signaling to the virtual motorboat), acrobatic maneuvers, and obstacle jumps (the slider, a kicker, and a jump ramp). The game will contain realistic physics, animation, and sound effects. Commentators, including (Megan Pedersen), will describe and evaluate the wakeboarder's performance. After each performance or routine, the player can use the video replay feature to observe and improve their tricks. Each of the seven unique locations will have an obstacle course that can be modified by the player before the competition begins. Players will be judged based on a 100-point system for their routine's technical difficulty ("execution," worth 33.3 points), the "in-air" acrobatics ("intensity," worth 33.4 points), and the seamless flow of the routine ("composition," worth 33.3 points). Like the real world of competition, each wakeboarder has a two-fall limit.

[special features and USP]

In the single-player mode, the player can practice his or her tricks on various obstacles and courses. In order to become a Pro Wakeboarder, the player must successfully show an understanding of the beginner, intermediate, and advanced tricks, grabs, spins, and inverts. (Megan Pedersen) will coach and evaluate the player as he or she progresses from novice to Pro Wakeboarder status. The beginner wakeboarder can learn simple air maneuvers and grabs like the Butterslide 180, the Surf Carve, and the Ollie Blind 180. Then the player can practice the intermediate tricks like

Chapter 5

the Indy Blind 180, the Scarecrow, and the Back Roll. Finally, the player can advance to the difficult inverts, spins, and grabs like the Whirlybird, the Elephant, and the Wrapped KGB.

The soundtrack for (Megan Pedersen)'s International Wakeboarding Open will have a rock/album sound with commercialized bands that will enhance the extreme gameplay, gain the teenagers' audio attention, and have the press commenting on the "hot" soundtrack.

[final selling sentence (wrap it up)]

(Megan Pedersen)'s International Wakeboarding Open will be a highly anticipated arrival into the extreme sports gaming world with its fast-paced, turbocharged acrobatic maneuvers, realistic sound effects, orchestrated ambient sound track, and commentators describing the wakeboarder's tricks, as well as having the (Megan Pedersen) name, a dominant female competitor in the world of extreme sports.

———◆———

Years ago, I met a student studying to become a medical doctor who was addicted to Mortal Kombat. He wanted to design a game where the player would be inside the human body combating real-life diseases like cancer. The cancer cells would invade the body and the player would gather his super force of red and white blood cells, the Chemo Team, and Radiation Sensations and use their martial art techniques to fight and destroy the disease. This game would not only be fun for the fighting genre fans but would also teach people about diseases (what the disease does, where it attacks the human body, symptoms, and what to look for as it progresses) and their treatments (the latest cures, various treatment options, and length of time needed to destroy a disease or put it in remission).

We worked together to expand this concept, including the entire human life (from infancy to old age).

We called this game Medical Kombat and felt that it would appeal to all ages, especially children 13 to 18 as well as medical students like my co-designer.

Several films have been made on this subject, such as *Fantastic Voyage* (1966) and *Osmosis Jones*. *Osmosis Jones*, a 2001 film starring Chris Rock, is about a white blood cell (Jones) and a cold tablet (Drixorial) who must in 48 hours combat a deadly virus called "the Thrax" inside its host body, Frank. In *Fantastic Voyage*, in order to save the main character who has a potentially fatal health problem, a miniaturized spaceship is injected into the bloodstream to quickly travel to the location of the problem so the crew can save the patient's life.

At the Walt Disney World Resort EPCOT's Wonders of Life pavillion is a simulation ride called Body Wars where the riders in a ship are shrunk before it enters the human body and explores the bloodstream as well as other organs such as the brain. The main mission is to travel to the location of a splinter penetration that is being attacked by white blood cells. (Fun fact: The simulation was directed by Leonard Nimoy in 1989.)

Medical Kombat

[the opening sentence]

Medical Kombat is a third-person POV, martial arts/first-person shooter that takes place in a real human body from birth to death as the good side combats diseases and viruses and players learn all about many diseases, their symptoms, and causes as well as the past and latest medical treatments.

[game concept overview (premise)]

The player, or players in multiplayer mode, will select an age range to play from, such as infancy, young childhood, or young adult to adulthood.

The infant diseases will include jaundice, convulsions, seizures, asthma, hernia, and so on.

The young childhood diseases will include viruses and ailments like mumps, measles (rubeola and rubella, or German measles), chicken pox, polio, allergies, acne, bee stings, hiccups, splinters, epilepsy, broken arms and legs, and so on. Other diseases will include bacterial diseases (like scarlet fever, whooping cough, typhoid fever, diphtheria, gangrene, cholera, conjuctivitis, and tuberculosis), viruses (like smallpox, influenza, anthrax, pneumonia, herpes, hepatitis, trachoma, and yellow fever), fungal diseases (like thrush and athlete's foot), nutritional diseases (like beriberi, rickets, and scurvy), and parasitic diseases (like malaria and bubonic plague).

The adult diseases will include leukemia, cancer (lung, skin, breast, and bone), tumors, gallstones, kidney stones, AIDS, heart problems, diabetes, Alzheimer's, arthritis, osteoporosis, ALS, muscular dystrophy, and emphysema.

Besides the aforementioned good guy teams, there will be vaccines and drug-injected superheroes like penicillin, insulin, and other medications. Some superheroes can fight an enemy one-on-one, some spin medicated webs trying to capture and destroy the unsuspecting enemies, and others shoot medication into the human body, blocking the pathways or locking the enemy inside a region. The super team uses the human body's blood transit system to travel through arteries away from the heart and through veins back to their headquarters (the heart). The object of each mission is to survive, and the player(s) will have several medical gauges and monitors that will give up-to-date tracking of the patient's progress.

[game marketing and sales pitch, USP]

Medical Kombat has unique cross-genre appeal since it is a martial arts fighting game, an FPS, and an educational game all in one. Parents will appreciate its educational benefit, and males and females ages 8 to 16 will

Chapter 5

be enthusiastic about the realistic and intense fighting and destruction of their enemies. Each year 15,000 to 19,000 high school students apply to medical colleges throughout the U.S. Several films have been made on this subject, like *Fantastic Voyage* and *Osmosis Jones*.

[similar and competitive games]

The platform for this game will be Windows Vista and XP as the first release, with Microsoft's Xbox and Xbox 360, Sony's PlayStation 3 and PSP (PlayStation Portable), and the Nintendo Wii and DS to follow. Similar fighting games like Namco Bandai's Soulcalibur IV (which retails at $59.95 for the Xbox 360 and PlayStation 3), Street Fighter IV (which retails for $59.95 for the PC, Xbox 360, and PlayStation 3), and Mortal Kombat vs. DC Universe (which retails for $59.95 for the Xbox 360 and PlayStation 3).

[target audience/demographics/market]

The intended audience is all ages, especially children 13 to 18 as well as medical students, fighting game fans, and game players who enjoy watching medical television shows such as *ER*, *Grey's Anatomy*, *Hopkins*, and *House*.

[final selling sentence (wrap it up)]

Medical Kombat simulates the first war that man ever fought, the first war you have ever fought, and the last war you will someday lose. The players will enjoy the thrill of real-life search and destroy as they battle their way through each mission and learn about life and death in the process.

Organic Game Design

Blizzard, a well-known game developer, frequently uses the organic game design style in games such as the Warcraft series and Diablo. Although the teams at Blizzard can spend months on a nondocumented concept (not following a GDD), they sometimes have to terminate the entire process for one reason or another.

This may seem like a complete waste of time and effort, but the process does generate an occasional great, innovative, original idea that improves their game and causes the entire gaming industry (players and developers) to stand up and praise them.

In the game design "creative process," thousands of great ideas and not-so-great ones are discussed and documented. For example, Blizzard wanted to test groundbreaking concepts for Warcraft 3. Some of the ideas thought of were not technically feasible and others were not "fun." Instead of following a rigid GDD, Blizzard tried numerous concepts and suggestions, redesigned them, and threw away the ones that did not seem to work. If a problem with a major design concept was found, the concept was completely scrapped and redesigned even if it had a year of development behind it. Not every concept works out as planned inside one's head.

Unfortunately, when a gameplay mechanic that was thought to be a new innovation turns into an adventure into boredom, it has to disappear (a difficult but an important decision to make).

The critical aspect of "organic design" is knowing when to terminate an idea, and to fully document the concept and why it was killed. If the concept is not documented with an explanation of what went wrong, why the team felt this idea had to go, and the issues surrounding this decision, then the concept may fall victim to "recycling." A poorly documented "kill" will resurface as a new innovative idea later if there is nothing to prevent this process.

Let's examine this recycling process as a "cool" idea is suggested and months of artwork and programming occur. The testers complain that this concept is boring and tedious. Nothing is written down about the concept and the reasons for killing it, so months later a team member suggests the original "cool" idea or something close to it. The team gets excited and starts new programming and artwork since the old development was completely thrown away. The team is now wasting time on a concept that again will be killed. The recycled idea could have been stopped when the suggestion resurfaced. The team could have checked the "killed" document and seen what the original idea was and why it was killed. Don't allow a killed concept to become a Frankenstein that villagers with torches must kill again. Remember that the "organic design" style is for experienced developers who are well financed and can waste time for the betterment of the final game.

Here are some tips for organic design:

- Removing a poor or flawed concept quickly and painlessly is best.
- Often rethinking the concept or replacing it entirely leads to a better implementation and game design.
- Organic design is not for the novice game designer, but it is an important concept to understand.

Workshop

Assignments

Assignment 1: Discuss the benefits and constraints of the game design styles.

Assignment 2: Discuss known games and what style the developers might have chosen.

Assignment 3: Discuss eye-catching marketing and sales pitches.

Assignment 4: Discuss current games and their demographics.

Assignment 5: Write the opening sentence for three game concepts.

Exercises

Exercise 1: List 10 publishers, including their main genre, platforms supported, and a few of their titles.

Exercise 2: List 10 licensed properties and describe each game in one sentence.

Exercise 3: List five known games and evaluate the expected demographics including gender, age, hobbies, and income level.

Exercise 4: In designing a baseball game, list several competing games' information such as the game's title, publisher, platforms supported, and price.

Unguided Exercises

Unguided Exercise 1: Write a One Pager based on a TV show (not a game show).

Unguided Exercise 2: Write a One Pager based on a film license (one not yet developed).

Unguided Exercise 3: List five games and analyze the publisher's promotional material to describe their marketing and sales pitch.

Unguided Exercise 4: Examine the marketplace and list five game genres and subjects that are heavily saturated and five game subjects that are unique.

Internet Reading Assignment

"What Makes a Game Good?" by Wolfgang Kramer
   http://www.thegamesjournal.com/articles/WhatMakesaGame.shtml

"34 Ways to Put Emotions Into Games" by Brad Kane
   http://www.gamasutra.com/gdc2003/features/20030308/kane_
   emotion_01.htm

Thoughts for Discussion

1. Brainstorm a few game design ideas and practice presenting a one-sentence pitch.
2. Discuss games and their USP.
3. How can emotions add to a game's design?
4. What is the importance of the "tension curve" over time? (See "What Makes a Game Good?" by Wolfgang Kramer.)
5. How would you add emotions to a game? Which emotions would you choose to use?

Chapter 6

Game Research

As game designers, we first get a great idea, our vision. Then we play a sample game in our head and have a very basic concept of our "fantastic" game.

Now begins the hard part, the reality of game design. We need to thoroughly understand the game's subject matter as though we are professionals at it. This is done in the phase called "research."

This is the first mountain that we must cross. Many "wannabe" game designers start the climb upward and eventually lose interest and quit. To the professional game designer, this is the fun phase, where the dream first hits the paper and the vision becomes real.

Over the years, I've helped many newbie game designers iron out their ideas and concepts (Pedersen Principle 9: Share Your Toys!). One of their first concerns is "If I tell you my great game concept, how do I know you won't steal it?" My answer has always been, "You are the one with a burning desire to create this vision and I'm not. There's a lot of hard work ahead, several months of painstaking decision-making work, and you have that determination to make your vision a reality. I have a lot of my own visions that to me are important to design. I don't have enough time to design my own visions, so why would I want to steal yours?"

I would prefer that the original visionary design the game and get rewarded later financially and get credited than steal the idea and work extremely hard on it for free. That's why I enjoy mentoring. Let others do their work and hopefully we'll all get rewarded at some point.

The best way to protect your game design is to spend $35 (online) or $45 (by mail) to register a copyright of your document(s). To copyright a document you need to get a form from the U.S. Copyright Office in Washington, D.C., fill it out, and return it along with your document(s) and filing fee. The forms are available online at http://www.copyright.gov/forms/. Then once it is copyrighted, place the copyright notice on at least the first page. I like to place this notice at the top of every page so if copies are made the notice is included. The notice should be of the form "© 2009 Roger E. Pedersen," where either the symbol © or the word "Copyright" precedes the copyright year and the copyright's owner.

The titles of films and books cannot be trademarked, but computer and video game titles can be. If the name of your game is unique and "catchy," you should spend the couple of hundred dollars to get a lawyer to perform a trademark search (to search a trademark, check out http://www.uspto.gov/main/sitesearch.htm) and then file a trademark for your game's name. The fact that your title is trademarked will help you later when talking to publishers. I worked for a game company that had a future game title on their website for several years. Before they had a chance to trademark and publish it, another company advertised their game by the same name. We contacted a lawyer and found that the other company had filed that name for a trademark. We decided not to fight the costly and most likely unwinnable fight to challenge the trademark, so we lost that title.

Remember, ideas are truly a dime a dozen. Concepts are worthless in gaming until the designer commits the idea to paper in a design document.

To prove that ideas without supporting documentation are meaningless, look at Chapter 4, "Game Concepts and Ideas," where hundreds of free gaming concepts from books, film, and history are listed.

Once the idea is properly researched and documented, it becomes golden. Proper research starts with setting research goals, identifying venues that offer research sources, satisfying your research goals by collecting information and answers to the goal criteria, and storing the found items for future access.

Research must be done to gain an expert understanding of your vision. Even if you are a professional on the game's subject matter, you'll need to document for others the background information, object specifications such as environment dimensions, sample objects that are needed in the environment, realistic sound effects, and character dialogue.

During research, you should collect documents, images, textures, sound files, various characters' attributes, and numeric information. Research should educate the entire development team and influence the game design process.

In this chapter, you will learn to set research goals based on the game's concept, vision, or licensed property; understand where to locate research sources that have the information you are looking for; and the specific information you need to research and questions to answer in order to design a realistic and believable game.

Research Goals

The first step in research is to set the "research goals" for your game and its design.

Every game has different research goals that need to be stated in order to properly locate the needed information that transforms a concept or vision into a realistic, believable, documented game.

Most games will have similar research goals such as facts about the concept including room, building, and outdoor measurements; background history; daily human interaction; and period-specific items such as clothing, common objects, transportation, and terms of speech. Another research goal is to collect drawings, photos, and pictures of people, buildings, architecture, and typical objects that are associated with the concept. A goal may be to collect background sounds, music, and sample voice-over dialogue and accents.

For sports games, the goals should be to collect interviews, a rulebook, video footage, and statistics of the teams and players. Gathering material from similar and competing games such as documenting how they market and promote their game, reviews and previews of these games, and playing these games are other goals to set and research.

Let's look at designing a soccer game (outside the U.S. it would be called "football") where all of the professional licenses have been secured by the publisher.

Goal 1: Get the dimensions and field markings for a soccer field.

Goal 2: Get pictures of the stadiums and uniforms (home and away) and team information for all teams in the league.

Goal 3: Obtain statistics and photos, especially the player's face, for each player on each team.

Goal 4: Find video or photos depicting goalie saves and top players' trademark shots and maneuvers.

Goal 5: Document each team's playing schedule and the method for determining the championship team.

Goal 6: Obtain general manager information such as methods for trading players, obtaining new players, contract negotiations, and financials such as pre-sold seats and ticket prices.

Goal 7: Get the official rules and referee book to understand penalties and warning calls, including the various referee stances for calls and signals. (NJ IGDA member Mike Sweeney suggests that every member of the sport game development team have a copy of the rulebook next to them at all times.)

Goal 8: Obtain actual video of a soccer match to understand the stadium's sounds ranging from cheering, stadium announcements, player grunts, and ball kick sounds to coach ranting. Gather the color commentaries of announcers for phrases, styles, and content used before, during, and after the game (including the wrap-up).

Goal 9: Gather reviews and promotional material for competing and similar soccer games, and play the competitors' games.

Goal 10: Gather additional information on legendary players and teams such as statistics, historical uniforms or old stadiums, signature kicks and maneuvers or goalie saves, and pictures of the players.

When I begin researching a gaming concept that I'm developing, I make a list of similar and competing games. Then I ask, "What current and past games are close to the game I'm developing?" and "What games in my game's genre are currently selling?"

Chapter 6

Even if you think your game is unique and there's nothing close to its concept, you'll need to explain your vision to publishers and convince them that it will be successful.

Research Sources

Once we have a set of research goals, we need to find sources of information, artwork (pictures, drawings, and photos), and sounds (audio clips and music) we can use to reach and achieve our goals. We must seek out venues where we can find these sources.

Libraries have books, magazines, and encyclopedias for you to use and take notes from. The Internet is an obvious source for information that may be more recent than what can be found in books, and it also allows you to search for pictures and sound samples needed for the game. If your library doesn't carry the books or magazines you need, check out what's available in bookstores or on Amazon.

One of the first places I look is magazines. I want to see what current products are reviewed in my game's genre and perhaps competitors to my game. Even more insightful are the advertisements of gaming retailers. They list a lot of games under genre headings and their prices. This is the useful information that you will later need, such as competitive selling titles, their platform (PC, PlayStation 2 and 3, Nintendo Wii and DS, or Xbox/Xbox 360), and their retail selling price.

The next place I look is the magazines' and gaming websites' lists of top games in each genre for the current and previous year. People associate future success with the current winners. You'll want to associate your game with the top-awarded games in your game's genre when you're selling your concept to a publisher.

Then I look at the similar and competing game publishers' websites to view how they are marketing their product so I can get an idea of how to market my game. Let their highly paid marketing and sales departments benefit you and get ideas to use for free. Read their descriptions and features and copy them down so your game will have the same features and gameplay. Look at any screenshots they display to see what the gamers are familiar with and how your screens should look. Some sites will include favorable reviews of their game, so collect them and make notes from the reviewers' comments.

Let's examine several research sources and each source's positive and negative aspects.

Source	Positive	Negative
Books	Reliable content that may contain pictures. A good reference. Easy to store and bookmark.	May contain outdated information.
Magazines	Good source for previews, reviews, and advertisements (marketing and sales promotion). Easy to store and bookmark.	Previews and reviews are opinions of the reviewer. Sometimes reviews can be thinly disguised advertisements.
Newspapers	Current and often reliable. Easy to store and bookmark.	Articles may be brief and centered on the writer's interest.
Encyclopedias	Reliable and good information. Often contain photos and diagrams.	May contain outdated information. Locating the information may require knowledge of the subject; for example, information about Gettysburg may be found under U.S. Civil War.
Dictionary/ Thesaurus	Good resource for spelling, references, and synonyms. Available in word processors.	Not a good source for subject research.
Microfilm/ Microfiche	A good source for indexed out-of-print magazine and newspaper information. Easy to copy and store.	May not be current or contain the latest information.
Interviews	Current, opinionated source for information and insights that can be very reliable if from experts. An easy source to copy, store, and mark up.	Opinions and may be slanted. May not contain all of the answers since cliffhangers and partial insights lead to more sales.
Recorded Device (DVD, CD, DAT, tape, video, download, podcast)	Easy to listen to, copy, and store. A great source for in-game audio and samples. Videos display action, especially in sports, and show professional production that the audience expects. A good way to familiarize yourself with music styles and sound effects.	Copyright rules must be followed if closely used. Time consuming to listen to and view these resources. Each piece must be documented for future usage.
Internet	A good source for current information, photos, pictures, textures, sounds, and advertisements. Accessible at any time for sound clips and effects, sample music, searching for and hiring freelance staff, and obtaining free and trial downloads.	Sometimes Internet information is not accurate, so check the reliability of the site. Copyright rules must be followed for photos, artwork, audio, and other content. Plagiarism must be avoided.

Chapter 6

You will also search other sources (magazines and websites) for reviews of similar and competing games. When I look at a review, I make a list with two columns labeled "Good" and "Bad." Under "Good," I write down the reviewer's favorable comments and the standard features that the game must have, plus any extras that the designer is being praised for. Under "Bad," I list the reviewer's unfavorable comments, like problems with the game or features designed that didn't work or weren't as good as they should have been. I pay special attention to graphic and sound issues. Features that were missing or not handled correctly are noted and later I address these so I don't fall victim to the same criticism by other reviewers and gamers.

The important issues are the game's interface (what does the gamer view and how does the gamer interact with the game?), the POV of the game (first- or third-person), the game's options, the computer's or platform's requirements (RAM, hard disk minimum space required, Windows version needed, CD speed required), and special devices required (driving wheel, force-feedback joystick or mouse, 3D accelerator card).

As a designer, I also value buying the top-selling games' hint books or strategy guides. These books discuss the game's basic strategy and give an in-depth look at the game design. Hint books reveal each side's or character's strengths and weaknesses. Many times gamers favor one side or character above the others without fully understanding or realizing the strengths and weaknesses they are dealt. Likewise, many gamers don't understand or realize the strengths and weaknesses of their opponents in the game. Hint books and strategy guides discuss these issues in detail.

Many gamers and designers don't have the time it would take to play all variations and situations for one side or one character, let alone all sides and all characters. This problem of not understanding the strengths and weaknesses of their characters and sides becomes more of an issue in online (web-based) games where the gamer's time and money (cost of playing, connection costs, and so on) are needed to play.

As designers, we need to understand the successful games' intricate design details and balanced play so we can have references to follow. Playing games is a great start in understanding the gamer's POV, but as designers we need to understand the game designer's POV. This viewpoint requires us to research and study these games as well as play them.

Hint books and strategy guides may also tell us the "why" behind the decisions that were made by the game designer. Internet games may suffer from latency (a slowdown) when the server(s) get too populated. To solve this technical dilemma, the game must move players from the current server to another less-populated server. For example, the gamer might experience a magical cloud that overshadows the terrain and teleports all of the players currently in that area into another area (one controlled by a less-populated server). The key is to make the gamers unaware of the "why" and still have a fun and meaningful experience.

Another interesting area is the designer's notes ("postmortem") that are included on many sites. The postmortem is where the development team, after the product has shipped, tells about the project — especially where things went wrong or if they could do it all again, what they would do differently.

If your desire is to become a game designer, you must master the trade by first learning from other masters as though you are an apprentice (by studying existing games, researching the game's subject matter, and playing games from the best to the near best). You can then become a master yourself by designing your vision through research, documentation, and play testing.

Items to Research

Now that we have our list of goals and know the sources to find information, we need to make a shopping list of "items to research." A good start to understanding and researching items that your game concept needs is to make a list of similar and competing games. Ask yourself, "What current and past games are close to the game I'm developing?" and "What games in my game's genre are currently selling?"

This research material can also be used to explain your vision to publishers and convince them your game will also be successful.

The information to find for the research phase is pictures of characters; locations such as towns, cities, and buildings; architecture; environment dimensions; realistic sights and sounds; historical background; and information for gaming variations and puzzle problems.

Let's look at an example of items to research for a coral reef game and the research needed to design a game based on an historic landmark.

Example: The Australian Great Barrier Reef Simulation

- Make a list of the fish (species and genus), coral, and plant life to be included and gather pictures of each object and other photos to be used later as textures and model reference guides.

- For each life-form, generate a list of where in the reef they would normally reside, their swim boundary (distance from home they can travel), the food they eat and time between feedings, the prey that enjoys eating them, friendly and unfriendly life-forms and symbiotic relationships (such as the shark and the sharksucker or the sea anemone and the clownfish), and the size and weight of each life-form and feeder type (herbivores, planktivores, benthic invertebrates feeders, omnivores, and piscivores) in the food chain.

- Learn terms such as "schooling," which is the organized movement of a group of fish in either polarized orientation (all fish facing the same direction) or nonpolarized orientation (nonspecific direction). Schooling has several purposes, such as to confuse a potential predator in thinking the group is a single larger fish, to force the predator to decide which fish will be eaten (aka "selfish herd"), and for predator detection (with so many eyes and viewing directions, the predator will be detected before it begins its attack).

■ Examine the coral reef structure (channel, bay or lagoon areas, water depth, fringing reef, and bank reef areas) and water temperature.

■ Learn about the man-made and environmental problems affecting the reefs that can be used as a puzzle, or activities that cause havoc in the ecosystem for the player to resolve.

Some man-made problems might include:

■ Overfishing (netting demanded fish and discarding others)

■ Contamination from chemicals such as sodium cyanide, chloride bleach, or quinaldine (forcing fish to lose their balance and exit their hiding places, poisoning some fish and other sea life)

■ Dynamite or blast fishing (killing both demanded and other fish and destroying the reef structure)

■ Muro ami fishing (pounding on the reef to force confused fish into awaiting nets while weakening the reef's structure)

■ Mangrove harvesting (mangrove trees, important to the coral reefs and where juvenile coral reef fish normally live, are harvested for fuel and building materials)

■ Oil leaks and spills (the cloudy water blocks sunlight, essential for photosynthesis) and oil's heavy metal attribute (destroys the coral's tissue, making it hard to reproduce, and destroys the symbiotic algae)

■ Industrial waste (entangles life-forms such as turtles, and sewage containing nitrogen kills algae and benthic organisms like clams)

■ Radioactive pollution (mutates or kills a wide range of fish species)

■ Greenhouse gases like carbon dioxide, methane, nitrous oxide, and chlorofluorocarbons (trap the heat, increasing the water temperature and UV (ultraviolet) rays, which cause coral bleaching where the symbiotic algae exits the polyp and makes coral die. Crown-of-thorn starfish that are usually afraid of the branching coral tentacles can then attack and eat the remaining coral.)

Natural and environmental problems include:

■ Eutrophication (adding nitrogen or phosphorus to the sea and coral reef, causing an explosion of algae growth)

■ Nitrification (adding organic waste to the sea, which causes the oxygen needed by fish to be depleted)

■ Agriculture (fertilizers that commonly contain nitrogen, phosphorus, and potassium as well as silt wash downstream and harm sea life)

■ Parasites and disease that destroy fish and plant life (wrasses feed on parasites)

■ Hurricanes (destroy the reef's structure) and abnormally heavy rains (decrease the salt-to-water ratio, unsettling all coral reef marine life)

Researching a Historical Landmark

Can you imagine telling an artist to design the Roman Coliseum and leaving it up to the artist to create it?

The designer is the visionary and the artist is the worker who uses his or her talent to create the designer's vision. The research provides photos and modern-day video of the Coliseum, ancient pictures and architectural plans depicting the Coliseum and other buildings from that era, pictures of ancient clothing, and descriptions of activities that would have occurred around the massive structure, all of which would be a huge aid as the artist starts the task. Remember, it is the game designer and the game design document that instruct the programmers, artists, audio engineers, and producer about the game being developed. These team members must be free to create within their craft, but not free to create their vision of the game.

Expressing Research Findings

An important concept in both researching and documenting your game is to assume that the player and audience know nothing about the subject matter and gameplay issues.

Do not assume anything!

Document your concept and research findings as though the player and audience are not technical and are totally new to the game concepts and ideas. Think of explaining these issues to a willing-to-learn and eager-to-be-taught, child-like audience.

Let's examine how to document a simple game I call Two Heads.

> The player flips a coin twice. If both tosses result in "heads," the player wins.

This simple game should be more accurately described with more details that explain the concepts and issues in greater depth:

> The player freely tosses a coin so that it randomly spins in the air (also called a "toss"). The coin is a metal, two-sided, flat disc. One side is called "heads" and the opposite side is called "tails." Commonly, a coin has a person's head on one side (like the head of a president or monarch), which is known as the "head's side." The opposite side of the coin often has a bird such as an eagle on it, so it is often known as the "tail's side."

If the first toss results in the "head's side" appearing on top, the player continues. If the "tail's side" appears on top, the player loses.

If play continues (the first toss resulted in "heads"), the player tosses the coin for a second time. If the result is another "head's side" on top, the player wins. Otherwise, the player loses.

The second description clearly expresses the game's rules in simple, understandable terms. The game object (the coin) is described with its identifying features. The game's process is described in detail with the common lingo explained for future reference. The winning and losing conditions are identified so the player(s) can easily understand the goals.

Researching a Licensed Property

A *licensed property* is an intellectual property from copyrighted mediums such as books, films, comic books, and other games (such as the three licenses in Sonic and Mario at the Olympic Games). The term *pseudo-licensed property* is used to describe household names that are not currently owned or copyrighted properties, such as a Bible story, the life of Amadeus Mozart, the U.S. Civil War, plays like *Romeo and Juliet*, and books like *The Odyssey* and *Candide*.

Games based on licensed products often cause players to make certain assumptions about those titles. There are preconceptions about the characters, gameplay, content, and target audience. In stores, it's the licensed titles that get noticed first, regardless of their marketing and advertising.

Games developed by PSI Software and author.

Game designers must understand this customer mentality. The designer must understand everything about that license in order to provide the kind of entertainment that the target consumers have anticipated.

For instance, a baseball game that uses a particular baseball team's manager in its title suggests a strategy sports game. Players would probably assume that they would be responsible for making decisions about the players and batting order. On the other hand, a licensed product linked to a professional baseball player would suggest an emphasis on sports action, such as pitching or batting.

There's a reason why licenses cost big bucks. Designers and producers can use the license and its characters in order to leverage consumer preconceptions to the title's benefit.

Licensed products also come from properties such as novels, cartoons, and TV shows, as well as cereal manufacturers, sports teams, and restaurant chains.

Let's go through each research stage of research goals, research sources, and items to research for a licensed comic book superhero, a TV show sitcom (situation comedy), and a science fiction film.

Research Goals for Licensed Properties

The research goals for a comic book superhero would be to identify the superhero's appearance, non-superhero identity and lifestyle, powers, strengths and flaws, friends and associates, and adversaries.

For the friends, associates, and adversaries, list their appearance, lifestyles, powers or how they aid the superhero, strengths, and weaknesses.

Most licensors will have what is known as a "three-position model sheet" depicting the character facing forward, a side view, and a back view. Commonly, they will have a book that details every story character, describing their first appearance, eye and hair color, birth date and age, personal background, whether they are right- or left-handed, hobbies, educational background, superpowers, strengths and flaws, interactions with the superhero, interactions with other characters and the adversaries, vehicles driven, weapons they are experts at, special abilities, and attack and defense capabilities.

Record and take notes of all the characters' favorite phrases, accents, and dialects. Understand the characters' education level and the vocabulary that they would use in conversations and words that fans will understand.

Learn the fans' favorite storylines, adversaries, and supporting characters.

Goals for a TV sitcom would be to identity the main characters' appearance, their personalities in terms of strengths and weaknesses, how they feel and interact with other characters and situations, and their hobbies and jobs. Examine where the characters meet, where they live, and where their world exists in terms of distance and diversity, such as a high-rise apartment, a comedy club, or a coffeehouse in a big city.

Understand the characters' backgrounds, where they come from, what their families are like, and what motivates them, excites them, and makes them go insane. Also, note the little hard-to-see items like a superhero's logo on his refrigerator, certain books located on a shelf, or the type of designer sunglasses or clothing he wears.

Gather pictures of the environment's architecture, sample building exteriors, parks, street scenes, and office and living quarter interiors.

List previously used storylines to reference or draw new storylines from, guest star appearances you can use to add "Easter eggs" (hidden storylines or treasures) by having them reappear in the game, and mentioned story titbits that can be further explored, such as a character mentioning a cruise vacation in an actual storyline and incorporating a cruise in your game.

Note and speak with writers and the show's producer to include inside jokes and themes in the game design.

Surf the TV show's fan websites and the production company's website to gather additional insights into the licensed property and the fan likes and dislikes.

Goals for a science fiction film would be to identify the characters' appearance, their personalities in terms of strengths and weaknesses, how they feel and interact with other characters and situations, and their hobbies and jobs. Examine the film's settings such as terrain and city depictions, as well as the characters' accents and dialogue, to understand the property. List a few possible storylines that differ from the film's linear script.

Examine other science fiction games such as those based on *Star Wars*, *Star Trek*, and *The Matrix*.

Read the reviews of similar and competing games from magazines and websites.

Document how the publishers of these games promote their game through advertising, packaging, and website information so your design will contain similar features such as the user interface, game mechanics, animation, graphics, cinematics, sounds, and system requirements. Pay special attention to the new features and the reviewer criticisms of similar products.

Collect sample photos, drawings, and location interior and exterior layouts from science fiction films, websites, books, and magazines.

If the film is part of a series, review past films to gather historical background information, gain a better grasp of the characters' past behavior and experiences, and learn about other characters that the audience would recognize from past films.

A licensed film project should have the script and photos of the location sets available and possibly an early preview of the film footage shot ("dailies").

Speak with writers and the show's producer to include inside jokes and themes in the game design and document (if possible, record) everything.

Surf the movie's fan websites and the production company's website to gather additional insights into the licensed property and the fan likes and dislikes.

Research Sources

The comic book superhero game needs research of past issues of comic stories, future storylines scheduled and planned by the writers, and the pen and ink concept art.

Visit the comic book's fan websites, where fans are more than willing to educate you in your game design of their favorite superhero. Also visit the comic book company's website to see how they market and promote their property.

A TV show sitcom game needs research of the previous shows. Chatting with the writers and producer about future show storylines and direction can also be good.

Gather pictures of the various venues in which the characters are often seen, such as living quarters, offices, coffee shops, and stores.

Like comic book websites, the fan websites for TV shows can help you in your design, and the show's website will let you see how they market and promote their property and deal with their fans.

Research all the sitcom actors' personal backgrounds, filmography, and previous TV work as well as the sitcom's key behind-the-scenes personalities such as the writers, producer, executive producers, and special guest stars.

List all of the sitcom's shows in show date order with a sentence describing each episode.

A game based on a science fiction film may be published to coincide with the film's release, making it difficult for the designer to find research information. Here, working closely with the licensor is critical and quick responses are crucial. Prerelease photos, dailies, and unedited film footage are needed to design the game's storyline and provide the artists with information they need to create character models and environments.

The movie distributor's or production company's website may have photos and sales and marketing promotional materials that a designer can use as reference material and for storyline concepts. This material can also help depict the main and supporting character relationships and positioning.

Discussing the film with the actors, writers, director, and producer would be invaluable, and videotaping interviews with these people would be a great addition to the game's CD or DVD (similar to the film's additional features).

Read the science fiction and film magazines for previews of the film you are working to design a game from.

Choosing an Appropriate Concept to Research

A "wannabe" game designer wanted my mentoring. He had three game design concepts that he thought would earn him millions and have the major publishers begging to sell his games.

His background was working as an international contract lawyer and he had a graduate degree in international business law and an undergraduate degree in paleontology (dinosaur scientist). He had played a lot of recent games, especially sims, RPGs, and FPSs. He played both single- as well as multiplayer versions of his favorite games on the Internet, but he had never designed a game, let alone worked on a game in any capacity.

Let's look at and critique his three concepts.

> Intergalactic Council is a space diplomacy and strategy simulation game where up to 10 players are members of the council. Each of the 10 players is a diplomat representing his or her galaxy. Each diplomat presents the council treaties, trade agreements, and his galaxy's requests (bills). If negotiations fail, the diplomats can declare war or boycott the council meetings.
>
> Each galaxy has its own inhabited planets, a galactic space armada (ships), and tradable resources.
>
> The laws and treaties follow the international laws for format and regulations established for venues outside the Earth.
>
> The goal of the game is for each diplomat to either successfully negotiate in order to create and get bills, treaties, and trade agreements passed, or by intergalactic warfare, force the acts to be accepted by the council.

How does this concept sound to you? Would it make for an interesting game? What issues need to be researched in order to get a better understanding of the rules and gamer's play options?

I thought the concept sounded interesting but wanted to see more of it developed through research. The designer's education and work gave him the expertise to design such a game. My concern was simpler: "Is this a game that a newbie game designer should start with?"

My thoughts were that even to a seasoned game designer with some international business law background, this design was a Herculean task. I suspected that trying to research and properly design this concept would take 6 to 12 months to complete, and that the new designer would most likely quit in the research phase. I advised him to put this design on hold and start his design career off with an easier, less complex concept.

After he'd had a few titles finished (not necessarily published), he'd feel more confident in tackling a major research and design project, and a publisher might be willing to be financially involved. It is equally important that the team (in this case, the designer) doing the project have credentials (proof that they can finish a started task).

The second concept was The Lost Kingdoms.

> The Lost Kingdoms is a fantasy simulation where the player(s) represent the kingdoms of humans, elves, dwarves, centaurs, trolls,

orcs, or giants. The kingdoms have coexisted in peace for hundreds of years where the human, elf, and dwarf kingdoms were allies; the centaurs were neutral; and the troll, orc, and giant kingdoms were evil. As the game begins, the evil kingdoms of trolls, orcs, and giants are expanding, looking for more land and food (they eat humans, elves, dwarves, and centaurs). The kingdoms must sign peacekeeping treaties or go to war.

How does this concept sound to you? Would it make for an interesting game? What issues need to be researched in order to get a better understanding of the rules and gamer's play options?

At first I felt that The Lost Kingdoms was somewhat similar to the Intergalactic Council game. Just like the first concept, this one is an enormous undertaking for a first game design. The concept is good and similar to the popular *Lord of the Rings* books. The races in this game are familiar to RPG and fantasy RPG players. Research is critical to show good judgment and an educated concern for the fans who know and understand these races.

While researching each race, you must be able to answer the following questions and do so through the eyes of an avid fan. (Substitute the specific race involved in the game where "elves" appears.)

- What do elves look like (male and female)?
- What do elves wear (daily dress and war clothing)?
- How do elves talk (common elf phrases)?
- What weapons and fighting styles do elves favor?
- What do elves do each day?
- What do elves cherish and care about?
- What do elves believe in (family, gold, customs, and ideology)?

These are just a few starting issues to research in this game. Your job is to understand like the avid fan does the characteristics and thoughts (social, political, and economical) of your game's kingdoms, races, and individual heroes.

Again, as in Intergalactic Council, I felt that The Lost Kingdoms was another good concept that would take at least six months to document and not an ideal first game to design.

The third concept was The Survival of the Fittest.

The Survival of the Fittest is a prehistoric simulation where mankind must survive from the Neanderthal man era to the Cro-Magnon man era. In solo and multiplayer versions, each player controls the destiny and daily activities of a clan. Hunting, fishing, and making clothes and shelter are necessities for survival. The goal is to survive through several generations and keep mankind from become extinct.

This third design, The Survival of the Fittest, is the most feasible and within the realm of a first-time game designer, especially one who has a degree in paleontology.

Chapter 6

The Survival of the Fittest is a nice twist from all those hunting FPS games that flooded the stores after Deer Hunter.

Let's do some research for our game, The Survival of the Fittest.

Researching a Simulation Game: The Survival of the Fittest

The time period for this simulation game is the Ice Age. Homo erectus, or the "upright man," is thought to have evolved around 1.5 million years ago. Then 200,000 to 250,000 years ago, the Neanderthal (or Neandertal) appeared. Around 25,000 B.C., the Cro-Magnon man became the fittest species.

In my research, I decided to include the Homo erectus in the design for the initial migration from Africa to Europe and Asia and for their primitive lifestyle.

Similar successful products would be the Deer Hunter series and the hundreds of products that mimicked it, as well as The Sims, since in this game you'll be monitoring and making decisions for tribe or clan members for several generations.

Comments on competing hunting games are:

Neanderthal man, reconstructed from a skull found in Amud, Israel. Used with permission from the Neanderthal Museum, Mettmann, Germany (www.neanderthal.de).

Good:

- Actual animal sounds, realistic 3D animations and graphics, true-to-life animal behavior and weather conditions.
- The game captures the essence of the outdoors. Accurate AI and the animals react to the hunter's sounds and scents.
- The ability to customize the input keys and option settings.
- The game ran well on an average computer.

Bad:

- Difficult to see the animals' tracks.
- Sounds were repetitious and did not have much variety.
- The game had little variance in the gameplay.

Homo Erectus

Homo erectus, or the "upright man," first appeared around 1.5 million years ago in Africa and later migrated to Europe and Asia. They were the first hunters and gatherers who used primitive weapons like stone axes and knives. They lived in the midst of the Ice Age, so traveling across bodies of water was as simple as crossing a vast terrain of frozen, natural ice bridges. It is thought they migrated north from Africa in search of food. They had the skills to make fire. Fire was an important key to life since it protected them against wild animals that feared fire, gave the tribe heat when traveling through cold regions, and allowed them to cook their food, thus killing possible diseases and softening their meat. The elders could share stories around the fire.

Homo erectus had a large face, a thick skull, a large, powerful lower jaw, and a receding forehead. They could grow to 5' 9" and often lived in caves. They traveled over 8,500 miles from Africa to Europe or China (8,700 miles) and the species survived for over a million years, following the herds that moved northward seasonally.

Neanderthals

Neanderthals, or Homo sapiens ("wise man"), lived approximately 200,000 to 250,000 years ago.

They lived in Europe (Germany, Italy, Switzerland, France, and Portugal), Asia (Siberia and Poland), and the Near East (Turkey, Syria, Lebanon, and Israel).

A clan was comprised of 6 to 25 members. Males lived to ages 40 to 45, while females, many dying in childbirth, lived to age 30. Clans often stole women from neighboring clans. Neanderthals were cave dwellers. The men hunted within their 30-mile territory. Since they lacked in-depth planning, they hunted in zigzag paths after their prey. Neanderthals cared for their wounded and disabled members and buried their dead in a ceremony where they painted the body of the deceased.

Neanderthals had brawny, short bodies, short arms, and broad trunks and were large brained (low, sloping foreheads). They walked with bent knees, heads leaning forward, and were very strong. They were well adapted for cold, harsh climates.

Neanderthals made elaborate use of stone tools. They had hand axes for skinning and cutting game into pieces and choppers for breaking bones to eat the marrow, pound meat, and chop wood. Denticulates could shape wood and remove bark.

Neanderthal male hunter and female gatherer, reconstructed from skulls found in La Chapelle-aux-Saints, France, and Forbes' Quarry, Gibraltar. Used with permission from the Neanderthal Museum, Mettmann, Germany (www.neanderthal.de).

Chapter 6

Scrapers could clean hides. Curved-back knives could cut flesh easily. Spears were cut with pointed ends or fitted with stone heads. Neanderthals made wooden clubs, and they used bones for needles and fish hooks. They could craft warm boots and make fire by spinning a pointed stick next to kindling.

They were hunters and used spears to kill animals as well as force herds off cliffs. They hunted reindeer, red deer, horses, wild cattle, gazelle, rabbit, sheep, and goats. They fished and speared salmon.

Neanderthals were also preyed upon by saber-tooth tigers, 10-foot-tall cave bears, foxes, cave lions, woolly mammoths, hyenas, and dogs with huge teeth.

Cro-Magnon Man

Cro-Magnon man, or "Homo sapiens sapiens," lived around 25,000 B.C. and followed their food throughout the seasons. In winter, they returned to their shelters while in summer they traveled, following the herds. Like their ancestors, they ate seeds, berries, roots, nuts, and salmon. They sweetened their foods with honey.

Cro-Magnon man could grow to six feet tall and could live to age 50 and beyond. They had huge frontal lobes and could plan ahead. They hunted in groups or individually. They had stone axes, knives, spears, harpoons, wooden bows, and sharp stone-tipped arrows. They used traps and fished with nets woven from vines. They built rafts and canoes to catch larger fish in the deeper waters.

Cro-Magnon man learned how to soften leather and use animal gut as thread and bones as needles. In summer, they wore woven grass and bark clothes. In winter, they wore animal skin clothing and moccasins. Their homes were portable and were made like tepees with branches or mammoth bones and covered with animal skins. Often the large home had a central hearth for a fire. Cro-Magnon men painted and tattooed their bodies, perhaps as a sign of social position. They had flint blades and oil lamps.

They created statues out of ivory, bone, and antlers. They made colored cave paintings that depicted hunts and animals (stick figures), and they often included outlines of the artist's hands. They made necklaces and pendants from shells, teeth, feathers, flowers, and bone.

They ate and were hunted by the same animals as the Neanderthals, except that the woolly mammoth and saber-tooth tiger were then extinct. Cro-Magnon man could store and cure food.

Final Thoughts

From this information, gameplay starts to run through your mind. Thousands of Homo erectus tribes leave Africa in search of food (herds) and travel over 8,500 miles into Europe and Asia (think both solo- and multiplayer versions).

During the journey, they must hunt with their primitive weapons and seek shelter (ideally a cave). Gamers will have the Homo erectus tribe perform daily duties (hunting, cooking, and seeking and making shelter and clothing) through 10 to 15 generations (depending on skill level). The Homo erectus tribe must not become extinct.

Upon successfully arriving at the tribe's final destination — Europe or Asia — Neanderthal clans of six members will emerge as the gamer's new tribe and gameplay will continue through six to eight generations (depending on skill level), with the clan's membership reaching 25 members.

Then Cro-Magnon man dominates the Earth and, through a more advanced intelligence and tool skill, are able to hunt better, survive the environmental conditions, and create art.

Gameplay in The Survival of the Fittest will have the clan or tribes hunting for food and skins with their era's primitive weapons. As the group is hunting, predators will be hunting them. Another possible scenario is a saber-tooth tiger or a 10-foot-tall cave bear will enter the cave when the clan is sleeping and attack them (another variation of being hunted). This aspect of the hunters being hunted adds to the simulation's realism and has the gamer using a carefully planned, cautious strategy throughout the game to keep his clan alive and healthy.

Researching a Classic Game: Poker

Poker is played by using a single deck of 52 cards. The deck has four suits: clubs ♣, diamonds ♦, hearts ♥, and spades ♠. Each suit has 13 cards ranked 2 through 10, jack, queen, king, and ace (the ace can be the highest or lowest card).

Poker games always begin with a shuffle to randomly sort the deck. A brand new deck always has the 52 cards in suit and rank order.

The Shuffle

Most computer languages have a random function, which is critical to most games.

A good idea is to set the initial randomizer to a truly unique number like the current time in military format — a 24-hour clock including hour (0 to 23), minute (0 to 59), second (0 to 59), and millisecond (0 to 999).

When the poker game is first entered and a poker variation is selected, the initial deck of suits and ranks in order should be initialized. Using two random numbers (called "A" and "B") from 1 to 52 (positions of the cards in the deck), you can exchange the cards so that the card in position "A" is relocated to position "B," and the card in position "B" is relocated to position "A."

The shuffle can repeat this exchange many times. Some designers like to make this number a prime or an odd number of exchanges. For the most part, a shuffle of 1,000 exchanges is fine.

After the first shuffle of the initialized deck, the remaining shuffles throughout the game start the next shuffle process with the current shuffled deck.

Hand Rankings

The following examples are in ranking order, meaning the best hand has a ranking of 1 and the worst hand has a ranking of 10.

Rank	Hand Name	Description of Hand/Example
1	Royal Flush	A, K, Q, J, 10 of same suit
		10♠, J♠, Q♠, K♠, A♠
2	Straight Flush	Five same suit consecutive cards
		4♦, 5♦, 6♦, 7♦, 8♦
3	Four of a Kind	Four cards of the same rank
		7♠, 7♣, 7♦, 7♥, 6♥
4	Full House	Three of a kind plus a pair
		3♦, 3♠, 3♣, K♠, K♥
5	Flush	Five cards of the same suit
		3♥, 7♥, 10♥, Q♥, A♥
6	Straight	Five cards in sequence
		5♣, 6♦, 7♣, 8♥, 9♠
7	Three of a Kind	Three cards of the same rank
		J♥, J♠, J♦, 8♥, 9♠
8	Two Pair	Two pairs of different rank
		5♥, 5♠, 9♣, 9♠, 8♥
9	One Pair	Two cards of the same rank
		A♠, A♦, 2♥, 4♦, 8♠
10	High Card	None of the other rankings
		K♠, 2♦, 4♠, 6♥, 8♦

Poker Variations

Poker has many variations, with each variation having its own rules.

The more popular poker variations are Draw Poker, Five-Card Stud, Seven-Card Stud, Chicago High, Chicago Low, Texas Hold 'Em, and Omaha. Most poker variations can be played with two to eight players. The cards are shuffled and distributed by a player called the "dealer." In all variations, the first card is given to the player to the left of the dealer. A round of betting consists of each player deciding whether he or she should bet (or raise after the first bet was made) an amount from the group's agreed-to minimum to maximum, fold (quit this round of play), or check (agree to cover the current amount due to the pot). When three raises to the original bet have been made or all players have checked, the betting round is completed.

In Draw Poker, all players make a small blind bet or ante before receiving any cards. Then players, starting with the player to the left of the dealer, receive cards until each player has five cards. Players carefully look at their cards and determine which cards to keep and which cards to discard. Players can discard up to three cards, four cards if they are keeping an ace. Before discarding, each player may bet or raise, fold (quit this round of play), or accept the current bet amount (check). Then the remaining players discard their cards. Another round of betting occurs where each player can bet, fold, or check. After all players have checked or three raises have occurred, the players must show their cards and the player with the highest hand wins the pot (all bets made). If only one player remains (no showdown), he wins and his cards can remain unexposed.

One variation of Draw Poker commonly played is Draw Poker Jacks or Better, where to open the first round of betting the player needs a pair of jacks or better (a better ranking like a higher pair or three of a kind) to bet. This lets the other players know that he has a hand containing a pair of jacks or better. If no player can bet (no hand has at least a pair of jacks or better), the cards are reshuffled and a new round begins (ante and all). This variation can build the pot quite large with antes, and players with bad hands can fold earlier.

Five-Card Stud is a variation where each player receives his first card face down (called the "hole"), the next three cards are dealt face up, and the last card is dealt face down. The player to the left of the dealer receives the first card. If played with a bring-in, the player with the lowest first up card must bet the minimum. Some variations have all players at the start ante up (a small bet). After all players have received that round's up card (cards two through four), betting occurs. Then after the fifth card (a down card) has been received by all players, the last round of betting occurs. In each betting round after the first, the player with the highest ranking hand showing (only the up cards) starts the betting process. If only one player remains, then he wins the pot and his cards can remain unexposed. Otherwise, the remaining players show all five cards, and the player with the highest ranking hand wins the pot.

Seven-Card Stud is a variation where the first two cards are dealt face down (the "hole") and the third card is dealt face up. It can also be played with a bring-in; otherwise, on the first up card, the player with the highest ranking card opens the betting round. Each player must either bet (raise), fold, or check. Cards four through six are dealt face up, and after all players have received that round's card, betting occurs. The last card (the seventh card) is dealt face down unless in an eight-player game all eight players remain, then the last card is dealt as a community card (shared by all players). If only one player remains, he wins (no showdown) and his cards may be left unexposed. Otherwise, all remaining players must show their cards, and the player with the highest ranking hand wins the pot. If more than one player has the highest ranking hand, then they split the pot or the player with the highest suit wins. The suit order is usually spades (the highest), hearts, diamonds, and clubs (the lowest).

Chicago High plays exactly like Seven-Card Stud except that the player with the highest spade in the "hole" splits the pot. The ace of spades is the highest card. If the last card (seventh card) is a community card, it cannot be used as a "hole" card.

Chicago Low plays exactly like Seven-Card Stud except that the player with the lowest spade in the "hole" splits the pot. Players must decide whether the ace of spaces is the lowest card or the two (deuce) of spades is the lowest. If the last card (seventh card) is a community card, it cannot be used as the "hole" card.

Over the last few years, Texas Hold 'Em and Omaha have become popular variations. Texas Hold 'Em is a seven-card poker game where each player receives two down cards and the remaining five cards are called "community cards," which are shared by all of the players. Each player must make his best five-card poker hand using five out of the seven cards (his two cards plus the five community cards). After the two down cards have been dealt to all of the players, the player to the left of the dealer must make a small blind bet. Then a round of betting occurs where each player must bet (raise), fold, or check. Then five cards are placed face down in the center as community cards.

The middle three community cards are turned over (face up) and another round of betting occurs. Then the first community card is flipped over (face up) and another betting round occurs. Finally, the fifth community card is turned over (face up) and the final round of betting occurs.

If more than one player remains, the player with the highest ranking hand wins the pot. Any combination of the player's own two down cards and the five community cards can be used to make the best five-card poker hand. The pot is split if a tie occurs.

Omaha is a form of Texas Hold 'Em that is popular in casinos and on "poker nights." Omaha is a nine-card poker variation where each player is dealt four down cards and the remaining five cards are dealt face down as community cards (for all players to use). Each player must create the best ranking poker hand by using two of his four cards plus three of the five community cards. Just as in Texas Hold 'Em, after the first four cards are dealt, the player to the left of the dealer must make a small blind bet. Then players must bet (raise), fold, or check. The middle three community cards are turned face up and another round of betting occurs. The first community card is flipped and another round of betting occurs. The last (fifth) community card is turned over and the last round of betting occurs. The players remaining show their cards, and the player with the best ranking poker hand wins the pot.

Special Considerations

A deck contains 52 cards. If there are eight players playing Seven-Card Stud, the number of cards needed is 56. If all eight players are still in the game, the seventh card dealt is dealt as a "community card," where all players must use the same card as their seventh (or down) card.

The same scenario can occur in Five-Card Draw, where there are eight players with five initially dealt cards and each player discards three cards, thereby totaling 64 cards needed. If additional cards are needed in Five-Card Draw, then before a player's discarded cards are added to the pile of discarded cards, the pile of discarded cards is shuffled and the discarding player receives his replacement cards. Then his discarded cards are added to the pile of discarded cards. This way no player can receive his discarded cards, and each player will receive replacement cards.

A player's hand is stored as a maximum of nine cards, where the first seven cards are used to analyze the player's hand value (ranking). A hand can hold five cards, as in Five-Card Draw and Five-Card Stud; seven cards as in Seven-Card Stud, Chicago, and Hold 'Em; or nine cards as in Omaha.

Researching a Baseball Game

The first and oldest rule in research is "check and recheck your facts."

Never assume that the data given to you by a reputable source is accurate and complete.

When I received the data for the game General Mills' All-Star Baseball, the data was missing important statistic fields and individual player statistics, had inaccurate or jumbled statistics (like 367 was 376), and needed

significant checking to verify the given data and supply the missing data needed.

The baseball data was divided into two major groups: team data and player data. Team data included the team name, team graphics (logo, 3D stadium, team uniform for home and away games, and so on), stadium location, franchise facts, ticket prices, and club owner. The player data was categorized by player bio, graphics, all batting information, fielding information, and pitching info (for pitchers).

Player bio information included the player's birthday, hometown, position (manager, coach, pitcher, catcher, infielder, or outfielder), salary, height and weight, and so on. The graphics included the player's face texture or skin file name, the player's uniform (including the number and special patches worn), and so on. The player's batting information included batting statistics, batting side (right, left, or switch hitter), special batting stance, batting swing, running to base animations, and so on. The fielding information included catches right- or left-handed, fielding statistics, special running and catching animations, and so on. The pitching information included the pitch type thrown, pitching statistics, pitching specialty (like relief pitcher or starting pitcher), and so on.

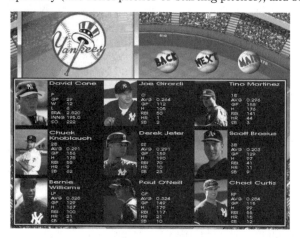

First, I checked other reliable statistics sources like the CBS sports and ESPN websites. I wanted the player's personal data (like birth date) to tell gamers interesting facts when they played the game, like "Today is the following player's birthday" and "This week is the birthday of these players too." This feature was easily accomplished by reading the computer's internal clock (date and time) and reading all of the player

birthdays from the database that was created and modified. Like baseball trading cards, I wanted to supply the player's height, weight, and hometown for announcers to add to their colorful commentary or as a statistic used along with the player's thumbnail photo as they came to bat. The player's hitting statistics were needed to properly compute the results of the game's hitting "eye and hand" twitch skills. A home-run hitter would more often strike out or hit triples and home runs over hitting singles and doubles. Pitchers, on the other hand, generally strike out or hit singles. Given exactly the same swing data (the same pitch type and strike zone location, the same hit type like a "power swing," and the same connection timing of the bat with the ball), you would expect that the real-world results would vary greatly if the batter was a home-run hitter rather than a pitcher.

One rule I decided early on in the data gathering process was to be consistent and able to explain my decisions to a hardcore fan. One such example of this was with American League pitchers who do not bat, except in certain games in the World Series. The first data I used was the last year the pitcher had a valid batting statistic. Then I would use that pitcher's lifetime statistics for batting. Lastly, I used any minor league or previous (to becoming a professional pitcher) batting statistic I could find. Generally, I found most of the statistics I needed.

One hard-to-find statistic I needed was the running and throwing speeds for all players in order to accurately calculate base running and field throwing to tag a runner out. I tried to find a 100-yard dash timing statistic to grade players into several speed categories (for both running, stealing, and throwing).

Let's examine the real world of baseball versus the computer, statistics-based AI we need to design. The situation to examine is a runner on first base when the batter hits the ball into center field. The experienced center fielder picks up the ball and throws it to the second baseman. This is an every-game, real-life situation. How can the computer accurately recreate this scenario?

Based on the twitch indicators and the batter's real-world batting statistics, the resulting hit or strike can be calculated. The twitch indicators include the type of pitch, the selected "aimed at" strike zone location, the type of batting power, and the "bat-to-ball" connection timing. The

Chapter 6

batter's real-world batting statistics are percentages for a strike, single, double, triple, home run, and fly ball. The ball's trajectory and speed can be accurately computed, including weather, wind, and gravity factors.

Now that the ball's flight and expected landing position are known (through calculations), each player in the field calculates, based on his present location and running speed, who can get to the ball the fastest (in this case the answer is probably the center fielder). The center fielder runs toward the ball's final location, which was already calculated. Upon picking up the ball (our calculations determined that a catch couldn't be made in time), he looks at the runner on first base. The first calculation needed is the distance from the first base runner's current position (he might have been leading off the base) to second base, multiplied by his standard base running time (remember that 100-yard dash statistic!).

Then the same calculation is made for the batter running from home plate to first base. A calculation is made for the center fielder, knowing the distance from his position to first base, his position to second base, and his throwing speed statistic. Each calculated scenario is compared: (1) the center fielder's throw to first base time versus the batter's running to first base time, and (2) the center fielder's throwing time to second base versus the first base runner's time to second base.

Obviously, whichever scenario is quicker for the center fielder to execute is the outcome of this play. In this case, the center fielder will throw to the second base player who (calculated as being closest to the goal of stopping or tagging out the runner who was on first base) is closest to that position. This is a simple description of simulating in AI the real-world thinking and spontaneous actions that we see every day.

Research Conclusion

The hardworking customers that will buy your game desire exciting, fun, and realistic games. Hype, superb graphics, and wonderfully orchestrated sounds might entice customers to buy the product, but to gain a true fan base, the praise of the reviewers, and respect from publishers and from the gaming industry, you as the designer must properly research your vision.

As we have seen, research can add new light and expand your initial vision. Organizing and planning your goals greatly helps the entire development team in maintaining your vision and accessing the information throughout the entire development process.

A poorly designed game, a game that annoys the fan base, or a game with hype and no substance will be devastating to your publisher (if you get one) and hurt your career as a game designer.

Invest your time in researching, and the experience and effort will pay off big throughout your career.

Workshop

Assignments

Assignment 1: Discuss the following topics:
1. Research sources, or where to find information.
2. What type of information a designer needs to find.
3. The importance of researching similar games and development postmortems.

Assignment 2: Discuss the research needed to design a basketball game.

Assignment 3: Discuss the research needed to design a fantasy-adventure game such as one based on *The Lord of the Rings*.

Assignment 4: Discuss the research needed to design a chess game and its variations and various piece representations.

Assignment 5: Discuss researching a favorite licensed property and describe the facts known and the facts that are not yet known but needed.

Assignment 6: Select characters from your favorite cereal manufacturer, restaurant chain (think hamburgers), cartoon, or children's show and list five points for each stage that are research goals, research sources, and items to research.

Exercises

Exercise 1: Answer the following questions:
1. What is the first step in beginning research?
2. Name three places to find research sources.
3. Name three sources to gather resource information.
4. What is the primary function of the game designer?
5. What phenomenon of fish behavior can confuse predators?
6. Storing data, filing paperwork, and copying CD/DVD sound recordings describe what research stage?
7. When developing a commonly known concept, should the designer skip simple and obvious instructions such as the winning and losing conditions?

8. Games based on televisions shows, films, and comic books are called what?

9. A comic book licensor usually has drawings of the characters called what?

10. Can the game designer or producer hire voice-over actors to narrate their characters' voices and write their own characters' script without consulting the licensor? Explain.

Exercise 2: Read the following description and follow the instructions.

A publisher has hired the student to design a AAA forensic investigator game title based on the popularity of several TV shows such as *CSI* and *Forensic Files*.

The publisher will provide access to the FBI Forensics Lab in Washington, D.C., and top-level forensic investigators to interview.

Marketing, sales, and demographic information:

From TV's *Quincy* to films such as *The Bone Collector*, *Seven*, and *The Silence of the Lambs* to television hits like *CSI* and *Forensic Files*, the mass audience eagerly watches. *CSI: Crime Scene Investigation*, which won the 2001 Favorite New Series Award, the 2001 Golden Globe, and the 2001 Emmy for best show, is watched by 28.7 million people in the USA, Europe, Asia, Australia, and South America. The demographics have *CSI* watched by a broad, affluent, and computer-savvy audience categorized by age ranges of 18-34, 18-49, and 25-54, including both genders. Court TV's *Forensic Files* has an audience of over two million that includes a demographic of ages 18-49 and 25-54, including both genders.

1. List 10 goals in order to design the game.

2. List five forensic disciplines, describe them, and document the research sources.

3. Obtain pictures, photos, or drawings for five of the forensic disciplines listed.

4. Answer three of the following four questions:

   a. Why do investigators photograph the crowd of onlookers at an arson or bomb site?

   b. Where would a forensic investigator use a camera?

   c. What is "blood splatter" and what evidence does it reveal?

   d. What is "criminal profiling"?

Unguided Exercises

Unguided Exercise 1: Review two similar games that are currently in the marketplace.

Unguided Exercise 2: Select a game concept and list 10 questions that need to be answered in order to design the game.

Unguided Exercise 3: Select a game concept and provide 10 facts that research should uncover.

Chapter 7

Innovation in Gaming

According to *Webster's New Collegiate Dictionary*, the word *innovation* means "a new idea, method, or device."

Is necessity the "mother of invention"?

Did Spore's massive amount of unusual, modifiable graphic and character creation make "procedural graphics" (algorithmic shapes) necessary?

Can a device or hardware help in innovating? Do we need a publisher's connection to innovate something like a Wii controller, a steering wheel, or a force-feedback joystick?

Would Guitar Hero have been as successful without its guitar device? Isn't Guitar Hero a finger version of Dance Dance Revolution? Perhaps we can piggyback on an existing technology or hardware with an innovation of our own.

In the early days of interactive gaming, the designer did not have the money people breathing down his neck yelling "Deliver us a hit!" Recently, I discussed innovation with an ex-Origin employee who praised the Ultima series as innovative and the Tabula Rasa MMO as wasting the designer's true talent since strict schedules and profits become more important than innovation and originality.

Innovation can be inexpensive to implement and a very powerful promotional edge for the game.

When I was designing games in the mid-1990s at Villa Crespo Software, several innovations were planned inside the games. One innovation grew from two sources that I was dealing with. The company was selling gambling games at $50 and wanted more sales the second year. At the same time, developers of shareware ("try and buy" games) complained about working with publishers and getting their games into stores. Shareware games did not have the budgets and polish that the top triple-A games had. After thinking about these issues, I suggested a low-cost game series of an abridged (less features) version of our $50 games, and working with the shareware developers on their game quality. The series was called the Coffee Break Series (CBS), and each sold for $14.95. The president of Villa Crespo Software numbered each title so the collector instinct in most gamers would make them want every game in the series. The stores were provided with holders that fit right in front of their cash registers, a location that normally costs thousands of dollars. (Publishers pay for premium store space and locations, and these innovations gave VCS's games great exposure at a discount.)

Stores that did not sell games at this price point usually had bargain bins that we convinced them to fill with the CBS titles. Stores reported to their headquarters that the winter holiday profits of just the CBS titles were paying their rent. Through the warranty cards, sales of the Coffee Break Series abridged titles confirmed the additional sale of the higher-priced counterparts, which were reduced to $40. The gambling games the second year outsold their first year sales and the CBS titles were hard to find in stores. Soon after the little publisher Villa Crespo Software released their innovation of quality, low-cost games, the giant publishers such as Microsoft, Sierra, and MicroProse started selling abridged versions or demos of their games.

When I designed the characters in Villa Crespo Software's Combination Lock, a trivia game show where the contestants were of different races, the EGA graphics format of 16 colors was the next step up from the four colors of CGA graphics and allowed for better, more discerning graphics with the ability to display a larger palette of pure and dithered patterns or colors. The game was one of the first to feature male and female contestants of all races, and the press ate this innovation up. The cost was minimal to have the artist provide the extra players.

When I was contracted by PolarWare (later bought by Merit Software) to design and develop a video game based on Don Bluth's film *All Dogs Go to Heaven*, the game was to output the entire digital sound track from the film through the PC speaker as well as the Covox, Adlib, and Creative Labs sound cards. In those days, this was a difficult task and not like today when Windows handles every device. The game featured an on-screen comic book with 10 mini-games that played the film's wonderful music digitally.

All Dogs was one of the first games to receive awards for innovation in game sound from these sound card manufacturers.

Films inspire future game innovation, such as *The Island*'s virtual boxing scenes, *The Paycheck*'s 3D screenless monitor, *2001: A Space Odyssey*'s voice communication chess game, and *Star Trek: The Next Generation*'s holodeck.

In my recent game Bingo Poker, I tried an innovation of making the game experience personal by requiring the player to enter his or her name and birthday (month and day). The NPCs (nonplayer characters) can make remarks using astrological data about the player and common facts such as famous people born under the same sign, favorite colors, their birthstone, lucky numbers, typical careers, favorable planets, and compatible and incompatible signs.

The full implementation of this innovation would be in an RPG or adventure hybrid game requiring the player to initially enter his or her name, birth date (month and day), city, state, and country.

Imagine playing a game after entering the aforementioned data and the game opens up in your bedroom where the walls are decorated with posters of your state's pro sports team. As you enter the kitchen, on the window ledge is your state's flower, and in your state's tree chirps your state's bird (or birds that live in your state). All of these sights and sounds are transparent to the player (perhaps the press will eat this innovation up), but these little items make the game unique to every player.

Let's design a scenario where we want the player to enter a room that is guarded by an NPC. There are several ways to achieve our goal. One way is to attack, insult, or challenge the player so that he or she instinctively wants revenge and enters the room (in actuality we have won since we want the player inside this room). The second way is to invite the player into the room through praise, potential promises, and flirtation.

An Aquarius individual, a person typically born between January 20 and February 18, is usually associated with a number of traits, including being contrary, detached, friendly, honest, humanitarian, independent, intellectual, intractable, inventive, loyal, original, perverse, unemotional, and unpredictable. Using this information, the gameplay can lure the player into an area or influence him or her to take a certain path.

The NPC can be an attractive female or male (for a positive invitation) or a hideous monster (negative taunt attacking the player).

Say a monster exclaims, "You're not smart enough to enter this room!" or "You are a disloyal person so do not try to enter this special room." The player, being proud of his loyalty or intellectual traits, will try to fight back at the monster and enter the room. Notice that as a designer you could substitute any of the Aquarius traits in the taunting sentences.

Now let's suppose that an attractive person of the opposite gender to the player smiles and remarks, "I see that you are a very friendly and inventive person and should enter this special room for people such as yourself" or "There is a dispute in this room and we need an honest person like yourself to help!" Once again, we can get the player into the room and substitute the other traits into these sentences or similar sentences. By using the appropriate traits of all 12 astrological signs in these sentences we can personalize the conversations of the NPCs for each player and make it appear that the NPCs are interacting with them. Every player will open the same game box and install the same game. As the player enters his or her own initial data, the entire game changes and is personalized. The interaction, the game challenges, and the sound and graphics are all customized to that player.

What did this innovation cost us? *Nothing*. Only a little research to match known facts with the player's entered data (the research described here took me less than a day using the Internet).

In Bingo Poker, the NPCs taunt the player before the match so he wants to beat the NPC. After the NPC wins, the final taunt tries to make the player feel bad so he will replay the game and try to win. When the player wins, the NPC gives him a positive congratulation using the astrological information.

Think of your own innovation or steal my innovation (but please give me a footnote credit).

Where is the Picasso of the game industry? How do we motivate designers to create innovative and exciting games? Where are the game mechanics that are as innovative as music's jazz?

Recent Gaming Innovations

Several innovations from recent games dealt with graphics, game mechanics, gameplay, audio, storytelling, and AI.

Deus Ex used an innovation that included stealth in order to avoid being captured or seen.

The 3D modding phenomenon of making games using another game's engine or creating machinima (discussed in Chapter 3, "Game Genres") spawned many games.

WarioWare used *mini-games*, smaller games within the game, as an innovative concept.

Unique use of time is an important innovation in some game mechanics. (Time mechanics are discussed in detail in Chapter 9, "Game Design Principles" in the section "Game Mechanics.") Some good examples of time innovations include reversing time as a "do-over" in Prince of Persia: The Sands of Time; slowing down time for the main character, as in Max Payne's "bullet time"; and the premise behind TimeShift, where even fire can freeze.

Innovations in presentation that recent games display include the POV (point of view) in FPS (first-person shooter) and 3PS (third-person shooter) games and using film-quality cut-scenes and cinematics.

Another innovation in games is the use of procedural landscape generation for trees, mountains, and terrain. In the Seven Cities of Gold, the environment was even deformable.

Music and audio innovations include adaptive music as used in GoldenEye 007. James Bond 007: Everything or Nothing had an originally written and performed soundtrack and an "A-list" of voice-over actors such as Pierce Brosnan, Dame Judi Dench, John Cleese, Shannon Elizabeth, and Heidi Klum and is considered the best James Bond game ever and possibly the greatest console first-person shooter ever made. The music mimics the actual gameplay, so as the player reacts quicker the soundtrack begins to speed up, and as the player slows down the music likewise plays slower.

The innovations in AI are highlighted in games such as Nintendogs (and offshoots) with its artificial pets.

Let's look at and examine a few game industry innovations that are noteworthy, such as Dance Dance Revolution, Guitar Hero/Rock Band, Spore, Second Life, and World of Warcraft, and hardware innovations such as the Wii remote (controller) and handhelds such as the Gameboy Advance (GBA), the PlayStation Portable (PSP), and the Nintendo DS.

Dance Dance Revolution

Dance Dance Revolution by Konami was released in 1998/1999 and was truly innovative as a rhythm and dance game that had the player(s) interactively following cues and modern rhythms with their bodies. The arcade and later the home console market took to this like the karaoke phenomenon. DDR was both original and unique, and even 10 years after its first release the game and its sequels and variations are still selling well. DDR's gameplay involves the player moving his or her feet to a set pattern, stepping in time to the general rhythm or beat of a song.

Guitar Hero/Rock Band

Guitar Hero/Rock Band, developed as a collaboration between RedOctane and Harmonix Music Systems, innovated the guitar device with popular rock music. Similar to DDR (I call it "finger DDR"), the game has had major sales. In just three years the Guitar Hero franchise sold over 19 million units. In 2006, Guitar Hero 2 sold over 1.3 million copies (all platforms or SKUs), and by December 1, 2007, 3.1 million copies of Guitar Hero II were sold. Guitar Hero World Tour sold over 534,000 units. In its first week, Guitar Hero On Tour for the Nintendo DS sold over 300,000 units.

Even the "geeks" want to be rock stars with the hottest guitar, compelling riffs, and screaming fans.

Rock Band is a one- to four-player version of Guitar Hero that allows players to simulate playing three different peripherals modeled after musical instruments, including two guitars (a lead guitar and a bass guitar), a drum, and a microphone. In three years Rock Band sold over four million units, and in December of 2008, Rock Band 2 was launched.

Spore

Spore, designed by Will Wright of Maxis, is innovative in many ways such as game mechanics, gameplay, and procedural graphics where the creatures can be created without prerendered models having predesigned animations. The player gets to customize/design his creatures and animate them. The universe of Spore has a vast game design and immense gameplay. Players can share user-created life-forms, buildings, and objects with other players and share recorded play sessions too.

World of Warcraft

World of Warcraft (commonly referred to as WOW) by Blizzard is a massively multiplayer online role-playing game (MMORPG) with more than 11.5 million subscribers in 2009 (which is more than 62% of the total number of online players) paying a $14.99 monthly subscription fee. (For those with slow calculators, that's over $165 million per month.) The game keeps growing, with each expansion pack costing $30 to $40 before paying the monthly subscription fees.

The majority of WOW players are 23- to 39-year-olds who play for an average of 23 hours a week.

In an area of the gaming industry where many MMOs have crashed and burned, WOW is innovative and making the money that any Hollywood blockbuster film would be proud of generating. When beginning World of Warcraft, there are simple tasks that let the player feel a sense of accomplishment and earn experience points, climbing up levels.

An innovation in WOW allows players to design their own "dashboards" to monitor their performance on certain tasks. The dashboard monitors give real-time feedback on that player's performance, and many other companies are trying to implement this in their own applications.

WOW motivates players and has them learning new skills they feel are worth investing their real time to learn.

Another innovation is the social aspect or "guilds" that players join to collaborate with each other, and as a team advance by earning experience points and thus achieve higher levels. The guild members become trusted friends, and although WOW doesn't require guild participation, players gravitate to join them as they advance.

Second Life

Second Life is Linden Lab's highly debated virtual world, game, or huge "chat room." Players can visit the world of Second Life (often referred to as SL) and meet friends and new people. As players buy property using real money, the terrain changes and a new shopping mall or a politician's headquarters adorns the once barren landscape. In SL, real-world items and services are for sale using your real money, where $1 U.S. equals 266 Linden dollars. The innovation of Second Life is in its community, where over 4.1 million players can interact with each other, and its ability to sell virtual property. Many colleges, universities, libraries, and government agencies use Second Life as a learning and meeting place. Political head-quarters and foreign embassies have opened buildings inside SL, and religious groups hold meetings on their SL property. Even artists have populated the terrain with artwork and statues, and sports teams have opened up virtual arenas and fields to entertain the SL audience.

Wii Remote

The Wii remote (controller) is an innovative device that makes the Wii games fun to play. The Wii wireless controller is capable of detecting the device's three-dimensional position for multiple devices as the game is being played. NPD, the leading global market research company, has Wii as the top-selling gaming console of its genera-tion, outselling the Xbox 360 and the PlayStation 3 (PS3).

The Wii sports games such as tennis, bowl-ing, golf, baseball, and boxing demonstrate the capabilities of the Wii remote's motion sensing. Women who rarely play video games are buying the Wii Fit because its 40 games of interactive exercises are fun and get the heart pumping. Each Wii Fit requires a Wii console and a Wii Balance Board. The Wii con-sole, devices, and games are selling to a huge market of people who previously were not interested in the gaming world.

Handhelds

Handhelds such as the Gameboy Advance (GBA), the PlayStation Portable (PSP), and the Nintendo DS have taken gaming portable. I can't go anywhere without seeing some child playing a handheld game, whether it is in restaurants, the dentist's office, or on buses and airplanes. The Nintendo Gameboy revolutionized the handheld gaming industry. The lightweight, portable gaming units have decent graphics, limited input, and allow you to play great, fun games. The Nintendo DS is an extension of the GBA (Gameboy Advance) with dual screens (the DS acronym) and even a touch screen. The Nintendo DS also has wireless connectivity and a microphone port. The microphone is especially cool to use in games such as Nintendogs, where you can name your dog and later call him or her to you through the microphone.

The innovative elements of the Nintendo DS are "PictoChat," which gives up to 16 people in a chat room the ability to chat wirelessly using the keyboard or stylus to draw pictures or write notes to each other. This ability is built into the Nintendo DS firmware (programmable system memory) and has a 60-foot range even through walls. This is a fun activity and could lead to innovative multiplayer games that use the stylus and keyboard.

Future Innovations

According to MyDigitalLife (www.mydigitallife.info/2007/10/14/awesome-brain-computer-interface-system-for-mental-controlling-second-life-avatars/), a brain-computer interface system (BCI) from the research team at the Biomedical Engineering Lab at Keio University in Japan has "developed a new BCI system, allowing the Second Life avatar to mentally control the simple movements." This technology will help the handicapped in many ways including playing games, and scientists such as astronauts who need to fix spaceship parts without physically using their gloved hands to turn or maneuver items will be able to use their brains rather than their brawn.

In 2007, Live Earth presented to a Tokyo audience the virtual reality singer of the Genki Rockets, Lumi, followed by a head-to-toe hologram likeness of former U.S. Vice President Al Gore, who materialized onstage as though he were really there and spoke about hope with expressions of amazement that overwhelmed the world-wide audience. (YouTube's video of this event can be found at www.youtube.com/watch?v=ebhv8X0njbk.) As game designers we can imagine with anticipation where this high-tech virtual technology is capable of going.

Mitch Kapor and Philippe Bossut of Kapor Enterprises, Inc. designed a prototypical interface using a 3D camera as an input device that demonstrates the possibilities for operating Second Life "hands free" without a mouse or keyboard.

Kapor states, "For the moment, our objective is to explore the possibilities for these new types of devices. We believe that these cameras will eventually make interacting with Virtual Worlds as comfortable as using a webcam. This will ultimately broaden the appeal of Virtual Worlds by  allowing new ways of online expression. It may also attract people who find the current gaming interface too hard to handle."

Readers are encouraged to check out the excellent video from Kapor Enterprises, Inc. at www.handsfree3d.com.

Second Life players can position their bodies to control their on-screen avatar's navigation and facial expressions and to edit objects. The player can actually lean forward or backward as his avatar walks forward or backward, and lean right or left to turn the avatar right or left. If the player stands still his avatar stops, and jumping up causes the avatar to jump in the virtual world.

If the player wishes to fly around the terrain like a bird, he just needs to raise his hands above his waist to take off, place his hands at waist height to level off, and move his hands below his waist to land. If the player angles his hands above his waist or leans one direction, that will turn the flying avatar in that direction. Whenever a player wants his avatar to jump off a cliff and land gracefully, he just places his hands behind his back.

Workshop

Assignments

Assignment 1: Based on a futuristic film's high-tech device or technique, such as *Star Trek*'s holodeck, *The Paycheck*'s screenless monitor, or *The Island*'s virtual boxing, design in a few sentences a game using this innovative technology.

Assignment 2: Explain how Guitar Hero is similar to and different from Dance Dance Revolution.

Exercises

Exercise 1: Describe your favorite game and explain how you could make the game more fun or better with an innovation.

Exercise 2: Research the original Tetris and its various clones, describing each clone's new gameplay variation and innovation.

Unguided Exercises

Unguided Exercise 1: Discuss which is more important: "innovation that makes the game more fun" or "innovation that makes the game more profitable."

Unguided Exercise 2: Discuss the importance, popularity, and differences between hardware and game innovation.

Internet Reading Assignment

"Innovation in Casual Games: A Rallying Cry" by Juan Gril
http://www.gamasutra.com/view/feature/1947/innovation_in_casual_games_a_.php

"Guitar Hero" Wikipedia article
http://en.wikipedia.org/wiki/Guitar_Hero_(video_game)

"50 Greatest Game Design Innovations" by Edge staff
www.Edge-Online.Com/features/50-greatest-design-innovations?page=0,0

Thoughts for Discussion

1. Discuss possible innovations for a sports game, a racing game, and a first- or third-person shooter.
2. Discuss being a game designer for a Nintendo game using a Wii controller and for Maxis (owned by EA) trying to design a mod for Spore.

Chapter 8

Game Design Documents

The Executive Summary and the Game Proposal

The Executive Summary (aka Five Pager or Design Treatment) is a publisher's or developer's document containing the basic summary of the game concept and a description of the game including the game's basic plot, the gameplay, the demographics (player's or target audience's gender and age), the flow of the game from the starting scenario to several typical endings (successful and unsuccessful), and the game's features (like graphics, audio presentation, hardware controls, and licensed properties). The Executive Summary is a short, concise informational and promotional document written for the executives that explains your game's concept, gameplay, and features.

The Game Proposal is written by developers seeking financial support from publishers. The difference is that the Game Proposal must include the staff's profile (its makeup and relevant work experience) and a budget with work completion milestones since the developer is not employed by the publisher and is an unknown risk. The One Pager or its information must be included in both the Game Proposal and the Executive Summary.

Before writing either document, you should perform a market analysis of similar games. You should know your:

- Publisher and potential publishers
- Competing products (publisher, license, platforms, retail price, sales figures)
- Past similar products, especially successful ones and similar genre games
- The entertainment marketplace, including books, films, TV shows, and games

Development Team Details

Let's look at the team makeup needed to develop a proposed game, especially for a start-up company. Chapter 10, "Knowing the Entire Team," discusses these roles in more depth.

Designer: One person to write the documents and keep the team focused on the game's vision.

Producer: One person to manage the team and project. The producer also liaises with the publisher, licensor, marketing and sales teams, and reviewers.

Programmers: Two to three game programmers and a network/Internet programmer. Possibly one or two level designers.

Artists: Depends on the game's graphic demands. Usually three to five artists to create environments and venues as well as characters.

Audio specialist: Usually one audio specialist for music and sound effects (SFX).

The following is an example of the basic requirements needed regarding software and hardware for a game project.

Each programmer needs a compiler such as Visual C++, C#, or other C++ compilers; a source control application to store their code, such as Source Safe, Darcs, CVS, or Subversion; a 2D graphics application such as Photoshop, CorelDRAW, or MS Paint (free with Windows); a word processing application such as MS Word; access to project management software such as MS Project or Intellisys Project; and 3D engine software and hardware, such as one to two computers. The development team should have access to video game consoles so they can compare their game to similar games, and the best games available on the Xbox, Xbox 360, PlayStation 2 and 3, PlayStation Portable (PSP), and the Nintendo Wii and DS, along with their input devices like the EyeToy, Rock Band instruments, and floor mats.

Each artist needs one or more 3D art packages such as 3ds Max, Maya Complete, Softimage, LightWave, or DeBabelizer, and 3D plug-ins, plus a 2D art package such as Photoshop or CorelDRAW.

The team will need an asset repository application such as NxN's Alienbrain, video capture software, and hardware such as one to two computers and a digital tablet. The art team may need a hi-res scanner, a color copy machine, and a high-quality (resolution) color printer.

My recommendation is to budget the same way for every project even if you already have these items and to charge the full retail price for each item. Many times during a project the team may need an additional computer or a new version of an application may be released, requiring an upgrade purchase. If the proposed budget includes these items at the retail price, the project can come in under budget (a feather in your cap), and if something happens requiring more money, your budget will provide for these unanticipated events. If a computer costs $3,000 and buying 10 computers gets you a discount of $500 per computer, then the $5,000 savings can be used for another needed purchase or for team bonuses at the end of the project. The budget money is usually an advance against royalties, so the money is allocated to the project. A producer who can negotiate better prices and discounts is a valuable asset to the project since there will be money for unforeseen events during the development process.

Other budgeted items would be for the audio engineers, such as audio software for composing and editing; video capturing and editing software; and digital cameras for capturing the QA testing session and gameplay for commercials, Internet trailers, and industry show promotional clips.

Other expenses to budget for the development include a high-speed Internet connection, network station, and server and other monthly expenses such as rent, utilities, phone service (office phones, fax, and employee cell phones), payroll services, package delivery services, office supplies and miscellaneous expenses, business insurance, magazine subscriptions and book purchases, overtime meals, travel expenses, and money for perks such as free snacks and coffee and for company functions such as employee birthday parties, holiday parties, and milestone completions. These are a few of the obvious items that need to be included in the budget for a 6- to 18-month project.

I suggest that any developer require a three-month advance plus initial costs to start a project. If a project gets cancelled (and how often does this happen?), the head of the company has the three months' advance payment to find another project before laying people off. The initial costs include the budgeted hardware and software items. The three-month advance includes the monthly expenses and payroll.

The initial costs may range from $50,000 to $250,000, depending on the platforms being developed and the number of people working on the project. The monthly ongoing costs may range from $5,000 to $12,000 a month.

The payroll budget dwarfs all other figures; a normal development project having 15 people earning an average of $60,000 a year (gross salary plus benefits and employer's social security contribution) is $900,000 a year and $1,350,000 for an 18-month project.

Let's look at the average salaries of a sample development team with some game industry experience:

Game designer	$90,000
Producer	$90,000
Technical director	$95,000
Art director	$95,000
Programmers (two)	$70,000 ($140,000)
Character artists (two)	$85,000 ($170,000)
Network administrator	$65,000
Environment artists (three)	$65,000 ($195,000)
QA testers (PT) (three)	$20,000 ($60,000)

2D texture artist	$45,000
Office manager	$35,000
Audio composer (PT)	$50,000

If you add up these yearly salaries, you would get $1,130,000 for your base yearly payroll.

An additional 10% for the employer's social security costs adds $113,000, and $1,000 a month per full-time employee for benefits (unemployment, medical, and dental insurance) would total $168,000.

The annual payroll inclusive would be $1,411,000 for this developer working on a game.

Obviously, the initial cost maximum of $250,000 plus the annual monthly cost of $12,000 (maximum) per month or $144,000 a year would not exceed $394,000, or one-third of the annual payroll.

Milestone Scheduling

Milestone scheduling is a delivery and payment agreement that came about to guarantee work promises and payment segments. In the old days, development was paid at timed intervals and promised work was delivered late, if at all. Now, the developers work on a deliverable and upon publisher's approval payment is given. Rarely are developers given a royalty for a "work for hire." If the developer is self-financed or has an intellectual property (or an "optioned" property), then a royalty agreement may be negotiated. When creating a milestone schedule, the timing of deliverables is key. You don't want to set unrealistic delivery dates since the development team would be in breach of contract if the milestone dates were missed. On the other hand, considering the project completion milestone as a year-long endeavor would not be realistic and waiting for payments at the end of completion would make it difficult to meet monthly expenses in order to keep the company in business.

Developmental progress is the main concern of the milestone schedule. Defining and achieving each step is the current method for measuring progress and thus getting paid for it.

A typical milestone schedule would have (1) a pre-demo date where the characters walking through the background are able to trigger all possible animations, (2) a playable demo where players can play a few key scenarios, (3) a fully playable level, (4) second fully playable level, (5) last fully playable level, (6) alpha version based on GDD and feedback from publisher and testers, (7) beta version, and (8) final version (the gold master) of the game.

Milestones set the developer's goals and determine what aspect and assets the developer must focus on.

In the past I have contracted for a fixed fee to work on a project. Usually as the project is being tested and the design is a real playable game, the publisher wants additional features added or different methods of interacting with the game such as a force-feedback joystick or new storyline paths. This additional work is called "feature creep." Feature creep can come from several sources such as the publisher, developer, licensor, and investors.

When publisher feature creep happens, I ask the publisher to make a choice. The first choice is for me to continue working on the contracted game with its deliverables for the agreed-to fee, and then negotiate the additional features after the original game is completed. The second choice is to be paid for the work thus far and end that project. Then a brand new project is started where new documentation is written combining the old documents with the added features, new milestones, and budget. Upon a new sign-off, the new project begins.

How Do You Get a Publisher to Want to Meet Your Team?

There are many ways to get the attention of publishers. For example, your team might be experienced or boast famous team members. Another way to capture the attention of publishers is to own an optioned license for a film, book, or even an actor. Pay for or at least make a down payment on the license so no one can steal your idea or concept.

Since many publishers are actively seeking new properties, a hot Internet game concept discussion can capture press and publisher interest. Even if you don't have the resources to publish your game commercially, a good review or a computer game magazine advertisement can get publishers' attention. Put your finished game in a box and get it reviewed or spend some capital for an advertisement in order to generate interest. (A game ad can be quite costly though, ranging from $10 to $30K.)

Finally, consider creating a great short demo to capture a producer's interest.

If the purpose of meeting with a publisher is to request demo and/or project funding, you must arrive at the meeting with the game design proposal, including the budget and other documents. Bring the development schedule (even if it was previously sent to get the meeting), relevant team experience (considered most important), artwork of key in-game scenes, and a video trailer or a quick demonstration of the game. The key team members who should attend this meeting are the company's president, the game designer, the lead producer, the lead programmer or director of development, and the art director or lead artist.

The pitch should highlight the game's marketing and sales demographics, the USP (unique selling proposition/point), and how this game will make the publisher money (lots of money).

The "cool" aspects of the game or how this game will destroy the current leading game are not as powerfully compelling to the publisher as charts and graphs showing profit.

If the purpose of the meeting is for a publishing deal only (no funding), then a game demo, sample artwork of key in-game scenes, or a quick playable version will suffice. The key team members who should attend a publishing deal only meeting would be the company's president, the game designer, and the producer. These deals can easily be done at conferences such as GDC and E3.

The designer must structure the pre-GDD documents according to the purpose of the project. An internal game for a publisher or well-funded developer requires less of a sell and explaining who the developer is.

If I gave you $2,000,000 to develop a game and several developers responded, who would you choose?

- A new developer with two experienced employees and one published game.
- A new developer with five experienced employees and no titles but willing to work for half the money.
- An experienced developer with two titles and six experienced employees.
- An experienced developer with five titles and all experienced employees.

Now reverse the situation since you are the developer seeking a game project from a publisher and write your excellent document to get the $2,000,000.

A Sample Game Proposal: 13 Mirrors

[opening sentence]

13 Mirrors™ is a 3D forensic science game combining the exploration of a third-person adventure involving solving criminal challenges and investigating crime scenes with an intellectual first-person strategy of running a true-to-life forensic lab, learning new forensic techniques from real forensic experts, and being the key expert witness in a dozen courtroom cases. After determining the perpetrator, the player will assist the police in the

13 Mirrors morgue scene where the player as a forensic scientist solves cases.

arrest that may lead to a chase throughout the city, inside multilevel buildings, or to the seedy part of town.

[pseudo-license and USP]

From TV's *Quincy* to films such as *The Bone Collector*, *Seven*, and *The Silence of the Lambs* to television hits like *CSI* and *Forensic Files*, the mass audience eagerly watches crime dramas. *CSI: Crime Scene Investigation*, which won the 2001 Favorite New Series Award, the 2001 Golden Globe, and the 2001 Emmy for best show, is watched by 28.7 million people in the U.S., Europe, Asia, Australia, and South America.

[demographics]

The demographics have *CSI* watched by a broad, affluent, and computer-savvy audience grouped by age ranges of 18-34, 18-49, and 25-54 including both genders.

Court TV's *Forensic Files* has an audience of over 2 million that includes a demographic of ages 18-49 and 25-54 including both genders.

[an overview]

In 13 Mirrors, the player is a forensic investigator who wears special contact lenses called "mirrors" that function as both a camera and computer screen and have voice transmitting ability to record and input information back into the computer system. The player, as Dr. Anthony "Mirror" Mirron, is given 12 randomly chosen cases in which he must investigate the crime scene and collect data and physical evidence leading to an arrest and conviction of the perpetrator. Each case must be solved within a specific amount of time, and new forensic techniques must be learned from real-life forensic experts. Successful cases give the player financial and status rewards. When the player collects certain pieces of evidence, a video clip depicting a view from the perpetrator's eyes will be shown (also known as a "reflection"). A surprise 13th "boss" case involving a serial killer is the finale.

[comparison to known games]

Many games like America's Army 3 and Tom Clancy's HAWX by Ubisoft are designed with a learn and practice phase followed by a field exercise testing the player's skill and learned knowledge. In 13 Mirrors, players will need to learn forensic techniques and procedures, practice using their laboratory equipment, and use this knowledge and skill to successfully complete each case leading to the arrest and conviction of the "right" person(s).

[platforms to develop on]

13 Mirrors will first be developed for the Xbox 360 (which we are registered developers for) and the Windows platform followed by the PlayStation 3 and PSP, and Nintendo Wii and DS.

13 Mirrors will be utilizing the latest 3D game engines such as the Vicious engine and the Torque engine (which we are registered developers for).

Similar games are Ubisoft's CSI: Crime Scene Investigation Hard Evidence for Windows, Nintendo Wii and DS, PlayStation 2, and Xbox 360 platforms for $29.99; CSI: New York for Windows Vista for $29.99; Ubisoft's Grey's Anatomy for Windows, Nintendo Wii, and DS for $29.95; NovaLogic's Delta Force: Angel Falls for Windows for $19.99; and Tom Clancy's HAWX for Windows, PlayStation 3, and Xbox 360 platforms for $59.99.

[the selling, wrap-up, closing sentence]

The mass audience of affluent, computer-savvy players who eagerly watch forensic TV shows and forensic movies now can play 13 Mirrors.

Relevant Team Experience

PSI Software Inc. Team Members and Experience

Roger E. Pedersen, Producer and Game Designer, President of PSI Software, Inc.

- Author of *Game Design Foundations* and *Game Design Foundations, Second Edition*, published by Wordware Publishing, Inc., 2003, 2009
- Author of award-winning Internet articles on Gamasutra.com, GameDev.net, and GigNews.com:
  - "Pedersen Principles of Game Design and Production"
  - "What I Did During My Summer Vacation, or, Developing a Game in 13 Weeks"
  - "Designing Great Games"
- Game industry experience since 1983 working as
  - Executive producer for Acclaim Entertainment
  - Director of product development for Merit Industries and Villa Crespo Software
  - Technical director for Phantom EFX
  - Film director, producer, and scriptwriter for PSI Productions
  - Game designer for Phantom EFX, American Alpha, Inc., KO Interactive, Cellufun, RealLife 3D Games (3D Open Motion), Hypnotix, Sports Simulation, Acclaim Entertainment, Merit Industries, Villa Crespo Software, Doubleday, CBS Software, Gametek, Hi-Tech Expressions, Merit Software, and PSI Software
  - Producer for RealLife 3D Games (3D Open Motion), Hypnotix, Corporate Communications Group, Doubleday, CBS Software, Gametek, Hi-Tech Expressions, Merit Software, Digital Embryo, and PSI Software

Michael R. Hausman, Senior Programmer

Michael R. Hausman is an experienced programmer who has worked on many AAA titles (listed below). Michael is a valuable team member for PSI Software, Inc. and programmer on the following titles:

Simon and Schuster: Deer Avenger, Deer Avenger 2: Deer in the City, Who Wants to Beat Up a Millionaire, Panty Raider, Bass Avenger, Miss Spider's Tea Party

Sierra: $100,000 Pyramid

Berkeley Systems: Ripley's Believe It or Not!

Pearson Software: Daria's Inferno

Knowledge Adventure: Sabrina the Teenage Witch: Brat Attack

Walker Boys Studio: War Between the States (demo)

General Mills: Big G All-Stars vs. Major League Baseball

Merit Software: All Dogs Go to Heaven

Villa Crespo Software: Amarillo Slim's Dealer's Choice, Amarillo Slim 7 Card Stud, Hearts, Dr. Thorp's Blackjack, Flicks! Film Review Library, Flicks! Trivia Game, Rosemary West's House of Fortune, Games Magazine: Word Games

Gametek: Press Your Luck, Wheel of Fortune, Jeopardy, Milton Bradley's Candyland, Go To The Head of The Class, Chutes and Ladders Parker Brothers' Sorry, Big Boggle Fisher-Price's Perfect Fit, I Can Remember, Fun Flyer

PSI Software: Cyber Cop, Zombies: Undead or Alive!

Hi-Tech Expressions: Swimware, Big Bird's Special Delivery, Ernie's Magic Shapes

First Star Software: Adventure U.S.A.

Pete Smith, Freelance Lead Artist

Pete Smith has been contracted to work on this project as lead artist. Pete has worked for over five years as lead artist on the following games:

3D6 Games: 3D character animator/modeler on Beastman for the Gameboy Advance

Pipedream Interactive/Majesco Games: 3D artist/animator on Blaster (GBA), Mercenary (PS2), Star Trek Voyager (PS2), Battling Robots: Beyond the Box (GBA), and Vampiress (cross-platform)

Awe Productions, Inc.: 3D artist intern on Big Dirt Trucks 2 Adventures (distributed by Mattel Interactive, 2000)

Experienced in 3ds Max, Character Studio, Maya Unlimited, Photoshop, QE Radiant, Nendo, Infini-D, DeBabelizer Pro, Adobe After Effects,

Adobe Premier, Illustrator, Director, Flash, QuarkXPress, Painter 3D, Sound Forge, Acid, and CoolEdit

Target Demographic

- The demographics are similar to the TV viewing audience who watches *CSI* and Court TV's *Forensic Files*.
- They are a broad, affluent, and computer-savvy audience grouped by age ranges 18-34, 18-49, and 25-54 including both genders.

The Competition

- Ubisoft's CSI: Crime Scene Investigation is based on the TV show and has *only five crimes* to investigate.
- Ubisoft and the licensor will not go beyond the "safe" TV audience realism of a crime scene.
- Ubisoft's CSI has the player as the TV show's character's apprentice and doesn't have the player utilizing real forensic lab equipment to solve the case.

13 Mirrors Feature Summary Sheet

- Thirteen exciting cases (more than twice Ubisoft's CSI cases)
- Training by the country's top forensic experts and real-life trainers
- Real-world crime scenes with an option for the level of realism
- Realistic 3D environments from actual crime scenes, the forensic lab, and the courtroom
- Easily recognizable main character for sequels

Gameplay Summary

13 Mirrors is a 3D forensic science game combining the exploration of a third-person adventure involving solving criminal challenges and investigating crime scenes with an intellectual first-person strategy of running a true-to-life forensic lab, learning new forensic techniques from real forensic experts, and being the key expert witness in a dozen courtroom cases. After determining the perpetrator, the player will assist the police in the arrest that may lead to a chase throughout the city, inside multilevel buildings, or to the seedy part of town.

In 13 Mirrors, the player is a forensic investigator who wears special contact lenses called "mirrors" that function as both a camera and computer screen and have voice transmitting ability to record and input information back into the computer system. The player, as Dr. Anthony "Mirror" Mirron, is given 12 randomly chosen cases in which he must investigate the crime scene and collect data and physical evidence leading to an arrest and conviction of the perpetrator. Each case must be solved within specific amount of time and new forensic techniques must be learned from real-life forensic experts. Successful cases give the player financial and status rewards. When the player collects certain pieces of evidence, a video clip depicting a view from the perpetrator's eyes will be shown (also known as a "reflection"). A surprise 13th "boss" case involving a serial killer is the finale.

Dr. Anthony "Mirror" Mirron is a forensic investigator who has a muscular, attractive appearance and should be as easily recognized as Lara Croft, Max Payne, and Mario are to the public.

Game Specifics

After the case is solved and the trial begins, the player will be called upon as the forensic expert witness and must correctly piece together the "reflections" (the video clips that were seen when certain pieces of evidence were collected). Winning a court case will give the player additional accolades, while losing a case leads to public scrutiny, problems with the boss, and being sent to class to learn much needed lessons.

An on-screen success score will have the player replaying cases to better his rating. After successfully completing 12 cases, the player will be given the option to play the bonus case (in single-player or multiplayer mode) involving a serial killer on a rampage throughout the city.

The 12 cases involve forensic investigative techniques such as fingerprinting, handwriting analysis, tracking people and vehicles, counterfeiting fraud, charred or altered documents, narcotic and dangerous drug analysis, identification and comparison, flammable liquids and fire debris, paint fragments, explosive materials and residue, ballistics, DNA analysis and toxicology, sexual assault, and trace evidence materials. The player must use the forensic lab to identify data, log items, properly store items, and follow standard procedures for evidence custody and lab requests. Each case depicts real-life crime scene scenarios that are often violent and grotesque in nature.

Game Modes

13 Mirrors has two levels of play, which are called "Associate mode" and "Professional mode."

In Associate mode, players are told what to do at each crime scene and are helped in the forensic lab. Also in Associate mode, determining the perpetrator and being the key courtroom expert is left up to your senior forensic investigator.

The maximum score for each case in Associate mode is 25 points (or 300 points for the 12 cases).

In Professional mode, players must read the preliminary report describing the crime scene and location, photograph and log a cautious walk-through of the entire scene as it appears when he arrives, mark special problem areas, carefully photograph each piece of evidence starting with items that could be easily lost or moved, log the location and position of each piece of evidence, and store it in its proper container.

The player must also secure the area by keeping out unauthorized personnel such as the press and wandering law enforcement personnel, and recording everyone who enters and leaves each room. Once in the forensic laboratory, he reserves the lab equipment and lab units to perform the required tests.

Logging requires case identifier, date, time, location, weather and lighting conditions, and condition and position of evidence.

The player photographs each piece of evidence from eye level to represent the normal view, the condition of the evidence before recovery (first take a photograph without the scale), the evidence in detail including a scale, the photographer's initials, and the date. Important evidence is photographed twice: a medium-distance photograph that shows the evidence and its position to other evidence, then a close-up photograph that includes a scale and fills the frame.

Additional materials needed include prior photographs, blueprints, or maps of the scene.

The player photographs the most fragile areas of the crime scene first, then all stages of the crime scene investigation, including discoveries; the interior crime scene in an overall and overlapping series using a wide-angle lens; and the exterior crime scene, establishing the location of the

13 Mirrors hotel crime scene (notice the dead body on the bed).

scene by a series of overall photographs including a landmark. The photographs should have 360 degrees of coverage. Consider using aerial photography, and photograph all entrances and exits.

A crime scene sketch must include case identifier, date, time, location, weather and lighting conditions, dimensions of rooms, furniture, doors, and windows, distances between objects, persons, bodies, entrances and exits, and measurements showing the location of evidence. Each object should be located by two measurements from nonmovable items such as doors or walls, and key, legend, compass orientation, scale, scale disclaimer, or a combination of these features.

Additional key instructions include the following:

- A search should be in a pattern such as a grid, strip or lane, or spiral.
- Wear gloves to avoid leaving fingerprints. Do not excessively handle the evidence after recovery. Seal all evidence packages at the crime scene.
- Obtain known standards such as fiber samples from a known carpet.
- Make a complete evaluation of the crime scene.
- Constantly check paperwork, packaging, and other information for errors.

Depending on the crime being investigated, this may require the investigator to use special equipment (fuming wand, fuming chambers, alternate light source, electrostatic dust print lifter) or special techniques (casting materials, blood spatter analysis, hand washings, chemical processing, bullet trajectory analysis, etc.).

The final check should entail the following: ensure all documentation is correct and complete, photograph the scene showing the final condition, ensure all evidence is secured, ensure all equipment is retrieved, and ensure hiding places or difficult access areas have not been overlooked.

The maximum score for each case in Professional mode is 50 points (or 600 points for the 12 cases).

Training

Training is available in latent fingerprint identification, DNA analysis, hair and fiber examination, firearm and toolmark identification, microscopy, photography, quality assurance, chemistry and instrumental analysis, computer forensics, evidence handling, public speaking, testimony proficiency, document examination, bomb disposal, polygraph testing, shoe print and tire tread analysis, and artist sketching.

In 13 Mirrors, video training by real-world forensic experts will instruct the player in forensic techniques, equipment usage, and investigative procedures.

Points Gained and Lost in 13 Mirrors

- Gain one point for photographing and logging a cautious walk-through of the entire scene as it appears when you arrive,
- Gain one point for securing the area by keeping out unauthorized personnel and recording everyone who enters and leaves each room.
- Gain one point for performing a proper final check.
- Gain one point for crime scene sketch with dimensions.
- Lose one point for forgetting to wear gloves and invalidate that item.
- Lose two points for forgetting to log in any item after signing it out, which invalidates that item.
- Lose one point for improperly sealing an evidence package at the crime scene, which invalidates that item.
- Gain experience and two points for using the proper lab and discovering important information.
- Gain up to five points for determining the perpetrator; accusing the wrong person lessens this point factor.
- Gain up to five points for successfully prosecuting the perpetrator; points vary according to the accuracy and skill quickness.
- Gain learning experience and one point for each training seminar attended.

Personalization of Gameplay

The player will register for the game entering his or her name, birth date, pets owned, city, and state. This will allow the player to see his state flowers in a vase on top of the kitchen table as the state bird perched on the state tree chirps outside the window.

13 Mirrors will tailor the game to that player. Inside the player's forensic lab office will be an empty award wall where each solved case replaces an empty location with an award.

The game will use the astrological information to change gameplay and use city and state references specifically designed to provide an immersive experience.

During the 13th case, the unknown serial killer will personalize messages and crimes based on the player's registration information.

Player Awards

For each case correctly solved, the player receives case solved congratulations.

For each courtroom case where the accused perpetrator is found "guilty," the player receives a citation.

Case Solved Congratulations		Citation Presenter	
1	Forensic Lab Senior Investigator	1	Forensic Lab Chief
2	Forensic Lab Senior Investigator	2	Forensic Lab Chief
3	Forensic Lab Senior Investigator	3	Forensic Lab Chief
4	Forensic Lab Senior Investigator	4	Forensic Association Chapter President
5	Forensic Lab Supervisor	5	Forensic Association National President
6	Forensic Lab Supervisor	6	Deputy Mayor
7	Forensic Lab Supervisor	7	Mayor
8	Forensic Lab Chief	8	Senator
9	Forensic Lab Chief	9	FBI Regional Deputy
10	Forensic Lab Chief	10	FBI Director
11	Deputy Mayor	11	Attorney General
12	Mayor	12	Vice President
13	Vice President	13	President

Budget

Initial setup costs:	Hardware:	$130,000
	Software:	$70,000
Monthly payroll:		$120,000
Monthly expenses:		$12,000
Forensic expert consulting fees:		$100,000
18-month budget:		$1,584,000
Initial payment:		$596,000

(payroll of three months + start-up costs)

Milestone Schedule

First 6 months:

Art department: Initial characters with animation
>   Background scenes and 3D world

Programming department: Script scenarios and scene investigation proce-
>   dures for each mode (Professional and Associate)
>   Architect load and save procedures, collisions, and playable
>   screen areas
>   Initial code using the 3D engine

Audio composer: Basic sound effects and ambient music
>   Initial voice-over script recorded and edited

Level designer: Personalized scenarios and placement of crime scene
>   objects
>   Court, lab, and forensic office objects placed and room
>   designed

Months 7 to 9:

Four crime scenarios working with lab, site investigation, and citation
>   awarded

Basic video tutorial and training sessions working

Months 10 to 12:

Eight crime scenarios finished and playable from initial investigation and
>   lab research to court decision

Months 13 to 14:

Final "boss" serial killer scenario from initial investigation and lab
>   research to court decision

Based on alpha and beta testing and last-minute publisher input, final
>   update of game

Candide 2517 Design Treatment

[opening sentence]

Candide 2517 is a space adventure game in third person containing major battles in space, land, and sea, one-on-one fighting, and games of chance in a range of settings from beautiful and glamorous casinos to seedy desolate towns and including natural disasters such as earthquakes, meteor storms, deluges, and snowy blizzards.

[marketing and sales pitch]

Candide 2517 is based on *Candide, ou l'Optimisme*, Voltaire's 1759 novel-ette. It describes the adventures of a young man who is pummeled and whipped in every direction by fate while he desperately clings to the belief that we live in the "best of all possible worlds." *Candide* has become

Voltaire's most celebrated work and has been read by millions of people throughout the years.

Candide and the Land of El Dorado have the power of name recognition, which attracts players just like the license of a film, television, or book property would without the expensive fees. Since 1956, playhouses from Broadway to London have performed an adaptation of Voltaire's work by Hugh Wheeler, named *Candide*, with original music by Leonard Bernstein.

Candide 2517 will have stunning venues that the audience for games like Myst enjoyed and space battles as good as the Star Wars games. In several venues ranging from street scenes to ship galleys to elaborate casinos à la Las Vegas, games of chance will be necessary in order to earn valuables.

[demographics]

The target audience is vast, from teenagers to adults, including both genders. The battles can be played as "twitch" games where quickness and timing win or as strategy versions where the player acts as the general of the space armada. Sci-fi fanatics and literature minded game players are among the intended audience.

[platform and hardware requirements]

The first platform will be Windows Vista using a 3D engine that supports vast, planet-sized outdoor terrains as well as indoor venues such as palaces, casinos, castles, small inns, and single-unit dwellings. The game will be developed in solo and multiplayer modes.

An Internet version would be developed next for players using Windows Vista and solo and multiplayer modes on the PlayStation 3, Nintendo Wii, Xbox, and Xbox 360 to play against the game's AI or human opponents in the various battles or adventure independently from planet to planet.

[game features]

The graphics will be highly touted with images ranging from stunning planets to harsh terrains, extremely high-polygon objects, and detailed characters to visually mesmerizing buildings like the casinos and palaces.

With the intensely captivating, ambient original sounds, Hollywood-quality voice talent, and unique sound effects, Candide 2517 is an auditory adventure.

Candide 2517: The Storyline (a Futuristic Version of Voltaire's Classic Novel)

On the planet of Westphalia, in the kingdom of the most noble Baron of Thunder-ten-tronckh, lives the Baron, one of the most powerful lords; the Lady Baroness, who weighs 350 pounds; Cunégonde, the 17-year-old daughter who is fresh-faced, comely, plump, and desirable; the Baron's son, who is young and in every respect worthy of the father from which he sprung; and Candide, the illegitimate nephew of the Baron.

The children are under the tutelage of the scholar Pangloss, who teaches "metaphysico-theologo-cosmolonigology," or that this world is "the best of all possible worlds."

Candide falls in love with the Baron's young daughter, Cunégonde. The Baron catches the two embraced and expels Candide from his terrestrial paradise.

The snow falls in great flakes and through the blizzard, Candide (almost frozen to death) crawls 100 miles in waist-high snow to the next town, which was called Wald-berghoff-trarbkdikdorff.

On his own for the first time, Candide meets two soldiers who offer him food and warmth. They draft him into the army of the Bulgars and fly him to their planet. Candide is given a small scout ship, which he accidentally launches into the atmosphere and crash lands.

Candide is court-martialed as a defector and sentenced to death or to run the gauntlet, a maze of torturous, mechanical devices, and be chased by the whole regiment. After running through the maze and receiving a few bumps and bruises, Candide begs to be killed. Blindfolded and in front of a firing squad, Candide kneels down just as the Bulgarian Majesty, receiving information about Candide's crime, decides to pardon him.

When Candide feels better, the Abbey takes Candide to the planet's gigantic and elaborate casino where Candide falls in love with the actress and entertainer Miss Clairon. Throughout each night he gambles and afterward waits for her to come by and chat with him.

(Here is where the player would play intergalactic games of chance as he watches the extremely sexy and entertaining Miss Clairon (think Jessica Rabbit). The player has to win the big jackpot to earn the favors of Miss Clairon, ranging from a kiss to an invitation to her private suite in the casino.)

Upon winning a night with Miss Clairon, she having cast her eye on two very large diamonds that are on Candide's finger, praises them in so earnest a manner that they were in an instant transferred from his finger to hers.

Along Candide's adventurous journey, he is reunited with the Baron's son, his true love Cunégonde, and his old mentor Pangloss. The final space battle against the Bulgars to reclaim the kingdom of Westphalia is intense and a wonderful ending that would make Voltaire applaud.

[marketing and sales pitch]

Candide 2517 contains the essential elements that players enjoy and desire in a game. Candide 2517 has adventure, lost treasures and planets, intergalactic fighting in "twitch" and strategy modes, and numerous paths to journey to get to the final victory.

Thanks to Voltaire, Candide 2517 has a rich and colorful storyline with exciting and interesting characters.

The pseudo-license of Candide and the Land of El Dorado as seen in the hit Disney film *The Road to El Dorado* will attract the mass market.

[ending sentence]

On September 11, 2001, America was shocked out of its blind optimism by the highjacking attacks. Voltaire and *Candide* is more in the public eye because of these terror attacks. Voltaire's *Candide* asks audiences to question why the world is like it is and makes people think how we can make it a better place for everyone.

Workshop

Assignments

Assignment 1: Discuss various teams' makeup based on the game design and property.

Assignment 2: Divide into two groups where one group is the publisher and the other group is the developer pitching a new game.

Assignment 3: Divide into two groups where one group is the publisher and the other group is the developer desiring to produce a hot, upcoming movie title as a game.

Assignment 4: Discuss the differences between a Game Proposal document and an Executive Summary using the case studies as samples.

Exercises

Exercise 1: List the components that define an Executive Summary and the Game Proposal.

Exercise 2: Explain how writing the One Pager document helps to write the Executive Summary and Game Proposal.

Exercise 3: Write your actual (or make up) relevant team experience with a description.

Unguided Exercises

Unguided Exercise 1: Write an Executive Summary or Game Proposal for a licensed, nongame-show property.

Unguided Exercise 2: Write an Executive Summary or Game Proposal (select the one not used in Unguided Exercise 1) for an unlicensed, original property.

Unguided Exercise 3: Price a single artist's development workstation including the computer, needed graphics applications, and an asset management system.

Unguided Exercise 4: Price a single programmer's development work-station including the computer, the compilers or IDE, and a basic graphics package.

Internet Reading Assignment

"Hiring Game Designers" by Arnold Hendrick
http://www.gamasutra.com/features/19980320/hiring_designers_01.htm

"Inside a Game Design Company" by Ernest Adams
www.gamasutra.com/features/20031201/adams_01.shtml

Thoughts for Discussion

1. Explain why a game designer may need an assistant.
2. What do you think of Hendrick's "acid test" and how would you score on it?
3. What suggestions are made "to get into the game business"?
4. Explain International Hobo's term "Zen game design."

Chapter 8

Chapter 9

Game Design Principles

As a game designer, you must understand and implement game mechanics, game balancing, AI (artificial intelligence), and pathfinding and be able to separate certain tasks into tiers or modules.

Each of these principles could easily be the subject matter for an entire book, so in this chapter we'll just cover the basics.

Game Mechanics

Game mechanics is the underlying framework and rules that determine the gameplay that produces an entertaining, interactive, and (hopefully) fun experience.

To learn game mechanics, you need to look beyond the monitor and study traditional games such as puzzles, board games, card games, and pen-and-paper games. In this section we'll examine a few of these games and their game mechanics.

When you walk into a store and look at computer and video games on the shelves or view these games on the Internet, what distinguishes similar games from each other?

There are dozens of FPS (first-person shooter) and 3PS (third-person shooter) games, as well as chess games and card games that have the same basic gameplay. Shooters (FPS and 3PS) have gameplay that involves immobilizing your opponent(s) by using your weapons full of ammunition and keeping your side alive. The gameplay in a chess game is to win the game by checkmate (capturing the king), win by time if a clock is used, or win by having the opponent resign (or surrender).

In a card game such as poker, the gameplay involves having the best ranked hand or by bluffing have all of your opponents believe that you have the best hand or a chance to have the best hand.

As a game designer, it is up to you to construct a game that is different or innovative so it stands out amongst similar games. No player will buy "just another" chess or poker game. Even with the popularity of shooters, players will not invest their time and money in "just another" FPS. Lest one forgets, the game you design must have a solid design and be entertaining and fun to play. A great innovation will not help a poorly designed or awkward game sell.

For a great example of a poor and awkward game with a huge Hollywood license attached to it, read Lesson One in Appendix D, "War Stories."

To stand out, a chess game must be the best one available for your platform or have a hook, commonly called a USP (unique selling point/ proposition) such as animated pieces, unique SFX (special effects like a mini-battle with smoke, fire, or lightning), an orchestrated ambient music score with interesting sound effects, or unique graphics with several different chess sets and boards.

The game mechanics in a poker game could play at an expert level, have animated, colorful opponents with interesting dialogue, allow for several variations of poker, and have Internet multiplayer capability. (See Chapter 15, "The Game Design Document," for more information about designing a poker game.)

If the game genre is a strategy game, the game mechanics would state whether it's a turn-based or RTS (real-time strategy) game. In a war game, does each player make his offensive and defensive strategy moves during his turn or are the strategic moves done simultaneously in real (actual) time? In a sports game like soccer (football outside the U.S.), are decisions, plays, and players on the field decided on-the-fly (real time) and based on turns, or does the offense select a strategy and on-field players and the defense sets its players and strategy? Based on the preset turn-based settings, the action (plays) can be animated to show the result of the play.

The game designer who knows and understands the game mechanics from popular games can borrow and implement them in his own games. The word "borrow" is used here because since common game mechanics, gameplay, game elements, and interactive devices cannot be copyrighted you are free to copy them as you wish.

Let's closely examine the game rules (mechanics) and gameplay from a few popular games.

In board games such as Risk and interactive games such as Pokemon and Magic: The Gathering, cards are used to select possible game actions or limit the player's choices as a game mechanic. The Magic: The Gathering card game uses as its game mechanic specific cards and their color to define playable attacks/offense, defensive plays, and food (mana) that gives warriors energy.

In the card game hearts, players try to avoid winning rounds that contain penalty cards and thus win the game by having the lowest points. In the card games of bridge and spades, players try to win the most rounds for points by having the highest ranking card of the played suit. Although different games, they all have similar game mechanics.

Othello

In Othello, the object of the game is to have the majority of your color discs on the board at the end of the game. Each player takes 32 discs and chooses one color to use throughout the game. Black places two discs and White places two discs in the middle of the 8x8 board. The game always begins with this setup.

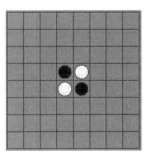

A move consists of "outflanking" your opponent's disc(s), then flipping the outflanked disc(s) to your color. To outflank means to place a disc on the board so that your opponent's row (or rows) of disc(s) is bordered at each end by a disc of your color. (A "row" may be made up of one or more discs.)

The first rule of Othello is that Black always moves first.

If on your turn you cannot outflank and flip at least one opposing disc, your turn is forfeited and your opponent moves again. However, if a move is available to you, you may not forfeit your turn.

A disc may outflank any number of discs in one or more rows in any number of directions at the same time — horizontally, vertically, or diagonally. (A row is defined as one or more discs in a continuous straight line.)

Backgammon

Backgammon is a game for two players, played on a board consisting of 24 narrow triangles called "points." The triangles alternate in color and are grouped into four quadrants of six triangles each. The quadrants are referred to as a player's home board and outer board and the opponent's home board and outer board. The home and outer boards are separated from each other by a ridge down the center of the board called the "bar."

Each player tries to bring his own checkers home and bear them off (remove) before his opponent does, hitting and blocking the enemy checkers along the way.

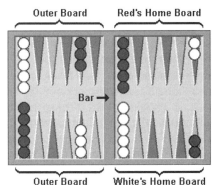

The points are numbered for either player starting in that player's home board. The outermost point is the 24 point, which is also the opponent's 1 point. Each player has 15 checkers of his own color. The initial arrangement of checkers is: two on each player's 24 point, five on each player's 13 point, three on each player's 8 point, and five on each player's 6 point.

Each player has his own pair of dice and a cup used for shaking. A doubling cube, with the numerals 2, 4, 8, 16, 32, and 64 on its faces, is used to keep track of the current stake (bet) of the game.

In backgammon, the object is for a player to move all of his checkers into his own home board and then bear them off. The first player to bear off all of his checkers wins the game.

Same Look, Different Game Mechanics

Games such as chess, checkers, and Othello play on an 8x8 board but are very different games with different game mechanics, gameplay, and goals. Games that use similar gameplay such as card-style rankings like pairs, three of a kind, straights, and full house can have completely different looks, as in poker, Rook, and Yahtzee. Rook is a Hasbro card game that has a deck of 56 cards in four colors, where each color has cards numbered 1 to 14.

Even a standard 52-card deck has play variations or different game mechanics such as poker, bridge, rummy, war, solitaire, blackjack, baccarat, cribbage, pinochle, and pai gow poker.

Dice games include Yahtzee, craps, numerous board games, and paper RPGs (role-playing games) such as Dungeons & Dragons, which is popular with college students.

Yahtzee (Milton Bradley/Hasbro) uses a set of five dice to determine a poker-like combination of rankings such as three of a kind, full house, and even five of a kind (a "Yahtzee"). Players must complete 13 combinations and rankings in two scorecard sections (upper and lower).

The paper-based RPG Dungeons & Dragons uses a special multisided die or pair of dice, such as a 12-sided die called a dodecahedron, that determine battle outcomes, locked door success or failure, and spellcasting.

The game mechanics of Dungeons & Dragons or D&D (TSR/Wizards of the Coast) use dice (or several die) rolls to determine actions and outcomes. The die or dice can be used to determine the character's initial ability scores during character creation, the character skills and experience, defense against an attack (armor strength), hit points gained or lost where no hit points left means "you're dead," saves against special attacks such as fireballs and magical spells, attack damage and its effect, and the benefits gained from training.

The official D&D rules state that "when a character makes an attack, a 20-sided die is rolled to determine success/failure." The 20-sided die is also used for saving throws, which determines the damage caused by magic, poison, and attacks from monsters and characters.

Craps is a dice game that uses the throw of a dice pair (two die) to determine the outcome that players wager on. On the first throw, called the "come out" throw, a "pass" bet wins ("don't pass" bet loses) on 7 or 11, while a "don't pass" wins (a "pass" bet loses) on a 2, 3, or 12 called "craps." Any other number thrown such as a 4, 5, 6, 8, 9, or 10 is called the "point." Players can bet on various numbers but the "pass" bets win if the point is thrown before a 7 is thrown. The "don't pass" bets win if a 7 is thrown before the point is thrown and ends that thrower's turn.

A game can have a game mechanic that increases in difficulty as the player approaches a winning condition. Perhaps more traps, more enemies, better AI, or smarter enemies become evident as the player gets closer to finishing a level or the game. Platform (action) games often use a difficult-to-beat monster called "the boss" to prevent players from finishing a level and ending the game.

Rock, paper, scissors is a game mechanic used in many computer and video games. The two players determine the winner of a confrontation where each player secretly selects either "rock," "paper," or "scissors." Simultaneously the two players reveal their selection as a hand gesture, trying to defeat that of the opponent. The gestures are resolved where "rock crushes (wins over) scissors," "paper covers or captures (wins over) rock," and "scissors cuts (wins over) paper." If both players reveal matching gestures, the tie requires another round until there is a winner.

A typical RTS game may have the "rock, paper, scissors" game mechanic where the infantry are vulnerable to tanks, tanks are vulnerable to helicopters, and helicopters are vulnerable to infantry.

The Goal in a Game

The goal in a racing game using vehicles such as cars, ATVs, Jet Skis, boats, motorcycles, or bikes is to cross the finish line first. The game mechanics involves driving or operating the vehicle within a physics-based environment; fast finger dexterity to control one or more devices such as an accelerator and brake; and maintaining the vehicle by keeping the tires in proper condition with the correct air pressure, a full gas tank, and full and clean oil and steering fluid.

Games such as military, racing, and sports games often contain a "training" mode to help players understand and become comfortable with the interactive game controls and features.

The goal in games such as Othello, Go, Diplomacy, and many multiplayer games is to occupy the largest territory for a specific duration.

Examining Game Mechanics

The game mechanics can change based on the level of play, where an easy or novice level has different rules, AI, and level of difficulty than its expert or top playing level.

In games such as Pac-Man and Space Invaders, the game mechanics use patterns to finish each level and pass its victory condition. Pac-Man involves knowing the correct pattern and timing to avoid the ghosts (enemies) and when to eat the blinking power-ups that turn the ghosts blue so that the Pac-Man can attack and eat the ghost. Space Invaders involves shooting rows and columns of aliens at the precise time and hiding behind the bases as protection before the aliens destroy them. Even Donkey Kong involves knowing the pattern of jumping and avoiding barrels and enemies to complete levels and eventually win the game with the high score. Donkey Kong players are fanatics and hold competitions to see who can get the highest score before the famous "Death Screen." Apparently since the game is on a ROM cartridge, the competition is to get a high score quickly before the memory problems creep into the graphics and crash (destroy/end) your game.

Resource management game mechanics are those in which the player(s) try to increase their game tokens or game points and spend or exchange their resources.

Games such as Scrabble have game mechanics that involve the placing of tiles onto an empty board to get points or accomplish strategic play leading to the game's winning condition.

One of the game mechanics that I find interesting deals with time. In Max Payne (Remedy Entertainment/Rockstar Games), there is a mechanic called "bullet time" where Max can freeze time and shoot the entire room of bad guys. In TimeShift (Saber Interactive), the player can freeze, slow down, and rewind time and walk through fire and shoot bad guys too.

In the film *Bill & Ted's Excellent Adventure*, the boys have a time machine and can use it to go to the past to get objects like keys and money to solve current problems. Each time they must write down in a notebook the scenario (object and its location) so they can leave these objects in the right place to obtain them in their future.

In Blinx: The Time Sweeper, time control in the game allows the player to reverse time on the environment and everything but Blinx, fast-forward time to move everything including Blinx forward, record time to allow Blinx 10 seconds to progress before the scene rewinds and Blinx and a shadow that follows Blinx's recorded actions as Blinx performs new ones, slow time effect to slow everything down except Blinx, and retry to rewind the entire game to a safe point.

In Braid by Jonathan Blow, time not only can be rewound many times but it can be rewound for any duration the player wants to go back. Braid has different sections that use time in a unique way. In one section, the player can rewind time and reverse the player's actions. Another section allows the player to reverse time and the actions but the objects are unaffected by time reversal. One section links time to the player's actions where moving left reverses time, moving right moves time forward, and standing still freezes time. Another section creates a shadow of the player so multiple actions can be performed (this effect was also used in Blinx: The Time Sweeper). In another section, a magic ring can be dropped to cause a time warp around itself so as objects move toward the ring they begin to slow down. The last section has time running in reverse as its normal mode so reversing time here sets the flow of time forward.

Prince of Persia: Sands of Time uses time so that if the player is killed he can return to a point in the game and get a second chance. (This game mechanic has limits based on the amount of "sand" you have, but your game can use this throughout.)

Imagine a game where the player plays through an entire level and then must replay that level backward. This time mechanic would have shot enemies using your bullet(s) to fire back at you and trap doors that open, requiring you to exit and then pull the lever. That would double your game experience without doubling your assets such as terrain (play area and rooms), characters, weapons, and audio and possibly make the gameplay more interesting and harder.

Victory Conditions

The game mechanics (rules) include the game's victory conditions, which differ from game to game and even in the same genre and in similar type of games such as simulations. The victory conditions could require defeating your opponent(s), acquiring the most points/money/terrain, or even being the biggest loser.

Imagine a game based on the Richard Pryor film *Brewster's Millions*, where a rich uncle leaves you $100,000,000 and the goal is to end up after 100 days with absolutely no money or valuables of any kind. The player must spend $100,000 per day for 100 days, and each item purchased has to have a valid purpose. The winner would be the player who lost everything and was penniless at the end of the 100 days.

In the first *Rocky* film (1976), Sylvester Stallone as Rocky Balboa, a small-time, struggling boxer, gets a chance to fight the world champion boxer Apollo Creed. Rocky is overwhelmed by this match and just wants to go the distance with the champ. This game mechanic victory condition would be to "avoid being beaten and go the distance."

In the popular "three match" games such as Call of Atlantis, 4 Elements, the Luxor series, the Zuma series, and the Bejeweled series, the game mechanic for the victory condition is "eliminate objects." When three objects of the same shape and color touch, the group disappears and points may be awarded. As colored shapes are added to the playing field, the player can maneuver them to create a "three match," thus eliminating those tokens (objects).

Since the early days of computer games when adventure games were the rage, solving puzzles of various types, ranging from moving physical objects to word logic, was the main game mechanic. Games have always had a connection to puzzle solving. Even platform (action) games require the player to determine that he must run to the western room to pull a switch, run to the eastern room to open the door, and return to the center room to beat the enemy and get transported to the next level. Now, that's a puzzle!

In the finals, swimmer Michael Phelps raced alone and with his amazing teammates for eight gold medals in the 2008 Olympics. The game mechanics were the same in the preliminaries as they were in the finals, but the victory conditions were significantly different. Phelps often took second in the preliminaries just to get into the finals and save his energy for his other races, but in the finals there was only one goal: to win and get the gold.

Combinational conditions could be the victory condition where over the course of several events such as in a triathlon (swimming, running, and bicycling) or decathlon (10 track and field events), the goal is to be the overall winner but not necessarily the winner of every event. In a strategy war game with several campaigns, the winner may be the player who has the most points even though he has not won every battle. (The quote that comes to mind is "I've won the battle but lost the war.")

Keep these ideas in mind when designing your game and its game mechanics (rules). Remember that you want to make your game rules and thus the gameplay interesting, compelling, and fun. As a game designer, you must work out how you want the winner to be decided.

Game Balancing

Game balancing means implementing fairness so that each side has an equal chance of winning by even play, handicap play, or odds play. Game balancing tries to level the field and uses the game's environment and resources to determine the equilibrium.

In chess and Go, the more experienced player may provide the lesser player a handicap by extra pieces (Go), removing a piece (chess), playing multiple opponents (simultaneous exhibition), or having less time to win the game (time odds). In sports such as bowling or golf, players often have a handicap where novices get extra points or are allowed to subtract strokes to make competing with more experienced players competitive. In bowling, a novice with a 50 handicap adds this amount to his final score, so if he bowls a 120, his opponent needs to bowl above a 170 to beat him.

Deliberate Imbalance

In game design, the plan to balance the game might require an imbalance where one side is favored so that a more experienced and skilled player has a challenge (handicapping one side).

Sports games might allow one side or team being crushed to catch up to present a more challenging and fun game rather than a pure, realistic simulation. A computer could destroy a human player if programmed to play faster or with a master level AI, but fine-tuning the NPC play requires understanding the overall game balance for all levels of players. The NPCs could be programmed to shoot and never miss or shoot 100s of rounds per second (faster than humanly possible), but few would want to play such a game.

Games of chance like those played in casinos have a built-in (intended) imbalance that gives the house an advantage. Even though the ornate casinos are built to make money, they continue to attract players. These players know that there is an imbalance but hope "to beat the odds."

Creative Balancing

In many games, designing a balance isn't as simple and easy to do as declaring "there are two sides, 'A' and 'B', which function the same way and have the same strengths and weaknesses."

When balancing characters, sometimes defeating them requires methods such as gaining a needed object (like Wonder Woman's lasso) or restraining them (like exposing Superman to Kryptonite). In game balancing, Lex Luther needs to be able to compete with Superman. If the game required Lex to defeat Superman, that would be impossible. The game should be balanced so Lex's goal would be to capture Superman in a Kryptonite cage. Superman could easily kill Lex, but that would ruin any sequels. Instead he should place Lex and his henchmen behind bars. Every superhero has powers and an Achilles' heel (a weak spot that enemies can use to their advantage).

Games need to balance weapons so that using a superweapon or power-up doesn't defeat everything in the game. A BFG (big freaking gun) is "cool" and fun to wipe stuff out with, but a weapon of this magnitude shouldn't make the entire game off balance. Perhaps linking the gun to game weapon credits or character energy would place a limit on its usage or effect. In a baseball game, a "super bat" would be used by every player and out-of-the-park home runs would become routine (since every player would knock the ball over the outfield wall). This would not only be unrealistic, but would cause the entire game to be imbalanced. Perhaps the "super bat" only gives players with a .250 average a 30% chance of hitting the home run, while a "slammer bat" gives every player a 50% chance of hitting a double, triple, or home run and a 50% chance of a pop out or strikeout.

Balancing magic in games can be implemented as the spellcaster loses energy or "magic" points when the spell is initiated. One idea could be that once a wizard knows a spell, it cannot be forgotten or lost, so the game must balance the magic such that spells like weapons do not have an infinite casting ability with equal result every time. The best way to implement balance in magic is to link its casting and effect to the caster's energy force or magic tokens. Thus, casting a spell after a successful round may require the caster to rest or to replenish his magic tokens.

The game balancing must deter players from "spawn camping," where the player(s) gains a huge advantage by positioning his character or team at an entry point into the game or by a teleporter called a "spawn point," so that unaware players can be immediately killed for points or other advantages.

Chapter 9

Extra Tidbits on Balancing

Dynamic game balancing (often referred to as DGB) tries to maintain balance so that the novice doesn't get frustrated by strong competition and the expert doesn't get bored by a game that is simple and doesn't provide a challenge.

Tutorials and practice modes allow the player to learn and understand the interface, game mechanics, and gameplay and to properly use items such as various weapons, which adds to the game's balance as players become more skilled and experienced.

AI (Artificial Intelligence)

Artificial intelligence, commonly known by its acronym AI, simulates to humans the illusion of intelligence in the behavior and actions of nonplayer characters (NPCs). For the AI to appear intelligent and challenge the human player, anything from complex algorithms, hacks, and cheats are valid solutions.

Artificial intelligence is a scientific term that gives nonhuman entities algorithmic and mathematical solutions for problem solving, simulating human thought, and decision making.

In films, this is often depicted as a mechanical robot trying to act human. In computer or video games; it is the heart and soul of the nonplayer characters (NPCs) controlling our enemies and allies.

Typically, we think of games such as chess, checkers, and backgammon as intellectual and sophisticated games; therefore machines that can simulate being an adversary (especially a masterful one) have been used by researchers to validate their AI techniques. Since computers can process mathematical instructions and perform iterations (repetitive processes) very fast, researchers in AI use these skills to simulate human thought.

As game designers, we must not only plan our vision but try to conceptualize each idea and how it can be expressed through a mathematical expression or logically arrived at through a database search or a script. You will discover that simple, everyday activities are in fact very complicated and complex processes.

In a chess game, White moves first and can make one of 20 moves (16 pawn moves and four knight moves). Normally, a good chess game will have an opening book of standard playable moves so the AI would not start until the game "is out of the book" (the database of normal moves no longer applies to the current position). The AI will play the current side to move, and based on each possible move calculate the opponent's possible moves. Each side to move is called a "play." The AI will examine a certain number of plays or stop if a threshold is evaluated (a "threshold" can be an evaluation number or based on a time duration or a victory condition such as a win, loss, or draw).

In Chapter 13, "Basics of Programming and Level Scripting," the Tic-Tac-Toe program uses its AI to evaluate the best move for the current player. If the player moving has a choice between a win and a loss, he would choose the win. If the player has a choice between a win and a draw (tie), he would choose the win. If the AI is examining the 20 moves in a chess position and in the first move the AI analysis evaluates that move as a win, then examining any other move would be a waste of time since the player cannot do better than the win.

In a fighting game, the NPC examines if the opponent is within an arm's length and throws its trademark punch (or one from a list of valid punches).

After the thrown punch, the fighter is prepared to react with a counter such as ducking, maneuvering away (perhaps a shuffle), or getting hit in a less vulnerable location. The AI must coordinate the fighter's punches at an acceptable speed (remember the computer can compute and respond faster than humanly possible). The punches or attacks in a martial arts match must deplete the energy and health of the opponent so that the opponent's attacks weaken during a prolonged match. Let's say that a punch to the head depletes the attack energy by 50% for 10 seconds and the defense energy by 30% during that time period. Another attack to the head, depending on how close to the first punch it's delivered, increases the total two-punch effect as to the energy lost and time duration of its effect. If the opponent is farther away from the NPC fighter than an arm's length, then the NPC must approach the opponent if the NPC's energy is equal to or more than 50%, and stay still to regain time and recoup energy if less than 50%.

Perhaps the AI could record the NPC's successful throws (punches) and combinations to use again and again until the opponent has a good counter for these actions. Also, any failed punch or combination would get a low list position so it can still be used but likely less often. These AI methods are valid and used by real fighters, so recording and tailoring an NPC's fighting style to that opponent is a good device and not considered "cheating." This information could be saved for future confrontations and other opponents.

In a baseball game, the pitcher throws the ball at the catcher as the batter from the opposing team tries to hit the ball and safely get on base. Most of us have seen this scenario many times on television or at the ballpark. There are many complex issues being processed in this simple example of a sports game. The batter's box is empty so the team "at bat" sends its next batter (based on the roster and batting order) to the plate. The pitcher may first check the runner on first base based on the following conditions: (1) there is a runner at first base, and (2) the first base runner is leading, or positioned off the base by a few feet or more.

The pitcher, who still has the ball even after it has been thrown to the first baseman, knows that a batter is "in" the batter's box and ready to receive a pitch. The ball is thrown based on a preset speed, type of pitch (curveball, fastball, slider, and so on), target position "in the strike zone," and real-world factors like typical pitches and number of strikes, balls, and wild pitches this pitcher throws. The batter responds by swinging at the ball or not swinging.

A pitch that is not swung at will be judged as a strike or a ball based on the pitcher's real-world factors previously mentioned. A swung at pitch will use the batter's real-world factors like number of strikeouts, singles, doubles, triples, and home runs; type of preset hit such as bunt, grounder, short hit (in-air hit in the outfield just outside the infield), or power hit (deep outfield or a possible "over the wall" home run); and point of contact with the ball (late swing, early swing, or perfectly timed swing).

The batter's real-world factors and player factors such as options selected and timing triggers are combined and a logical result should be determined. For example, a selected option to bunt would not result in an "over the wall" home run nor would a batting pitcher typically hit a home run or even a triple. The algorithm should include for a batting pitcher an extremely small (one in 10,000) chance of hitting a home run and a little better chance (one in 5,000) of hitting a triple even if the real-world factors indicate this is unlikely to occur. As the batter hits the ball into "fair" territory, the players in the field must follow the hit ball and respond if they are currently the closest to the ball. A ball hit to left field may have the shortstop initially moving, but as it passes by or over his head, he stops moving and the already moving left fielder continues moving until he acquires the ball. There are certain logical (predetermined) movements, such as the pitcher backing up the catcher on certain plays or the shortstop backing up the third baseman or second baseman, especially if they are the player moving after the ball.

Let's look at a situation where the center fielder has just acquired the ball after it has hit the ground (so a caught fly out is not possible). There are runners at second base and first base as the batter who just hit the ball is advancing to first base. The center fielder can throw the ball to the third baseman, putting out the runner from second base; throw the ball to the second baseman, putting out the runner from first base; or throw the ball to the first baseman, putting out the batter advancing to first base.

What decisions does the experienced center fielder make in the real world?

If the situation occurred when the team at bat had two outs, that would be vastly different than if the team at bat had no outs. (Remember, three outs retires the side.)

The way I handled this situation in my baseball endeavor started by taking the fact that each base is 90 feet from another. The database had a factor for each player's 100-yard dash speed (300 feet) and a factor for each player's throwing speed and accuracy. Before acquiring the ball, the computer calculated the distance from the point of acquisition of the ball to each base (first base, second base, and third base) and factored in the center fielder's throwing speed and accuracy to each of these bases against the runner's speed and his distance to the next base or his current position (remember the runner could be leading off the base when the ball was hit) to the next base. The action that would result in a guaranteed out would be selected first. If no out situation was possible, then throwing the ball to the most advanced base or third base to stop further advancement would be the default selected.

Let's assume that this scenario would have the center fielder throwing the ball to the second baseman. The second baseman would put out the runner from first base. If this was the third out, then the action would terminate and the at-bat team would be finished, and possibly the sides would exchange places (batting side taking the field and vice versa). If the out at second base was not the third out, then the second baseman would have to evaluate the current situation, just like the center fielder had done (second base runner is running to third base, is on third base, or is running home or batter is running to first base, is on first base, or is running to second base).

These factors would result in another throw by the second baseman to the first baseman, to the third baseman, to the catcher, or possibly held until all action is halted and the runners are safe (stationary, not advancing) on first and third bases. Then, the second baseman would throw the ball to the pitcher. The batter's box would again be empty and the cycle continues.

This seems like a lot of calculating and planning, but as designers we must express our vision to the other team members such as the programmers who must translate our vision into concrete instructions, the artists who must provide models and artwork needed for each of these scenarios and actions, and the sound engineers who provide realistic sound effects to add life to this realistic and intelligent creation.

In our design, we must be consistent and fair. If a pitcher has no batting statistics (this is possible nowadays), then have a planned criteria such as minor league or college statistics followed by an average division, league, or professional statistic for pitchers.

When designing a game like chess or poker, design the best or championship skill level first and then lessen its strength. Lower strength levels can have threshold criteria placed on the player, shorter search path depths, or time limits to determine the best move found. In chess, you may exhaust all paths of analysis for the expert, set a limit to the depth of each path or a threshold value (such as "situation is valued at half a pawn or better" end analysis) for a club player, and select one of several random "non-losing" moves for a novice player.

The method known as "procedural narrative," which is used by companies such as Valve, uses the AI to analyze the player's progress and skill level. This information adjusts the AI and NPC's skill and difficulty level accordingly so a novice player won't get frustrated and an expert player won't get bored.

Chapter 9

Cheating AI

Sometimes the AI for an NPC must cheat to make the game more challenging. This technique is known as "rubber banding." For example, in a racing game where the player could fly past Jeff Gordon, the NPC car that has fallen far behind could gain speed and power with its newly acquired "magical gasoline" to instantly cruise into a competitive position. Obviously, in a real-world, physics-based racing game, these AI routines would only be triggered upon certain conditions to make the game more fun and exciting. After all, are we designing a true simulation or a fun game? You're the visionary, so you decide what's best for your design.

Emergent AI, such as in Creatures, Black & White, and Nintendogs, allow the NPCs to learn from the player's actions and modify the NPC's behavior.

In GoldenEye 007, the AI would react to player's movements and actions, have the NPCs take cover, perform defensive rolls to avoid being shot, and throw grenades at the optimum moment.

In Perfect Dark, the NPC enemies were programmed to recover weapons from "dead" NPCs.

In Halo, the AI had NPCs using vehicles and moving in basic team formations as well as recognizing threats such as active grenades and approaching vehicles.

In Far Cry, the NPCs reacted to the player's strategy style and even surrounded the player if possible.

Document in your game design the level of AI you expect the NPCs to have and the variations of the AI you desire for the player's skill and play level.

Pathfinding

Pathfinding is probably the single most popular and frustrating game AI problem in the industry.

Pathfinding involves moving the NPCs through the terrain and environment in a logical, realistic way. Finding the shortest distance to traverse the Grand Canyon or cross the Amazon River probably isn't the best path to your destination. Pathfinding has grown in its importance in interactive gaming and is a complex AI project that should not be scheduled at the end of development. Pathfinding's goal is to move in straight lines where possible, but also avoid obstacles and potentially hazardous terrain such as cliffs, mountains, and rivers.

Basic Pathfinding Algorithms

The current basic pathfinding algorithms (methods) are A*, Dijkstra, and the Manhattan method.

A* (pronounced A-star) is an algorithm that begins with a "start node" (a position) and adds all possible nodes (accessible locations) to an open list (a list such as MapQuest's turn-by-turn driving directions). The "open list" nodes are assigned a heuristic (an equation that provides a good solution, ignoring whether the problem can be proven to be correctly solved), which sorts the list in an optimal path or route to the "destination node" (final location).

Let's examine how the A* or flood fill method is similar to a graphics application's paint tool, which will completely color a given area.

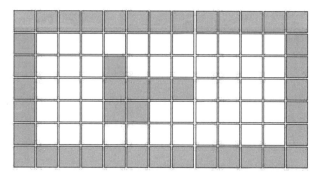

If we were to flood fill the white area with black, it would continue filling until it hit a non-white spot.

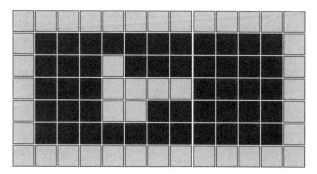

If we were to start at location "A," the fill would traverse in all directions until the new space was non-white.

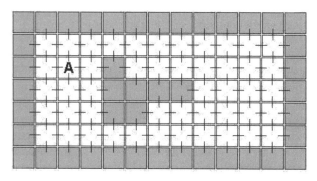

Chapter 9

Each space or "node" would check its neighbors in the four directions, and if the neighbor was white it would be changed to black. This recursive (repeating) process would repeat until all four directions starting with node A returned a "false," or no non-white connecting nodes left.

Dijkstra's algorithm is based on the A* algorithm without the heuristic and is slower since it expands equally in all directions.

The Manhattan method is pathfinding on horizontal and vertical units (no diagonals) as though the path is traversing city blocks. This method is easy and quick to implement but often overestimates the path's distance.

The pathfinding method used in a demo I worked on with Michael Hausman for War Between the States (Walker Boys Studio) should be called the Pedersen-Hausman method or the "blind person's algorithm." Michael and I sat in a room after researching the basic pathfinding algorithms and attempted to answer the question, "How does a blind person find his or her way from a room in a house to the front door of that house?" Secondly, "How does that blind person find the fastest and best path?"

A blind person hears someone knocking on the front door (the final destination point) and marks his current position, such as a chair in the room. The blind person walks straight ahead in the direction of the knocking sound, let's assume north, and counts the steps as he travels. The blind person hits a wall and feels the wall, first moving west and counting his steps. The blind person is looking for the room's door. After a certain number of steps a door is found. Let's say the blind person returns to the starting point, the chair, and walks north again counting his steps, and touches the wall again. Instead of now walking west since that path was already done, an easterly traverse of the wall is done until the door is found. Again the steps from the wall point with an east traversal to the door are counted. The quick analysis will determine the shortest distance from the starting point, the chair, to the door. If the blind person had a long string, he could attach it to the starting point and the door and retrace that path, looking for obstacles. For the first pass, let's assume that there were no obstacles. Now let's say the blind person is at the room's door listening to the knocking on the front door, and holding the long string the blind person walks toward the noise. Assume for this example that a simple turn east from the room's door leads to the front door. The string from the starting point to the front door shows the quickest and shortest path without the A* or Dijkstra's algorithmic processing.

Now that we understand the basic principle of the "Pedersen-Hausman" method, we can add the obvious "what-ifs." As the blind person encounters a river in an outdoor adventure, he has several choices such as building a bridge or traversing the river.

The river is walked along in two directions counting each step and looking for a break in the river, an existing bridge, or a point that is shallow enough to safely cross the river. Once this point is found, the string from the last point is connected to this point. The same principles apply to steep cliffs, where the elevation drop is more than twice the size of the person, and mountain terrain where the climbing height is so great that the path direction is impractical (perhaps this is the only path so it stays low on the path option list). Obstacles such as trees are tall but can easily be walked around. Obstacles such as boulders are wide and may be tall but again are easily walked around, although the best path selection would have to determine which side of the boulder to walk around. Houses are similar to large boulders in that they can be walked around. The distance calculated by the AI will decide which side of the house (object) is best to add to the path. Since large objects block the line of sight, discovering what's on the other side of the house is crucial. Players at the top of a mountain have a long line of sight as do those in a valley.

The "Pedersen-Hausman" Method (Blind Person's Algorithm) Further Explained

The typical path from a character's current position to the destination (waypoint) usually passes directly through one or more obstacles.

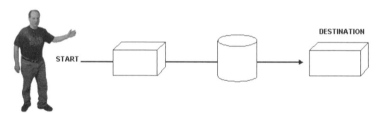

The first solution in avoiding these obstacles is to "ride the rail," or walk around the object's surface until you're free to continue toward the destination.

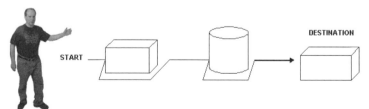

Although the "riding the rail" algorithm solves the problem of avoiding obstacles, it looks silly and unrealistic; sort of a blind person's path solution.

The next solution is to make the path less blocky by connecting the points of the hypotenuses of the triangles.

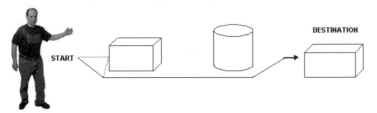

The last issue to make the path to our waypoint truly realistic is to curve the path.

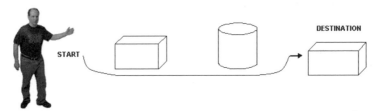

The way to simulate a realistic character movement in 3D is to plot a straightforward path from the character's current position to its destination and record all of the obstacles from a world table that lie on this straight line. For each obstacle, calculate the original collision point and the two tangent points on either side of the obstacle. The point closest in distance is the one selected to be connected as the hypotenuse of the triangle.

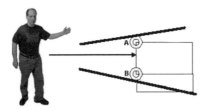

Selecting a side of an object to add to the path.

Other Pathfinding Solutions

The objects that are on the map as collision areas should include static objects like buildings, water, fences, and so on, as well as dynamic, move-able objects like vehicles, people, and floating bridges. The game design may include the ability to destroy objects like buildings and bridges, thereby modifying the original list of static objects. Another game design might require that characters avoid areas due to hazardous conditions (such as a toxic gas spill) that may be in effect under certain conditions or for a certain time period, or specific areas belonging to tribes and clans.

These avoidance issues greatly change the terrain path created. One solution would be to dynamically (on-the-fly) set these areas when needed as an obstacle block or zone and let the pathfinding function handle this as though it were a large building to walk around.

The solutions discussed thus far don't take into account various terrain elevations. In nature, rivers run downhill and our characters would probably prefer a downhill path to town rather than a Mount Everest climbing shortcut. The distance over Everest may be the shortest, but its elevation and other factors make that path less desirable. If each node had an elevation factor, then the path created would be the shortest path within reason. Otherwise, the character's morale and fatigue factors would be greatly increased, causing negative results later. The elevation factor could also be used in the character's line of sight functionality. If a character is standing in a ditch, then that character probably wouldn't see the massive horde of enemy troops heading toward him in the distance. On the other hand, a fort on top of a mountain would have its residents' line of sight able to see quite a distance and its cannons able to fire a long way.

If a character is standing on one side of a building, then the enemy approaching from the other side would not be noticed since the character's line of sight is blocked by the building.

These factors add to the realism of the game and that's what players demand, so that's what your game design should include.

Other pathfinding issues could include formations (groups of moving objects), the turn radius, and the ramping up or down speed to initialize a movement and to terminate a movement.

In some fighting games, a formation is a group of characters all moving independently but as a group. Soldiers in two columns march behind their leader. As the leader turns, so does the entire troop. They all must maintain their relative distance from the row in front of them, march at the same speed (pace), and turn their bodies relative to their path line. The leader may be marching north as the last soldier in the line is still marching east 50 feet behind the leader. Formations also must not collide and bounce off each other like billiard balls. These are complex structures that must be in your game design and algorithmically understood by the team developing your vision.

Humans are bipeds, so if they are moving the wrong direction they can turn on a dime and reverse their movement toward the goal. Vehicles and horses need more space to create a turn radius. For example, for you to circle or turn your car around when reversing from the road south to the road north you use a "U-turn" or "K-turn" maneuver. People can perform this maneuver with an "about face" motion.

People, horses, and vehicles don't accelerate their pace instantly and don't stop on a dime at will. Moving objects need to increase their speed (velocity) and must decrease it before coming to a complete stop. All of these factors must be incorporated into the game design for a realistic look and feel in your game.

Chapter 9

Because these complex physics issues are difficult to implement, they should be addressed in the design documents and discussed as the game is being developed. Often, ideas, concepts, and features that are in the design document hit the cutting room floor (do not make it to the final product). The design document items should be frequently discussed and addressed to determine their status as to whether they are "in," "out," or "on hold" for the final product. Most items can be implemented, given enough development time and money. In reality though, developers don't have the luxury of unlimited time and finances.

Designing the Game System Architecture in Tiers or Modules

While working at a game company with recent graduates from a prestigious gaming college I analyzed their code and noticed that it was extremely "academic." No experienced programmer in any industry would have architected a system like theirs. I asked each programmer, each of whom was talented and intelligent, about the system design that they had used for their demos. The game development techniques they described were poorly planned not only from an IT standpoint but also from a game developer's standpoint.

You may already be familiar with the "n-tier" (or modular) programming architecture. In "n-tier" architecture (where n stands for a multiple, as in three-tier), the tiers contain separate and self-contained code such as a graphics tier, an audio/music tier, a game mechanics (logic and rules) tier, a language tier, and possibly a database tier.

Let's assume that you want your game on multiple platforms, available in multiple written languages, and possibly using multiple databases. The development team has designed the game in tiers for a platform such as Windows. A publisher sees your demo or finished game and wants to finance your game (a) on another platform, (b) internationally on the current platform, or (c) using its own database.

If the game was not architected in tiers, then these needed modifications might be a huge programming endeavor. In the tiered architecture, we know that the game mechanics (logic and rules) tier is universal and will work correctly on any platform. The graphics and audio/music tiers need to have similar functionality for the publisher's desired platform. The good news here is that once this code is written, any future game can reuse this code for that platform. The database tier can be rewritten so any game mechanic code that calls a database function will now be redirected to the publisher's database (as a sub-tier in the database tier). The language tier handles all displayed text. The code throughout the system may refer to a variable called "Player Name," and based on the default language being English, the language tier will return the English.Name of "name." If the player decides to change the language option to Spanish, the language tier for Spanish.Name would return "nombre," and if the language option was French, French.Name would return "appelez-vous."

Now you can see the power of the tiered architecture, where complex modifications are made simple and do not affect other working tiers. If you can effectively communicate this method of programming to the game's technical team, it will benefit your game and let the publisher know you can quickly port the code to future games because the code developed for your game is solid and easily modifiable.

Workshop

Exercises

Exercise 1: Discuss the difference between game mechanics and gameplay.

Exercise 2: Discuss the benefits and potential problems of pathfinding.

Exercise 3: Design a balanced system of play for a main character, NPCs, and the adversary.

Unguided Exercises

Unguided Exercise 1: Describe the game mechanics, gameplay, AI, and pathfinding methods involved in designing a sports game.

Unguided Exercise 2: Describe the game mechanics, gameplay, AI, and pathfinding methods involved in designing a role-playing game.

Unguided Exercise 3: Describe the game mechanics, gameplay, AI, and pathfinding methods involved in designing a strategy game.

Internet Reading Assignment

"Collaborating in Game Design" by Noah Falstein and David Fox
    www.gamasutra.com/features/19970601/collab_in_game_design.htm

"Defining Boundaries: Creating Credible Obstacles in Games" by Gareth Griffiths
    http://www.gamasutra.com/view/feature/3709/defining_boundaries_creating_.php

"Defining Boundaries: Creating Credible Obstacles in Games, Part 2" by Gareth Griffiths
    http://www.gamasutra.com/view/feature/3771/defining_boundaries_creating_.php

Thoughts for Discussion

1. Discuss the game mechanics for a sports game such as wrestling, martial arts, or American football.
2. Discuss the game mechanics for a role-playing game.

Chapter 9

3. Discuss the game mechanics and gameplay for a comic book superhero game.

4. Discuss pathfinding methods for adventurers such as Lewis and Clark, Harry Potter at Hogwarts, or astronauts exploring the lunar surface.

5. Discuss strategies of using AI and pathfinding techniques.

Chapter 10

Knowing the Entire Team

The game designer must know the other team members and their skills.

Some time ago I designed a poker game for Phantom EFX entitled Reel Deal Poker Challenge (see Chapter 15, "The Game Design Document"). Phantom EFX is a company that creates television advertisements for clients such as casinos and local businesses in Iowa. The company had high-end graphic computers and six artists plus a professional sound studio, and I was the designer and the only gameplay programmer for the game. The design of the poker game was tailored to take advantage of the team's capabilities with photorealistic characters in the four-player mode and exquisite 3D casino backgrounds with wonderful ambient music and character voice-over performances.

If the design of this game had required massive programming efforts and little art and sound assets, then for this team, the design would be completely wrong since it would be ignoring the development team dynamics. On a game where there are many programmers and one artist, the game design strategy would be to make the game with limited art assets and have it be code intensive.

Modern gaming systems are capable of eye-popping graphics, ear-pleasing music, and high-speed polygon creating graphic processors. The players are demanding more realism, animation, dialogue, and gameplay storyline paths. These demands mean complex gaming systems, which require large development teams to transform a designer's vision into a final, playable game.

The multi-billion dollar gaming industry needs talented specialists and competes for programmers with banks and brokerage firms; artists with advertising and media companies; and audio specialists with the film, television, and recording industries.

The game development team members include game designers, producers, programmers, artists, audio engineers, composers, and QA (quality assurance) testers, plus external team members such as writers (can also be staff members), actors, and translators. Each of these disciplines has levels of experience, skills, and specialties. All positions require computer and communication skills as well as being an avid gamer and a team player.

When reading the following information about job titles, keep in mind that in the real world of business, frequently many jobs take on the role of multiple titles and one can easily be substituted for another. For example, a "senior producer" may perform the same duties as an "executive producer." Also know that many gaming companies frequently use job title monikers simply as a show of seniority rather than an increase in job responsibilities. The information and descriptions of the positions are based on a composite of recent job postings and research.

Game Designer

Senior Game Designer

The Senior Game Designer reports to the Producer. The Senior Game Designer leads the vision with game features and mechanics as well as communicating and supporting gameplay design details to the entire development team. The Senior Game Designer storyboards the experience (mechanics, menus, and UI (user interface)) and key game scenarios; manages the prototype development; and envisions, writes, and maintains the Game Design Document (GDD) throughout the project life cycle.

The Senior Game Designer works closely with Lead and Junior Designers, programmers, artists, producers, and clients (licensors) and mentors the Lead and Junior Designers, providing instruction, guidance, and feedback to advance their careers.

The Senior Game Designer protects the game's core features and keeps the excitement high during the production, and writes the Technical Design Document (TDD) with the Technical Director and programmers. The Senior Game Designer keeps the entire design team current with industry trends and game design techniques; oversees the testing to ensure game balancing; designs a "fun" and easy-to-use gameplay experience, features, and mechanics; and modifies the game design based on feedback from QA, consumer test groups, and other team members. The Senior Game Designer thoroughly understands the game design elements of story, dialogue, player interface, character interaction, mission, environment design, AI, combat mechanics, game strategy, gameplay flow, and levels of difficulty.

Lead Game Designer

The Lead Game Designer reports to the Senior Game Designer. If there's no Senior Designer, the Lead Game Designer performs the duties of the Senior Designer.

The Lead Game Designer provides leadership, creative focus, and the drive to ensure that the game design vision is successfully executed by the team; maintains the best industry standards and tools for the programming, art, and audio teams; and directs and mentors the Junior Game Designers, Game Level Designers, and Game Content Designers.

The Lead Game Designer understands level scripting, basic programming (possibly Lua, Python, C/C++), and basic art application software (Maya, 3ds Max, LightWave, ZBrush, and Photoshop).

Technical Game Designer

The Technical Game Designer works closely with the Senior Game Designer to help develop, document, and communicate game and function designs to the entire development team.

The Technical Game Designer functions as a designer the majority of the time and implements the game using a scripting language the rest of the time. The Technical Game Designer gathers the product and business requirements; creates functional prototypes; implements game logic; and documents game and functional designs to best communicate the player's experience, game flow, player interactions, and platform-specific controls and integration. The Technical Game Designer creates and maintains current game flow diagrams and logical design documents; keeps current on game industry trends; and plays current games, understanding their UI, play patterns, and "fun" elements. The Technical Game Designer communicates and works on a daily basis with the programmers, artists, and QA testers.

The Technical Game Designer is knowledgeable with applications such as scripting (MaxScript, MEL (Maya Embedded Language), ActionScript, Python, Lua); graphics software (Maya, 3ds Max, Virtools); languages like HTML and XML; and game level editors; and is skilled using Microsoft Office tools such as MS Project, Excel, Word, PowerPoint, and Visio as well as production, project tracking, and version control software such as Perforce.

Game System Designer

The Game System Designer has a strong design ability and owns the game systems and drives the design with the ability to create, implement, and tune a compelling game system. The Game System Designer implements and balances the NPC's abilities, traits, clans, and trade skills; designs compelling mini-games and missions; and balances the economic model for RPGs and RTS games and the combat system for action-shooters (FPS and 3PS). The Game System Designer understands level scripting and basic programming (possibly Lua, Python, C/C++), and gives formal presentations supporting the design decisions and strategy. The Game System Designer works with the Senior or Lead Designer to communicate the design, and understands and provides feedback on the creative vision for all game features and systems.

Chapter 10

Game Designer

The Game Designer reports to the Senior Game Designer. The Game Designer creates a detailed, well-written, understandable, and interesting GDD (Game Design Document); creates the game interaction, balancing, and events; understands storytelling and the structure of stories; and has a keen eye for aesthetics and an immersive, engaging gameplay experience. The Game Designer is an innovative and creative thinker, enthusiastic, and skilled in creating and tuning the gameplay. The Game Designer reviews, plays, and tests the game, comparing it to the written documents, and documents a competitive analysis of similar games. The Game Designer works on PC, console, and handheld platforms and is experienced using the Microsoft Office suite, Visio, Flash, Photoshop, and 3D graphics applications such as LightWave, Maya, or 3ds Max.

Game Content Designer

The Game Content Designer reports to the Game Designer. The Game Content Designer designs world objects, gaming zones, engaging missions, and object (item) placement using a scripting language (possibly an object-oriented script framework or XML). The Game Content Designer collaborates with the Senior or Lead Designer to fine-tune the game mechanics, implementation, and balancing. The Game Content Designer uses various tools to conceptualize and implement game concepts; is able to write technical documents and convey verbal and written ideas and concepts in a clear, detailed, and organized manner; and multitasks while understanding the big picture as well as the minute details. The Game Content Designer uses tools such as MS Office suite, Visio, and 2D graphics applications such as Photoshop.

Game Level Designer

The Game Level Designer scripts and creates level layouts, places objects (items) in levels, and designs puzzles and creates the terrain and game world in a natural but engaging way. The Game Level Designer is knowledgeable in many aspects of gaming such as art, coding, landscape, architecture, city planning, spatial awareness, and particle effects such as fire, lightning, and water flow. The Game Level Designer uses scripting languages such as MaxScript, MEL (Maya Embedded Language), ActionScript, Python, and Lua.

Producer

A producer would be the project's manager in the real world of business. The producer is in charge of ensuring that the project gets done on time and on budget. The entire development team reports in some manner to the Producer (directly or indirectly).

Executive Producer (Project Manager)

The Executive Producer manages Senior Producers and organizes the development team for the game projects. If an external developer is hired, the Executive Producer visits the developer's site and evaluates their tools (programming, art, and audio), the hardware, and team skills and experience.

The Executive Producer manages and oversees Senior Producers and Junior Producers and the QA Lead Tester on each project; maintains the milestone schedule (deliverables) and budget for each project; and is the liaison between the developers and sales, marketing, and PR (public relations). The Executive Producer keeps updated on current and upcoming games, the latest devices (joystick, controller, air guitar), game conferences, the latest Internet gaming news, and software tools.

On a daily basis, the Executive Producer reads every project's "bug" report, meets with each producer to discuss each assigned project and understands their status, and spends time watching the QA testers playing the games. The Executive Producer works with clients and licensors on current and future games and meets with them and the designers frequently. The Executive Producer interviews with the press for magazine and Internet previews, reviews, and planned rumors and interviews employee candidates and developers who want to work with the company.

Senior Producer

The Senior Producer manages production, defines the milestone schedule for each project with the collaboration of the team leads and the publisher, and is the key liaison for the game to the publisher, licensor, QA, platform vendors, and external consultants. Other duties include mentoring, training, and supervising producers and understanding current game production methodologies, pipelines, and technical requirements. The Senior Producer balances production considerations of quality and features with schedule deadlines, available resources, and budget constraints. The Senior Producer is an organized, excellent manager who hires employees and external developers; evaluates team members, hardware, and software tools; negotiates with the team, publisher, and licensors; and mediates and resolves conflicts. The Senior Producer manages other producers as well as several game titles on multiple platforms (SKUs). The Senior Producer scouts for new games that meet business and marketing goals by various methods, including game submissions, developer e-mail lists, and developer connections made at trade shows.

Game Producer

The Game Producer reports to the Executive Producer and the Senior Producer. The Game Producer manages the development team on one to two titles on one or more platforms (SKUs) and is the liaison to marketing, scheduling, quality assurance, sales, third-party relations, and promotions (PR). Other duties include informing upper management of the budget and performance status of current projects, localizing the game in the language and culture of the market, and scheduling and preparing for beta testing periods and sufficient quality assurance testing. The Game Producer improves documentation to make the production process more efficient, manages the post-launch process of optimizing game features for technical performance and sales conversion, including an analysis of the game lineup to find areas for improvement, and understands market opportunities to offer insights into improving the company's industry position.

Third-Party Producer

The Third-Party Producer works for a platform or device manufacturer and interfaces with the publisher's development teams that are developing games for their platform or device. The Third-Party Producer educates and supports the development team, ensures efficient development with a quick ramp up time, and promotes innovation. The duties include end-to-end support (game concept to final version). The Third-Party Producer must be enthusiastic, an avid game player, and knowledgeable in programming, 3D graphics, and game design.

External Producer

The External Producer works for a publisher and oversees one or more external development teams. The External Producer communicates daily with each development team leader; updates the publisher's upper management on the current status of each game and platform according to the schedule and milestones; works with QA testers, marketing, sales, and PR on issues regarding that game; and interviews with the press on previews and reviews as well as in-game code cheats (popular in North American gaming magazines).

Associate Producer (Assistant/Junior Producer)

The Associate Producer (Assistant Producer or Junior Producer) assists the Producer in tracking and coordinating the development process using software tools such as Windows, MS Word, MS Project, Excel, PowerPoint, Explorer, and Visio. The Associate Producer maintains the schedule and delivery of project milestones, maintains the asset pipeline(s), and gathers, prepares, and handles assets and other tasks assigned by the Producer (this position is also known as the Producer's "gofer").

Programmer

Technical Director (Director of Development/Engineering or Software Director)

The Technical Director (sometimes titled as Director of Development, Software Director, or Director of Engineering) is the head of the technical team (programmers, engineers, and network staff). The Technical Director manages the engine/tools team, the network server team, and the game development team (graphics, gameplay, audio, AI/physics programmers). The Technical Director hires the technical staff (reviews resumes, interviews, and negotiates external consulting technical staff); architects the technical pipeline; oversees the code reviews and sets the coding standards; helps in authoring the Technical Design Document (TDD); evaluates middleware and third-party software; and keeps current with technology, new platforms, and competing engines and tools.

The Technical Director works with the Game Designer on the IT milestone schedule issues, the Art Director on the art and animation tools, the Audio Director on audio and SFX tools, and the QA Manager to ship "bug and problem free" games and patches. The Technical Director manages the internal and external technical staff and understands project management methodologies, multitasking, budgeting, resource management, scheduling, and P&L (profit and loss). The Technical Director solves technical issues and identifies, prioritizes, resolves, documents, and communicates multiple solutions and trade-offs of technical, operational, and business issues.

Senior Tools/Engine Programmer

The Senior Tools/Engine Programmer reports to the Technical Director and develops and maintains a cross-platform, next-generation game engine. The Senior Tools Programmer works closely with the Producer, Game Designer, artists, QA testers, and other engineers/programmers to implement and fine-tune game features. The Senior Tools Programmer understands IDEs (integrated development environments) such as Windows and Linux and APIs (application programming interfaces) such as Direct3D and DirectX (DirectSound, DirectPlay, DirectInput, and so on), physics tools such as PhysX and Havok, and Windows and platform environments. The Sr. Tools Programmer understands coding in C++, C#, Java, Assembly Language, and low-level systems; scripting languages such as Perl, Python, Lua, and MEL (Maya Embedded Language); and tools such as Perforce, PIX, and VTune. The Senior Tools Programmer writes robust, maintainable code; designs and implements in-game engine editors; and maintains the data-driven tools pipeline, enabling efficient and independent authoring of game content by nontechnical team members. The Senior Tools Programmer understands the file formats for importing and exporting of 2D and 3D art packages and audio/video files. The Senior

Chapter 10

Tools Programmer develops and maintains plug-ins and stand-alone applications used in the creation and preprocessing of geometry, textures, animation data, and scripts. The Senior Tools Programmer understands 3D programming, 3D mathematics, and physics.

Senior System Programmer

The Senior System Programmer reports to the Technical Director and designs, builds, tests, and documents major game systems. The Senior System Programmer communicates with the artists and designers, solving problems and implementing system tools such as a level script interpreter, combat and movement mechanics, camera positioning and movement, and low-level platform-specific coding. The Senior System Programmer understands client/server methodologies and programming; IDEs (integrated development environments) such as Windows and Linux and APIs (application programming interfaces) such as Direct3D and DirectX (DirectSound, DirectPlay, DirectInput, and so on); the Windows and platform environments; and coding in C++, C#, STL (Standard Template Library), and Java.

AI (Artificial Intelligence) Programmer

The AI Programmer instructs the entities (objects and characters) in a game to appear to behave in an intelligent manner by implementing complex AI algorithms using simple rules and heuristics and other innovative methods. Working with the Game Designer(s) to understand their vision, the AI Programmer selects an approach that exhibits the necessary behavior without consuming excessive resources such as CPU and memory budgets. The AI Programmer understands decision trees, pathfinding, finite state machines, neural networks, genetic algorithms, and fuzzy state logic to instruct actions and responses such as entity movements, computer player strategy, and enemy tactic systems. The AI Programmer writes code that is reusable, optimized, and easily maintainable; helps in authoring the TDD; and keeps current in the latest AI research and advanced technical theories.

Physics Programmer

The Physics Programmer reports to the Technical Director and implements real-world physics algorithms in the tools and engine application. The Physics Programmer works with physics middleware or codes algorithms for forces such as gravity, wind, fluid dynamics, inverse kinetics, collisions, and conservation of energy (kinetic and potential energy).

Server/Network Engineer (Programmer)

The Server/Network Engineer reports to the Technical Director and implements networking systems and related game features such as matchmaking, UI, and community features. The Server/Network Engineer selects an appropriate networking strategy for a project and solves problems related to the impact of all platforms on the networking systems. The Server/Network Engineer deals with the complexity of issues related to latency, bandwidth, synchronization, determinism, replication, and prediction. The Server/Network Engineer maintains the existing network code based on I/O completion ports with TCP/IP (Transmission Control Protocol/Internet Protocol) that already supports multiple gateways, servers, and instances. The Server/Network Engineer maintains the multiplayer game features such as account authorization, cross-server chatting, and grouping and server load balancing. The Server/Network Engineer understands network protocols, network topologies, and various networking strategies for games including Xbox Live, PSN (PlayStation Network), and DWC. The Server/Network Engineer works with TCP/IP, sockets, SQL (Structured Query Language for database queries), OpenSSL, Linux servers, shell scripting, JavaScript, Web Services, HTML, XML, Apache, OpenGL, DirectX, .NET Framework, MSMQ (Microsoft Message Queuing), WCF (Windows Communication Framework), WF (Windows Foundations), and programming languages such as C++, C#, and Java.

Audio Software Programmer

The Audio Software Programmer (or Engineer) works closely with the metal (audio processor), creating great sound and audio libraries and tools that output audio and import and export audio formats on all platforms. The Audio Software Programmer understands audio processing, DSP (digital signal processing), voice, speech, audio codecs, 3D (surround) audio, audio scripting, MIDI, MP3, and interactive XMF as well as programming languages such as C++, C#, XML, Python, Java, and Assembly Language. The Audio Software Programmer creates audio tools, plans architecture, and keeps current on audio formats and methodology. The Audio Software Programmer works with OpenGL, DirectSound, and other multimedia tools and formats (WMF, AVI, MPEG). The Audio Software Programmer researches, analyzes, and writes technical designs and project plans and enhances the production environment pipeline.

Lead Programmer

The Lead Programmer manages the implementation of the project's technical vision and mentors the other engineers and programmers. The Lead Programmer is in charge of the high-level technical design and collaborates with the designers, artists, and engineers/programmers to best integrate game design, art, and technology. The Lead Programmer works with the Technical Producer in the performance appraisal process for the technical team and evaluates the technical risks associated with the game's proposal, development plans, and milestone schedule. The Lead Programmer mentors the technical team and helps establish technical requirements, profiling, performance analysis, and performance tuning. The Lead Programmer researches and develops the latest technology

Chapter 10

methodologies and middleware solutions and makes technical recommendations to the production team. The Lead Programmer understands 3D mathematics, algebra, and game programming aspects such as animation systems, graphics, AI, audio, gameplay, and physics.

Senior Software Engineer

The Senior Software Engineer understands the latest graphics research (such as pixel and vertex shaders) and has strong AI, physics, and mathematics skills using complex algorithms and computational techniques. The Senior Software Engineer reports to the Lead Programmer and mentors other game programming team members. The Senior Software Engineer programs in languages such as C++, C#, XML, Python, Java, and Assembly Language. The Senior Software Engineer implements game code conforming to performance guidelines, coding standards, designs, and code integration.

3D Software Programmer

The 3D Software Programmer reports to the Technical Director on designing and implementing the 3D graphics and math code and APIs in the game engine, tools, and game client. The 3D Software Programmer codes in C++, C#, Java, and Assembly Language; debugs code; understands memory management, runtime optimization, multithreading, game art and artifact usage, low and high polygon model formats, software configuration management systems such as Perforce, SVN, SourceSafe, and CVS; and uses scripting languages (MaxScript, MEL (Maya Embedded Language), ActionScript, Python, and Lua) and programming shaders.

Senior Graphics Programmer

The Senior Graphics Programmer is responsible for the game's graphics quality, implementing and maintaining rendering solutions for all platforms. The Senior Graphics Programmer works closely with designers, artists, and other engineers/programmers to implement and fine-tune the game's graphic features and provides support. The Senior Graphics Programmer understands 3D mathematics; physics; the graphic APIs such as Direct3D and OpenGL; programming shaders such as HLSL (High Level Shader Language), GLSL (OpenGL Shader Language), and Cg (C for Graphics, Nvidia's HLSL); code optimization and profiling tools such as VTune; and programming languages such as C++, C#, Java, and Assembly Language.

Game Programmer

The Game Programmer implements and maintains the game content for all platforms and helps write and update technical documents. The Game Programmer works closely with the technical, design, and QA teams to meet milestone and completion deadlines and implement the gameplay vision and assets (audio and art). The Game Programmer designs and implements game-specific systems that interpret the Game Level Designers' and artists' scripts. The Game Programmer reports to the Lead Programmer or Senior Programmer. The Game Programmer communicates with the engine/tools programmers and designers to understand the capabilities of the engine and tools pertaining to the game's design. The Game Programmer understands 2D and 3D graphics; mathematics; APIs (application programming interfaces) such as DirectX and OpenGL; computer languages such as C++, C#, and Java; and scripting languages and user interfaces.

Junior Programmer (Entry-Level Programmer)

The Junior Programmer is an entry-level position for programmers new to the game industry and recent "computer science" college graduates with game course experience. The Junior Programmer has game engine or scripting experience; programs in C++, C#, or Java; is an avid gamer; and has worked on a game project, game demo, or game mod.

Artist

Art Director

The Art Director is a senior manager who works with other senior team members and guides the development art team as well as brainstorms game ideas, conceptualizes the art style and vision, and suggests art solutions with the team. The Art Director manages art schedules with the Producer and documents the art reference guide. The Art Director hires, trains, and mentors the entire art team as well as critiques and gives feedback to subordinates. The Art Director creates the artistic style and vision for the game with the Lead Designer and supervises the outsourced art production for quality and based on milestone schedule. The Art Director is responsible for team art delegating and quality for art style, concept creation, models, textures, lighting and animations of all game art assets, and maintains all art assets with revision IDs. The Art Director communicates clearly and effectively the art goals, milestones, and design to the art team and has the ability to plan, document, and maintain the art schedule, budget, and staffing from preproduction to post-launch for the entire art team. The Art Director also has the ability to balance a game's creative and visual requirements with schedule, budget, and staffing limitations and designs, implements, and maintains the art pipeline for all games, managing both internal and external development. The Art Director identifies art issues and problems with design, programming, and audio teams. The Art Director works with art tools such as 3ds Max, Maya, Softimage, LightWave, DeBabelizer, and Photoshop and understands the art capabilities of all platforms, art file formats, and current and upcoming game art trends.

Art Technical Director

The Art Technical Director works with the lead artists creating rigs for characters, sets, and props. The Art Technical Director implements the art pipeline with a hierarchy, finds solutions to art issues, and keeps current on art tools and techniques. The Art Technical Director performs character setups, weighting, and skinning, and works with scripting languages such as MaxScript, MEL (Maya Embedded Language), ActionScript, Python, and Lua.

Senior Cinematic Environment Artist

The Senior Cinematic Environment Artist collaborates with the Game Director and Art Director. The Senior Cinematic Environment Artist creates game environments and maps and comprehensively understands form, color, lighting, modeling, texturing, collision development, asset optimizing, effects and game world animations, architecture, and natural landscapes. The Senior Cinematic Environment Artist has experience and knowledge of various art styles, concept drawings, and tools such as 3ds Max, Maya, LightWave, Softimage, ZBrush, Photoshop, and DeBabelizer.

Senior Environment Artist

The Senior Environment Artist creates 3D environments from conception to in-game assets using tools such as 3ds Max, Maya, LightWave, Softimage, ZBrush, Photoshop, and DeBabelizer. The Senior Environment Artist works with the Producer, Game Director, and Art Director on defining the visual art style of the game environments. The Senior Environment Artist has an extensive background in fine arts; creates and designs high-quality 2D and 3D art; and understands the basic elements, principles, and practices of form, color, and composition of landscapes, architecture, and various forms of level building such as collision development, creating models, lighting, environment and texture effects, sky dome creation, level optimization, and game world animation. The Senior Environment Artist combines ideas and methodologies of environment production to create an efficient and streamlined pipeline that other environment artists can follow. The Senior Environment Artist understands each platform and its capabilities and limitations, especially the next-generation platforms in regard to memory, polygon output, texture limitations, efficiency in building collisions, and the ability to build streaming and loading levels, characters, and lighting.

Lead Environment Artist

The Lead Environment Artist reports to the Art Director and manages and mentors junior artists. The Lead Environment Artist creates immersive, living, and fully-realized environments through lighting, atmosphere, object placement, populating the world, models, and textures. The Lead Environment Artist creates visually stunning 3D game environments, and works with the entire team to balance art assets and solutions related to technical and aesthetic issues. The Lead Environment Artist understands lighting and shadows in games, including radiosity, ray tracing, HDRL (high dynamic range image-based lighting), dynamic lighting, lightmaps, vertex lighting, photography, composition, color, space, structure, and form. The Lead Environment Artist works closely with other artists, programmers, and designers on all platforms using art tools such as 3ds Max, Maya, LightWave, Softimage, Photoshop, ZBrush, and DeBabelizer.

Environment Artist

The Environment Artist reports to the Senior or Lead Environment Artist or Art Director. The Environment Artist creates highly detailed, realistic environment art assets and beautiful, photorealistic 3D models and textures with a strong understanding of color, scale, proportion, and lighting. The Environment Artist also works with lighting assets, programming, scripting languages (MaxScript, MEL (Maya Embedded Language), ActionScript, Python, and Lua), character modeling, photography, and texture assets and mentors other artists to make the best game art possible.

3D Environment Artist

The 3D Environment Artist reports to the Art Director and Senior or Lead Environment Artist. The 3D Environment Artist models and textures assets for a multitude of environments, understanding form, color, shade, and 2D and 3D art assets. The 3D Environment Artist follows art and design concepts, reviews and critiques art, and collaborates with the designers and programmers. The 3D Environment Artist balances the creative and visual requirements with the milestone schedule and is skilled in concept drawing, illustration, and animation. The 3D Environment Artist creates 3D environments from conception to in-game assets using tools such as 3ds Max, Maya, LightWave, Softimage, ZBrush, Photoshop, and DeBabelizer and scripting languages such as MaxScript, MEL (Maya Embedded Language), ActionScript, Python, and Lua.

Visual Effects Artist

The Visual Effects Artist works closely with the Lead Artist and creates spectacular visual effects. The Visual Effects Artist sets the game's visual effect art style with regard to the game's technical and aesthetic decisions. The Visual Effects Artist understands the latest platform's texture and shader creation skills; the game creation processes and pipeline; tools such as 3ds Max, Maya, LightWave, Softimage, ZBrush, Photoshop, and DeBabelizer; and scripting languages such as MaxScript, MEL (Maya Embedded Language), ActionScript, Python, and Lua.

Chapter 10

Special Effects Artist

The Special Effects Artist reports to the Art Director and works closely with programmers. The Special Effects Artist creates all aspects of 2D and 3D game effects such as particle systems, animating textures, polygonal effects meshes, and procedurally programmed assets. Using 3D software, the Special Effects Artist simulates and renders animations of in-game effects for proof of concept and game demos and realistic effects such as smoke, fire, and explosions. The Special Effects Artist meets project deadlines and milestones and is technically skilled using tools such as 3ds Max, Maya, LightWave, Softimage, ZBrush, Photoshop, and DeBabelizer and scripting languages such as MaxScript, MEL (Maya Embedded Language), ActionScript, Python, and Lua.

Technical VFX (Visual Special Effects) Animator

The Technical VFX Animator reports to the Technical Art Director or Technical Lead Artist to produce high-quality set piece events and VFX sequences as they apply to real-time technology for the current platforms. The Technical VFX Animator solves technical production issues, especially issues related to animation and VFX, builds large rigs to handle large set piece events in a real environment, and prototypes technical rigs from production of animation tests to in-game use of final production animation. The Technical VFX Animator works with programmers and tool/engine teams to develop scripts, tools, and plug-ins to streamline VFX and animation workflow. The Technical VFX Animator works closely with Technical Artists and team leads to produce the best VFX; works with the pre-visualization department on across-the-board projects and VFX prototypes; and understands rigging and weighting techniques, dynamic and rigid body dynamics, scripting and animation principles, kinematics, and high-quality keyframe animation. The Technical VFX Animator understands game engines, tools, pipelines, and the game development process.

Lead VFX (Visual Special Effects) Artist

The Lead VFX Artist creates real-time special effects and understands what makes special effects work in a game. The Lead VFX Artist works closely with the art and design leads, graphic developers, and the audio lead to produce great effects. The Lead VFX Artist researches effects technology and sets up and maintains tools and workflow related to special effects such as particle systems, post processing effects, and shaders (specular and normal maps).

Senior VFX (Visual Special Effects) Artist

The Senior VFX Artist creates game effects that include multi-pass textures, character skinning, skeletal animation, rigid body dynamics, particles, and shaders to simulate effects such as explosions, smoke, fire, steam, fog, rain, flowing water, and natural phenomena such as leaves and debris flowing in the wind. The Senior VFX Artist follows concept art, storyboards, written descriptions, and scripts to create dynamic effects mockups for evaluation to final game production. The Senior VFX Artist understands physics, animation, and rendering. The Senior VFX Artist works with tools/effects system programmers under deadlines and schedules in a dynamic team environment. The Senior VFX Artist is skilled at using both proprietary tools and commercial game development tools such as 3ds Max, Maya, LightWave, Softimage, ZBrush, Photoshop, and DeBabelizer and scripting languages such as MaxScript, MEL (Maya Embedded Language), ActionScript, Python, and Lua.

Lead Character Artist

The Lead Character Artist manages the character artist team, clearly communicating the art direction and evaluating and giving constructive feedback to work in progress. The Lead Character Artist maintains and manages the character pipeline, which includes streamlined asset creation and techniques; collaborates with the software engineers to ensure that the presentation is rendered properly in the game; and helps the team create bleeding-edge, believable, stylized characters in rich cinematic scenes utilizing in-house art tools, various art applications, and the game engine. The Lead Character Artist reports to the Art Director, oversees the creation and delivery of the character art assets, establishes the aesthetic and technical character art standards, and works with the team leads and production team on art deliverables and the milestone schedule. The Lead Character Artist works in art applications and tools such as Maya, LightWave, 3ds Max, Softimage, ZBrush, MudBox, and Photoshop and understands 2D photo manipulation, painting software, and scripting languages such as MaxScript, MEL (Maya Embedded Language), ActionScript, Python, and Lua.

3D Character Modeler

The 3D Character Modeler works closely with the Lead Character Artist creating stylized character and object models from start to completion. The 3D Character Modeler works from existing concept art and model sheets or creates new concept art sheets to build from.

The 3D Character Modeler works in all aspects of creating 3D models and objects including meshes, textures, shaders, normals, and other technical and aesthetic considerations. The 3D Character Modeler understands texture painting, normal generation, UV mapping, animation, rigging, skinning, and creating characters in a human form with proportion and scale. The 3D Character Modeler works in art applications and tools such as Maya, LightWave, 3ds Max, Softimage, ZBrush, MudBox, and Photoshop and understands 2D photo manipulation, painting software, and scripting languages such as Unreal Editor, MaxScript, MEL (Maya Embedded Language), ActionScript, Python, and Lua.

Chapter 10

Character Animator

The Character Animator creates visually stunning 3D game animations for characters and objects, working within a team environment to balance art solutions related to technical and aesthetic issues. The Character Animator works closely with the designers, programmers, and other artists. The Character Animator works in art applications and tools such as Maya, LightWave, 3ds Max, Softimage, ZBrush, MudBox, and Photoshop, and understands 2D photo manipulation, painting software, and scripting languages such as Unreal Editor, MaxScript, MEL (Maya Embedded Language), ActionScript, Python, and Lua.

Character Rigger

The Character Rigger designs and sets controls for animation sequences (animation) from facial rigs, rag doll setup, and skin weighting to setting up all character and object movements (actions). The Character Rigger understands facial rigging such as join and blender shapes, object hierarchies, axis locks, degrees of freedom, forward kinematics (FK), inverse kinematics (IK), and different sized rigs for various proportioned characters and sets up, copies, and transfers skin weights to characters and costumes. The Character Rigger collaborates with other character artists and animators. The Character Rigger understands workflows for skeletons, rigs, and animation and analyzes and debugs skin weight issues.

Senior Cinematics Animation Artist

The Senior Cinematics Animation Artist will collaborate closely with the art, creative, and game directors in order to satisfy the cinematic needs of a specific project. Specific tasks include working on the vision process for cinematic content of game, creating storyboards based on the game's script, ensuring cinematic aesthetics complement the in-game aesthetics, and creating complex rig/skin animation setups. The Senior Cinematics Animation Artist understands the language and structure of film cinematography and editing in order to implement camera movements and cuts, keyframe animating of characters and objects, cinematic compositing and finishing, scheduling, and tasking of other animators and modelers to meet schedules and milestones.

Cinematics Artist

The Cinematics Artist works with the Art Director and the Senior Cinematic Animation Artist, creating high-quality in-game cinematics (IGCs) and full-motion videos (FMVs), and meets production schedules and deadlines. The Cinematics Artist turns storyboard concept drawings into layout files for IGCs and FMVs and places characters and cinematic assets into shots. The Cinematics Artist uses 3D tools and Adobe After Effects and Premiere and exports and implements the camera, characters, and script data into the game engine.

3D Artist

The 3D Artist designs, models, lights, and renders 3D content with a thorough understanding of physical motion, weight, balance, texture, and form. The 3D Artist works closely with 2D artists and programmers. The 3D Artist understands traditional illustration and character animation and has solid conceptual and design skills. The 3D Artist works in art applications and tools such as Maya, LightWave, 3ds Max, Softimage, ZBrush, MudBox, and Photoshop.

Lead Animator

The Lead Animator manages a small team of animators in the creation of compelling and realistic moving objects and characters. The Lead Animator authors the animation guideline documents, researches and informs the team of the latest methodologies and practices, and sets art milestone schedules. The Lead Animator understands human anatomy; 2D artwork such as digital and traditional painting, textures, life drawings, and concept art; 3D artwork such as traditional sculpting and modeling of characters, objects, and environments with 3D motion capture data; and keyframing including facial expressions and lip synching. The Lead Animator reports to the Art Director and works with the Game Designer and Level Designer to produce the art style, understands the platform's limitations, and maintains high art standards. The Lead Animator works with the Lead Character Artist and Senior Technical Artist to collaborate on the proper technical requirements and enhancements to animation tools such as rigging, AI, and physics. The Lead Animator researches animation techniques used in other games and films. The Lead Animator works in art applications and tools such as Maya, LightWave, 3ds Max, Softimage, ZBrush, MotionBuilder, Character Studio, and Photoshop.

Senior Animator

The Senior Animator defines the structure and technical setup of how the animation team works on the game. The Senior Animator works with game leaders on the game vision and collaborates with the Concept Artist and Character Modeler. Supervisory and art direction is given by the Senior Animator to the animation team. The Senior Animator understands drawing and concept art; creates dynamic in-game animations including human anatomy and natural and expressive movement; and models, textures, skins (vertex weighting), and rigs in-game assets. The Senior Animator also understands CG (computer graphics) and traditional animation fundamentals such as posing, timing, and character weights as well as keyframe animating, forward kinematics (FK)/inverse kinematics (IK) switching, constraints, and facial rigs. The Senior Animator works in art applications and tools such as Maya, LightWave, 3ds Max, Softimage, ZBrush, MotionBuilder, Character Studio, and Photoshop.

Chapter 10

Technical Animator

The Technical Animator creates and rigs character animations including humans and creatures with tails and multiple legs and wings. The Technical Animator works on painting deformation weights on character outfits and animates mechanical and organic props. The Technical Animator understands anatomy, skeletal animations, and natural and expressive movement, and models, textures, skins (vertex weighting), and rigs in-game assets. The Technical Animator works in art applications and tools such as Maya, LightWave, 3ds Max, Softimage, ZBrush, MotionBuilder, Character Studio, and Photoshop.

Animator

The Animator works closely with the Lead Animator (or Senior Animator) and Lead Artist developing, defining, and maintaining high-end animation content for games. The Animator produces the designer's vision and all technical and aesthetic considerations for the game's animation requirements. The Animator understands storytelling; basic game design; rigging; and traditional animation including action, acting, cinematics, blend shape, facial expression, and lip synching. The Animator also knows anatomy and animation principles, technology, processes, and dependencies. The Animator develops an IP (intellectual property) from conception to completion using concept artwork, 3D models, and texture maps provided by other team artists. The Animator works in art applications and tools such as Maya, LightWave, 3ds Max, Softimage, ZBrush, MotionBuilder, Character Studio, and Photoshop.

Intermediate Animator

The Intermediate Animator creates, exports, and implements fluid and smooth quality animation in the game. The Intermediate Animator works with senior and technical artists and programmers in regard to improvements and resolution of problems in the asset creation and export pipelines, tools, and other art resources in the game. The Intermediate Animator reports to the Lead Animator for work critiques on all completed and in-process animations for in-game play. The Intermediate Animator works with programmers and artists to create the optimum balance between smooth, seamless movement and optimized performance on each platform within the production schedule.

The Intermediate Animator understands animation theory; 3D keyframe animation; traditional animation principles; and fundamentals such as squash and stretch, staging, timing and motion, anticipation, exaggeration, follow-through, and arcs. The Intermediate Animator works in art applications and tools such as Maya, LightWave, 3ds Max, Softimage, ZBrush, MotionBuilder, Character Studio, and Photoshop.

Lighter

The Lighter adds the light to games, creating atmosphere and realism, tone, and depth in a scene. Lighters create visually balanced individual elements that enable other game artists to produce a convincing image or environment. The Lighter's images look aesthetically pleasing and are easily rendered. Lighters ensure a consistency in lighting, color balance, and mood between the many elements in a shot or game scene. Lighters emphasize drama and narrative and establish details such as location, weather, time of day, and season. Lighters work with the animators and designers to establish the art style. Lighters know math and art theory and practices, computer animation, photography, film, and physics. Lighters also understand color theory, composition, light, and form plus rendering, lighting, shading networks, polygonal modeling, and texture UVs. Lighters work from reference materials, identify and translate key lighting details into applicable information, and light moderate to complex interior and exterior scenes. Lighters work in art applications and tools such as Maya, LightWave, 3ds Max, Softimage, ZBrush, Houdini, and Photoshop.

Senior Technical Artist

The Senior Technical Artist manages a small highly talented team and reports to the Art Director and Technical Director. The Senior Technical Artist sees that the artwork has concrete visual quality as per the system requirements. The Senior Technical Artist creates experimental art assets for iterative implementation and manages the outsourcing processes for the art asset production. The Senior Technical Artist creates concept art, models (low- and high-polygon), textures, and animations. The Senior Technical Artist works in art applications and tools such as Maya, LightWave, 3ds Max, Softimage, ZBrush, MotionBuilder, Character Studio, and Photoshop.

UI (User Interface) Artist

The UI Artist conceptualizes, designs, and implements the user interface of the game using a diverse visual range of 2D and 3D elements. The UI Artist works with 3D computer models, textures, and animations to create and implement front-end menus, backgrounds, HUD (heads-up display) elements, icons, mini-game assets, and 2D and 3D game assets. The UI Artist maintains a consistent look and feel for the user's experience throughout the game. The UI Artist reports to and communicates with the Lead Artist, Art Director, and Producer, meeting deadlines and being an active team member. The UI Artist understands FMV (full-motion video) and works with art applications and tools such as Photoshop, Flash, Adobe After Effects, Illustrator, Maya, LightWave, 3ds Max, Softimage, and ZBrush.

Chapter 10

Front End Graphic Designer

The Front End Graphic Designer reports to the Art Director, creating front-end screens and user interfaces (UI) and setting forth design styles to integrate into the game. The Front End Graphic Designer works closely with the design team to ensure the front end meets the game's vision. The Front End Graphic Designer understands color, composition, and utilizing type and images. The Front End Graphic Designer works in art applications and tools such as Maya, LightWave, 3ds Max, Softimage, ZBrush, and Photoshop.

Texture Artist

The Texture Artist creates and applies textures to element surfaces to achieve a quality result to complete 3D CG (computer-generated) characters, sets, and objects. The Texture Artist works closely with the Art Director, Modeler, and Lead Technical Artist to create models in the required art style. The Texture Artist understands UV layouts, texture projections, and 2D texture painting. The Texture Artist works in art applications and tools such as Maya, LightWave, 3ds Max, Softimage, ZBrush, MotionBuilder, Character Studio, and Photoshop.

Senior Concept Artist

The Senior Concept Artist creates original and imaginative concept art for characters, objects, backgrounds, environments, and other art assets. The Senior Concept Artist understands traditional and digital drawing formats and has expert skills in drawing human and animal forms with proportion and scaling in a unique, stylized manner. The Senior Concept Artist reports to the Lead Artist, Art Director, and Senior Artist to develop and put on paper the artistic vision of the game's design. The Senior Concept Artist creates finished artwork for preproduction, in-game production (storyboards), and marketing/sales materials. The Senior Concept Artist mentors and guides the Junior Concept Artists and manages external Concept Artists, defining the look and style of the game. The Senior Concept Artist supplies the 3D Animators clear 2D art concepts on which the game's 3D characters, objects, and environments are based.

Concept Artist (Junior Concept Artist)

The Concept Artist creates original, unique, and creative concepts to render in a clear, detailed, and timely manner. The Concept Artist has a strong attention to detail approach to creating visually appealing concept artwork. The Concept Artist understands human and animal anatomy, architectural and environmental design, lighting, composition, color theory, atmosphere materials, and textures. The Concept Artist reports to the Senior Concept Artist and helps create balanced solutions to all related technical and aesthetic issues.

Audio Engineer and Composer

Audio (Music) Director

The Audio (Music) Director manages in-house and external audio contractor development of audio resources/components such as SFX (sound effects), music, cut-scene soundtracks, voice-over dialogue samples, and interface sounds for all game projects.

The Audio Director trains the audio team in sound generation tools, understands the game integration tools and techniques, keeps current on new audio equipment and software, and maximizes the effectiveness of existing audio tools and equipment. The Audio Director analyzes and plans the milestone schedule and audio budget for current and upcoming titles on all platforms and clearly defines the necessary additions and modifications to the existing audio pipeline(s). Other duties include supervising external audio contractors to deliver on-time, quality assets; managing audio assets by revision generation; overseeing music composition, recording sessions, and mixing; and directing voice-over (and casting VO talent) and SFX recording sessions. The Audio Director sets the standards and tools for creating scores, works with the engine/tools programmers to maximize the audio component of the game, and prototypes music that is creative and fits the mood of the game. The Audio Director knows the audio capability of all of the platforms and is a versatile composer. The Audio Director is a good audio producer who has a strong sense for high-quality audio, has musical instrument experience, is a strong team leader, and loves games.

Senior Sound Designer

The Senior Sound Designer provides high-level detail and high-quality game audio. The Senior Sound Designer works and communicates with designers, programmers, and artists and provides all types of audio assets for in-game implementation. Duties include field recording; creating SFX (sound effects); managing sound assets; and troubleshooting audio issues. The Senior Sound Designer possesses skills such as Foley, DSP (digital signal processing), and mixing, and creates SFX manually and with software tools such as Wwise, FMOD, Logic Pro, Adobe Audition, Sound Forge, Pro Tools, Waves, Cubase, cSound, Max/MSP, Pure Data, Reactor, and Ableton Live.

Technical Sound Designer

The Technical Sound Designer understands the technical constraints of each platform's audio design and capabilities. Other duties include designing, mixing, implementing, and managing high-quality game audio. Working in 3D environments, the Technical Sound Designer integrates sound with characters, items, and object and game locations. The Technical Sound Designer works closely with the Audio Director, designers, artists, and programmers to best solve audio issues and problems; provides audio expertise to contractors, vendors, and clients (licensors); and communicates with and manages the audio team. The Technical Sound Designer is a highly creative and imaginative specialist with a keen ability to solve problems and learns new tools and skills quickly. The Technical Sound Designer uses tools such as SCREAM, Xact, Wwise, and FMOD and creates and mixes film-quality SFX using audio packages such as Pro Tools, Nuendo, Sound Forge, and Peak.

Sound Effects Designer

The Sound Effects (SFX) Designer understands the SFX needed in the game and records, edits, synchronizes, and mixes digital sound effects and music using commercial and proprietary audio tools. The SFX Designer works closely with the Game Designer, Audio Software Programmer (Engineer), and Producer to enhance the audible game experience.

Music Composer

The Music Composer will create original ambient, high-quality orchestrated music under the direction of the Audio Director, Game Designer, and Producer. The Music Composer is familiar with transcribing parts and laying out note patterns, mixing/mastering, audio postproduction, current and upcoming game and film music and audio formats, MIDI sequences, and DAWs (digital audio workstations).

Audio Mixer

The Audio Mixer uses tools such as Pro Tools to combine sound channels such as music, SFX, ambient sounds, and dialogue into a single channel. The sounds are cleaned up, the output frequency and volume set to a uniform level, and dynamic and panoramic positional sounds and effects such as reverb and delay (for an echo effect) are manipulated. A good Audio Mixer can add aesthetic, ear-pleasing audio inside the game, creating a valuable dimension to the play experience.

Audio Editor

The Audio Editor selects the best music, and adds ambient sounds, SFX, and verbal dialogue to the game scenes, characters, world items, and game locations using DAWs (digital audio workstations) such as Pro Tools. The Audio Editor reports to the Audio Director and Senior Sound Designer.

Audio Scripter

The Audio (or Sound) Scripter creates and modifies audio for game development and implements, mixes, and manages high-quality game audio content. The Audio Scripter works with the programmers to implement the SFX, audio systems, and features in the game. Other duties include using proprietary and custom game audio tools such as SCREAM, Xact,

Wwise, FMOD, Pro Tools, Nuendo, Sound Forge, and Peak, as well as scripting languages. The Audio Scripter works closely with the Audio Software Programmers (Engineers), has a highly creative and imaginative sense for problem solving, and quickly learns new audio tools and gaming platforms.

Audio Assistant

The Audio Assistant reports to the Senior Sound Designer and is responsible for the audio integration, audio debugging, and some SFX creation. The Audio Assistant communicates with the audio team verbally and in writing about audio issues in the game.

QA (Quality Assurance) Tester

QA Manager

The QA Manager provides overall management and leadership to the testing operations group and sets strategic implementation of policies and procedures to the QA testing team. The QA Manager develops and implements comprehensive test strategies for QA standards, risk assessment, problem resolution, and organizational processes and controls and manages a full spectrum of tests throughout the entire life cycle including automated tests, functional and non-functional testing, gray-box testing, test plans, and tracking of QA efforts.

For the QA test operations' managers and team, the QA Manager provides technical, tactical, and strategic leadership and planning methods and sets goals for organizational and product quality that are understood by the QA team. The QA Manager mentors the QA team and supports the entire game development organization. The QA Manager thoroughly understands the software development life cycle, plans and coordinates software and middleware test methodologies, and represents the QA team as its leader and liaison between key development groups (design, programming, art).

QA Lead Tester

The QA Lead Tester reports to the QA Manager and the Producer. The QA Lead Tester is in charge of managing the entire testing process on a game title including creating test schedules, reports, and task lists; taking ownership of the "bug" database; clarifying the issues with the development team; and resolving these issues in a timely manner. The QA Lead Tester manages that game's QA team and resources (hardware and software), is the liaison with the other development groups involved with this game, and mentors, trains, and develops the team.

Chapter 10

QA Tester/Analyst

The QA Tester/Analyst reports to the QA Lead or Senior Tester and possibly the QA Manager. The QA Tester/Analyst evaluates and tests game submissions to the organization using excellent problem solving and analytical skills with a strong attention to detail. The QA Tester/Analyst evaluates the game design, game rules, UI, and overall quality of the "game experience." The QA Tester/Analyst knows and uses Microsoft Word, Excel, MS Project, and PowerPoint and clearly documents the evaluation results. The QA Tester/Analyst executes regression tests of resubmitted assets and builds.

QA Senior Tester

The QA Senior Tester reports to the QA Lead Tester and is responsible for applying software engineering principles to test, verify, and integrate the game and its components.

Duties include full life cycle participation in testing the game from planning; conducting and documenting tests; creating a "bug" report (errors, play issues, graphic problems, and inconsistencies); and performing regression tests, integration tests, and other software quality control functions. The QA Senior Tester clarifies the found issues to the other development team members such as artists, programmers, and the audio engineer/specialist.

The QA Senior Tester conducts automated tests using tools such as WinRunner, QuickTest, Rational Robot, and TestDirector. The QA Senior Tester has an acute attention to detail, good communication skills, both written and verbal, and is capable of working alone and as a valuable team member. The QA Senior Tester understands networking fundamentals and is very comfortable working with various hardware and software.

QA Tester (Entry Level)

The position of QA Tester is usually the entry point for most gamers who have no game industry experience or skills such as programming, art, or audio. This position reports to a QA Senior Tester and requires a love of gaming since the average work week can be 40 to 60 hours.

Since every teenager dreams of playing games for a career, this job pays very little (the old "supply vs. demand" economic theory in practice). The QA Tester must have good communication skills, both verbal and written, must follow directions provided by the supervisor, and must be a good team member. The QA Senior Tester gives the QA Tester test plans and test cases to run on the game. The testing must uncover gameplay, graphics, and audio anomalies, and the QA Tester documents how they manifest themselves in the game environment. Some QA teams record all test sessions to show (playback) the events that led up to a problem or display the problem itself. The SMPTE (time code) of the recorded media is used to mark the cited bug or issue found. Sometimes this position is a temporary to permanent one where candidates are hired for one to three months and if competent become full-time QA Testers.

Other Positions

Other positions at a gaming company include marketing and sales, public relations (PR), customer service, community relations, and build coordinators.

The marketing and sales staff works on the company's advertising, distribution (the product as it pertains to the market needs, product pricing, and product promotion), and selling of products.

The public relations staff disseminates information about the company and its products to their audience to get exposure. PR tries to build a rapport with employees, customers, investors, and the general public.

The customer service staff's mission is to keep the current and potential customers satisfied and positive toward the company.

The community relations staff publishes newsletters and organizes contests, community outreach programs, tournaments, and live chats, as well as assisting in forum moderation and working with the appropriate development teams to provide valid community feedback.

The build coordinators create the game using the latest code, art assets, sound files, and other data such as text or XML files.

External or outsourcing positions work best for artists, audio engineers and composers, customer support, and programming of a closed system such as code to convert PNG files to BMP files. Critical work that needs daily to hourly monitoring must be done internally unless the budget cannot afford this. Often outsourcing can be negotiated as a flat fee or a preset hourly fee so the total budget for a task is agreed to by all parties.

Workshop

Assignments

Assignment 1: Play a recent game and e-mail the publisher or developer with a list of positive suggestions to make the next version (sequel) better and improve gameplay. Share these comments with the class or friends.

Assignment 2: What would be an ideal team working on a small casual game under a limited budget of $100K for six months?

Exercises

Exercise 1: When designing a game based on a given topic, what key roles should be present and how could those persons influence the design decisions?

Chapter 10

Exercise 2: When designing a game based on a license, what key roles should be present and how could those persons influence the design decisions?

Exercise 3: What are the roles during game development of the Designer, Producer, Art Director, Technical Director, and Marketing Director?

Unguided Exercises

Unguided Exercise 1: Select and combine two game genres and the best team to develop the game. Explain your reason for the team's members.

Unguided Exercise 2: Select two game platforms to develop a game for and the best team to develop the game. Explain your reason for the team's members.

Internet Reading Assignment

"Effective Art Directors: Gaming's Something Something"
by Ben Cammarano
   www.Gamasutra.com/view/feature/3857/Effective_Art_
   Directors_Gamings_.php

"Peeking inside Insomniac: A Conversation with Ted Price"
by Christian Nutt
   www.Gamasutra.com/view/feature/3850/Peeking_inside_
   Insomniac_a_.php

Chapter 11

Game Narrative Scriptwriting

In 1995, I decided to learn all I could about the movie-making business. The film industry is a well-established medium similar to game design and production, with its own rules and theories.

I have said for some time that if a movie were made like a video game, the audience would walk out after five minutes. In game design and implementation, we often lack solid and interesting storylines. (That's why I recommend "borrowing" masterpieces from other disciplines like classic stories, movies, and history in Chapter 4, "Game Concepts and Ideas.")

The gaming business blames our shortcomings on technology issues like slow computer speed, insufficient memory or RAM, lack of storage space available on CD or DVD, and lag time or slow Internet transmission rates. However, we pay little attention to important visual issues like lighting, camera POVs, actor positions and the verbal impact on their delivery, and sound effects. I've heard it said — and I agree — that technology is a tool and not the basis for designing a great game. Stories, character development, interesting puzzles, and interaction make great games.

The film business is just that — a business — and many game publishers and developers fail to understand and operate like a profitable business. I have seen companies that ran their business haphazardly and without plans, documentation, or any goals except to finish the current game at some point.

The film business has several phases such as preproduction, production, and postproduction. Preproduction is where the script is written, the shooting schedule is prepared and documented, the entire film's budget is documented, the in-front and behind the camera crews are hired, and the filming locations are scouted out and selected. After 6 to 18 months of extensive planning that has been researched, documented, and communicated to all personnel involved, two to eight weeks of expensive filming begins. Then postproduction begins with the first dailies (each day's or previous day's shooting) reviewed to ensure that the film is usable. If the director is satisfied with the currently shot footage, then production is ready to continue. Otherwise, the production team must reshoot scenes or make cutting room decisions. Postproduction also includes editing (which takes should be in the final film and which POV or shooting angle looks best) and voice audio (the shooting dialogue is only a placeholder as actors and actresses rerecord all of their lines in a soundproof room for the final merging with the film).

When film is shot, the film itself contains no usable sound. The audio is recorded on another medium like audio or digital tape and later merged with the film in the editing room. Obviously, film contains both audio and video, but almost always the audio is redone in postproduction.

Also in the postproduction phase ADR (automated dialogue replacement or additional dialogue recording) and Foley (recording natural, everyday sound effects such as walking noises) are added to the film.

It is in postproduction that a film may go through several staff and audience viewing tests to see how people react to various versions of the film.

As a film producer, you would be expected to understand the filming process like lighting, camera angles, and camera techniques as well as dealing with your crew, actors, writers, and studios.

As a game producer, you should be equally skilled.

This book is about game design and not filmmaking. These skills, although they may be interesting to learn, fall more into the realm of the game producer. The skills that the designer needs to understand are the preproduction skills mentioned earlier, which include scriptwriting, scheduling, budgeting, determining the characters that are needed, and stage direction (how you envision the screen to depict a scene like "CLOSE-UP on George as he enters the room seeing his wife dead for the first time").

A brief introduction of these skills is discussed in this chapter. Through your research in the library or a favorite bookstore, you can learn additional insights about the film business, preproduction, and postproduction.

Film is a linear (one beginning, one middle, and one ending) type of medium where the audience is passive (only watches the presentation). Games are usually nonlinear, and we'll look at an example of a nonlinear game shortly.

In writing a script for actors to follow, there are certain standards in formatting your masterpiece. Standard items in your script would be "slug lines" or scene identifications, the action in this scene (a description of any action), the character who is speaking, the dialogue or line spoken by this character, any action the character is performing (such as "he lights a candle as he walks toward the hallway"), the camera and stage directions (information to the camera person like CLOSE-UP, CUT TO, FADE-IN), and scene notes that the writer wants to briefly convey.

Typical information included in a "slug line" is location (the courthouse steps, in the evil doctor's laboratory, outside in front of John's house), the time of day and weather conditions (nighttime, around 10 P.M. as the rain is pouring down), stage instructions (dark room lit by a flickering candle, blindingly sunlit room with an open window), cues and special effects (like lightning, explosions, ringing telephone), and background music.

Slug lines include "INT." for an interior shot and "EXT." for an exterior shot, along with the time of day. For example:

EXT. PEDERSEN HOUSE - NIGHT

INT. BEDROOM - MOMENTS LATER

EXT. THE PARKING LOT - DAY

Camera POV information may include instructions like (CU) or CLOSE-UP, PULL BACK, TIGHTEN - ADAM AND EVE, ANGLE - ON THE BOOK, (MS) or MEDIUM SHOT - MICHELE AND BROOKE, CAMERA PANS RIGHT.

When typing the script, column (or pica) 60 is where you put the camera start of scene or end of scene instructions like CUT TO:, DISSOLVE TO:, and FADE IN/OUT:. When a character is speaking but not shown on the screen, we call this a "voice-over" (VO) and after the character's name we place the (VO) indicator, as in ROGER (VO) meaning that Roger is speaking off camera.

Stage directions are always in parentheses like (crying), (laughing), and (looking at the book).

The cover page should begin with the script's name (or game's name) with relevant episode information one-third to halfway down the page and centered, followed by (on the next line) the "by" or "written by" (again centered), and then on the next line the author's name centered. At the bottom-right corner of the cover page should be separate lines that are composed of the author's or representative's name; street address; the city, state, and zip code; the phone number; and the fax number. At the bottom-left corner of the cover page should be the copyright notice (for example, "Copyright 2009, Roger E. Pedersen"). I prefer to include the copyright notice on all pages in either the header or footer in case the script magically disappears or gets reproduced without authorization.

The entire script should be typed on white paper, 8.5 inches by 11 inches (20 pound weight), with 1-inch margins all around. You begin the first page of your script (using Courier 12-point type) with the film's (or game's) title placed seven lines down from the top of the page and typed in all capitals, underlined, and centered. Then five lines below the title (on line 12 from the top of the page) you type "FADE IN:". Then two lines down from that (on line 14) you write your first scene.

Remember to always check your spelling and punctuation (especially since modern word processors include spell checking features). A script should be bound with a plain card stock cover secured by two or three brass brads.

Chapter 11

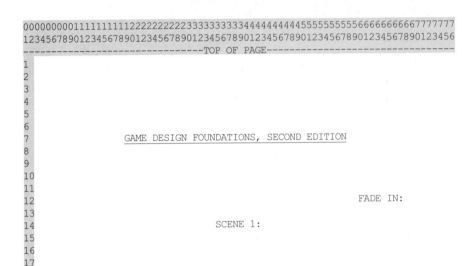

```
000000000011111111112222222222333333333344444444445555555555666666666677777777
123456789012345678901234567890123456789012345678901234567890123456
---------------------------------TOP OF PAGE---------------------------------
1
2
3
4
5
6
7          GAME DESIGN FOUNDATIONS, SECOND EDITION
8
9
10
11
12                                                    FADE IN:
13
14              SCENE 1:
15
16
17
18
19
```

The script contains other important items such as the name of the character, the character's dialogue, the dialogue directions, and the page number.

The character's name is always in all capitals and starts on the 40th
space or pica. The dialogue starts on the 30th space or pica and ends on
the 60th space or pica. The dialogue directions begin on the 35th space or
pica. The page number begins on the 75th space or pica and is two lines
from the top. All sound effects are in all capitals.

```
000000000011111111112222222222333333333344444444445555555555666666666677777777
123456789012345678901234567890123456789012345678901234567890123456
                              (Roger walks in the room tired.)

                                   ROGER
                         What a busy and tiring day!
                         Let's see what I received in
                         the mail today.
```

The rule of thumb for scripts is that "one page equals one minute in the
film."

So that game scripts look professional, they should follow the film
industry's standards, which help ensure that the actors and film crew
understand the vision in their own terms.

The script will provide documentation for cinematic action, cut-scenes,
voice-overs, and various storytelling paths as well as for the entire development team.

Linear vs. Nonlinear or Games vs. Films and Books

In a linear format like a book or a film, the author (or scriptwriter) is in control, leading the reader or viewer on a journey from the beginning to a single conclusion.

In a nonlinear format like a game, the player decides on the journey from the author's presented beginning or from the player's current situation. The multiple paths from this starting point vary depending on the player's decisions, and the ending will depend on how the player satisfies the author's view of success or failure. The author can use NPC (nonplayer characters) to influence the player, assist the player, or compete against the player.

Linear format mediums control the entire world and can be represented as an event or chapter leading into another event or chapter, where the order and connection is extremely important. For example, all events and characters in chapter four must happen and be known before chapter five occurs.

Nonlinear format mediums can be represented by numerous closed boxes, where the player can open up any one of the boxes and discover the events and characters independent from previous information that has been acquired. The order in which the player opens the boxes is part of the game; perhaps in one game the order is not important and in another game the order in which a box is opened greatly changes the entire story being revealed.

Unlike linear formats, in nonlinear games a box can be opened more than once, and each time it's opened the events and characters can remain constant or change entirely. The first time you open the box you might be greeted by a simple "Hello," whereas the second time you open the box you may be greeted by "I'm glad to see you again."

A Linear Format Story

To illustrate the subject of linear format, let's look at one of my favorite stories by Lewis Carroll, called *Alice's Adventures in Wonderland*. In the next section we'll revise the story into a nonlinear format game. (For those who have not read or seen on film this exciting adventure story, there are many Internet sites where you can download the entire book, including the original drawings.)

A worthy game about Alice in Wonderland is Electronic Arts' American McGee's Alice, where upon Alice's return to Wonderland she learns of its chaotic and demented state and she must return the world to its proper happy state. This theme is similar to the film *Journey Back to Oz*, which was based on Baum's *Ozma of Oz* and a few characters and situations from *The Marvelous Land of Oz*.

Alice in Wonderland statue in Central Park, NY. Pictured are Alice, the Mad Hatter, the March Hare, the Dormouse, and the Cheshire Cat.

An Overview of Lewis Carroll's Alice in Wonderland

Alice, her cat Dinah, and the Cheshire Cat

Chapter 1, A: Alice, a young girl who owns a cat, Dinah, sees a White Rabbit with a waistcoat and a pocket watch run across her lawn exclaiming, "Oh, dear! Oh, dear! I shall be late!"

Chapter 1, B: Alice follows the rabbit down the large rabbit hole under the hedge.

Chapter 1, C: Alice falls down the hole slowly. She sees cupboards, bookshelves, maps, and pictures upon pegs as she falls.

Chapter 1, D: Alice touches down and follows the White Rabbit down a long corridor lit by a row of hanging lamps.

Chapter 1, E: Alice ends up alone in a hall filled with locked doors. A three-legged glass table appears with a tiny golden key on top of the table. Alice finds a small 15-inch door behind a curtain that the little golden key fits. A liquid in a "Drink Me" bottle is swallowed by Alice, who begins to shrink to 10 inches. Alice leaves the golden key on top of the glass table. An "Eat Me" cake is eaten and Alice grows to 9 feet high.

Chapter 2: White Rabbit appears, dropping his white kid gloves and a large fan after seeing large, giant Alice. Giant Alice cries, creating a pool of tears. Using the White Rabbit's fan, Alice begins to shrink.

The White Rabbit

Chapter 3: Alice is swimming with several animals and birds that assemble on the bank of the pool. To dry off, the group consisting of Alice, a lory, a dodo, an eaglet, a duck, a magpie, a canary, and two crabs (a mother and her daughter) runs in a circle or "caucus-race." Alice gives everyone candy and presents herself with a thimble.

Chapter 4, A: The White Rabbit commands Alice to go to his house and return with a pair of gloves and a fan. Alice travels to the White Rabbit's house and collects a pair of gloves and a fan. Alice finds and drinks from an unlabeled bottle and begins to grow, filling up the entire house. The White Rabbit, a lizard named Bill, and two guinea pigs begin to throw pebbles that turn into little cakes when they hit the floor near Alice. Alice eats one of the cakes and begins to shrink.

Chapter 4, B: Alice runs into the woods. She sees an enormous puppy that playfully wants to fetch a stick. Alice escapes into a flowered, grassy area where on top of a large, growing mushroom sits a large hookah-smoking caterpillar.

Chapter 5: The caterpillar tells Alice that eating one side of the mushroom will make her grow and the other side will make her shrink. Alice eats the right side and begins to shrink. Alice manages to eat the left side and grows enormously. A pigeon flying overhead sees Alice's head and long neck and assumes that Alice is a serpent. Alice tries pieces of the mushroom: left-hand pieces to grow, right-hand pieces to shrink, until she is back to a normal size.

Chapter 6: A Fish Footman and a Frog Footman are chatting as the door shuts. The door opens and Alice enters a large kitchen filled with smoke where the Duchess sits nursing her baby on a three-legged stool while her cook stirs a cauldron of peppered soup. Sitting on the hearth is a wide grinning Cheshire Cat. The cook begins to throw pans, plates, and dishes at the sneezing Duchess and her baby, whom she is violently tossing in the air. Alice steals the baby, who turns into a pig, and she lets it go trotting away. Alice chats with the Cheshire Cat who tells her that traveling to the right leads to the Mad Hatters' and traveling to the left goes to the March Hare's.

Chapter 7: At a large table under a tree, the March Hare and the Mad Hatter are drinking tea with the half-sleeping and half-awake Dormouse between them.

Chapter 8: A large rose garden of white roses is being painted red by three playing cards. Ten diamond suit card soldiers, 10 heart suit card royal children, the Knave of Hearts, the White Rabbit, and the King and Queen of

The Mad Hatter

Hearts attend the Royal Croquet game where hedgehogs are croquet balls, flamingos are the mallets, and the playing cards are the arches. During croquet, Alice chats with the Cheshire Cat.

Chapter 9: The Duchess, who has been imprisoned, is freed and walks with Alice until the Queen of Hearts appears and the Duchess flees. Alice meets the Gryphon and they visit the Mock Turtle.

Chapter 10: The Lobster Quadrille (a sea dance with lobsters) happens.

Chapter 11: The Knave of Hearts is accused of stealing the Queen's tarts. In the court are the King and Queen of Hearts, a pack of cards, the Knave of Hearts in chains, the White Rabbit, the Gryphon, the guinea pigs, and Lizard Bill. The first witnesses are the Mad Hatter, the March Hare, and the Dormouse. The next witnesses are the Duchess' cook and Alice.

Chapter 12: In court, Alice grows large. Finally, giant Alice realizes that everything in court is nothing but a pack of cards. Alice's sister awakens her as Wonderland disappears.

Get involved with your vision as the author joins Alice in Wonderland with open arms.

Nonlinear, Game Interactive Format

In a "nonlinear, game interactive format," the chapters of the linear format become self-contained boxes, allowing the player to select from the available boxes or places to explore.

The storytelling or control of the plot rests in the hands and skills of the player. The designer's job is to give numerous paths and options for the player to operate therein. Think of this as an amusement park where the individual rides are entirely self-contained, but they are located near other rides of a similar theme in that section of the park. Selecting amusements and rides in various orders may result in a variety of outcomes; for instance, eating and then riding three roller coasters may produce a result much different stomach-wise than riding the roller coasters first and then eating a big meal.

Become one with your vision and put yourself into your work.

The designer sets the stage and provides paths and possible storylines. For each path an outcome is determined. Some areas can be entered only once, while others can be entered multiple times. Some areas must be entered in a specific order, and in others the order produces different outcomes.

Let's examine a nonlinear game based on the linear story of *Alice in Wonderland* called… Alice in Planet Wonderland.

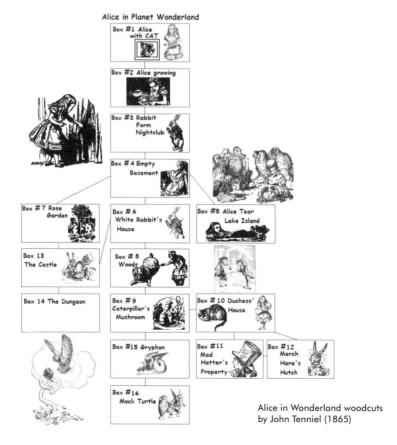

Alice in Planet Wonderland

Box #1 Alice with CAT

Box #2 Alice growing

Box #3 Rabbit Form Nightclub

Box #4 Empty Basement

Box #7 Rose Garden

Box #6 White Rabbit's House

Box #5 Alice Tear Lake Island

Box 13 The Castle

Box #8 Woods

Box 14 The Dungeon

Box #9 Caterpillar's Mushroom

Box #10 Duchess' House

Box #15 Gryphon

Box #11 Mad Hatter's Property

Box #12 March Hare's Hutch

Box #16 Mock Turtle

Alice in Wonderland woodcuts by John Tenniel (1865)

Chapter 11

Alice in Planet Wonderland

Box 1: (enter initially only)

Alice sits at her CAT (Computer by Advanced Technologies) computer (Dinah) playing solitaire. She is about to be 33 years old on March 3. On her 13th birthday, her mother, also age 33, died unexpectedly. Divorced and lonely, she stares at her computer screen night after night. She was raised by her aunt along with her older sister. After high school, she had to work instead of attend college, where she wanted to study medicine or law.

An e-mail pops up.

"Oh, Dear! Oh, Dear! I shall be late! Download the Wonderland program." (signed) The White Rabbit

Curious, Alice downloads and executes the 3D Virtual Wonderland program and in first-person POV sees a 3D White Rabbit run across the screen and down a hole located under a row of hedges.

Alice places her finger on her computer screen on top of the hole under the hedge and her finger disappears.

Amazed, Alice drinks her cup of tea, which has magically turned purple. She is instantly transported into the 3D virtual Wonderland world.

She enters the surprisingly large rabbit hole in hope of adventure.

Box 2: (an initial entry)

As 33-year-old Alice floats down into the abyss, she turns 28 and sees objects from her past. Soon she turns 23, and more familiar objects from those years appear around her as she continues to fall. Then she turns 18 and notices the world around her is the same as it was in those late teenage years. Finally, Alice lands on the ground as she has become 13 again. The White Rabbit is seen running down a long corridor.

Box 3: (multi entry)

"The Rabbit Form," a dark nightclub with pulsating music dimly lit by a row of hanging lamps, is owned by the White Rabbit. Cards, dominoes, and chess pieces are dancing to the music. In the back there are stairs leading to a basement.

Box 4: (multi entry)

An empty basement with several locked doors, a sofa, two comfortable chairs, and a coffee table holding cakes and glasses of purple, green, and yellow juices. Also in the basement is a three-legged glass bookcase with a golden key lying on the top shelf. Each door leads to a different "box" or story pathway, but only three doors lead to continuing adventure paths. The other doors lead to puzzles and return to the empty basement.

If Alice partakes of the "Eat Me" cakes on the coffee table, she will turn 18 years old. Then with another bite, she'll become 23 years old. Then after another mouthful, she'll turn 28 years old, and lastly become 33 years old again. If Alice drinks from any of the glasses, she'll lose five years from her life so if she's 18 years old, she'll turn 13 again. She can never get older than 33 or younger than 13. She needs to be at least 23 to acquire the key and 13 to unlock and open any door.

The first door enters the Alice Tear Lake Island. The second door is the entrance to the White Rabbit's House. The third door enters the white rose garden leading to the King's Castle. Other doors have puzzles that must be solved to return to the empty basement.

Box 5: (multi entry)

Alice Tear Lake Island is the island where the "caucus race" happens and was created by the first Alice's tears. This is where Alice interacts with other virtual 3D characters such as a lory, a dodo, an eaglet, a duck, a magpie, a canary, and two crabs (a mother and her daughter).

Connects to Box 4: An Empty Basement.

On the first time here (or if Message One flag is not "On") Alice learns that, after the original Alice's first visit, the Queen of Hearts has been placed in the dungeon for beheading half the kingdom and for unjustly accusing the Knave of Hearts of stealing her tarts. The Mad Hatter rules now since he won the "caucus race" while everyone else was trying to solve his "riddle of the day" that had no sensible answer.

After the first time, try to win the caucus race to win the prized thimble.

Box 6: (multi entry)

The White Rabbit's House, where the White Rabbit, the messenger and herald for the King, lives. The White Rabbit has many employees who have cottages on his estate, such as the housemaid, Mary Ann; the butler, Pat; and the gardener and handy-creature, Lizard Bill.

At the White Rabbit's House acquire the pair of gloves and a fan.

Connects to Box 4: An Empty Basement and Box 13: The Castle.

Box 7: (multi entry)

The Rose Garden in front of the King's Castle, where the gardeners — the Two of Hearts, the Five of Hearts, and the Seven of Hearts — paint the white roses red and prune the luxurious gardens. Often in older days croquet was played here with flamingo mallets, hedgehog balls, and playing card arches.

Box 8: (multi entry)

The woods, where an enormous puppy playfully wants to fetch a stick. The woods are located just north of the Caterpillar's Mushroom.

Connects to Box 6: The White Rabbit's House and Box 9: The Caterpillar's Mushroom.

Box 9: (multi entry)

The Caterpillar's Mushroom. A flowered, grassy area where on top of a large, growing mushroom sits a large hookah-smoking Caterpillar. The Caterpillar explains that eating the left side of the mushroom will make one grow older and the other side will make one grow younger.

A pigeon flying overhead attacks grown-ups (over 23 years old). This is located just south of the woods (beware of the giant puppy).

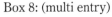

Box 10: (multi entry)

The Duchess' House, where a Fish Footman guards the entrance and inside the large kitchen filled with smoke a Duchess sits nursing her baby on a three-legged stool while her cook is stirring a cauldron of peppered soup. Occasionally sitting on the hearth is a wide grinning Cheshire Cat who can disappear and often gives great advice. Quite often the cook throws pans, plates, and dishes at the sneezing Duchess and her baby, whom the Duchess violently tosses in the air.

From the Duchess' House traveling to the right leads to the Mad Hatter's Property and traveling to the left goes to the March Hare's Hutch.

Box 11: (multi entry)

Mad Hatter's Property. Located on the front lawn of the Mad Hatter's domicile is a large table under a tree reserved for drinking tea. Currently, the Mad Hatter and his "mad as a March Hare" companion reside at the Castle where it's always "tea time."

Connects to the Duchess' House and the March Hare's Hutch.

Box 12: (multi entry)

The March Hare's Hutch. The hutch, which is in the shape of a large rabbit, is where the March Hare resides. It is cluttered with piles of carrots and bags of tea.

Connects to the Duchess' House and the Mad Hatter's Property.

Box 13: (multi entry)

The Castle is where the Mad Hatter rules in riddles and drinks tea with his companions, the March Hare and the forever sleepy Dormouse. The Hatter gets very few things done but at least he's not running around chopping everyone's head off like the now imprisoned Queen of Hearts did.

In a nice room inside the castle resides the King of Hearts. The Frog Footman runs errands for the Hatter and the Hare, but not very often. The Mad Hatter enjoys watching the Knave of Hearts carry the royal crown, especially in the castle's dungeon where the raving and angry Queen of Hearts sits. (Remember, the Queen accused the Knave of stealing her tarts at one time.)

Box 14: (multi entry)

The Castle's Dungeon is a large room. On one side is a metal-barred prison (room) with a bed, and on the adjacent side is a foyer for visitors and guards to sit at the table or move the chairs toward the prisoner.

Currently, the Queen of Hearts resides here and is visited daily by the Knave of Hearts, who delivers a fresh tart each morning and leaves it on a chair in front of the barred prison just out of reach of the Queen.

The King, who lives in his lofty room upstairs in the castle, has long forgotten his wife and her annoying, belittling behavior toward him.

Box 15: (multi entry)

Gryphon's Mountain Cave. From the mountain cave of the Gryphon (half lion and half eagle) it is just a short trip to proceed to visit the Mock Turtle on his sandy beach upon solving the Gryphon's puzzle.

Box 16: (multi entry)

Mock Turtle's Sandy Beach. The sandy beach area by the sea is where the Mock Turtle lays on a rock sobbing and telling marvelous stories and puns. The Mock Turtle will eventually explain how to defeat the Mad Hatter in a song of riddles.

Possible story lines:

- In the dungeon, Alice learns that the Caterpillar will help her get home.

- The Caterpillar gets Alice to grow tall and a bird whispers to her to visit the Gryphon with a series of answers to the riddles.

- Alice answers the Gryphon's riddles and learns from the Mock Turtle how to defeat the Mad Hatter. Alice wins the caucus race on Alice Tear Lake Island and receives the prized thimble, gathers carrots from the March Hare's Hutch, and steals the Mad Hatter's family tea-cup while avoiding the conflict of the running baby pig and flying objects from the Duchess' house. Finally Alice must confront the March Hare and the Mad Hatter in a tea ceremony with the collected objects to win the game.

Possible endings:

- Alice stays in Wonderland forever.
- Alice returns home in time for her 33rd birthday.
- Alice returns home as a 13-year-old and her mother lives past 33.
- Alice returns home as an 18-year-old and goes to college.
- Alice returns home as a 23-year-old and meets a handsome doctor.
- Alice joins the Queen of Hearts in the dungeon.
- Alice becomes the new Queen of Wonderland.
- Alice goes mad and becomes a wicked witch who gets visited by a girl named Dorothy and her dog Toto (but that's another story).

Nonlinear Game-Oriented Scripting Standard

Since nonlinear or "game-oriented" scripts can jump from scene to scene as the player (now in charge) commands, there must be a way to connect dialogue with the dynamically created story. By labeling each section of dialogue and allowing "condition" comments, we can design our vision using the same scenario with varying responses based on preexisting conditions.

Many RPG and adventure games incorporate dialogue trees or "narrative based on character interaction" that allows the player a selection of relevant topics to speak about with characters and NPCs. This method gives the illusion of intelligent NPCs since there is no repetitive chatter and the conversations focus on current events, important information to tell the player, gossip, rumors, and the latest news.

Label: ALICE-06-001 (Chapter 6, first time)
Condition: Alice enters the Duchess' kitchen (first time).

> ALICE
> Hello. I'm Alice.
> What a nice baby you have.

Label: ALICE-06-002 (Chapter 6, after first time)
Condition: Alice enters the Duchess' kitchen (after first time).

> ALICE
> Hello. Nice to see you again, Duchess.
> My, has the pig, eh…, baby grown.

Label: ALICE-06-005 (Chapter 6, after first time)
Condition: Alice enters the Duchess' kitchen (after first time).

> ALICE
> Hello, again.
> Boy, I sure come here often.
> May I hold the baby?

The dialogue does not follow a linear story; therefore the scripting should follow the game flow and the dialogue should be formatted exactly like a standard script. This technique assures us that the game will have all of the script conditions and voice-over parts to shoot, and that the talent (which we will be working with from outside the gaming industry) will view us as professional and understand the work we need them to perform. By providing our needs in this format, we can get the talent to read their lines based on our game's conditions and accurately estimate the costs for their efforts, and we will have many verbal variations so our game players won't be bored or frazzled by hearing the same repeated dialogue every time they enter the Duchess' kitchen.

Scheduling a Shoot or Voice-Over Session

Scheduling a shoot session is an important and often underappreciated skill that when correctly planned can save a lot of time and money. (Think budget!)

A good method to start the process is to create a table and list all of the actors' (real names if selected) or characters' names in one column followed by each scene and act (by venue/location) in the following columns.

A scheduling example:

Actor Name	Scene					
	1	2	3	4	5	6
Mary	X	-	X	X	X	-
John	-	X	X	X	-	X
Michele	-	X	X	X	-	-
Roger	X	-	-	X	X	-
Brooke	-	-	X	X	X	X
Megan	-	X	X	X	X	-

Now the shoot scheduler must analyze this table of actors or characters along with their scenes.

In the analysis phase of the scheduling using the example, let's examine the scenario where the actor Roger is a famous, award-winning thespian whose work will enhance the sales and marketing of our game. Roger's time is both valuable and expensive compared to the other actors in our shoot.

Ideally, we'd want to shoot his (Roger's) scenes first and work around his schedule. In the example, Roger appears in scenes 1, 4, and 5. Let's look at a shooting schedule that begins on a Monday. Roger's agent tells us that he is only available for one scene a day and is free on Tuesday, Wednesday, and Friday.

In this scenario, we'd shoot the scenes in the following order:
Monday is for shooting Scene 3 (Roger is not available).
Tuesday is for shooting Scene 4 (Roger is available).
Wednesday is for shooting Scene 5 (Roger is available).
Thursday is for shooting Scene 2 (Roger is not available).
Friday is for shooting Scene 1 (Roger is available and finished).
Saturday (last shooting day) is for shooting Scene 6.

This analysis for the schedule would have the following effect:
Mary works on days 1, 2, 3, and 5.
John works on days 1, 2, 4, and 6.
Michele works on days 1, 2, and 4.
Brooke works on days 1, 2, 3, and 6.
Megan works on days 1, 2, 3, and 4.

This schedule accommodates the specific schedule of superstar Roger and tries to minimize the other actors' schedules that may require costly overnight lodging, meals, and transportation. Try to maximize the "act and leave" process and minimize the nonworking ("off") days.

Another criterion to examine is location-dependent situations, such as renting an authentic World War II fighter airplane. Renting such a vehicle might be less expensive in the off season or midweek (on Tuesday through Thursday) since air shows occur on weekends and transporting to the air shows probably occurs on Friday to travel to the show and Monday to return to the "home base."

If a scene needs to be shot with an authentic World War II fighter airplane, then this scene with all of the actors involved would have priority for a scheduled midweek shoot. The earlier the better (like on Tuesday rather than Thursday), since the scene might have to be reshot. (For example, a botched Tuesday shoot could be reshot on Wednesday, whereas a Thursday bad shoot would have to be reshot the following Tuesday and cost more time and money.)

If a venue or location is rented for the day, then all scenes and acts that take place at that venue must be scheduled for that day's shoot. The venue's shoot day is more important than the actors' schedules, and the production scheduler must weigh all of the scenarios and costs involved (actor time and venue and prop rentals) to properly construct the entire production schedule.

During a location shoot, the costly actor's scenes are shot first, followed by the scenes that would dismiss the most actors, so as the day progresses fewer actors remain (aka "act and leave").

When developing a script for cut-scenes, in-game character voices, or cinematics, scheduling included in the design document not only helps the producer and development team but is needed for budgetary considerations such as the number of shoot days, number of actors and crew, location setups (needed actors, crew, and props and equipment), and a fallback or contingency plan for bad weather (such as rain or snow) and absent personnel (such as those who are sick or accidentally detained).

The schedule helps in set building (when needed, transporting the sets), props needed, scheduling rehearsals, and actor stand-ins for camera adjusting and lighting the scene.

There are lots of books on scheduling filming, writing scripts to Hollywood standard format, and storyboarding that you can learn techniques from if your game vision incorporates cinematics, cut-scenes, motion capture, and actors (human and 3D characters and NPCs).

Workshop

Suggested Activities

Discuss the cinematics, cut-scenes, and narration of a current game and how it worked in the game flow and brought the player into the game, or didn't work and could have been better implemented.

Assignments

Assignment 1: Watch a game trailer and write down the dialogue. Discuss how the visual and dialogue in the trailer promote interest in the game.

Assignment 2: Select and combine three genres and write a description of how that game should promote itself in a trailer with suggested visuals and dialogue.

Exercises

Exercise 1: Write the first page (title page) for your game script.

Exercise 2: Select a children's story such as "Goldilocks and the Three Bears," "Little Red Riding Hood," or "Jack and Jill," and write two pages of dialogue using the Hollywood standard script format.

Exercise 3: Using the selected children's story in Exercise 2 ("Goldilocks and the Three Bears," "Little Red Riding Hood," or "Jack and Jill"), write two situations with at least three path options for a game script's dialogue.

Unguided Exercises

Unguided Exercise 1: Write a one-page review of a current game, describing its camera angles, dialogue, sound effects (SFX), and any cut-scenes and cinematics.

Unguided Exercise 2: Write a one-page review of a current game's trailer, describing its camera angles, dialogue, sound effects (SFX), and cinematics.

Internet Reading Assignment

"Writing a Video Game Script" by Keira Peney
http://www.isotx.com/wordpress/?p=225

"PC and NPC Interaction in Video Games" by Keira Peney
http://www.isotx.com/wordpress/?p=471

Chapter 12

Character Design Document

When I worked as producer and codesigner for Acclaim Entertainment on DC Comics' game called Justice League of America, they had a thick book entitled *Who's Who in the DC Universe*. The book contained character profiles that included information such as personal data on the characters (alter ego, occupation, marital status, known relatives, group affiliation, base of operation, height, weight, eye color, and hair color), the background of the character, and descriptions of the character's powers and weapons plus pictures of the character.

In 1998, I designed, produced, and coprogrammed with Michael R. Hausman Big G All-Star Baseball Game for BrandGames' (through Hypnotix) client General Mills. According to Wikipedia (http://en.wikipedia.org/wiki/Advergaming), this game was the first "advergaming" product. Advertised on over sixty million boxes of cereal, General Mills' Big G All-Star Baseball required two box tops and $1 to purchase the CD-ROM. (The first in-box CD-ROM cereal box advergame was Chex brand's Chex Quest, which featured Chex Warrior in a Doom-type scenario battling invaders.)

In designing General Mills' Big G All-Star Baseball, I used professional baseball player statistics such as hits (singles, doubles, triples, home runs), walks, strikeouts, caught hits (pop outs), and pitching or fielding data as well as each player's personal data such as bats (right-side, left-side, or either), catches (right-handed or left-handed), 100-yard dash speed, baseball position, team name, and so on. The 100-yard dash speed was used to calculate running to a base or for moving in the field to catch, throw, or go after the ball.

Since General Mills had no "Who's Who" book about their characters that contained statistical information (data) such as right- or left-handed and baseball stats, we derived the information for each character by combining Major League Baseball player statistics that would be similar to what the character was thought to play like. For the pitchers that had a designated hitter, their statistics were either any previous statistics or their league's average statistics for pitchers.

During the development of the game, a Character Design Document was written and implemented. In the document, all of the General Mills characters were described, along with their baseball statistics as well as the top nine players of every American and National League Baseball team (the collected data used was previously described). Between the innings, other General Mills characters provided entertainment and cheering.

The creation and usage of the Character Design Document helps the artists working on the game, which helps the licensor and publisher to understand the designer's view of the art style and vision. The Character Design Document is created by the Game Designer and updated as 2D and 3D artists provide their concept and model artwork.

This description of part of the information collection process required for a cartoon-based baseball game is included to give you an idea of the information you will need when you begin your own game.

Here's an example of what I mean: In 1996, when I was a Candidate Chess Master (U.S. Chess Federation rating of 2100+), I asked International Chess Grandmaster Sam Reshevsky to play a 45-minute game each week and explain his every move. I wanted to get inside his head to see how top chess players "saw" the board. The rest of this chapter will place you, the reader, inside my head as we look at the Character Design Document for a game that I designed called Bingo Poker.

When creating any design document such as the Game Design Document (GDD) or the Character Design Document (CDD), I suggest surfing the Internet for sample photos and pictures of people, places, backgrounds, and textures. Many online search engines let you set your search for image files relative to what you are looking for.

Bingo Poker

For the game Bingo Poker™ I designed for the casual game market I wanted a background story and interesting opponents to challenge the player.

One creative way to start a game design is to design an advertisement for the game that shows how you think it should be presented to the player.

As a competitive chess player, I am familiar with the process of registering to play in a competition and paying entry fees. I wanted the Bingo Poker player to have a similar setup with a welcome to the competition screen featuring a registration desk and information about the game and fees.

From the main screen, the player can sign up as a new player or select his or her name from a list of registered players. From this main screen, there is access to the trophy case (on the left), a Help tutorial, an Options screen to set options, a Payout link to view the game results point payouts, and a credits screen to give my staff

recognition for their work on the game. Upon successful registration including the player's name and birth date (month and day), the player can compete in a five-round Master's Challenge and a nine-round National Championship Tour, playing against any of the 41 colorful opponents and being romanced by a mysterious "Secret Admirer."

Since casual games (see Chapter 14, "Game Design Outlets") at this time are primarily a gaming outlet dominated by a female audience, I wanted a Harlequin romance, *Sex in the City*, *Cosmopolitan* magazine secret admirer feature (à la Mr. Big and Princess).

The background story told in Bingo Poker's opening animation is as follows:

> Fired from your job for playing Bingo Poker, your skills allow you to enter the five-round Master's Challenge, playing for trophies and the coveted Master's Challenge Champion's Gold Trophy leading to the nine-round National Bingo Poker Championship Tour to earn the National title and a check for $100,000.
>
> Each of the 41 colorful characters challenge the player and increase in competitive strength each round, as wonderful ambient music and film-like sound effects add to the compelling gameplay. Each of the 21 men and 20 women has a personality profile describing their background and interests. The characters are equally diverse in where they live, their nationality, race, and occupation, but all are worthy competitors. Each screen or room has its own unique ambient music and sound effects. Play statistics for each level of skill are saved. In the Trophy Room, the trophy case contains plaques praising these accolades as well as top scoring silver and gold trophies won in tournaments.

The original hand drawn artwork   The in-game artwork with red stapler.

The opening animation features you, the player, playing Bingo Poker at work and setting a new record. An e-mail congratulates you and invites you to join the Bingo Poker National Tour and televised competition. (One of the benefits of being the game designer is being able to put your name and a cartoon image of yourself in the game.)

Just then… your boss, Nodon, walks into your office.

"You're FINISHED!" boss Nodon yells. (What, you want me to get sued by saying "You're FIRED!" This is funnier anyway and may get more press publicity.)

Notice the e-mail message on the computer screen, the coffee cup featuring a spade

design, and a deck of cards on your desk, as well as the designer required *Office Space*'s red Swingline stapler.

I wanted a balanced, diverse group of players containing both genders and all races that any player would respond to visually and personality-wise. When faced with the task of designing characters, I often borrow images and characters from film, music, and television. I want the player to know my character upon sight and by reading their colorful description.

Supplying the game's artist with reference material saves his or her time and the project's budget money because the artist is told what the designer's vision is and can create the art based on that vision.

I listed many well-known female and male stars and people of varying races, and tried to even the demographics of the final selections to be put into the game. I also try not to use too many names starting with the same letter. The names of the characters were taken from books, TV, and films. If you have trouble coming up with names for your game's characters, you can look at lists of names in baby name books or on baby name websites. These sources are especially good for listings of the most popular names over the years and for common foreign names.

From Bingo Poker's original Character Design Document:

> These characters will appear in the Master's Challenge and may be selected as the "Secret Admirer." Depending on the player's gender, the Secret Admirer must be of the opposite gender of the player and not appearing in that game.
>
> The characters will be presented with their biography and before and after each character challenges the player. Each opponent will randomly deliver the first of their trash talk lines (10 or more available lines specifically written for that character) and a player-based astrological line of trash talk.

During the Bingo Poker National Championship, the player will be followed by a Secret Admirer who will send a note after each round describing him or herself, and upon winning the Championship will be revealed along with the check for $100,000. Each Secret Admirer character will have a description to get the player guessing who their admirer is. Also, each character will have at least 10 rant lines (personal sayings) to exclaim to the player after the game of Bingo Poker is over.

When the player registered to compete in Bingo Poker, he or she entered a birth date (month and day). This information allowed me to add astrological information in my game. I believe that there are two ways to control a player's decisions: through positive reinforcement and through negative reinforcement.

If the designer wants the player to enter a room, a computer-controlled character (NPC, or nonplayer character) can praise or intimidate the player by using information based on the player's astrological attributes.

For example, a sexy, attractive character could tell the player that "only *intelligent* or *well groomed* people can enjoy the pleasures inside this room," which might get the player to enter the room. The attributes "intelligent" and "well groomed" would be selected from a list of the player's astrological attributes.

Another example is what I call the "Roxbury Boys Scenario," where an ugly monster or snide character states, "You're *too weak* and *dumb* to pass me and enter the room," which might cause the player to want to triumph over the monster or character by entering the room. The movie *A Night at the Roxbury* featured two "nerds" who wanted to get into clubs and places that excluded or rejected them. The attributes "too weak" and "dumb" could be selected from a list of negative attributes based on the player's astrological sign.

The character descriptions include the character's birthday (month and day and years old, not year of birth, so the player doesn't age as the years go by), right- or left-handed, astrological sign, height, eye color, hair color, and city that they were born in, as well as facts about themselves.

As you read through the character's descriptions and speaking lines, notice the amount of research that went into these areas such as understanding the character's profession, city, and hobbies and using humorous film dialogue based on the actor's films.

A Humorous Story about Bingo Poker Game Mechanics

When the original publisher had signed a contract for Bingo Poker, their legal team asked that the game not have playing cards, since poker cards are equated to gambling and the courts have issues with gambling games. The 52 playing cards were removed and stored for use in other future games. The new game mechanics used a set of dominoes of pink, green, cyan, and yellow that used the first 13 letters of the Phoenician alphabet. Each Phoenician letter also stood for a word such as "aleph" (which means ox), "beth" (which means house), and "gimel" (which means camel). The name of the game was even changed to King Solomon's Squares.

The publisher's QA testers started playing the demo of Bingo Poker/King Solomon's Squares, and after two days reported that the 13 colored dominoes with Phoenician letters seemed to be just like playing cards and questioned why regular playing cards weren't being used. The lawyers checked with the courts, explaining Bingo Poker's multiplayer tournament mode mechanics. In Bingo Poker tournament mode, the publisher's (or portal running the tournament) server shuffles the deck and selects 25 cards, where every player has exactly the same deck to start with. Then each player's deck is shuffled and one card at a time is dealt to the player. The player must freely place that card in any unoccupied (available) square on the 5x5 board. The courts in New York ruled that Bingo Poker tournament mode played for cash prizes is a game of skill as defined by the aforementioned game mechanics.

Later, the original publisher went out of business as a publisher and returned all rights to the developer. (Lesson: Never throw away art assets and never underestimate the QA testers' findings!)

Bingo Poker Characters

Fabio Balboa

One of the male characters I designed was a combination of Rocky Balboa and the male supermodel Fabio, whom I named "Fabio Balboa." As you read this sentence, you are picturing this character based on those characteristics, which makes his design and recognition easy.

The artist, Gifny Richata, was given photos of Sylvester Stallone as Rocky Balboa and Fabio and asked to merge the two based on the biography of Fabio Balboa.

From the author's personal movie memorabilia photo collection. Press Kit SS4B1. (c) 1976

From the author's personal movie memorabilia photo collection.

Fabio Balboa is described as:

A one-time boxing champion who has traded in striking opponents for striking a pose as the first male supermodel. Balboa was born with natural athletic talent and street smarts rather than intellectual smarts. With his muscular physique and an unbroken nose, Fabio and his patient acting coach struggled through and made several national TV commercials, which turned into a contract to model sportswear. Today, Fabio Balboa can be seen swaggering across the stages modeling for workout magazines and fitness ads. In his spare time, Balboa plays tic-tac-toe and has hired a Bingo Poker trainer since boxing has left him punchy. Can you believe Fabio is still single?

Fabio Balboa has the following hints as a Secret Admirer:

Birthday: July 6, Age: 40, Birthplace: Philadelphia, PA, Height: 5' 10",
Handed: Right, Hair Color: Blond, Eye Color: Blue,
Occupation: Model and Ex-Boxer, Work Town: Philadelphia, PA

- I was born under the sign of Cancer.
- I like to oil paint and admire the work of Leonardo da Vinci.
- I like to fight and dance.
- I'm not handsome in the classical sense.
- I do enjoy a good cigar and "Bollywood" movies.
- I jog 10 miles every day.
- I have an athletic build.
- I'm a tic-tac-toe champion.
- I like to eat meat after I pound it.
- Sometimes I'm driven to get Carter.
- I often say life's a cliffhanger.

Fabio Balboa has the following trash talk/personal sayings (I obviously watch a lot of films):

- Women weaken legs!
- I just want to say hi to my ex-girlfriend, okay?
- Who am I kiddin'? I ain't even in this person's league.
- I feel like a Kentucky Fried idiot.
- Do you like having a good time? Then you need a good watch!
- Was ya ever punched in the face 500 times a night? It stings after a while, ya know.
- I won! But I didn't beat him!
- You don't look so bad to me.
- You ain't so bad, you ain't so bad, you ain't nothin'.
- Nature's smarter than people think.
- This ain't no pie eating contest.

The animations needed while the character is playing Bingo Poker are playing, thinking, and looking in a sequence (e.g., play, think, play, look, play).

Play animation sequence:

Think animation sequence:

Look animation sequence:

Besides these animations, each character has a "greet," a "win," and a "loss" animation.

Upon meeting the player, each character displays a five-frame "greet" animation sequence.

If Fabio Balboa beats the player, his five-frame "win" animation sequence is displayed.

If Fabio Balboa loses to the player, his five-frame "loss" animation sequence is displayed.

Johnny Rocket

The character "Johnny Rocket" is described as:

> Johnny Rocket is known for two activities: winning car races and eating hamburgers. Johnny is an adrenaline junkie and quite the ladies' man. Johnny says, "Give me a fast car or a fast woman and I'm in love." Johnny Rocket loves danger as he travels around the country and internationally looking for the perfect bridge to bungee jump from, the perfect building to BASE jump off, and that treacherous cliff to climb up. As a teenager, Johnny wore silver-colored braces, played the violin, and took ballet lessons. People are amused that Johnny dropped out of Harvey University Law School a week before graduation, then broke his leg in the World Championship Skateboard Triathlon in California. Can Rocket find a copilot in his life?

Johnny Rocket was based on Johnny Knoxville, star of *The Dukes of Hazzard*, along with a humorous association with a burger franchise and with "Rocket" as a race car driver's last name.

From the author's personal movie memorabilia photo collection.

Our artist created the race car driver Johnny Rocket to look more like Danny Zuko of *Grease* or "The Fonz" of *Happy Days*. My original vision was of a race car driver wearing a jacket covered with sponsor logos, but we decided that using actual logos might lead to legal and trademark problems. To solve this problem I searched the Internet for a suitable race car driver type of jacket and found one that featured an American flag. The artist then transferred the new American flag jacket onto Johnny Rocket and his animation sequences.

Johnny Rocket has the following hints as a Secret Admirer:

Birthday: March 11, Age: 37, Birthplace: Knoxville, TN, Height: 6' 1", Handed: Right, Hair Color: Brown, Eye Color: Blue, Occupation: Race Car Driver, Work Town: Indianapolis, IN

- I was born under the sign of Pisces.
- I suffer from asthma.
- My dad wanted me to take over his used car dealership.
- I have a scar on my head from getting punched by a professional heavyweight boxer.
- I loved the TV show *Hazzard County Dukes* and the Three Stooges.
- In one week as a child, I had the flu, pneumonia, and bronchitis.
- I played the violin and love Bach's Sonata No. 5 in F minor.
- I can do pirouettes and grand-pliés.
- I have beautiful, straight, white teeth from years of wearing silver-colored braces.
- On a dare, I bungee jumped down the Hoover Dam.
- I went BASE jumping off of Italy's Leaning Tower of Pisa.
- I've climbed El Capitan in Yosemite National Park, California.
- I destroyed the LSATs and then did it to Harvey University's law school.
- After I won the World Championship Skateboard Triathlon, I said "Tony who?"

Captain Richard Kelly

Another character was Captain Richard Kelly (based on Nicholas Cage), described as:

> Airline pilot Captain Richard Kelly is the major airline's most senior pilot. After a stressful day of flying coast to coast, Kelly enjoys relaxing by playing handheld video games and Bingo Poker. Captain Kelly spends his vacations either visiting famous cities and venues such as Philadelphia's Independence Hall, San Francisco's Alcatraz, Las Vegas, Manhattan, and Brooklyn or traveling by ship on luxury cruises. Captain Richard Kelly learned to fly in the Air Force and was stationed in Italy for four years. In Italy, Richard learned to play the mandolin and became passionate about Italian opera like Verdi's *Rigoletto*. Captain Kelly has an empty right seat in his love life as he is always looking for that perfect "copilot."

[Notice the references to the films of Nicholas Cage. Players knowledgeable about the film will enjoy the charming attention of these references and the other players will appreciate the colorful character comments.]

The original artwork of Captain Richard Kelly (on the left) did not show the pocket emblem or the correct number of stripes on the sleeves. The photo of an actual airline pilot helped the artist draw a more realistic version of Captain Richard Kelly.

Captain Richard Kelly has the following hints as a Secret Admirer:

Birthday: January 7, Age: 44, Birthplace: Bronx, NY,
Height: 6' 1", Handed: Right, Hair Color: Brown, Eye Color: Blue,
Occupation: Airline Pilot, Work Town: Fort Worth, TX

- I was born under the sign of Capricorn.
- I enjoy playing handheld video games like Tattoo Lizard and Dinner Man.
- I enjoy visiting Philadelphia's Independence Hall, the Liberty Bell, and the Betsy Ross House.
- Each year, I visit San Francisco's Alcatraz, or "The Rock," the wharfs, and the wine country.

Chapter 12

- In Las Vegas, I let my dice fly over the craps table before I leave.
- When I fly to JFK Airport, I spend a few days in Manhattan visiting the museums and old churches.
- For one week a year, I travel by ship on a luxury cruise to venues like Brazil and Europe.
- I've learned to never break up with a flight attendant when she's carrying hot coffee.
- I flew an F-18 Hornet in the Air Force.
- I was stationed in Italy for four years and would like to say to you *"ti amo con tutto il cuore."*
- In Italy, I learned to play the mandolin and wrote you a song.
- I am passionate about Italian opera like Verdi's *Rigoletto*.

Dr. Drake Ramore

The description of successful Dr. Drake Ramore (based on the soap opera character played by Joey (Matt LeBlanc) on the TV show *Friends*) is:

Dr. Drake Ramore is a Beverly Hills doctor with a promising practice in plastic surgery.

Dr. Ramore's client list reads like a "Who's Who" in Hollywood. His waiting room is harder to get into than the Academy Awards. Drake enjoys swimming and can often be seen playing golf or tennis with his celebrity friends and patients. Drake was an extremely overweight adolescent who lost over 80 pounds through dieting, a gastric bypass, and liposuction. Dr. Ramore frequently dances and drinks the night away at LA's private clubs where he mingles and parties with his friends as well as his current and future patients. Will there ever be amore for Ramore?

The original artwork of Dr. Drake Ramore (on the left) did not show the elegant and expensive suit that one would expect a single doctor in Beverly Hills to wear. A modern suit worn by a model found on the Internet helps give a better impression and style for Dr. Drake Ramore.

Dr. Drake Ramore has the following hints as a Secret Admirer:

Birthday: July 25, Age: 41, Birthplace: Bronx, NY,
Height: 5' 10", Handed: Right, Hair Color: Brown, Eye Color: Brown,
Occupation: Doctor, Plastic Surgeon, Work Town: Beverly Hills, CA

- I was born under the sign of Leo.
- I was an obese child.
- While in college, I worked as a male model.
- I have a license as a carpenter.
- I enjoy the thrill of parachute jumping and car racing.
- I like to relax with my good friends at a coffeehouse.
- I enjoy photographing landscapes and animals.
- I vacationed in Australia last year and ate kangaroo.
- I really like the half hour comedy.
- I love eating nacho chips and drinking cola.
- Sometimes I feel that I'm lost in space.
- I enjoy dancing and partying.
- I swim 20 laps every day.
- I love playing tennis and golf.

As I previously mentioned, I based the characters in Bingo Poker on famous people and sent the character artist many sample photos of the uniforms or clothing that they should be wearing. I wanted the artist to create his interpretation of the famous person rather than an exact but cartoonish version of the person. In many casual games, the players do enjoy cartoonish characters such as in Diner Dash's Flo and Cake Mania's Jill.

Diner Dash is a registered trademark of PlayFirst, Inc. Cake Mania is a trademark of Sandlot Games.

Following are samples of some of the other characters from Bingo Poker.

[Note that at the request of one publisher that I was dealing with on Bingo Poker, the names of colleges and companies were changed into puns. Also notice the references to the colorful characters, especially relating to their "based on" personality.]

Ariel Nikon

(Based on Tyra Banks, model and TV talk show host)

[The last name, Nikon, was an attempt at humor for a professional photographer's name.]

Professional photographer Ariel Nikon has graced the covers of numerous magazines with her photos of models and exotic locations. Ms. Nikon is involved in all aspects of the production of daily photo shoots including acquiring the talent, contracting and hiring the models and negotiating with their management, and location and model scouting. Ariel selects and assembles the needed equipment according to the day's shoot, the anticipated weather conditions, and the functions and limitations of the various cameras, their lenses, and accessories. Ms. Nikon measures the light level and uses lighting equipment or flash units if needed. Will the darkroom of Ms. Ariel Nikon's love life be illuminated and developed into a picture-perfect photo album of love?

Ariel Nikon has the following hints as a Secret Admirer:

Birthday: December 4, Age: 38, Birthplace: Baltimore, MD, Height: 5' 11", Handed: Right, Hair Color: Brown, Eye Color: Brown, Occupation: Photographer, Work Town: New York, NY

- I was born under the sign of Sagittarius.
- I wear a size nine shoe.
- I do not drink alcohol.
- At 13 years old, I was 5 feet, 7 inches tall.
- At 12 years old, I was 50 pounds overweight.
- I was on the TV show *America's Top Model Photographers*.

- I love sports and going to basketball games or watching basketball on TV.
- I love sports and going to baseball games or watching baseball on TV.
- I enjoy reading mystery books.
- I am an amateur astronomer and own a powerful telescope.
- I like to visit the planetarium and can spend hours in the observatory.
- Every night, I stare at the stars and wish for you.
- I enjoy traveling and I want you as my traveling companion.
- I picture us together forever, constantly developing.

Aries Warmonger

(Based on Dwayne "The Rock" Johnson and Colin Powell)

A New York Military Academy graduate with top honors, General Aries Warmonger climbed through the ranks during three tours of duty and by using his diplomatic skills in several treaty negotiations. As the oldest son of a Naval Admiral, rebellious Aries elected to attend the Military Academy in New York. Army Cadet Warmonger majored in engineering and excelled as the school's top athlete, participating in football, wrestling, and shot putting on the track team. When his busy schedule permits, General Aries Warmonger enjoys playing first-person shooter video games and tournament Bingo Poker. General Warmonger has never been defeated but longs for someone to capture his heart.

[General Colin Powell's uniform is shown on the right as a military uniform reference. Also note the name Aries, a variation for the God of War, and Warmonger, a humorous attempt at a last name.]

Aries Warmonger has the following hints as a Secret Admirer:

Birthday: May 2, Age: 45, Birthplace: Annapolis, MD,
Height: 6' 4", Handed: Right, Hair Color: Brown, Eye Color: Brown,
Occupation: U.S. Army General, Work Town: East Point, GA

- I was born under the sign of Taurus.
- My dad was a Naval Admiral. I say "Go Army!"

Chapter 12

- I played QB and tight end in college football.
- I enjoy karate, wrestling, and shot putting.
- I love video games, especially Bingo Poker and Doomination.
- In wrestling, I invented the "Rock Elbow" maneuver.
- My college alumni include Ulysses S. Grant, Stonewall Jackson, and Robert E. Lee.
- My college alumni include Bradley, Eisenhower, MacArthur, Pershing, and Patton.
- I am a huge fan of the Marx Brothers and the Three Stooges.
- Although in great shape, I have a weakness for donuts.
- I am a skilled sharpshooter and light tackle saltwater fisherman.

Dr. Ashley Suuri

(Based on Lucy Liu)

[In Japanese, "suuri" means "mathematical principle."]

Dr. Ashley Suuri is a professor of applied mathematics at the Institute of Technology and committee head of the Program in Mathematics for graduate and undergraduate students. Dr. Suuri received her bachelor's degree from Barnyard College and her master's and Ph.D. from New York College. Ashley is a member of American Mathematics Society and officer and member of American Females in Mathematics. The magazine *U.S. Mathematics* named Dr. Suuri the top innovator for her theories and she won the prestigious Isaac Newton Award and the Euclid Plaque in Advanced Geometric Mathematics. Do the numbers add up for Ashley to find her equal?

[I wanted Ashley to have an Asian look, so placing a kimono-like outfit on her helps give this impression to the player.]

Ashley Suuri has the following hints as a Secret Admirer:

Birthday: December 3, Age: 40, Birthplace: San Francisco, CA, Height: 5' 3", Handed: Right, Hair Color: Black, Eye Color: Brown, Occupation: Mathematics Professor, Work Town: Cambridge, MA

- I was born under the sign of Virgo.
- I speak fluent Mandarin Chinese… *Wo ie ni.*
- As a child, I learned to play the accordion.
- I enjoy amusement parks and rock climbing.
- Every winter, I go to Vail and spend days skiing.
- My hobbies include being an equestrian.
- I enjoy competitive backgammon and chess.
- I go to Vegas and Reno to play roulette and craps.
- I create Sudoku puzzles for newspapers.
- I cannot cook but can microwave popcorn and pizza.

Chaz Rivers

(Based on Justin Timberlake)

Fitness center and health club owner and personal trainer Chaz Rivers trains a diverse clientele with goals such as fat reduction, body shaping, and improved sports performance. Chaz Rivers received his M.Ed. in exercise physiology and sports administration. The Rivers gym is over 12,000 square feet, and has a fully-equipped weight training gym featuring the best in virtually every type of state-of-the-art training equipment. Besides being a black belt in Tae Kwon Do and a competitive aerobics competitor, Chaz teaches toning, kickboxing, aerobics, box aerobics, and yoga. He is an XYZ Certified Senior Fitness and an ABC Certified Personal Trainer. In college and high school, Chaz participated in baseball, football, soccer, wrestling, cross-country, tennis, golf, and bowling. Can a female personally train Chaz Rivers to improve his lonely, unloved cardiovascular muscle and like a black belt sweep him off his feet?

Chaz Rivers has the following hints as a Secret Admirer:

Birthday: January 31, Age: 37, Birthplace: Memphis, TN, Height: 6' 1", Handed: Left, Hair Color: Blond, Eye Color: Blue, Occupation: Fitness Club Owner, Work Town: Boise, ID

- I was born under the sign of Aquarius.

- I teach and actively compete in aerobics to keep in excellent shape.
- I am a black belt in Tae Kwon Do and practice kickboxing.
- To relax, I practice yoga and box aerobics.
- I sing and enjoy bass fishing.
- In school, I was the pitcher on the baseball team.
- In school, I played quarterback on the football team.
- In college, I played goalie on the soccer team.
- In school, I wrestled and ran cross country.
- I enjoy playing golf, tennis, and bowling a few games.
- I exercise and tone my body so it is in sync with my intelligent mind.

Professor Daniel Potter

(Based on Sean Connery, the name is a combination of Daniel Radcliffe and Harry Potter)

Mystery book author Professor Daniel Potter consistently has his books on the top 10 best-selling lists. When not on his world wide book tours, Daniel resides in his New Hampshire log cabin located on prime deepwater frontage or his prestigious Scottish estate of 105 acres of stunning wooded sheep farm with a lake and lush green highlands. Professor Potter gained worldwide recognition when his book *Soup Questions* won a Paul Litzer Prize. Professor Daniel Potter speaks, reads, and writes in several languages besides English including French, Scottish, Latin, Russian, and Greek. Daniel enjoys sitting in front of his fireplace reading a good book and sipping bourbon. Can a "woman in red" intrigue Daniel and rewrite the next chapter in his life?

Daniel Potter has the following hints as a Secret Admirer:

Birthday: August 25, Age: 58, Birthplace: Edinburgh, Scotland, Height: 6' 2", Handed: Left, Hair Color: Gray, Eye Color: Brown, Occupation: Author, Work Town: Nashua, NH

- I was born under the sign of Virgo.

- I enjoy the foliage and the White Mountains of New Hampshire.
- I own a prestigious Scottish estate situated among medieval abbeys, great gardens, and magnificent castles.
- In French, I'll say *"je t'aime."*
- I'd like to say in Scottish, *"tha gradh agam ort."*
- In Latin, I'd look at you and whisper *"te amo."*
- In Russian, I'd kiss you and say *"ya tyebya lyublyu."*
- If it's Greek to me then I'd look into your eyes and say *"Eime eroteumenos me 'sena."*
- Romance to me is lying next to a roaring fire, reading a good book, and sipping bourbon.
- I entered the Mr. Universe contest, finishing third in the tall man's division.
- I enjoy reading Fleming's spy novels.
- While in college, I worked as a coffin polisher and a milk delivery man.

Donna Dallas

(Based on Beyonce Knowles)

Fashion designer Donna Dallas is from Omaha, NE, where her fashion preferences were jeans and boots. Her love for fashion magazines led her to New York's School of Design, and she interned at KDNY. Her designs caught the eye of CEO Karen Diaz, and Donna's designs ended up being in the KDNY fall collection. Upon graduation, Ms. Dallas was offered the position of assistant designer, but since every design Donna Dallas created was revolutionary, she quickly became a senior designer with her own line called "Dallas." Donna Dallas has been tearing up the runways in New York, Paris, and London with her wild fashions and rumors of her passionate flings with rock stars and blue-collar Joes. Donna needs a man who will be more than an accessory to walk down the bridal runway with her as well as attend fashion shows and Broadway plays and go horseback riding.

Donna Dallas has the following hints as a Secret Admirer:

Birthday: September 4, Age: 31, Birthplace: Omaha, NE,
Height: 5' 7", Handed: Right, Hair Color: Brown, Eye Color: Brown,
Occupation: Fashion Designer, Work Town: New York, NY

- I was born under the sign of Virgo.
- I love and own a few cats.
- I am allergic to perfume.
- I read and speak French fluently.
- I'm teaching myself Italian and Japanese.
- Can I take you to Paris or Milan next week for a fashion show?
- I rather date you than any rock star I've bonked.
- I love attending plays in New York City and London.
- I go to a lot of loud rock concerts and get VIP backstage passes.
- I enjoy going horseback riding on country trails.
- I like weekending in New England during foliage season.

Elizabeth Julia

(Based on Jennifer Lopez)

TV sportscaster Elizabeth Julia works for the National Sports Channel in Charlotte, NC, where she grew up as the daughter of sports legend Coach Julia. Coach Julia was a pro-football quarterback who went on to coach for the University of North Carolina's football team and was the director of the Atlanta Olympics. From an early age, Elizabeth was inside the announcer's booth and added her young commentary to college football games and worked at the Atlanta Olympics as a sportscaster for women's gymnastics and basketball. After receiving her communications degree from the University of Noted Dames and being the "Voice of the Fighting Irish" at their football, basketball, and baseball games, the National Sports Channel hired Ms. Julia to anchor and sports report in her hometown of Charlotte, NC. Will every man strike out with Elizabeth?

Is there any man confident and sports minded enough to score her heart?

Elizabeth Julia has the following hints as a Secret Admirer:

Birthday: July 24, Age: 38, Birthplace: Charlotte, NC,
Height: 5' 6", Handed: Right, Hair Color: Brown, Eye Color: Brown,
Occupation: Television Sportscaster, Work Town: Charlotte, NC

- I was born under the sign of Leo.
- My grandparents were from Ponce in Puerto Rico.
- I enjoy eating Mexican and Cuban food.
- In high school, my nickname was "Super Nova."
- I speak fluent Spanish… *"Te amo."*
- I do not drink alcohol.
- I wear a size six sneaker.
- Love me and love sports.
- I am a "Fighting Irish" Latino looking for my number one draft choice.
- At work, I'm an aggressive bitch, but at home I want to be all yours, coach.
- I want a confident, intelligent man of any size and age.

Dr. Emily "Jersey" Jones

(Based on Pam Anderson and Indiana Jones)

Archeologist and relic hunter Dr. Emily "Jersey" Jones received her doctorate in anthropology from Princetown University in New Jersey. Having the last name "Jones," it wasn't long before her colleagues nicknamed her "Jersey" Jones. Currently a professor who teaches graduate students when she's not globetrotting in search of relics for museums, "Jersey" Jones enjoys rock climbing, jogging 10 miles every day, and working out in her karate dojo. Dr. Jones went on an archeology dig in Peru, where it is believed that King Solomon sent two fleets to the biblical city of Ophir — the site of King Solomon's gold mines — and discovered containers of gold with Phoenician and Hebrew writing on them. Can any man provide fortune and glory, entitling their story "Jersey Jones and the Love Crusade"?

[She is a sexy, female version of Indiana Jones complete with the brown felt hat.]

Dr. Emily "Jersey" Jones has the following hints as a Secret Admirer:

Birthday: July 1, Age: 41, Birthplace: Vancouver, Canada,
Height: 5' 7", Handed: Right, Hair Color: Blond, Eye Color: Blue,
Occupation: Professor and Archeologist, Work Town: Edison, NJ

- I was born under the sign of Cancer.
- I am a vegetarian but I will eat fish and eggs.
- I am an animal rights activist.
- I do not wear or buy fur.
- At bars, I prefer Canadian beers.
- I listen to the music of Bob Dylan and Mick Jagger.
- I speak several old languages such as Greek, Latin, Egyptian, and Hebrew.
- I speak many modern languages including Japanese and Russian.
- I enjoy rock climbing, scuba diving, and skydiving.
- I jog 10 miles every day.
- I work out in a karate dojo and specialize in weapons.

Ethan Wong

(Based on a young Jackie Chan)

San Francisco restaurateur and Food Channel's master chef Ethan Wong is a state-of-the-art chef known for his cutting-edge Chinese cuisine and for his sauces.

Elegance in Wong's cooking and his presentation is important in preparing exquisite meals served on Wedgwood china shown on TV or in his highly acclaimed restaurant in the Bay City. Ethan enjoys singing and playing the guitar. When Ethan Wong is not visiting the Sonoma and Napa vineyards, he competes in domino and Bingo Poker tournaments or watches martial arts films starring Bruce Lee and Van Damme. Will Ethan Wong's fortune cookie read "Love is just around the corner"?

Ethan Wong has the following hints as a Secret Admirer:

Birthday: April 7, Age: 52, Birthplace: San Francisco, CA,
Height: 5' 9", Handed: Left, Hair Color: Brown, Eye Color: Brown,
Occupation: Restaurateur and TV Chef, Work Town: San Francisco, CA

- I was born under the sign of Aries.
- I enjoy watching martial arts films and Kung Fu shows.
- I take vocal lessons and enjoy singing in the kitchen and in the shower.
- On some weekends, you can find me by the bay playing my guitar and singing.
- I often travel sideways to Sonoma and Napa to taste the wines that I'll serve.
- I can be seen in Chinatown playing dominoes and Go.
- I want to give your mouth a special Chinese treat.
- I can be seen in your home every day… on the Food Channel.
- I speak and write in Chinese just like my cooking… in Mandarin and Cantonese.

Madison St. Claire

(Based on Jessica Simpson)

Belgian chocolates were once the height of premium chocolate before the creation of C&Y Bars. Madison St. Claire began her chocolate and confectionary business in a small storefront on the Virginia Beach boardwalk where she made and sold every C&Y Bar and other candies. Once film star and chocoholic Johnny Wilder put chocolate C&Y Bars in his Motion Picture Award winning film, people from all over the world started ordering C&Y Bars by the caseload. Soon Ms. St. Claire had to enlarge her operations and opened a C&Y Bar factory. *Chocolate Lovers Magazine* awarded chocolate C&Y Bars its top accolades and declared them "the best chocolates in the world." Is there a special someone who can give Madison the ingredients for romance, melting her heart and giving her a rich, dark, mouth-watering kiss?

[Notice the chocolate bar-shaped C&Y earrings and the revealing, bright-colored clothes.]

Madison St. Claire has the following hints as a Secret Admirer:

Birthday: July 10, Age: 38, Birthplace: Hershey, PA,
Height: 5' 3", Handed: Left, Hair Color: Blond, Eye Color: Blue,
Occupation: Chocolatier, Work Town: Virginia Beach, VA

- I was born under the sign of Cancer.
- I love receiving pink roses.
- I had Lasik eye surgery and can see you perfectly.
- I love animals and own a small dog.
- Can I give you my sweet kisses?
- Looking for a man to make me scream "I wanna love you forever!"
- I collect fashion dolls.
- I enjoy singing, especially while jogging or driving my sports car.
- I go to Japanese sushi restaurants often.
- I love the ocean and would love for you to see me in a bikini.
- I want a sweet, intelligent man for my life partner.
- A man with a good sense of humor makes my head spin.

Olivia Bloom

(Based on Penelope Cruz)

Olivia Bloom is a CPA for a top accounting firm and the daughter of well-known CPA Leo Bloom. Olivia supported herself through college working as a model. Her interest bearing figure has many clients wanting to show her their assets. Inside that gorgeous head is a brilliant mind and number-cruncher that makes Ms. Bloom an outstanding accountant. Olivia's hobbies include Scrabble, tournament Bingo Poker, and chess and she's an amazing billiards player. Olivia studied classical ballet for over nine years and her father taught her how to repair and maintain an automobile. Ms. Bloom speaks Spanish and Greek fluently. Will Olivia Bloom find a man in which to invest her time and analyze his portfolio with a smile?

[Comment: The surname Bloom came from Mel Brooks' *The Producers*]

Olivia Bloom has the following hints as a Secret Admirer:

Birthday: April 28, Age: 39, Birthplace: Santa Fe, NM,
Height: 5' 5", Handed: Right, Hair Color: Brown, Eye Color: Brown,
Occupation: CPA (Accountant), Work Town: Albuquerque, NM

- I was born under the sign of Taurus.
- Besides English, I speak fluent Spanish and Greek.
- I enjoy playing Scrabble and chess but want a partner.
- I play competitive bridge and need a partner, not a dummy.
- In college, I did some modeling for fashion magazines and catalogs.
- As a youth, I studied classical ballet for over nine years.
- I am an amazing billiards player, winning several tournaments and hustling many guys in bars.
- My father taught me how to repair and maintain an automobile.
- I'm looking for an honest man who doesn't itemize.
- I don't date actors or producers.

Congresswoman Penelope Park

(Based on Tia Carrere)

Congresswoman Penelope Park is a Democrat from Cleveland representing the 10th District of Ohio in the United States House of Representatives. Penelope Park received her bachelor's degree from Ohio State College and her master's in public administration (finance & budget) from Kennel College. Congresswoman Park serves on the Committee of Financial Services and chairs the Financial Services' Subcommittee Financial Institutions and Consumer Credit, which focuses on banks, depository institutions, deposit insurance, and the overall safety and soundness of the banking system. Congresswoman Park often speaks to the Cleveland Women Voters, the Ohio Businessperson's Association, the Ohio Agricultural Trade Commission, and Cleveland's City Club. Congresswoman Penelope Park is a member of

the Ohio Women's Hall of Fame. She enjoys singing and reading and is an avid skier and twin engine pilot.

[Notice the American flag lapel pin and neutral, gray suit.]

Penelope Park has the following hints as a Secret Admirer:

Birthday: January 2, Age: 41, Birthplace: Cleveland, OH, Height: 5' 8", Handed: Right, Hair Color: Brown, Eye Color: Brown, Occupation: Congresswoman, Work Town: Washington, DC

- ■ I was born under the sign of Capricorn.
- ■ I was born a Buckeye.
- ■ I climbed Campbell Hill.
- ■ My father owned a farm and raised corn and wheat.
- ■ I am a huge advocate of women's issues.
- ■ I sing for charity and at karaoke bars.
- ■ I enjoy reading several newspapers every day.
- ■ I am an avid skier and enjoy tango dancing under the stars.
- ■ I take flying lessons and own a twin-engine airplane.
- ■ I am learning ballroom and Latin dancing but need a steady partner.
- ■ At Kennel College, I was the student body president and the sorority president.

Ryan Getty

(Based on Owen Wilson)

Texas cattle rancher and oil tycoon Ryan Getty resides on 10,000 acres outside Houston with his two dogs. He has an in-ground Olympic swimming pool and hot tub, tennis courts, and a heliport complete with his own helicopter. Getty's estate has fenced pastures, three ponds, and two live creeks. Ryan's large herd of cattle and dozens of horses graze alongside his 20 oil rigs. Every morning Ryan rides his horse alongside his ranch hands to round up and inspect the cattle herd. Ryan can still rope and tag with the best wranglers, riding western saddle or bareback. Twice a week, Ryan Getty inspects his entire operation as he

pilots his own helicopter. Ryan Getty serves on the prestigious board of directors for the Texas Oil Association. Is there a woman who can reach "deep in the heart" of Texan Getty?

[Notice the typical cowboy hat for single stallions and the string tie.]

Ryan Getty has the following hints as a Secret Admirer:

Birthday: November 18, Age: 45, Birthplace: Houston, TX,
Height: 5' 11", Handed: Right, Hair Color: Blond, Eye Color: Blue,
Occupation: Cattle Rancher/Oil Tycoon, Work Town: Houston, TX

- I was born under the sign of Scorpio.
- I'm a huge John Wayne movie fan.
- I support the arts such as the rodeo.
- I own two dogs who love to roam my cattle ranch.
- I enjoy fishing in my three ponds and two live creeks.
- I need a partner for Wednesday night line dancing.
- I enjoy swimming laps in my Olympic swimming pool.
- After a hard day, a relaxing soak in the hot tub while drinking whiskey is pacifying.
- A few sets of tennis is a great way to burn off my chef's gourmet barbeque lunch.
- I enjoy riding one of my stallions amongst the herds of cattle at dawn.
- I wish to rope and tag you instead of one of my prized cattle.
- If you'd like to see my entire ranch, we could fly around it in my helicopter.
- I go to Houston often to attend the Texas Oil Association's Directors meetings.

Tyler Franks

(Based on Tyson Beckford)

Sports agent Tyler Franks has seen the money and represents superstars and supermodels. "Bo not only knows Tyler" but has Tyler on speed dial. Tyler has clients on every channel, field, court, and racetrack. At Twolane University, Tyler played varsity baseball as the starting shortstop, played soccer as a halfback, and ran the 400-meter solo and relay races. After two years of starting for North Carolina's triple-A baseball team as shortstop and never getting to the "show," Tyler Franks joined Maguire's Sports Management International as an associate sports agent. Now, Tyler Franks is at the top of his game as senior vice president and the sports world's most well-known agent and negotiator. Will some lady "complete him"?

Tyler Franks has the following hints as a Secret Admirer:

Birthday: December 19, Age: 38, Birthplace: Alpharetta, GA, Height: 6' 2", Handed: Left, Hair Color: Brown, Eye Color: Brown, Occupation: Sports Agent, Work Town: Atlanta, GA

- I was born under the sign of Sagittarius.
- I enjoy shopping to buy expensive clothes and shoes.
- I party with super athletes and the beautiful people.
- In high school, I was voted "the most likely to succeed."
- I earned an athletic scholarship to Twolane University.
- At Twolane University, I played starting shortstop on the varsity baseball team.
- At Twolane University, I played starting halfback on the varsity soccer team.
- At Twolane University, I ran track, participating in the 400-meter solo and relay races.
- For two years, I played triple-A baseball in North Carolina.
- I am a romantic and always go after what I desire.
- In a relationship, I always say "Show me some loving, honey!"

District Attorney Venus Vette

(Based on Halle Berry)

Jacksonville District Attorney Venus Vette represents the state of Florida in criminal cases and works with Jacksonville law enforcement officers in the investigation and preparation of cases to be heard before the criminal courts. D.A. Venus Vette received her Juris Doctor degree from Pennsylvania's Villiansover University School of Law. D.A. Vette is a member of the Florida District Attorney's Association, an officer in the Jacksonville County Bar Association, and an active member in Florida's Violence Against Women Association. D.A. Venus Vette speaks conversational Spanish, enjoys boating, is a certified scuba diver, and jogs 10 miles every morning before work. If any man steals D.A. Venus Vette's heart, she might give him life as her husband.

Venus Vette has the following hints as a Secret Admirer:

Birthday: August 14, Age: 40, Birthplace: Philadelphia, PA, Height: 5' 7", Handed: Left, Hair Color: Brown, Eye Color: Brown, Occupation: District Attorney, Work Town: Jacksonville, FL

- I was born under the sign of Leo.
- I am lactose intolerant.
- In high school, I was the honor society president.
- I was the high school prom queen.
- I was the captain of the cheerleading squad.
- I speak conversational Spanish.
- My word is my bond. I'll always be a jinx to you.
- I enjoy vacationing in the Caribbean and going scuba diving to explore the coral reefs.
- On weekends, I enjoy cruising in my boat and catching some sun in my sexy bikini.
- I enjoy sitting patiently with my cats.
- I want a perfect lover, not a perfect stranger.
- I love storms, especially lightning storms.
- I jog over 10 miles to work each morning, then shower and change clothes there.

Zip Martin

(Based on the Ewan McGregor character in *Down with Love*)

Zip Martin works at the National Space Program as a scientist and dreams of someday traveling to Jupiter. Zip is a shy bachelor who loves *War of the Stars*, especially episode 3. As a teenager, Zip visited Cape Canaveral, FL, and got stuck inside a space simulator ride for hours. From that moment, Zip Martin vowed he'd one day become a "rocket scientist." Zip studied astronomy and computers, and became a ham radio operator and earned a "technician class" license. Zip Martin's ham radio call sign is "AP11NA," which Zip proudly claims is short for "Apollo 11 Neil Armstrong." Zip Martin received both a BS and an MS in engineering from Pittsburgh's Carnegie Watermellon University. Zip

Martin hopes to meet his Venus if he can get his head out of the clouds long enough.

Zip Martin has the following hints as a Secret Admirer:

Birthday: March 31, Age: 41, Birthplace: Corpus Christi, TX, Height: 5' 10", Handed: Right, Hair Color: Red, Eye Color: Green, Occupation: Astro-Scientist, Work Town: Houston, TX

- I was born under the sign of Aries.
- In college, I took up space studies.
- I like to use Morse code.
- I traveled to France last year.
- I wanted to become an Air Force pilot but I wear glasses.
- I ride motorcycles and go on long rides around the country.
- I have parachuted and climbed high mountains.
- I love science fiction, especially George's *War of the Stars* films.
- I like vacationing on the island.
- I collect gnomes.

Lord Nigel Smythe

Lord Nigel (based on Hugh Grant) is a distant cousin to Prince Charles and considered a playboy who enjoys polo and yachting and is a master dart champion. The Smythe 400-acre estate houses one of the finest wine cellars in Great Britain and magnificent stables where Nigel enjoys brisk morning rides. Lord Smythe participates in wine tasting events at the finest wine cellars in Great Britain with his Oxhard

University crewing mates. When Nigel isn't vacationing in Paris, Rome, or Venice, he helps out charities that are dear to his heart such as The National Ballet or The Princess Memorial Fund Project that ensures access to cancer services for all ethnic groups. Can a lady coxswain steer Lord Smythe's love boat to the finish line?

Dr. Michael Einstein

Pedersen Prize-winning physicist Dr. Michael Einstein knows all about subatomic particles and does the crossword puzzle in ink in under five minutes. Michael was a member of the National Institute for Technology team that card counted an eight-deck shoe to win a million dollars from a Las Vegas casino. Growing up, Michael's mother taught him to cook and two years ago he learned gourmet French cooking in Paris. Dr. Einstein speaks and reads Japanese and German, is a master at Go, and has an addiction to spicy Mexican food. Theoretical attraction is easy for Dr. Michael Einstein to calculate, whereas female attraction remains a mystery to him.

[Notice the photo ID badge and game designer privilege of adding my last name in the description. The last name, borrowed from Albert, was another attempt at humor and easy recognition.]

Dr. Isabelle Dupree

Marine biologist Dr. Isabelle Dupree works in Miami, FL, and specializes in coral reefs and the behavioral ecology of cnidarians (hydroids, jellyfish, anemones, and corals) and fishes. Dr. Dupree surveys the Florida Keys and spends her time in the field collecting samples and

diving and in the lab analyzing and reporting her findings. Besides deep sea diving, Dr. Dupree is a thrill seeker enjoying sky diving, roller coasters, and going to the track to race high-performance sports cars. Isabelle became obsessed with aquatic life-forms after watching *Finding Jaws*, an animated shark-out-of-water film. Dr. Dupree frequently dines at Japanese sushi restaurants. There are plenty of fish in the sea, but is there a high-adrenaline merman out there for Isabelle?

[A marine biologist, Dr. Isabelle Dupree is wearing a mermaid style, ocean blue dress (she is based on Angelina Jolie.]

Workshop

Assignments

Assignment 1: Describe your favorite game character and what about that character appeals to you.

Assignment 2: Discuss why a designer may want to create memorable iconic characters such as Mario, Sonic, Mega Man, or Lara Croft.

Exercises

Exercise 1: Design a game based on six nursery rhymes and create a biography with sample photos of each character that matches your vision (use Internet searches for images).

Exercise 2: Select your favorite sitcom and prepare a Character Design Document that describes each main character in detail.

Exercise 3: Select a comic book hero film and recast it with your selected actors and describe your decision.

Unguided Exercises

Unguided Exercise 1: Describe a film with an Oscar-winning or nominated actor or actress or supporting actor or actress. After describing the film, explain your analysis of the person's performance.

Unguided Exercise 2: Design a game based on the first 10-person mission to Jupiter and create a Character Design Document for these characters.

Internet Reading Assignment

"Lessons in Color Theory for Spyro the Dragon" by John Fiorito and Craig Stitt

http://www.gamasutra.com/view/feature/3173/lessons_in_color_theory_for_spyro_.php

"Innovations in Character: Personalizing RPGs, Retaining Players" by Anders Tychsen

http://www.gamasutra.com/view/feature/3704/innovations_in_
character_.php

"A Veteran with Character: Roger Hector Speaks" by Brandon Sheffield
http://www.gamasutra.com/view/feature/3672/a_veteran_with_
character_roger_.php

Thoughts for Discussion

1. Discuss the character profiles for an 1860s western USA (cowboy era) game.

2. What type of characters would suit a game about lawyers, doctors, or police officers?

3. Discuss the characters for a Bible story and then discuss several actors and actresses who could be cast.

4. In a comic book game about villains and criminals, discuss several innovative characters and their descriptions.

Chapter 13

Basics of Programming and Level Scripting

Programming is like being a general in the military and giving absolute commands to your troops. You say "march" and 100 soldiers begin to move forward. You say "halt!" and they all stop immediately. This is programming. You tell a dumb machine that can only do a few things, such as add one plus one, to answer the question "does one equal one?" Simplistic? Yes. Realistic? Yes.

Commands (let's call them "instructions") are processed in order similar to the way some things in life are processed in order:

At 7:00 A.M.: You get up out of bed.
At 7:15 A.M.: You walk into the bathroom.
At 7:16 A.M.: You turn on the water in the shower.
At 7:17 A.M.: You get into the shower.
At 7:18 A.M.: You soap yourself.
At 7:19 A.M.: You rinse off.

Repeat three more times

At 7:20 A.M.: You soap yourself.
At 7:21 A.M.: You rinse off.
At 7:22 A.M.: You soap yourself.
At 7:23 A.M.: You rinse off.
At 7:24 A.M.: You soap yourself.
At 7:25 A.M.: You rinse off.

(end of the loop or repeated commands)

At 7:26 A.M.: You exit the shower and dry off.

This is life, but it can also be looked at as a set of instructions (or programming).

A Look at Programming

Architects design plans, builders create blueprints, and engineers draw schematics. Computer engineers (including programmers) draw flowcharts to visually explain the system's or module's flow that they wish to design and program.

Let's start our look at programming with a few common terms and concepts.

All programs and scripting languages store values in *variables*, which can be of various types such as character, numeric, and date/time.

Programs are not linear, and therefore the main routine will interact with subroutines and subroutines will call other subroutines.

A subroutine can be passed variables as input parameters.

A subroutine that returns a value is called a *function*; for example, ADD(2,3) would return 5.

A *character* or *char* is an 8-bit (numbers from 0 to 127) storage location that is used for alphanumerics (numbers, letters A-Z, and symbols).

A *boolean* or *bool* is an 8-bit storage location that is TRUE (non-zero) or FALSE (a zero value).

An *integer* or *int* is a 16-bit storage location that is used for numbers –32,767 to 32,767.

An *unsigned integer* is a 16-bit storage location that is for positive-only integers or numbers 0 to 65,535.

A *long* is a 32-bit storage location that is used for numbers –2.1 billion to 2.1 billion.

An *unsigned long* is a 32-bit storage location that is for positive-only longs or numbers 0 to 4.2 billion.

A *float* is a 16-bit real number (decimal or fraction).

A *string* is a group of characters (char format) that are referenced by a common name and have a NULL (or zero) ending delimiter.

An *array* is a group of common elements, such as an array of integers, an array of longs, or an array of strings.

A *structure* is a group of elements of various types. A structure wraps these elements together under one heading. A sample of a structure called "Employee" may contain the employee's name (a string), the employee's address (a string), the employee's salary (a float), and the employee's age (an integer).

A *class* is similar to a structure where various types of elements and functions related to these elements are combined. Similar to the "Employee" structure, we could have a class "Employee" that includes the employee's name (a string), the employee's address (a string), the employee's salary (a float), the employee's start date (a date structure of three integers defining the month, day, and year), and employee's birth date (a date structure). The class "Employee" can also contain the function for the employee's age (no longer an integer but a function based on today's date and the employee's birth date), a yearly salary review based on the employee's start date, and a birthday e-mail function to send the employee an "E-card" on their birthday (based on the birthday variables).

ASCII stands for American Standard Code for Information Interchange.

Operating Systems

There are several operating systems and system graphic libraries such as Windows, Microsoft DirectX, OpenGL, and Linux.

Windows NT is a Microsoft Windows personal computer operating system designed for users and businesses needing advanced capability. NT's technology is the base for the successor operating system, Windows 2000. Windows NT (which unofficially may have originally stood for "new technology") is actually Microsoft NT Workstation and Microsoft NT Server combined. Workstation was designed for business users who needed a more reliable and faster performance system than Windows 95 or Windows 98.

Windows CE (which unofficially may have originally stood for "consumer electronics") is based on the Microsoft Windows operating system but designed for including or embedding in handheld computers and as part of cable TV set-top boxes.

Windows 2000 (W2K) is a version of Microsoft's evolving Windows operating system that was called Windows NT 5.0. At its release Microsoft emphasized that Windows 2000 was evolutionary and "built on NT technology."

Windows XP is a version of the Windows desktop operating system for the PC that was touted as the most important version of Windows since Windows 95. Windows XP was built on the Windows 2000 kernel and comes in a Professional version and a Home Edition version.

Windows Vista is the latest version of Windows and is available in six versions. *Vista Starter 2007* is a 32-bit version for PCs outside the U.S. There is no support for the Aero interface, and it allows only three concurrent applications to run at once. *Vista Home Basic* is a version that supports 8 GB of memory, but not the Aero interface. *Vista Home Premium* is a version that supports 16 GB of memory and the Aero interface, including the Media Center Edition interface introduced with XP. *Vista Business* is a version that supports 128 GB of memory and includes IIS Web server, Remote Desktop, a backup utility, and support for dual processors. *Vista Enterprise* is the same as Vista Business with BitLocker encryption, limited virtualization (Virtual PC Express), and Subsystem for Unix Applications (SUA). *Vista Ultimate* is a version that combines the Home Premium and Enterprise versions plus support for podcasting and advanced gaming.

Vista adds numerous features, including improved security and greater support for digital rights management. Vista requires more memory than Windows XP — at least 1 GB is recommended, with 2 GB being a safer bet. The next major upgrade to follow Vista is expected in 2010.

DirectX is an application programming interface (API) for creating and managing graphic images and multimedia effects under Microsoft Windows. DirectX includes DirectDraw (an interface for creating two-dimensional images), Direct3D (an interface for creating three-dimensional images), DirectSound (an interface for sound), DirectPlay (a plug-in for Internet and multiplayer applications), and DirectInput (an interface for input from I/O devices).

OpenGL (Open Graphics Library) is the computer industry's standard API for defining 2D and 3D graphic images across numerous platforms and operating systems. OpenGL is similar to DirectX's DirectDraw and Direct3D.

Linux is a Unix-like operating system that includes a graphical user interface, an X Window System, TCP/IP (file transfer, electronic mail, remote logon), and Emacs (customizable open source text editor and application development system) with a reputation as a very efficient and fast-performing system. Unlike Windows, Linux is publicly open, and because it conforms to the Portable Operating System Interface standard user and programming interfaces, developers can write programs that can be ported to other operating systems. There are approximately 18 million Linux users worldwide.

Programming Commands

Let's look at the basics of programming commands or statements through three styles: flowcharting, BASIC (Beginner's All-purpose Symbolic Instruction Code) language, and C (or C++) language.

Conditional Statements (Also Called "if" Statements or Decision Blocks)

Flowchart	BASIC	C or C++
Does A equal B?	If A=B then	if(A==B){
Is A less than B?	If A < B then	if(A < B){
Is A less than or equal to B?	If A <= B then	if(A <= B){
Is A greater than B?	If A > B then	if(A > B){

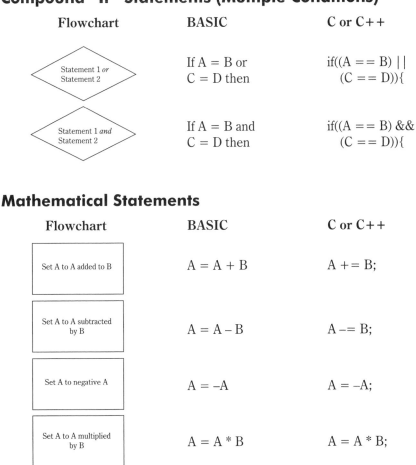

Flowchart	BASIC	C or C++
Is A greater than or equal to B?	If A >= B then	if(A >= B){
Is A not equal to B?	If A <> B then	if(A != B){
If not A (A is not zero)	If not A then	if(!A){

Compound "If" Statements (Multiple Conditions)

Flowchart	BASIC	C or C++
Statement 1 *or* Statement 2	If A = B or C = D then	if((A == B) || (C == D)){
Statement 1 *and* Statement 2	If A = B and C = D then	if((A == B) && (C == D)){

Mathematical Statements

Flowchart	BASIC	C or C++
Set A to A added to B	A = A + B	A += B;
Set A to A subtracted by B	A = A – B	A –= B;
Set A to negative A	A = –A	A = –A;
Set A to A multiplied by B	A = A * B	A = A * B;
Set A to A divided by B	A = A / B	A = A / B;

Set A to A multiplied by 2	$A = A * 2$	$A = A << 1;$ $A = A * 2;$
Set A to A divided by 2	$A = A / 2$	$A = A >> 1;$ $A = A / 2;$
Set A to A added by 1	$A = A + 1$	$A++;$ $++A;$
Set A to A added by 10	$A = A + 10$	$A += 10;$
Set A to A subtracted by 1	$A = A - 1$	$A--;$ $--A;$
Set A to A subtracted by 10	$A = A - 10$	$A -= 10;$

A "loop" Statement

Set an array "Q" with 10 indexed storage spaces where each index is multiplied by 2.

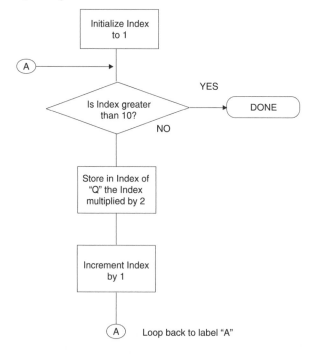

BASIC program for the "loop" flowchart (' indicates a comment):

```
FOR INDEX = 1 TO 10    'INDEX will start at 1 and end after it
                       'increments to 10
Q(INDEX)= INDEX * 2    'Store in index of Q, INDEX multiplied by 2
NEXT INDEX             'Increment INDEX and loop back to FOR
```

C or C++ program for the "loop" flowchart (// indicates a comment):

```
for(INDEX=1; INDEX <= 10; INDEX++) // INDEX will start at 1, check to
                                   // see if it's still less than or
                                   // equal to 10 and then increment
                                   // INDEX by 1
Q[INDEX] = INDEX << 1;             // Store in index of Q, INDEX
                                   // multiplied by 2
```

This process can also be initialized as:

```
// C starts with index of zero
       int Q[11] = { 0, 2, 4, 6, 8, 10, 12, 14, 16, 18, 20};
```

Computer Concepts

The first concept we will examine is called a "stack" or a "queue." Let's compare this to a checkout line in a grocery store that opens up and there is no one in the line. A customer enters the line and the cashier begins to ring him up. Another customer enters the line behind the first customer, and then another customer enters the end of the line behind the second customer. The first customer pays for his groceries and leaves. The second customer is rung up as another customer enters the end of the line.

This everyday occurrence is known as a queue or a stack, where the first person in line is the first person processed. We call this FIFO, or First In, First Out.

FIFO's cousin is FILO, or First In, Last Out, which occurs in situations like cooking pancakes. The first pancake is nice and brown and is tossed onto a plate. The next pancake is finished and tossed on top of the first pancake. Another pancake is cooked and tossed on top of the second pancake. Then you sit down at the kitchen table ready to eat the fruits (or pancakes) of your labor. The first pancake you begin to eat is the last pancake you cooked (the pancake on top). The next pancake you eat is the second one cooked and the last pancake you eat is the first one cooked. This method is an example of FILO, as the first pancake cooked is the last one eaten.

Min-Max Gaming Theory (with Alpha-Beta Pruning)

Let's pretend that we are playing a game and it is our turn. On our turn we have two choices, "A" and "B." By selecting choice "A," we will lose the game, and by selecting choice "B," we will win the game. The obvious choice would be "B" for the win. If we have 10 choices and the first choice gives us a win, the remaining nine choices can be ignored since any other choice will not produce a result better than the first choice, which results in a win. This is the theory called "min-max with alpha-beta pruning." You seek to find your best result and your opponent seeks to find your worst result (or his best result). If choice "A" for your opponent leads to you winning and choice "B" for your opponent leads to you losing, your opponent will choose "B," leading to your loss (or his win). As you evaluate each level or turn to be made, you seek a positive, winning result while your opponent seeks a negative (losing for you) result.

Once the maximum or a preset cutoff (threshold) result has been found, all remaining decisions (or paths) are unnecessary to examine. Many "n-player" games like chess, Othello, and checkers utilize these gaming theories to quickly evaluate and determine the machine's strategy (also called AI, or artificial intelligence, since we are simulating intelligent thinking).

Before we look at instructing a machine to process our commands, let's look at a simple gaming process on paper and then replicate it through a flowchart (a diagram explaining our process) and then use various methods of writing our instructions (also known as "coding" or "programming").

Tic-Tac-Toe

Let's look at a simple game that we all know and have played called Tic-Tac-Toe. The three-by-three board is filled by two players ("X" and "O"), and the winner is the player who successfully connects three of his Xs or Os in a row (horizontal, vertical, or diagonal).

1	2	3
4	5	6
7	8	9

In Tic-Tac-Toe, the player who goes first (say, "X") can choose one of nine spaces to mark with an X (as in the above diagram spaces one to nine). Then "O" has a turn and can mark any of the remaining eight empty spaces. This gameplay continues until either player has won (three connecting marks) or all of the spaces are filled (no player wins). In mathematics, we call this process "factorial," and in Tic-Tac-Toe it is 9!, or nine factorial (9 * 8 * 7 * 6 * 5 * 4 * 3 * 2 * 1).

This means that the full tree structure or game path would have 9! ending states (or "nodes"), which is 362,880 win, lose, or draw (tie) states.

When playing Tic-Tac-Toe, there are two methods of selecting a space to mark with your X or O: randomly marking an empty space or logically examining each empty space through an iterative process and selecting the space that leads to a non-losing result (a winning or tying result). All games use one of these methods, but obviously the second, non-random method gives us a better game and stronger competition.

The following sample game will indicate the side to play (X or O) and the next available space to mark.

(A) "X" mark 1	(B) "O" mark 2	(C) "X" mark 3	(D) "O" mark 4	(E) "X" mark 5	(F) "O" mark 6	(G) "X" mark 7

X	2	3		X	**O**	3		X	O	**X**		X	O	X		X	O	X		X	O	X		X	O	X
4	5	6		4	5	6		4	5	6		**O**	5	6		O	**X**	6		O	X	**O**		O	X	O
7	8	9		7	8	9		7	8	9		7	8	9		7	8	9		7	8	9		**X**	8	9

X wins (3, 5, 7 diagonal connection).

The "min-max" search would return a result of 1 for X and –1 for O, meaning a win for the player "X" worth 1 point and a loss to player O worth –1 point. The process would terminate or prune lower branches, since the game is over at step (G). The result of –1 in step (F) would trigger a more favorable result for O to find elsewhere.

O evaluates the next empty space, which is space 7 in step (F), in lieu of the losing choice step (F) marking space 6.

(F) "O" mark 7	(G) "X" mark 9 (win)

X	O	X		X	O	X
O	X	6		O	X	6
O	8	9		O	8	**X**

X wins (1, 5, 9 diagonal connection).

Again the "min-max" search would return a result of 1 for X and –1 for O, meaning a win for player X worth 1 point and a loss to player O worth –1 point. The process would terminate or prune lower branches since the game is over at step (G). The result of –1 in step (F) would trigger a more favorable result for O to find elsewhere.

O evaluates the next empty space, which is space 8 in step (F), in lieu of the losing choice step (F) marking space 7.

(F) "O" mark 9	(G) "X" mark 7 (win)

X	O	X		X	O	X
O	X	6		O	X	6
7	8	**O**		**X**	8	O

Finally O evaluates the next empty space, which is space 9 in step (F), in lieu of the losing choice step (F) marking space 8.

(F) "O"	(G) "X"
mark 9	mark 7 (win)

X	O	X
O	X	6
7	8	**O**

X	O	X
O	X	6
X	8	O

After looking at the various paths, O will evaluate step (D), O mark 4, as the critical mistake and evaluate (D), O mark 5. In step (E), X must stop O from winning by marking space 8 (forced move).

(D) "O"	(E) "X"
mark 5	mark 8 (forced)

X	O	X
4	**O**	6
7	8	9

X	O	X
4	O	6
7	**X**	9

In step (F) below, O finds the next free space and marks space 4.

In step (G), X must once again stop "O" from winning by marking space 6 (forced move).

In step (H), O must stop "X" from winning by marking space 9 (forced move).

(F) "O"	(G) "X"	(H) "O"
mark 4	mark 6 (forced)	mark 9 (forced)

X	O	X
O	O	6
7	X	9

X	O	X
O	O	**X**
7	X	9

X	O	X
O	O	X
7	X	**O**

Finally, X marks space 7, the only remaining space, and a tie or draw occurs.

Let's examine the following Tic-Tac-Toe scenario:

X	O	3
4	**X**	6
7	8	9

This scenario has player O select and mark an empty space. The iterating method would require that each empty space (spaces 3, 4, 6, 7, 8, and 9) be examined and evaluated. After spending time and effort evaluating the empty spaces, the process would recognize that player O is forced to mark space 9 to prevent player X from winning. The best method of handling the selection and marking of our next space would be to first check to see if any empty space would give us the immediate win and then if we can't win, check if any empty space would give our opponent the immediate win before examining each empty space in order.

Forced Move

Our thinking would lead us to the following thought process:

TOP:

Set current Tic-Tac-Toe board to current scenario.

Is there an empty space to mark so that I win?

If YES, select and mark this space and set result to WIN.

If NO, continue.

Is there an empty space to mark so that I won't lose?

If YES, select and mark this space and set result to Forced Mark.

If NO, continue.

Are there any empty spaces left?

If YES, continue.

If NO, set the result to the game is over (a tie).

Place your mark on the next empty space.

Set side to play to the other player.

Go back to label TOP.

To properly design the function "Forced Move," we need to know which player is to mark X (marked as +1) or O (marked as –1). This function will return a +100 value if we win, a –100 value if our opponent could win (we are forced to block), and a zero if no winning situation is found. We know that to win at Tic-Tac-Toe, we must have three connecting spaces marked with matching Xs or Os.

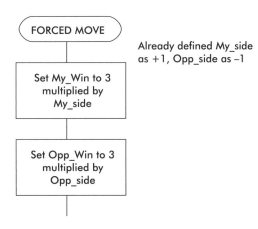

FORCED MOVE

Already defined My_side as +1, Opp_side as –1

Set My_Win to 3 multiplied by My_side

Set Opp_Win to 3 multiplied by Opp_side

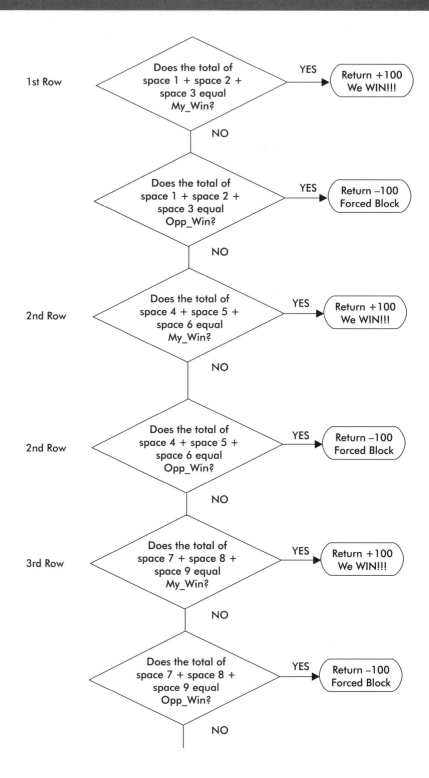

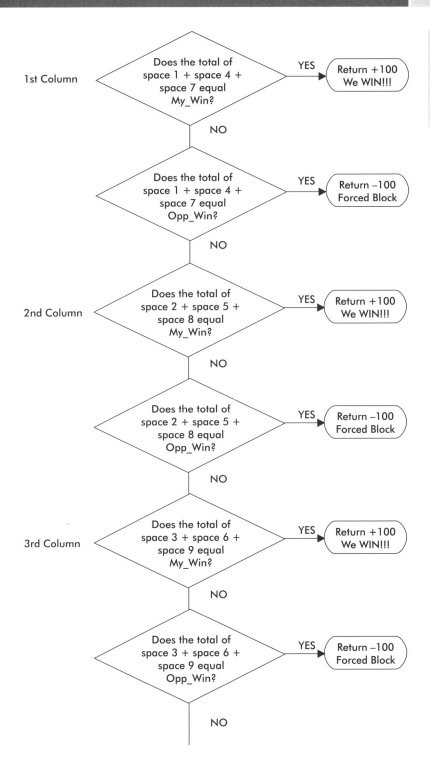

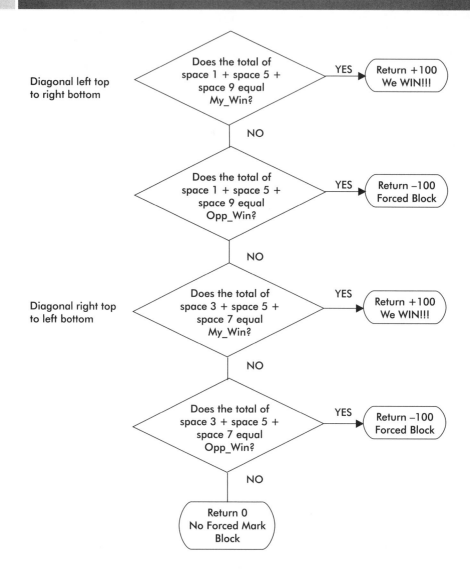

Diagonal left top
to right bottom

Does the total of
space 1 + space 5 +
space 9 equal
My_Win?

YES → Return +100
We WIN!!!

NO

Does the total of
space 1 + space 5 +
space 9 equal
Opp_Win?

YES → Return −100
Forced Block

NO

Diagonal right top
to left bottom

Does the total of
space 3 + space 5 +
space 7 equal
My_Win?

YES → Return +100
We WIN!!!

NO

Does the total of
space 3 + space 5 +
space 7 equal
Opp_Win?

YES → Return −100
Forced Block

NO

Return 0
No Forced Mark
Block

Forced Move Revised

The flowchart describing a "Forced Move" looks (obviously) like a process that can be better defined and easier to express. We can define an array called wp (win path), which has two dimensions — paths and linked spaces.

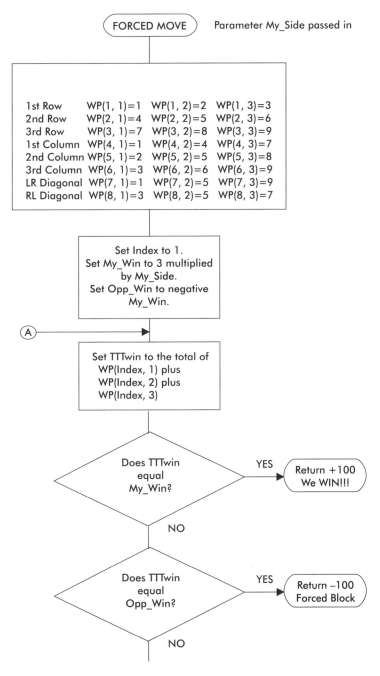

FORCED MOVE — Parameter My_Side passed in

1st Row	WP(1, 1)=1	WP(1, 2)=2	WP(1, 3)=3
2nd Row	WP(2, 1)=4	WP(2, 2)=5	WP(2, 3)=6
3rd Row	WP(3, 1)=7	WP(3, 2)=8	WP(3, 3)=9
1st Column	WP(4, 1)=1	WP(4, 2)=4	WP(4, 3)=7
2nd Column	WP(5, 1)=2	WP(5, 2)=5	WP(5, 3)=8
3rd Column	WP(6, 1)=3	WP(6, 2)=6	WP(6, 3)=9
LR Diagonal	WP(7, 1)=1	WP(7, 2)=5	WP(7, 3)=9
RL Diagonal	WP(8, 1)=3	WP(8, 2)=5	WP(8, 3)=7

Set Index to 1.
Set My_Win to 3 multiplied by My_Side.
Set Opp_Win to negative My_Win.

(A)

Set TTTwin to the total of WP(Index, 1) plus WP(Index, 2) plus WP(Index, 3)

Does TTTwin equal My_Win? — YES → Return +100 We WIN!!!

NO

Does TTTwin equal Opp_Win? — YES → Return −100 Forced Block

NO

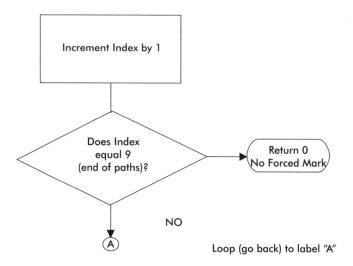

Let's look at how we can use the knowledge we just learned to program Tic-Tac-Toe in Visual Basic and Visual C++ (the code can also be found on the book's companion CD).

Visual Basic Tic-Tac-Toe

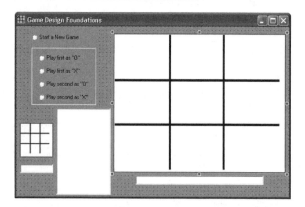

Our user interface (shown above) lets the player start a new game, decide whether the player would like to go first or second as either X or O, and lists the moves (spaces marked). The larger "big" board is where the current game is played and the player marks their desired space. The smaller board displays the computer thinking as calculated by the min-max with alpha-beta pruning search algorithm.

FORM1

```
Private Sub Form_Load()

Dim i As Integer
```

```
Form1.BorderStyle = 0

Text1.Text = "                    " + "Moves" + "                    "
Frame1.Visible = False

InitVariables
playerMark = -1
End Sub

Private Sub Option1_Click(index As Integer)

    Picture1.Enabled = True
    Picture1.PaintPicture BigBoard, 0, 0
    Picture2.PaintPicture SmBoard, 0, 0

    InitVariables
    showBigBoard
    showSmallBoard

    playerMark = (2 * (index Mod 2)) - 1 '-1 is "O", 1 is "X"

    playerDONE = 1                      ' Computer goes first
    Option1(index).value = False        ' Reset selected value
    Frame1.Visible = False
    Option2.Enabled = True
    Option2.value = False
    Option2.Visible = False

    If index < 2 Then                   ' Player's turn
        Text5.Text = "Your turn, please mark a space"
        Picture1.Enabled = True         ' Player goes first
        playerDONE = 0
    Else                                ' Computer's turn
        opening
    End If
End Sub

Private Sub Option2_Click()

  Frame1.Visible = True
  Text1.Text = "                    " + "Moves" + "                    "
  Option2.Enabled = False
End Sub

Private Sub Picture1_Click()

Dim i   As Integer
Dim flag As Integer

  If playerDONE = 1 Then Exit Sub
  flag = -1

' Check the area the player has selected to mark
  For i = 0 To 8
    If PmouseX >= (15 * BigBoxXY(i, 0)) And PmouseX <= (15 *
                (BigBoxXY(i, 0) + 120))
    Then
        If PmouseY >= (15 * BigBoxXY(i, 1)) And PmouseY <= (15 *
                (BigBoxXY(i, 1) + 95))
```

```
          Then
            If ttt(0, i) = 0 Then
                ttt(0, i) = playerMark
                Text1.Text = Text1.Text + "You marked space " +
                    Str(i + 1) + "         "
                Text4.Text = "Marked " + Str(i + 1)
                showSmallBoard
                ' Display current path scenario of board
                playerDONE = 1
                showBigBoard
                opening
                Exit Sub
            End If
        End If
    End If
  Next i
End Sub


Private Sub Picture1_MouseMove(Button As Integer, Shift As Integer,
    X As Single, Y As Single)
  PmouseX = X
  PmouseY = Y
End Sub

Private Sub Picture1_Paint()
  showBigBoard
End Sub

Private Sub Picture2_Paint()
  showSmallBoard
End Sub

Public Sub showBigBoard()

Dim i As Integer

For i = 0 To 8
    If ttt(0, i) = 1 Then
        Picture1.PaintPicture markX, 15 * BigBoxXY(i, 0), 15 *
            BigBoxXY(i, 1)
    End If
    If ttt(0, i) = -1 Then
        Picture1.PaintPicture markO, 15 * BigBoxXY(i, 0), 15 *
            BigBoxXY(i, 1)
    End If
Next i

Clevel = 0
showSmallBoard
End Sub

Public Sub showSmallBoard()

Dim i As Integer

For i = 0 To 8
    If ttt(Clevel, i) = 1 Then
        Picture2.PaintPicture smarkX, 15 * SmBoxXY(i, 0), 15 *
```

```
            SmBoxXY(i, 1)
    End If
    If ttt(Clevel, i) = -1 Then
        Picture2.PaintPicture smarkO, 15 * SmBoxXY(i, 0), 15 *
            SmBoxXY(i, 1)
    End If
Next i
End Sub
```

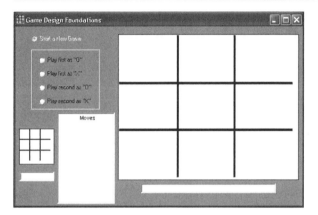

MODULE1

```
' Since C++ starts arrays at index zero we will too
' Set the global variables

Public ttt(0 To 9, 0 To 8)          As Integer
Public wp(0 To 7, 0 To 2)           As Integer
Public BigBoxXY(0 To 8, 0 To 2)     As Integer
Public SmBoxXY(0 To 8, 0 To 2)      As Integer
Public playerMark                   As Integer
Public Path                         As String
Public playerDONE                   As Integer
Public PmouseX                      As Integer
Public PmouseY                      As Integer
Public markX                        As Picture
Public markO                        As Picture
Public smarkX                       As Picture
Public smarkO                       As Picture
Public BigBoard                     As Picture
Public SmBoard                      As Picture
Public caption1                     As String
Public Clevel                       As Integer
Public L1nextspace                  As Integer
Public Level1Data(0 To 9)           As Integer


Sub InitVariables()

Dim i As Integer
Dim j As Integer
```

```
' Change the path according to your directory

    Path        = "C://Wordware//VBTicTacToe//"
    Set BigBoard = LoadPicture(Path + "TicTacToeBigBoard.bmp")
    Set SmBoard  = LoadPicture(Path + "TicTacToeSmBoard.bmp")
    Set markX    = LoadPicture(Path + "BigX.bmp")
    Set markO    = LoadPicture(Path + "BigO.bmp")
    Set smarkX   = LoadPicture(Path + "SmallX.bmp")
    Set smarkO   = LoadPicture(Path + "SmallO.bmp")

    Clevel = 0

    Form1.Picture1.Enabled = False

' Initialize the Tic-Tac-Toe boards (all levels) to zero
    For i = 0 To 9
       For j = 0 To 8
          ttt(i, j) = 0
       Next j
    Next i

' We start the arrays at zero to match our C code

' Rows
    wp(0, 0) = 0: wp(0, 1) = 1: wp(0, 2) = 2
    wp(1, 0) = 3: wp(1, 1) = 4: wp(1, 2) = 5
    wp(2, 0) = 6: wp(2, 1) = 7: wp(2, 2) = 8
' Columns
    wp(3, 0) = 0: wp(3, 1) = 3: wp(3, 2) = 6
    wp(4, 0) = 1: wp(4, 1) = 4: wp(4, 2) = 7
    wp(5, 0) = 2: wp(5, 1) = 5: wp(5, 2) = 8
' Diagonals
    wp(6, 0) = 0: wp(6, 1) = 4: wp(6, 2) = 8
    wp(7, 0) = 2: wp(7, 1) = 4: wp(7, 2) = 6

' Define our two Tic-Tac-Toe boards

    BigBoxXY(0, 0) =   0: BigBoxXY(0, 1) = 0
    BigBoxXY(1, 0) = 125: BigBoxXY(1, 1) = 0
    BigBoxXY(2, 0) = 243: BigBoxXY(2, 1) = 0
    BigBoxXY(3, 0) =   0: BigBoxXY(3, 1) = 101
    BigBoxXY(4, 0) = 125: BigBoxXY(4, 1) = 101
    BigBoxXY(5, 0) = 243: BigBoxXY(5, 1) = 101
    BigBoxXY(6, 0) =   0: BigBoxXY(6, 1) = 196
    BigBoxXY(7, 0) = 125: BigBoxXY(7, 1) = 196
    BigBoxXY(8, 0) = 243: BigBoxXY(8, 1) = 196

    SmBoxXY(0, 0) =  0: SmBoxXY(0, 1) =  0
    SmBoxXY(1, 0) = 22: SmBoxXY(1, 1) =  0
    SmBoxXY(2, 0) = 44: SmBoxXY(2, 1) =  0
    SmBoxXY(3, 0) =  0: SmBoxXY(3, 1) = 22
    SmBoxXY(4, 0) = 22: SmBoxXY(4, 1) = 22
    SmBoxXY(5, 0) = 44: SmBoxXY(5, 1) = 22
    SmBoxXY(6, 0) =  0: SmBoxXY(6, 1) = 44
    SmBoxXY(7, 0) = 22: SmBoxXY(7, 1) = 44
    SmBoxXY(8, 0) = 44: SmBoxXY(8, 1) = 44

    Randomize (Timer) ' Initialize the random number function
```

```
End Sub

' Copy a new Tic-Tac-Toe board starting with the previous board

Sub Copy_ttt(level As Integer)

Dim index As Integer

If level < 1 Then Exit Sub
If level > 8 Then Exit Sub

Clevel = level            ' For small tic-tac-toe board

   For index = 0 To 8
      ttt(level, index) = ttt(level - 1, index)
   Next index
   Form1.showSmallBoard
End Sub

' Let's verify if there's an empty space to fill

Function SpaceEmpty(level As Integer) As Integer

Dim index As Integer


   For index = 0 To 8
      If ttt(level, index) = 0 Then
         SpaceEmpty = index + 1
         Exit Function
      End If
   Next index
   SpaceEmpty = 0         ' No empty space was found
End Function

' A function to check if the current board position is a winning one
' for either player

Function IsThereaWin(level As Integer, MySide As Integer) As Integer

Dim ttWin     As Integer
Dim OppWin    As Integer
Dim MyWin     As Integer
Dim wpindex   As Integer
Dim i         As Integer

  OppWin = -3 * MySide
  MyWin  =  3 * MySide

  For wpindex = 0 To 7    ' For each win (3 rows, 3 columns, and
                          ' 2 diagonals)
     ttWin = 0
     For i = 0 To 2       ' Add the 3 spaces as per direction to check
        ttWin = ttWin + ttt(level, wp(wpindex, i))
     Next i

     If ttWin = MyWin Then    ' I have 3 connecting marks
        IsThereaWin = 100     ' I win plus space to move to
        Exit Function
```

```
      End If

   If ttWin = OppWin Then   ' Opponent can get 3 connecting marks
      IsThereaWin = -100    ' Forced plus space to block
      Exit Function
   End If
 Next wpindex

 IsThereaWin = 0
End Function

' Let's check to see if there's a forced move to make
' A forced move is a winning space or a blocking space to stop a loss

Function Forced_Move(level As Integer, MySide As Integer) As Integer

Dim index   As Integer
Dim trys    As Integer
Dim ttWin   As Integer
Dim OppWin  As Integer
Dim MyWin   As Integer
Dim wpindex As Integer
Dim i       As Integer
Dim FMove   As Integer
Dim sgn1    As Integer

   OppWin = -3 * MySide
   MyWin  =  3 * MySide

   For trys = 0 To 1
      For index = 0 To 8

         If level > 0 Then Copy_ttt (level)

         If ttt(level, index) = 0 Then   ' Empty space

            If trys = 0 Then             ' Can we win on this turn
               ttt(level, index) = MySide
            Else                         ' Can our opponent win if we
                                         ' don't block on this turn
               ttt(level, index) = -MySide    ' Opponent
            End If

            FMove = IsThereaWin(level, MySide)

            If FMove <> 0 Then sgn1 = 1

               If FMove < 0 Then sgn1 = -1

               Forced_Move = sgn1 * (Abs(FMove) + index + 1)
               If level > 0 Then Copy_ttt (level)
               Exit Function
            End If

         End If
      Next index
   Next trys

   If level > 0 Then Copy_ttt (level)
```

```
    Forced_Move = 0            ' No forced move
End Function
```

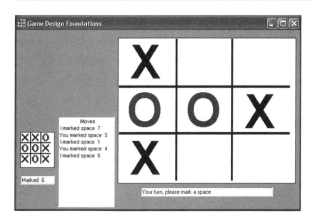

```
Sub Tic_Tac_Toe()

Dim X       As Integer
Dim MySide  As Integer
Dim spaceon As Integer
Dim FMove   As Integer
Dim i       As Integer
Dim value   As Integer

    X = 0: MySide = -playerMark

    If SpaceEmpty(0) Then    ' Game still on

' A forced move to win or to block a win is the best mark move

        X = Forced_Move(1, MySide)
        spaceon = Abs(X) Mod 100

        If X <> 0 Then          ' A forced move has been calculated
            ttt(0, spaceon - 1) = MySide ' either a '1' or a '-1'
            Form1.Text1.Text = Form1.Text1.Text + " I marked space "
                + Str(spaceon) + "        "
        End If

' Find a space that's not forced

    If X = 0 Then

' Initialize level 1 available mark spaces to an extremely low value
        For i = 0 To 9
            Level1Data(i) = -999
        Next i

' Call Min-Max function where Alpha is very low and Beta is very high

        X = MinMaxValue(1, MySide, -999, 999)   ' Find the best move

' Find the best space to mark from level 1 list of valid spaces
```

```
        spaceon = SpaceEmpty(0) - 1
        X = -999

     For i = 1 To 9
        if Level1Data(i) > X Then
           spaceon = i
           X= Level1Data(i)
        End If
     Next i

     ttt(0, spaceon - 1) = MySide      ' Mark the best space

     Form1.Text1.Text = Form1.Text1.Text + " I marked space "
             + Str(spaceon) + "        "
  End If

  Form1.Text4.Text = "Marked " + Str(spaceon)
  Form1.showSmallBoard              ' Display current path scenario
                                    ' of board
End If

Form1.showBigBoard
playerDONE = 0

FMove = IsThereaWin(0, playerMark)

If FMove <= -100 Then       ' Be prepared to see this message often
   Form1.Text1.Text = Form1.Text1.Text + "      " + "HURRAY!
          I WON!" + "           "
   Form1.Text1.Text = Form1.Text1.Text + "    Play me again?"
   Form1.Text5.Text = "Would you like to play me again?"
   playerDONE = 100
   Form1.Option2.Visible = True
   Exit Sub
End If

If FMove >= 100 Then       ' You may never see this message
   Form1.Text1.Text = Form1.Text1.Text + "      " + "WOW!
          YOU'VE WON!" + "           "
   Form1.Text1.Text = Form1.Text1.Text + "    Play me again?"
   Form1.Text5.Text = "Would you like to play me again?"
   playerDONE = 100
   Form1.Option2.Visible = True
   Exit Sub
End If

If FMove = 0 Then           ' No win found and all spaces marked

   playerDONE = 0
   Form1.Text5.Text = "Your turn, please mark a space"

   If SpaceEmpty(0) = 0 Then    ' No more empty spaces to mark
      Form1.Text1.Text = Form1.Text1.Text + "                " +
           "DRAW!" + "              "
      Form1.Text1.Text = Form1.Text1.Text + "    Play me again?"
      Form1.Text5.Text = "Would you like to play me again?"
      Form1.Option2.Visible = True
      Exit Sub
   End If
```

```
      End If
End Sub

' Just like a chess opening database, here are standard
' Tic-Tac-Toe opening marks

Sub opening()

Dim i As Integer
Dim j As Integer
Dim k As Integer

   Form1.Text5.Text = ""      ' Clear message

' Check to see if we go first or second
   j = 0

   For i = 0 To 8
      If ttt(0, i) <> 0 Then
         j = j + 1
         k = i
      End If
   Next i

   If j > 1 Then

      Form1.Text5.Text = ""
      Tic_Tac_Toe     ' Find a space to mark
      Exit Sub
   End If

   If j = 0 Then      ' We go first
      i =(Rnd * 5)     ' Valid first marks are spaces 1, 3, 5, 7, and 9
      i = i * 2        ' We have a random number 0 through 4 so we
                       ' double it
      ttt(0, i) = -playerMark
      Form1.Text4.Text = "Marked " + Str(i + 1)
      Form1.Text1.Text = Form1.Text1.Text + " I marked space " +
          Str(i + 1) + "       "
      playerDONE = 0
      Form1.showBigBoard
      Form1.Text5.Text       = "Your turn, please mark a space"
      Form1.Picture1.Enabled = True    ' Player goes
      Exit Sub
   End If

   If j = 1 Then                 ' We go second

' Valid moves are center and the opposite corner if the opponent
' marked a corner space

      i = -1                     ' A flag

   If k = 4 And i = -1 Then    ' Center space marked
      AAA: i = Int(Rnd * 4)    ' Valid first marks are spaces 1, 3,
                               ' 7, and 9
   If i = 4 Then GoTo AAA       ' Can't mark the center space
      i = i * 2                 ' We have a random number 0 through 4
                               ' so we double it
```

```
   End If

   If i = -1 Then                    ' Center space was not marked
      i = 4                          ' Mark center space (space 5)
   End If

   ttt(0, i) = -playerMark
   Form1.Text4.Text = "Marked " + Str(i + 1)
   Form1.Text1.Text = Form1.Text1.Text + " I marked space " +
         Str(i + 1) + "        "
   playerDONE = 0
   Form1.showBigBoard
   Form1.Text5.Text        = "Your turn, please mark a space"
   Form1.Picture1.Enabled = True    ' Player goes
   Exit Sub
   End If
End Sub
```

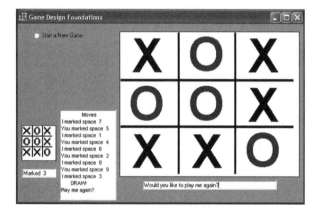

```
Function MinMaxValue(level As Integer, MySide As Integer, alpha As
      Integer, beta As Integer) As Integer
Dim WIN       As Integer
Dim index     As Integer
Dim MTlist    As Long
Dim nextspace As Integer
Dim X         As Integer
Dim succval   As Integer

' Reset current level board

   Copy_ttt (level)

   If SpaceEmpty(level) = 0 Then
      MinMaxValue = 0
      Exit Function
   End If

' Find a space that's not forced
' List all open spaces
```

```
    MTlist = 0     ' List all the open (unmarked) spaces on this level

    X = Forced_Move(level, MySide)     ' Is there a forced move (a win
                                       ' or a block of a win)


    If X <> 0 Then                     ' A forced move has been flagged
       MTlist = Abs(X Mod 100)         ' Space is 1 to 9
    Else
       For index = 0 To 8
          If ttt(level, 8 - index) = 0 Then    ' Subtract from 8 for
                                               ' ascending order
             MTlist = MTlist * 10 + (9 - index)
          End If
       Next index
    End If

    While MTlist > 0
       nextspace = MTlist Mod 10              ' Next space to mark
       MTlist = (MTlist - nextspace) / 10 ' Remainder of possible
                                          ' spaces to mark

       Copy_ttt (level)
       ttt(level, nextspace - 1) = MySide

       Form1.Text4.Text = "Marked " + Str(nextspace)
       Form1.showSmallBoard                   ' Display current path
                                              ' scenario of board

       WIN = IsThereaWin(level, MySide)

       If WIN >= 100 Then
          succval = WIN
       Else
          succval = -MinMaxValue(level + 1, -MySide, -beta, -alpha)
       Endif

       If level = 1 Then                      ' Save this space's value
          Level1Data(nextspace) = succval
          If succval = 100 Then               ' Winning line found
             MinMaxValue = succval
             Exit Function
          End If
       End If

' The Alpha-Beta pruning code

       If succval >= beta Then
          MinMaxValue = beta
          Exit Function
       End If

       If succval > alpha Then alpha = succval

    Wend

    MinMaxValue = alpha                        ' Return a draw

End Function
```

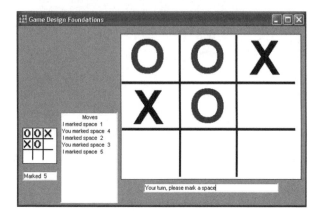

Visual C++ Tic-Tac-Toe

```
//since C++ start arrays at index zero we will too
int ttt[8][8]={{0,0,0,0,0,0,0,0},{0,0,0,0,0,0,0,0},
    {0,0,0,0,0,0,0,0},{0,0,0,0,0,0,0,0},{0,0,0,0,0,0,0,0},
    {0,0,0,0,0,0,0,0},{0,0,0,0,0,0,0,0},{0,0,0,0,0,0,0,0}};

int wp[8][3]={{0,1,2},{3,4,5},{6,7,8},    // Rows
             {0,3,6},{1,4,7},{2,5,8},    // Columns
             {0,4,8},{2,4,6}};           // Diagonals

// Copy a new Tic-Tac-Toe board starting with the previous board
void Copy_ttt(int level)
{
   int index;

   if(level<1) return;                    // Invalid parameter
   for(index=0; index<9; index++)
     ttt[level][index]= ttt[level-1][index]
}

// Let's verify if there's an empty space to fill
int SpaceEmpty(int level)
{
   int index;

   for(index=0; index<9; index++)
     if(ttt[level][index]==0) return(index+1);
   return 0;                              // No empty space was found
}

// Let's check to see if there's a forced move to make
// A forced move is a winning space or a blocking space to stop
// a loss
int Forced_Move(int level, int MySide)
{
   int index, trys, ttWin;
   int OppWin= -3 * MySide;
   int MyWin=   3 * MySide;
```

```
for(index=0; index<9;index++)
   for(trys=0; trys<2; trys++){
      if(level>0) Copy_ttt(level);

      if(ttt[level][index] == 0){                // Empty space
         if(trys ==0)ttt[level][index]= MySide;
         else         ttt[level][index]=-MySide;  // Opponent

      ttWin= ttt[level][wp[index][0] + ttt[level][wp[index][1] +
            ttt[level][wp[index][2];

      if(ttWin == MyWin)return(100 + index);
         // I win plus space to move to
      else
      if(ttWin == OppWin)return(-(100 + index));
         // Forced plus space to block
      }

   return 0;   // No forced move
}
void Tic_Tac_Toe()
{
int x=0, MySide= 1, spaceon;

   while(SpaceEmpty(0) && x < 100){        // Game still on
      x= Forced_Move(1, MySide);
      spaceon= abs(x)%100;
      if(x != 0)ttt[0][spaceon]= x/100;    // Either a '1' or a '-1'
      else{                                // Find a space that's not forced
         BestMove(1);                      // Find the best move
      }

      x= 0;                                // Reset 'x'
   }
}
```

(This code and the C++ code can be found on the book's companion CD.)

Basic Level Scripting

In the early days of game programming, the programmer wrote all of the code including gameplay, AI (artificial intelligence), sound routines, animation, physics, and so on.

Today's games need fine-tuning and game balancing based on QA (quality assurance) testing and other team members' feedback. Programmers are among the most highly paid team members, and their skills and time are extremely valuable.

In "the old days of gaming," the programmer would set up the code with game parameters and then testing would occur. The testing would show problem areas in balancing the game and the strength of the NPCs (nonplayer characters), and the code would be modified. This process would continue until a satisfying game passed the testing. A smart programmer would set up the initial and current parameters in an external (to the code) file.

In order to avoid spending the programmer's valuable time testing and tweaking the game's parameters, a new position of "level designer" was created. The level designer uses a scripting language that is similar to programming where the parameters and game logic is tested and tweaked. The programmer is only concerned with the game rules, AI, physics, UI (user interface), sound, and animation. The level designer is concerned with designing the missions, placing the characters and objects in the world, designing the terrain, and building the environment.

Scripting is the "code" that controls the game parameters and goals. Here is an example of a basic script scenario:

A miner Bob needs to sleep for 8 hours, eat meals at 7 A.M., 12 P.M. (noon), and 6 P.M., and upon collecting four gold nuggets he needs to deposit them at the bank.

A simple script would be:

Set start of game time to 6 A.M. Every cycle the time is incremented by 30 minutes.

- If Time is 6 A.M. Miner Bob awakens.
- If Time is 7 A.M., Miner Bob needs to go home and eat.
- If Time is 12 P.M., Miner Bob needs to go home and eat.
- If Time is 6 P.M., Miner Bob needs to go home and eat.
- If Time is between 8 A.M. and 6 P.M., Miner Bob needs to go to the mine if he has less than four gold nuggets.
- Miner Bob has four gold nuggets and needs to go to the bank.
- Miner Bob is at the bank and deposits four gold nuggets. Add four gold nuggets to Miner Bob's total. Miner Bob has no gold nuggets.
- Miner Bob is in the mine and every 30 minutes collects one gold nugget.
- If Time is 7 P.M., Miner Bob goes to sleep.

This process of Miner Bob's daily life becomes a simple scripting program.

If Miner Bob's daily life needs tweaking, the level designer can change the times, the number of nuggets needed for a bank deposit, and the time increment of each passing phase without the programmer's involvement.

There are several scripting languages that are used in gaming, especially with 3D game engines, such as Lua, Python, and ActionScript. The game code is completely separate from the generic engine code and the script doesn't require a time-consuming compiling phase (converting code into a format readable by the computer). It is easy to add innovative missions and interactions to the script in a quick modify, run game, and test scenario.

Workshop

Suggested Activities

Activity 1: Discuss the programming roles that an FPS, MMO, and casual game would need in order to develop that game.

Activity 2: Discuss how the programming team and the level design team should work together to make a great game such as an FPS, 3PS, or RTS game.

Assignments

Assignment 1: What is the importance of AI, pathfinding, physics, and engine code?

Assignment 2: Explain how level designing is similar to and different from programming.

Exercises

Exercise 1: List the titles of five 3D games, their publisher, and their developer, and describe the 3D engine used as well as its benefits.

Exercise 2: Describe the differences between scripting languages such as Lua, Python, and others that you have researched.

Unguided Exercises

Unguided Exercise 1: Make a list of 3D games and the scripting language used and describe that scripting language.

Unguided Exercise 2: Write a list of game languages used to program video console, computer, handheld, mobile, and Internet games.

Internet Reading Assignment

"What I Did During My Summer Vacation: Developing a Game in 13 Weeks" by Roger Pedersen
   http://www.gamasutra.com/features/20011211/pedersen_01.htm

"Beginning Level Design, Part 1: Level Design Theory" by Tim Ryan
   http://www.gamasutra.com/features/19990416/level_design_01.htm

"Defining Dialogue Systems" by Brent Ellison
   http://www.gamasutra.com/view/feature/3719/defining_dialogue_systems.php

Chapter 14

Game Design Outlets

So you've decided you want to be a game designer, and reading and working through the exercises in this book have given you the tools to become one. Now you need to put your talents to good use by researching the gaming industry and publicizing your abilities and worth.

The Top Publishers in the Gaming Industry

Who are the top publishers in the gaming industry and how do you let them know about your talents and skills?

> **Note:** Please realize that every day studios merge, get bought out by other publishers, or are closed down, so use this information as a great starting point. If you play games from these publishers and their studios, send them e-mail comments on the game such as "this feature was good" or "this feature would have been better if..." and you may get a job as a tester or make valuable connections to pitch your game design to someone inside the company. When contacting any company, ask for their producer or a producer named in the credits. No company ever screens calls to the producer, and it's the producer who usually recommends future games to be developed.

Activision is located at 3100 Ocean Park Boulevard, Santa Monica, CA 90405 (www.activision.com).

Activision's top series are Call of Duty and Guitar Hero, and their top movie-based titles are Spider-Man 3, Transformers, and Kung Fu Panda.

Activision Blizzard was formed with Activision and Vivendi's four studios (Blizzard Entertainment, Sierra Entertainment, Sierra Online, and Vivendi Games Mobile). Activision's studios are Beenox (Quebec City), Bizarre Creations (Liverpool, UK), Infinity Ward (Encino, CA), Luxoflux (Santa Monica, CA), Neversoft (Encino and Woodland Hills, CA), Raven Software (Middleton, WI), RedOctane (Sunnyvale, CA), Shaba Games (San Francisco), Toys For Bob (Novato, CA), Treyarch (Santa Monica, CA), Vicarious Visions (Troy, NY), and Z-Axis (Foster City, CA).

Atlus U.S.A., Inc. is located at 199 Technology Drive, Suite 105, Irvine, CA 92618 (www.Atlus.com).

Atlus' current and upcoming titles for the Nintendo DS are Trauma Center: Under the Knife, Izuna 2: The Unemployed Ninja Returns, Master of the Monster Lair, Luminous Arc 2, and Persona 4. For the Wii their most popular title is Dokapon Kingdom, for the PSP a recent title is Yggdra Union, and for the Xbox some of their titles are Spectral Force 3, Zoids Assault, and Operation Darkness.

Disney Interactive Studios (formerly Buena Vista Games) 500 South Buena Vista Street, Burbank, CA 91521, Tel. 818-553-5000, Fax 818-567-0284 (http://disney.go.com/disneyinteractivestudios/).

The company's most popular titles are based on Disney films and televisions shows and include American Dragon: Jake Long, Cars, Chicken Little, Cinderella, Enchanted, Finding Nemo, Hannah Montana, Herbie, High School Musical, Kim Possible, Meet the Robinsons, Nightmare Before Christmas, Pirates of the Caribbean, Power Rangers, Princess, Ratatouille, Santa Clause 3, That's So Raven, The Cheetah Girls, The Chronicles of Narnia, The Little Mermaid, The Suite Life of Zack & Cody, and Wall-E.

The Disney Interactive Studios include Avalanche Software (Salt Lake City), Fall Line Studio (Salt Lake City), Propaganda Games (Vancouver, BC), Black Rock Studio (Brighton, UK), and Junction Point Studios, Inc. (Austin, TX).

Capcom U.S.A., Inc. is located at 475 Oakmead Parkway, Sunnyvale, CA 94086 Tel. 408-774-0500, Fax 408-774-3995 (megamail@capcom.com, www.capcom.com).

Capcom's franchises include the Street Fighter and Mega Man series. Their other well-known titles are the Resident Evil series, Onimusha, the Devil May Cry series, Dino Crisis, and the vs. Capcom titles (SNK vs. Capcom and Marvel vs. Capcom).

Capcom's studios include Capcom Interactive (Los Angeles), Cosmic Infinity (Burlington, ON), Flagship (Tokyo), Team 1 (Osaka), and Team 2 (Osaka).

Electronic Arts corporate headquarters is located at 209 Redwood Shores Parkway, Redwood City, CA 94065, Tel. 650-628-1393, Fax 650-628-1422 (www.ea.com and jobs.ea.com/home.aspx).

EA's powerful franchises include Madden Football, The Sims, FIFA, Need for Speed, and Rock Band.

EA's studios include BioWare (Edmonton, AB, and Austin, TX), Black Box (Vancouver, BC), Bright Light (Guildford, UK), Criterion (Guildford, UK), DICE (Stockholm, Sweden), EA Montreal, EA Salt Lake, EA Canada (Burnaby, BC), EA Los Angeles, Maxis (Emeryville, CA), Mythic Entertainment (Fairfax, VA), Pandemic Studios (Los Angeles), Phenomic (Frankfurt, Germany), EA Tiburon (Orlando, FL), and Viceral Games (formerly EA Redwood Shores) (Redwood City, CA).

Konami is located at 209 Redwood Shores Parkway, Redwood City, CA 94065, Tel. 650-628-1500, Fax 650-628-1422 (www.konami.com).

Konami's franchises include Dance Dance Revolution, Castlevania, Death, Jr., Frogger, Karaoke Revolution, Pro Evolution Soccer, Silent Hill, and Yu-Gi-Oh! Konami publishes the Bomberman series, Hellboy: The Science of Evil, Winx Club, Go Pets: Vacation Island, and the PS3 title Metal Gear Solid 4.

Konami's studios include Blue Label Interactive (Los Angeles), Hudson Soft (Tokyo, Sapporo, San Francisco), Konami Computer Entertainment (Tokyo), Konami Software (Shanghai), and Kojima Productions (Tokyo).

LucasArts is located at 1110 Gorgas Avenue (P.O. Box 29908), San Francisco, CA 94129 (www.lucasarts.com).

Owned by George Lucas, the company's titles include the Star Wars series, the Indiana Jones series, Fracture, Thrillville: Off the Rails, and the LEGO series.

Microsoft Game Studios is located at 1 Microsoft Way, Redmond, WA, 98052-6399, Tel. 425-936-8080 (www.microsoft.com/games).

Microsoft's popular titles include the Age of Empires and Age of Mythology series, the Halo series, Gears of War, and Project Gotham Racing, as well as Mass Effect, Ninja Gaiden II, and Lost Odyssey. Xbox Live offers one of the largest online gaming subscription services and casual games.

Microsoft's studios include Lionhead Studios (Guildford, UK), Microsoft Game Studios Japan (Tokyo), Rare (Twycross, UK), Turn 10 Studios (Redmond, WA), SpawnPoint Studios (Lake Mary, FL), XBox Live Productions (Redmond, WA), and Wingnut Interactive (Wellington, NZ).

Midway Games corporate headquarters is located at 2704 West Roscoe Street, Chicago, IL 60618, Tel. 773-961-2222 (www.midway.com).

Midway Studios in Chicago remains one of Midway's major studios, having developed Blitz: The League for the PlayStation 2 and Xbox and Stranglehold for the PlayStation 3, Xbox 360, and PC. Midway Home Entertainment in San Diego is developing and completing the game Rise and Fall: Civilizations at War. Surreal Software in Seattle developed The Suffering: Ties That Bind. The Mortal Kombat series, Unreal Tournament 3, the NBA Ballers franchise, and titles based on the Happy Feet movie license are other profitable titles.

The company also operates Midway Studios in Austin, TX, and its offices in Europe are Midway Games Ltd. (London), Midway Games

GmbH (Munich), Midway Studios Newcastle, and Midway Games SAS (Paris).

Namco Bandai is located at 4555 Great America Parkway, Suite 201, Santa Clara, CA 95054 (www.namcobandaigames.com, jobs@namcobandaigames.com).

Namco Bandai Games publishes the Soul Caliber, Naruto, Tekken, Ridge Racer, Dragon Ball Z, and Tamigotcha series. Other titles include Dead to Rights, the Pac-Man franchise games, Time Crisis, We Love Katamari, The Fast and the Furious, Ace Combat, and Gunpey.

Namco Bandai's studios include Banpresoft (Tokyo), Bec Co., Ltd. (Tokyo), Namco Tales Studio, Ltd. (Tokyo), Namco Bandai Games America (San Jose, CA), and Namco Bandai Games Ltd. (Yokohama, Tokyo).

NCSoft corporate headquarters is located in Seoul, South Korea. Its North American subsidiary, NC Interactive, is located at 6801 N Capital of Texas Highway, Building 1, Suite #102, Austin, TX 78731-1780, Tel. 512-498-4000 (www.ncsoft.com, jobs@ncaustin.com).

NCSoft's current tiles are Dungeon Runners, Guild Wars Platinum Edition, Lineage II, and Tabula Rasa. Upcoming titles include Tower of Eternity, Soccer Fury, and more of the Lineage series.

Other subsidiaries are NCsoft West (Seattle), NC Northern California (Mountain View, CA), Carbine Studios (Orange County, CA), AreaNet (Bellevue, WA), and NCsoft Europe (Brighton, UK).

Nintendo of America is located at 4820 150th Ave. NE, Redmond, WA 98052, Tel. 425-882-2040 (www.nintendo.com).

In case you were born yesterday, the current Nintendo games for the Nintendo DS include the Pokemon series, the Mario games, the Legend of Zelda series, Kirby games, and Crossword DS. For the Wii, Nintendo publishes Wii Sports, Mario games, Donkey Kong games, Excite Truck, and Zelda games. Other Nintendo top sellers are Brain Age 2, Super Smash Brothers Brawl, Mario Kart Wii, and Wii Fit.

Retro Studios, which is wholly owned by Nintendo and based in Austin, TX, developed the Metroid series.

SCi/Eidos is located at 651 Brannan St. # 400, San Francisco, CA, 94107, Tel. 415-547-1200 (www.edios.com).

Eidos has several development studios, including Crystal Dynamics (San Francisco), IO Interactive (Denmark), Eidos (Montreal; Hungary; Shanghai, China), Beautiful Game Studios (UK), and Pivotal Games (UK). They partly own Rocksteady (UK).

SCi/Eidos games include Tomb Raider, Hitman, Commandos, Deus Ex, Legacy of Kain, Thief, TimeSplitters, 25 to Life, LEGO Star Wars: The Video Game, and Fear Effect.

Sega Sammy Holdings/Sega of America is located at 650 Townsend Street, San Francisco, CA, 94103, Tel. 415-701-6000 (www.sega.com).

Sega franchise titles include the Sonic series, Yakuza, Golden Axe, The House of the Dead, Medieval, and NiGHTS. Their most popular titles include Samba De Amigo, Space Siege, Mario and Sonic at the Olympic Games, Sega Superstars Tennis, Iron Man, The Incredible Hulk, Beijing 2008, Brain Assist, and The Club.

Sega's studios include Creative Assembly (West Sussex, UK; Fortitude Valley, Australia), Secret Level (San Francisco), Sega Shanghai Studios (Shanghai), Sega Studios (Tokyo), Sega Studios USA (San Francisco), and Sports Interactive (London).

Sony Computer Entertainment America, Inc. (SCEA) is located at 919 East Hillsdale Blvd., 2nd Floor, Foster City, CA, 94404-4201 (www.us.playstation.com).

SCEA popular titles include the Ratchet & Clank, SOCOM, Gran Turismo, Uncharted: Drake's Fortune, and God of War series.

Sony's studios include Bigbig Studios (Warwickshire, UK; Bend, OR; San Diego; Cambridge, UK; Bangalore, India), Contrail (Tokyo), Evolution Studios (Cheshire, UK; Foster City, CA), Guerrilla Games (Amsterdam), Incognito Entertainment (Salt Lake City, Liverpool, London), Polyphony Digital (Tokyo, Santa Monica, Seoul); SN Systems (Bristol, UK), Sony Online Entertainment (Austin, Denver, Los Angeles, San Diego, Seattle, Taiwan, and Tokyo), Zener Works (Tokyo), and Zipper Interactive (Redmond, WA).

Square Enix is located at 999 N. Sepulveda Boulevard, Third Floor, El Segundo, CA 90245, Fax 310-846-0403 (hr-jobs@square-enix-usa.com, www.square-enix.com).

Square Enix's franchise titles are Final Fantasy, Dragon Quest, Heroes of Mana, Valkyrie Profile, and Kingdom Hearts.

Square Enix's studios include Community Engine (Japan), Taito Corp. (Japan), Square Enix China (Beijing), and Square Enix Tokyo.

Take-Two Interactive is located at 622 Broadway, New York, NY 10012, Tel. 646-536-2842 (www.take2games.com).

Take-Two Interactive's best sellers are the Carnival Games series and Grand Theft Auto series.

Take-Two Interactive publishes games from Rockstar Games, 2K (Novato, CA), 2K Czech (Brno, Czech Republic), 2K Boston (Quincy, MA), 2K Australia (Canberra), 2K Marin (Novato, CA), Cat Daddy Games (Bellevue, WA), Firaxis Games (Hunt Valley, MD), Kush Games (Camarillo, CA), PAM Development (Paris), Rockstar Leeds (Leeds, UK), Rockstar North (Edinburgh), Rockstar San Diego, Rockstar Toronto, Rockstar Vancouver, and Visual Concepts (San Rafael, CA).

THQ ("Toy HeadQuarters") is located at 27001 Agoura Road, Calabasas Hills, CA 91301, Tel. 818-871-5000 (www.thq.com).

THQ's internally created franchises include Saints Row, Frontlines: Fuel of War, Red Faction, MX vs. ATV, and Company of Heroes.

THQ's studios include Big Huge Game (Timonium, MD), Blue Tongue Entertainment (Melbourne, Australia), Heavy Iron Studios (Los Angeles), Juice Games (Warrington, UK), Kaos Studios (New York), Locomotive Games (Santa Clara, CA), Mass Media (Moorpark, CA), Paradigm Entertainment (Dallas), Rainbow Studios (Phoenix), Relic Entertainment (Vancouver, BC), Sandblast Games (Seattle), THQ Studio Australia (Queensland), Vigil Games (Austin), and Volition, Inc. (Champaign, IL).

Ubisoft is located at 3200 Gateway Centre Blvd., Suite 100, Morrisville, NC 27560 (www.ubi.com/US/ and http://jobs.ubisoft.ca/en/).

Ubisoft's popular titles include Assassin's Creed, Prince of Persia, Rayman, Tom Clancy's Splinter Cell, Tom Clancy's Rainbow Six, Brothers In Arms, Far Cry, Heroes of Might & Magic, The Settlers, and Driver racing game. Ubisoft has film and television properties such as CSI, Lost, and Peter Jackson's King Kong.

Some of Ubisoft's studios include Red Storm (Morrisville, NC), Ubisoft (Quebec and Montreal), Reflections (UK), Blue Byte and Related Design (Germany), and a studio in Pune, India.

Vivendi is located 240 W 35th Street, New York, NY 10001, Tel. 212-601-5000 (www.vivendi.com, www.vgmobile.com, and (for Activision Blizzard) www.vivendi.com/corp/en/subsidiaries/index_games.php).

Vivendi's hottest franchises are World of Warcraft, F.E.A.R., Starcraft, Diablo, Empire Earth, Leisure Suit Larry, Ground Control, Tribes, Crash Bandicoot, and Spyro the Dragon.

Vivendi's studios include Blizzard Console (Aliso Viejo, CA), Blizzard Entertainment (Irvine, CA), Blizzard North (San Mateo, CA), High Moon Studios (Carlsbad, CA), Massive Entertainment (Malmo, Sweden), Radical Entertainment (Vancouver, BC), Sierra Entertainment (Bellevue, WA), Swordfish Studios (Birmingham, UK), and Vivendi Games Mobile (Los Angeles; San Mateo, CA).

The Outlets

Often those who want to become "game designers" look at today's games with their massive amount of graphics, engaging stories with numerous pathways, orchestrated music and realistic sound effects, a large team of professionals, and budgets in the millions and wonder "How can I design a game to compete in today's market?"

I have studied and worked in the independent film industry. The standard belief in the film industry is that the work and effort involved in the development of a short film (less than 30 minutes) from preproduction to postproduction requires the same process (although scaled down) as today's three-hour, $100 million blockbuster epic. The process involved in filmmaking includes writing the script, location scouting, auditioning and hiring the cast and crew, determining the shooting schedule, preproduction planning, actual shooting from early morning dailies to the entire day of shooting and delivering film to the processing lab, postproduction with film editing, matching the audio to the visuals, adding music, sound effects, and ADR (automated dialogue replacement or additional dialogue recording), and distributing the film to theaters or film festivals.

Just like in the film industry, in the gaming industry the processes required to complete a simple cell phone game, Internet game, casual game, or mod (a modification of an existing FPS, RPG, or RTS game) are the same as those needed by multi-million dollar, 100+ member development team projects supported by publishers and large developers.

The game design process and the practices learned in this book are the same as (or close to) the ones used throughout the game industry. The more you understand, the more you practice your craft, the more games you play from the designer's POV (point of view), and the more you refine your game design skills, the better game designer you will be.

In the old days, apprentices studied under their masters for years until they learned the skills and techniques required to become a master. For those who are fans of *Star Wars*, think of the Jedi Master and his young padawan (student) who eventually with training will become the master. Pretending to be "Darth Gamer," read this several times aloud: "I was once the student game designer and you were the master game designer. Now, I am the master game designer!" All of us can be creative and innovative.

Let's assume that you have a desire and perhaps a great game idea. (If you are drawing a blank, reread Chapter 4, "Game Concepts and Ideas.") We'll also assume that your funds are limited (even if you're rich, you'll want to save your own money). The outlets that I would suggest looking into for your game are the casual game space, Internet games, cell phone games, 3D game engines, machinima, handhelds, and home-brew gaming.

If you're contemplating working on an Internet game, a casual game, a mod, or a homebrew game, search the Internet for some of the many design contests that would provide you with great promotion for your game just by entering.

Also look into and consider digital distribution methods that are becoming more common, such as Steam, D2D, and Internet portals such as www.manifestogames.com. (ManifestoGames states "We're here to create for games what indie music and film provide: an audience and market for creativity and individual vision, defying the big publishers' mediocrity and hype.")

The Thinnox program (www.Thinnox.com) for junior high and high school students teaches GarageGames Game Builder, Torque Game

Engine modding, and Gameboy Advance handheld emulation development from the available free Internet tools using the C programming language (see Chapter 13, "Basics of Programming and Level Scripting").

The Torque products available on www.garagegames.com/products/torque are the Torque Game Builder, the Torque Game Engine (with porting path to the Xbox 360 and Nintendo Wii), and the Torque Game Engine Advanced (uses modern shaders and post processing).

The Torque engines are available for a free 30-day trial period. The price for the Torque Game Builder is $100 for indies and $495 for commercial developers. The Torque Game Engine price is $150 for indies and $745 for commercial developers. The Torque Game Engine Advanced price is $295 for indies and $1,495 for commercial developers. GarageGames states "If you or your company earn less than $250,000 per year, you qualify as an indie and can purchase GarageGames products at our special discount for indies."

Internet Games

Internet game development uses tools such as Microsoft's Silverlight, Adobe's Flash and ActionScript (Adobe Flash CS4 Professional software is available for $699 with a trial version at www.adobe.com/products/flash), Java (available for free at http://java.sun.com/javame/downloads/sdk30ea.jsp), Python (www.python.org), and C/C++ from Microsoft and Borland. The tools to develop Internet games are free or can be used under a limited trial period. The Internet games that are commonly referred to as web-based games are games that are launched from a web page with no prior installation of software required.

For casual games that are downloaded the common development languages used are Flash, Shockwave, Java, and C++ where games are delivered in an ActiveX control.

The IGDA White Paper on web and downloadable games (www.igda.org/online/IGDA_WebDL_Whitepaper_2004.pdf) claims that "when it comes to purchases of downloadable games, the female skew becomes even more significant with some sites reporting as much as 70% of sales coming from females over 30."

The end result of this endeavor is to develop a demo or "proof of concept" that you can show a publisher or a developer who may work with you to make this game a reality. You can also use an Internet portal to directly sell your game to the public. This step takes your design from mere words in a document to a product and allows the money and decision making people to actually experience your design.

Machinima

One of the coolest aspects of modding a 3D engine is called "machinima," which is the convergence of cinema (film) and interactive entertainment (3D shooters and worlds).

On the book's CD is what I consider the best explanation of this process. Frank L. Fox's movie *What Is Machinima?* uses the Grand Theft
Auto (GTA) engine to describe the creative design process of machinima
using the GTA characters, vehicles, props, and locations.

I would like to thank Frank for his permission to present his work to
you on the book's CD and encourage you to visit his website
(http://flingfilms.com).

In 2008 at the annual NJ Filmmaker's Conference, I was one of the key-
note speakers and presented a lecture to an independent film audience.
These filmmakers had great enthusiasm and ideas but did not have the
budgets to make "Hollywood" films. (Sound familiar?)

I asked the audience, "Who has played 3D games and shooters?" and
lots of hands went up. I asked, "Who has played or heard of GTA?" and the
sea of hands continued to fill the air. I asked, "Who has seen or heard of
machinima?" and everyone in the entire room lowered their hand. At this
point, I asked, "Who in the audience would like to have at their disposal
over 100 actors, 1,000 vehicles and props, and 1,000 locations for free?"
The entire room was listening and very interested.

I explained that buying 3D games that allowed modding from game
developers such as id Software (Quake and Doom), Valve Software
(Half-Life series), Bethesda Softworks (The Elder Scrolls and Fallout 3),
Crytek (Crysis and Far Cry), Relic Entertainment (Company of Heroes),
Epic Games (Unreal), and Rockstar (GTA) would provide these abilities.
Then I showed the audience Frank L. Fox's movie *What Is Machinima?*
and the audience was amazed and had lots of questions regarding making
films and prototyping for future film production. The video quickly and
simply explained the process of how to make an inexpensive film or map
out the entire film to the non-technical film audience.

The Casual Game Market

The "casual game market" is a great outlet to consider when you design,
develop, and sell your game. The casual game market is dominated (60%
to 70%) by females ages 35 to 55 who do not consider themselves
"gamers" but spend as much time playing as the hardcore gamer.
Wikipedia states "The term casual game is used to refer to a category of
electronic or computer games targeted at a mass audience. Casual games
usually have a few simple rules and an engaging game design, making it
easy for a new player to begin playing the game in just minutes. They
require no long-term time commitment or special skills to play, and there
are comparatively low production and distribution costs for the producer."

Casual games are usually free online or to download and try, but may
provide revenue by in-game advertising or a small purchase price of $20
or less. The most popular casual game genres have been puzzle, word,
easy action, card, and board games that can be played in short durations,
have simple gameplay, and only require limited input devices such as a
one-button mouse.

The cost to get your game to the player is inexpensive. A portal owner negotiates an agreement to sell your game on their website (hopefully not an exclusive agreement, as you want to have many sites selling your game). The portal collects the money from the player and sends you a check every agreed-to period. The website will take care of the ordering and billing process, advertise your game with the other games, and keep track of your game's account.

I would advise that you also set up a website describing your game(s) and allow players to order the game from you directly at full retail price (you don't want to underprice your other website sellers). Players can search for your game, read your game's description, and see screenshots from your game to decide if they'd like to buy your game. You should also promote your game through relevant blogs, sites that feature game news, reviews and interviews with game designers and developers, and possibly show the game's artwork on art sites. Anything that creates a buzz about your game and promotes sales of your game is helpful. One developer who created an "Indiana Jones" adventure style game went to the opening of a new *Indiana Jones* film and handed out demos and trial play versions of the game, assuming that the film's audience was also their game's audience.

Take your game demos and trial versions to distribute for free at computer shows where hardware and software is sold and game competitions where professional players are competing for prizes. Go to where your audience is, whether it's a location or a magazine. The game information industry such as magazines and Internet game sites love getting previews, screenshots, and news.

A few years ago, a group of game developers from New Hampshire wanted to make an RTS sci-fi/fantasy game. They put together some preliminary artwork and started a website with a blog and an area where Internet game surfers could post comments and add design aspect suggestions to this game. The site became so popular that they began having weekly discussions about the game.

From these discussions, several magazines wrote articles about this innovative, "next hit on the horizon" game as though it were in development. The group (which I became a member of) even became sought after by many of the top publishers and developers listed at the beginning of this chapter. They wanted to see demos and some even wanted to finance the entire development. The only thing stopping us from accepting the million dollars being offered to us was the fact that the game didn't exist. The entire buzz was based on a game concept and communication about it through weekly chats and the blog.

This is the power of marketing and promoting your game and getting the basic concepts playable as a demo or trailer.

Modding a 3D Game Engine

The time and money (especially salary expenses) it takes to develop a world-class 3D engine and then develop a game that highlights the engine's features is an endeavor very few companies can afford to do.

Even THQ's Kaos Studios in New York developed Frontlines: Fuel of War using the Unreal 3 engine. As previously stated, I suggest that new game designers and developers get the GarageGames Torque Engine or Torque Game Builder as a great, inexpensive yet powerful starting application to build their game with. Creating a mod for your 3D game design or even to express your creative, cinematic skills is a great way to show others your talents. Be a game designer and get your vision made so that others can enjoy it. You don't want to spend two or more years with physics and mathematics experts developing your own super 3D engine. As mentioned in the section on machinima, other companies with excellent 3D mod engines are id Software (Quake and Doom), Valve Software (Half-Life series), Bethesda Softworks (The Elder Scrolls and Fallout 3), Crytek (Crysis and Far Cry), Relic Entertainment (Company of Heroes), Epic Games (Unreal), and Rockstar (GTA).

Cell Phone Games

The IGDA Mobile Gaming White Paper (www.igda.org/online/IGDA_Mobile_Whitepaper_2005.pdf) predicted that in 2009 U.S. mobile gaming revenue would surpass $1.79 billion. A typical mobile game takes three to six months for a small budget game and six months to a year for a 3D game developed with a team of two to five people. The main issues to plan for with mobile games are screen resolution, input keys, and the graphics capabilities of the cell phone.

According to ScreenDigest (www.screendigest.com/reports/08mobilegamevchain/08mobilegamingvalue-pdf/view.html), "From 2009 onwards, North America will become the largest mobile games market. Mobile games revenues in the U.S. will double over the next five years to just over 1.1 billion Euros [$2.2 billion U.S.]."

For cell phone games using a Nokia device, you can use the following (free) platforms: Symbian C++ or Open C/C++ for S60; Java, Micro Edition (Java ME) for the Nokia Linux; Flash Lite for S60; or Python for S60. Gameloft, EA's premier mobile studio, develops mobile games in Brew and J2ME. (A free software development kit is available for Brew through http://brew.qualcomm.com/brew/en/. Eclipse J2Me can be freely downloaded from http://eclipseme.org/docs/index.html, and Sun's J2ME, now called Sun Java Wireless, can be downloaded from http://java.sun.com/products/sjwtoolkit/download.html for free.)

Since most cell phones can only store a couple of games in memory at a time, a popular game may be purchased by the same player several times. The game may be played for a while, erased to play other cell phone games, and then repurchased to play again on the same cell phone.

Handhelds

The Gameboy Advance has lots of emulation tools available on the
Internet, and is it is easy to develop GBA games from your Windows PC.
Jonathan Harbour has written an excellent book called *Programming the
Gameboy Advance: The Unofficial Guide* that is available as a free download
(http://theharbourfamily.com/jonathan/?page_id=89).

A few of the GBA emulators include Visual Boy Advance, VBA Link,
BatGBA, and Boycott Advance (http://www.gameboy-advance-roms.com/
gameboy_advance_roms.htm). I have used several of these with the C
programming language and found that within a day, a simple GBA game
can be developed and played on your PC emulating a GBA. I have also
downloaded my game onto a ROM cartridge and then placed that ROM
cartridge into a GBA to play my game. Now that's cool.

Although I have used homebrew Nintendo DS emulators, my game
played on the emulator but I couldn't get the game to run on an actual
Nintendo DS, so be warned! (Hopefully the homebrew development programmers can fix this issue eventually.)

Homebrew Games

There is an entire retrogaming market of players who own old systems
such as the Atari 2600.

You can learn to design and develop simple, homebrew games for the
Atari 2600 from the AtariAge website (www.atariage.com/2600/program-
ming/index.html). You may be surprised to know that the Atari 2600 sold
over 30 million units and many of them are still being used. Every year,
more than 20 new Atari 2600 games are developed and sold by a number
of different companies and independent publishers.

There are even several magazines and newsletters published monthly
that focus on retrogaming and have news about new game releases.

The Atari 2600 homebrew community is among the largest groups
developing original games for classic video game consoles. If you sold

1,000 copies of your homebrew Atari 2600 game at $20 each with a $5 cost of goods expense, you'd earn $15,000 for your game. Not bad for two to three months of work. For more information, please see the Internet reading assignment at the end of the chapter called "Postmortem: Pixels Past's SCSIcide."

Workshop

Suggested Activities

Activity 1: Explain how your game design would fit in and sell well as a casual game, an Internet game, a cell phone game, or a 3D game mod.

Activity 2: Discuss developing a game for one of the suggested outlets and how your development would change if a publisher wanted to back your entire game and company budget.

Assignments

Assignment 1: How has "machinima" changed the way we view interactive 3D entertainment?

Assignment 2: How can independent filmmakers use "machinima" to produce an entire film or prototype a film?

Exercises

Exercise 1: For each genre mentioned in Chapter 3, list which publisher you would want to contact to pitch your game design to and why. List a second choice if needed as a fallback.

Exercise 2: Describe the difference between the retail game world and (a) casual games, (b) Internet games, (c) cell phone games, and (d) 3D game mods.

Unguided Exercises

Unguided Exercise 1: Write an e-mail to a publisher or developer whose name or logo appears on a game you've recently played and give them valuable criticism such as "I like these features...," "These features could have been better if...," or "Future features for this game should be...." (Notice that there is no "I hated this..." or "These features were really bad because....")

Unguided Exercise 2: Write a short marketing or PR document on your game idea that could be placed on a gaming news website.

Chapter 14

Internet Reading Assignment

Go to the IGDA (International Game Developers Association) website's white papers and select the latest report about casual games, mobile games, or online games.

www.igda.org/content/reports.php

"Postmortem: Pixels Past's SCSIcide" by Joe Grand

www.gamasutra.com/features/20030226/grand_pfv.htm

The Game Design Document

The Game Design Document (GDD) is the designer's entire vision spelled out in detail, which includes all of the storyline, character dialogue, world maps, city views, and detailed room specifications such as sample wallpaper, artwork, and rug designs. It also includes audio content for background or ambient sounds, sound effects, character dialogue (with accents and speech patterns), programming, and AI considerations.

This document is often called the "Design bible," since it is the document written by the designer for the entire team to follow, including the programmers (game, engine, and technical programmers), the artists (both scenery and character), audio specialists (composer, special effects, background sound engineers, ADR, and Foley specialists), and game testers. The concept is "If something exists in the game, it must appear and be described in the design document." It is the common point of reference that the entire team understands and follows to create the designer's vision. It is from this document that programmers (usually the lead programmer or technical director) and artists (usually the head artist) refer to when documenting the technical spec (or specification), which explains in detail the in-depth technical issues of all the game code, the engine code, and the artwork and audio files (including each file's name, size, and description).

> **Important note:** In order to avoid confusion, when the GDD is updated, you should *destroy* all previous copies. You can also use a different color cover page and label every page with a new version number.

Background

In late May 2001, I met with Phantom EFX in Iowa to discuss a follow-up game to Reel Deal Slots. My previous "casino" games included products from Villa Crespo Software such as video poker (Stanford Wong Video Poker and Dr. Wong's Jacks+), black jack (Dr. Thorp's Black Jack), craps, roulette, and poker games (Amarillo Slim's Dealer's Choice, 7-Card Stud, and Ruckus Poker). The meeting determined that the product was to be a poker game and some basic game design issues were discussed and written down.

In June 2001 the project was underway as design, programming, and artwork progressed concurrently. The distributors wanted a Christmas product, and that meant a mid- to late-August deadline (a gold master reproduced and boxed by the end of August). That was a 12-week project life cycle. My friends in the industry laughed when I chatted with them about the project, claiming that the time needed to complete a game of this size was 6 to 12 months.

This case is *not* (I repeat *not*) the usual project life cycle. Several important issues had to be resolved to meet these critical deadlines, such as numerous daily meetings in the beginning to flesh out the game design, total control of the project by the programmer (me), and working six to seven days a week, 10 to 16 hours a day. Needless to say, the official design document was never written. The design discussed daily was written down, and artwork submitted to programming had to be documented (filename, screen positions, file format).

The project shipped on time with a few items dropped from the original design document, and the Internet component placed in the first patch (downloadable update).

The Game Design Document of Reel Deal Poker Challenge reproduced in this chapter shows the design as originally planned. In brackets (e.g., [this was dropped from the game because…]) I'll include issues and reasons for changes, later implementations, or dropping the issue from the game.

I have often read articles and books on game design that discuss game documents in theory. In this chapter, I will show you in detail what goes into a Game Design Document.

This document is provided as a tutorial so you can start with this template and create your own, much better design documents for your visions — the games of the future.

Reel Deal Poker Challenge Design Document

PUBLISHER: PHANTOM EFX
GENRE: CASUAL GAME WITH ADVENTURE ELEMENTS
PLATFORM: WINDOWS 98/2K/ME/XP WITH DIRECT X 8.0
DESIGNERS: (in alphabetic order)
Roger E. Pedersen
Aaron Schurman
Danny Stokes
Marty VanZee

Table of Contents

Qiangsheng (aka "Q")
    Profile
    Poses
    Mouth Animations
    Animated Eyes
Lou
    Profile
    Poses
    Mouth Animations
    Animated Eyes
Special Floor: World Championship Poker Room
    Trevor
        Profile
        Poses
        Mouth Animations
        Animated Eyes
    Trevor Has Been Beaten (Red Dress Dance)
Eight-Player Poker Characters
Cards
    Whole Cards
    Discarded Cards
    No Alpha Round Cards
    Fake Drop Round Cards
    Fake Drop Shadow Cards
Cashier's Cage
    VIP Casino Card
    VIP Clipboard
    Cashier's Cage
Credits Screen
Statistics Screen
The Prize Vault
Chips
Tournament First Prizes
    Floor 1: $5,000 Tournament Prizes
    Floor 1: $25,000 Tournament Prizes
    Floor 2: $25,000 Tournament Prizes
    Floor 2: $100,000 Tournament Prizes
    Floor 3: $100,000 Tournament Prizes
    Floor 3: $500,000 Tournament Prizes
    Special Floor: $2,500,000 World Championship
Exit Game
Betting/Raising
Scriptwriting
    Yvette
    Sven
    Hoyt
    Melvis

> Jacqueline
> Mortimer
> Lou
> Q
> Lizzie
> Trevor
> Cashier, Bouncer, and Manager
> Programming
> Basic Poker AI
>> Draw Poker (No Openers and Jacks or Better to Open)
>> Five-Card Stud
>> Seven-Card Stud, Chicago Low, and Chicago High
>> Texas Hold 'Em and Omaha
> Game Variations Order of Play
>> Draw Poker No Openers and Jacks or Better to Open
>> Five-Card Stud
>> Seven-Card Stud, Chicago Low, and Chicago High
>> Texas Hold 'Em
>> Omaha

Overview

Reel Deal Poker Challenge takes place in the Poker Palace where players from each level's lobby enter the Cashier's Cage, the Slot Room, the Poker Room, or the Poker Tournament Room.

The goal of Reel Deal Poker Challenge is to advance through each of the three levels by winning tournaments and finally beating the World Champion in a winner-takes-all showdown.

Poker games variations available are Draw Poker, Draw Poker with Jacks or Better, Five-Card Stud, Seven-Card Stud, Chicago High, Chicago Low, Omaha, and Texas Hold 'Em. [Omaha, a variation of Texas Hold 'Em, was added due to its Internet and casino popularity.]

Based on the successful features from Reel Deal Slots and Video Poker, Reel Deal Poker Challenge will incorporate two addictive features such as the prize vault and "VIP" player areas. Players enjoy guessing what prizes they can win and earning prizes in their prize vault, as well as earning the right to access upper levels where there are better players and higher stakes. The Internet play through the Game Spy site will allow players (up to eight) to play a selected poker variation and increase their chip inventory against other human players.

Each room and lobby will have its own unique theme from "Oriental" to "Roman" to "Egyptian" accompanied by ambient (background) music in the lobby and in each room.

The Slot Room will be an extension to the Poker Palace to show off (and gain sales for the slot game) and increase the player's chip inventory.

[Although the players could enter the Slot Room and play several slot games, the money lost or won in the Slot Room was not added to the player's chip inventory. The prior product written in Linux and Windows under a different compiler using a special library for graphics and sound combined with the extremely short development cycle made this feature a low priority. Finally, it was implemented as a separate room with an "order this great product" screen before returning to the Poker Palace lobby. These are the issues that separate a design document and your vision from the realities of getting the product on the shelf in the time required (which is usually beyond most of the team's control).]

Rules of Poker

Poker is played by using a single deck of 52 cards. The deck has four suits: clubs ♣, diamonds ♦, hearts ♥, and spades ♠. Each suit has 13 cards ranked 2 through 10, jack, queen, king, and ace (the ace can be the highest or lowest card).

Poker games always begin with a shuffle to randomly sort the deck. A brand new deck always has the 52 cards in suit and rank order.

Hand Rankings

The following examples are in ranking order, meaning the best hand has a ranking of 1 and the worst hand has a ranking of 10.

Rank	Hand Name	Description of Hand/Example				
1	Royal Flush	A, K, Q, J, 10 of same suit				
		10♠,	J♠,	Q♠,	K♠,	A♠
2	Straight Flush	Five same suit consecutive cards				
		4♦,	5♦,	6♦,	7♦,	8♦
3	Four of a Kind	Four cards of the same rank				
		7♠,	7♣,	7♦,	7♥,	6♥
4	Full House	Three of a kind plus a pair				
		3♦,	3♠,	3♣,	K♠,	K♥
5	Flush	Five cards of the same suit				
		3♥,	7♥,	10♥,	Q♥,	A♥
6	Straight	Five cards in sequence				
		5♣,	6♦,	7♣,	8♥,	9♠
7	Three of a Kind	Three cards of the same rank				
		J♥,	J♠,	J♦,	8♥,	9♠
8	Two Pair	Two pairs of different rank				
		5♥,	5♠,	9♣,	9♠,	8♥
9	One Pair	Two cards of the same rank				
		A♠,	A♦,	2♥,	4♦,	8♠
10	High Card	None of the other rankings				
		K♠,	2♦,	4♠,	6♥,	8♦

Poker Variations

Poker has many variations, with each variation having its own rules. The more popular poker variations are Draw Poker, Five-Card Stud,

Seven-Card Stud, Chicago High, Chicago Low, Texas Hold 'Em, and Omaha. Most poker variations can be played with two to eight players. The cards are shuffled and distributed by a player called the dealer. In all variations, the first card is given to the player to the left of the dealer. A round of betting consists of each player deciding whether to bet (or raise after the first bet was made) an amount from the group's agreed-to minimum to maximum, fold (quit this round of play), or check (agree to cover the current amount due to the pot). When three raises to the original bet have been made or all players have checked, the betting round is completed.

In Draw Poker, all players make a small blind bet or ante before receiving any cards. Then the players, starting with the player to the left of the dealer, receive cards until each player has five cards. Players carefully look at their cards and determine which cards to keep and which cards to discard. Players can discard up to three cards (four cards if they are keeping an ace). Before discarding, each player may bet or raise, fold (quit this round of play), or accept the current bet amount (check). Then the remaining players discard their cards. Another round of betting occurs where each player can bet, fold, or check. After all players have checked or three raises have occurred, the players must show their cards, and the player with the highest hand wins the pot (all bets made). If only one player remains (no showdown), he wins and his cards can remain unexposed.

One variation of Draw Poker that is commonly played is Draw Poker Jacks or Better, where to open the first round of betting the player needs a pair of jacks or better (a better ranking pair or three of a kind) to bet. This lets the other players know that the player has a hand with a pair of jacks or better. If no player can bet (no hand is at least a pair of jacks), the cards are reshuffled and a new round begins (ante and all). This variation can cause the pot to become quite large with antes and allow players with bad hands to fold earlier.

Five-Card Stud is a variation where each player receives one card face down (called the "hole"), the next three cards are dealt face up, and the last card is dealt face down. The player to the left of the dealer receives the first card. If played with a bring-in, the player with the lowest first up card must bet the minimum. Some variations have all players at the start ante up (a small bet). After all players have received an up card (cards two through four), a round of betting occurs. Then after the fifth card (a down card) has been received by all players, the last round of betting occurs. In each betting round after the first, the player with the highest-ranking hand showing (only the up cards) starts the betting process. If only one player remains, he wins the pot and his cards can remain unexposed. Otherwise, the remaining players show all five cards and the player with the highest ranking hand wins the pot.

Seven-Card Stud is a variation where the first two cards are dealt face down (the "hole"), the third through sixth cards are dealt face up, and the seventh (last) card is face down. It can also be played with a bring-in;

otherwise, the player with the highest ranking up card opens the betting round. Each player must either bet (raise), fold, or check. Then cards four through six are dealt face up, and after all players have received that round's card, betting occurs. The last card (the seventh card) is dealt face down unless in an eight-player game all eight players remain, then the last card is dealt as a community card (shared by all players). If only one player remains, he wins (no showdown) and his cards may be left unexposed. Otherwise, all remaining players must show their cards and the player with the highest-ranking hand wins the pot. If more than one player has the highest-ranking hand (a tie), they split the pot or the player with the highest suit wins. The suit order is usually spades (the highest), hearts, diamonds, and clubs (the lowest).

Chicago High plays exactly like Seven-Card Stud except the player with the highest spade in the "hole" splits the pot. The ace of spades is the highest card. If the last card (seventh card) is a community card, it cannot be used as a "hole" card.

Chicago Low plays exactly like Seven-Card Stud except that the player with the lowest spade in the "hole" splits the pot. Players must decide whether the ace of spaces is the lowest card or the two (deuce) of spades is the lowest. If the last card (seventh card) is a community card, it cannot be used as the "hole" card.

Over the last few years, Texas Hold 'Em and Omaha have become popular variations.

Many of the top poker players consider Texas Hold 'Em to be the most challenging and sublime of all the poker games. Texas Hold 'Em is the game played to determine the undisputed champion at the World Series of Poker at Binion's Horseshoe in downtown Las Vegas.

Texas Hold 'Em is a seven-card poker game where each player receives two down cards and the remaining five cards are called "community cards," which are shared by all of the players. Each player must make his best five-card poker hand using five out of the seven cards (his two cards plus the five community cards). After the two down cards have been dealt to all of the players, the player to the left of the dealer must make a small blind bet. Then a round of betting occurs where each player must bet (raise), fold, or check. Then five cards are placed face down in the center as community cards.

The middle three community cards (the "flop") are turned over (face up), and another round of betting occurs. Then the first community card (the "turn" card) is flipped over (face up), and another betting round occurs. Finally, the fifth community card (the "river") is turned over (face up), and the final round of betting occurs.

If more than one player remains, the player with the highest ranking hand wins the pot. Any combination of the player's own two down cards and the five community cards can be used to make the best five-card poker hand. The pot is split if a tie occurs.

Omaha is a form of Texas Hold 'Em that is very popular in casinos and on "poker night." Omaha is a nine-card poker variation where each player is dealt four down cards and the remaining five cards are dealt face down as community cards (for all players to use). Each player must create the best ranking poker hand by using two of his four cards plus three of the five community cards (Omaha players often say "Two from the hand, three from the board"). Just like in Texas Hold 'Em, after the first four cards are dealt, the player to the left of the dealer must make a small blind bet. Then the players must bet (raise), fold, or check. The middle three community cards are turned face up, and another round of betting occurs. The first community card is flipped, and another round of betting occurs. The last (fifth) community card is turned over, and the last round of betting occurs. The players remaining show their cards, and the player with the best ranking poker hand wins the pot.

Start of the Game (or After the Game Icon Is Clicked On)

The Cashier's Cage

Players start their first game in the Cashier's Cage, where they must register to proceed into the lobby. In the Cashier's Cage, players can turn on or off the Four-Player Poker Room's character comments, turn on or off ambient sound (background music), look at their statistics for each poker variation (should I call if I'm only holding a pair of aces in Draw Poker?), register as players and get their name and unique ID number on their VIP Casino Card, or see the credits (the people who worked night and day to provide you with this fine entertainment).

The cashier's cage   VIP registration

VIP Register

The VIP registration screen has several required fields that must be entered before proceeding to play the game, such as the player's title (Mr., Mrs., or Ms.), the player's first and last name (two separately entered fields), and the player's birthday (month and day as two digits each). Optional fields are the player's address, city, state, and zip code (allow up to 10 digits). "CANCEL" will clear all fields and "DONE" will check the required fields for completeness and validity (the birth date check will validate the day based on the number of days in the month). This screen matches the previous product's screen, where there is a method for customers to register their product by sending the publisher their mailing information contained on this screen. [This feature of downloading the registration was not implemented by the publisher.]

The entry of "Mr.," "Mrs.," or "Ms." flags the return "welcome" verbal greeting of "Nice to have you back, (Sir or Miss)" and "Play well, (Sir or Miss)," which adds a nice touch to the game. (How did it know?)

The last player to play the game is the player that the game assumes is playing. If not, the new or returning player must indicate so.

In the Cashier's Cage players can request additional funds when they are below the highest floor allowed or minimum tournament entry fee.

If the player is only allowed on the first floor and his current chip inventory is below $250, he can receive an additional credit of $2,500. The credit is added to his current chip inventory and noted in the casino record (see the section titled "Statistics Screen").

If the player is only allowed on the first or second floors and his current chip inventory is below $1,250, he can receive an additional credit of $5,000. The credit is added to his current chip inventory and noted in the casino record (see "Statistics Screen").

If the player is allowed on all three floors and his current chip inventory is below $5,000, he can receive an additional credit of $25,000. The credit is added to his current chip inventory and noted in the casino record (see "Statistics Screen").

Otherwise, the player is given a sound bite of "Your account balance is not low enough to receive additional funds."

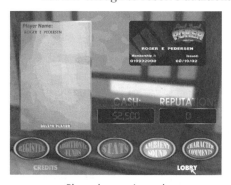

Player has registered

Prize vault birthday celebration

The "cash" area displays the player's current chip inventory in dollars, and the "reputation" area displays points earned by participating in poker tournaments.

The birth date information will be utilized in the game when the player enters the Prize Vault. If the current date is near the player's birthday, he will receive a cake and a one-time present (a $100 chip).

The Lobbies

There are three lobbies and a special level to play the World Champion in a winner-takes-all poker battle.

The first floor's motif is based on the Roman era with Doric columns, carved wooden doors, and a mirrored ceiling reflecting the plush Corinthian rug.

The second floor sends the player into the Orient, where Ming vases shoot out spirals of flames that light up walls hung with famous works of art from the Han dynasty. The floor is cushioned by rare Oriental rugs and the room has a simplistic wooden ceiling.

The third floor transports the player to the edge of the Nile, where pharaohs once ruled, and the players enjoy visions of authentic Egyptian hieroglyphics, rare Egyptian doors from the Throne Room of King Tutankamen, and an exotic rug from the temple of Cleopatra. The symbol of Ra, god of the Sun, appears as the wall torches flicker, adding to the illumination of the magnificent array of constellations that shine through the high, glass ceiling.

If a player hasn't earned enough reputation points to enter the elevator to the next floor, a security guard blocks the entrance to the elevator.

The Prize Vault

The Prize Vault (or Trophy Room) is where players store their first-place tournament prizes. There are 15 prizes to be placed in the Prize Vault. Winning them and discovering what they are is an addictive part of the fun (as experienced from the previous product, Reel Deal Slots and Video Poker). There is only one of each type of prize to win (prizes once earned cannot be removed). If a prize is clicked on, its description and a larger picture of that prize appears on the screen.

If the date is within seven days before the player's birthday and seven days after that date, the "happy birthday cake" and message will appear. Only the first time it does will a $100 chip be given as a birthday present (mark Chip Given and Year).

Audio

- All voice-over audio recorded
- Floor 1 (Roman) ambience (background music): Several to be intermixed and not repetitive
- Floor 2 (Oriental) ambience (background music): Several to be intermixed and not repetitive
- Floor 3 (Egyptian) ambience (background music): Several to be intermixed and not repetitive
- Special Floor ambience (background music): Several to be intermixed and not repetitive
- Player input sound effects for actions such as a button press or a mouse click
- Ambience (background music) for the other rooms on each floor such as the Cashier's Cage, Elevator (arriving and exiting sounds), Poker Room, Tournament Room, Prize Vault, and entering the Slot Room
- In-game sounds for card flipping, chip click when thrown on the table, chip rake when gathering your winnings, and a shuffle sound
- Music for winning a tournament and credits screen

Artwork

As a designer, your job is to (to the best of your knowledge) list all the needed artwork and communicate the vision you have of your game to the artists. But they have to see the same vision you do. Since this is an internal design document and not a product for sale, provide detailed photographs and pictures of your world from any source such as the Internet, books, and magazines and get on paper the closest visuals possible.

Lobbies

General

Multiplayer button and multiplayer mouse over

Next level congratulations

Poker Rooms for Four and Eight Players

Bet indicator	Marks the player who initially started the betting
Deal indicator	Marks the player who is dealer

First and Second Floor Card Icons

IconG5carddraw	Icon on green table for Five-Card Draw Poker
IconG5carddrawjb	Icon on green table for Five-Card Draw Poker Jacks or Better
IconG5cardstud	Icon on green table for Five-Card Stud Poker
IconG7cardstud	Icon on green table for Seven-Card Stud Poker
IconGChicagoHi	Icon on green table for Chicago High Poker
IconGChicagoLow	Icon on green table for Chicago Low Poker
IconGOmaha	Icon on green table for Omaha Poker
IconGTexasholdEm	Icon on green table for Texas Hold 'Em Poker

Third Floor Card Icons

IconB5carddraw	Icon on blue table for Five-Card Draw Poker
IconB5carddrawjb	Icon on blue table for Five-Card Draw Poker Jacks or Better
IconB5cardstud	Icon on blue table for Five-Card Stud Poker
IconB7cardstud	Icon on blue table for Seven-Card Stud Poker
IconBChicagoHi	Icon on blue table for Chicago High Poker
IconBChicagoLow	Icon on blue table for Chicago Low Poker
IconBOmaha	Icon on blue table for Omaha Poker
IconBTexasholdEm	Icon on blue table for Texas Hold 'Em Poker

Tournament

A tournament is a four-player game for a preset "entry fee" where the winner gets an additional money prize and in some rooms a "prize" to be added to his Prize Vault (or trophy room). All players keep their winnings. Early exiting from the room forfeits the entry fee. Reputation points needed to advance to the other floors are gained by participating in tournaments. The player with the most money after 20 hands of poker (any variation but only one per tournament) wins.

Tournament Information

Floor	Level	Next Floor Points	Ante Min	Ante Max	Entry Fee	VIP Points (1st-4th)
1	1	100	$20	$50	$1,000	15, 10, 5, 3
	2	100	$50	$200	$5,000	25, 20, 10, 5
	3	100	$250	$1,000	$25,000	35, 25, 15, 10
2	1	1100	$50	$200	$5,000	150, 100, 50, 30
	2	1100	$250	$1,000	$25,000	250, 200, 100, 50
	3	1100	$1,000	$5,000	$100,000	350, 250, 150, 100
3	1	1100	$250	$1,000	$25,000	1500,1000, 500, 300
	2	1100	$1,000	$5,000	$100,000	2500, 2000, 1000, 500
	3	1100	$5,000	$20,000	$500,000	3500, 2500, 1500, 1000
4	1	0	$20,000	$50,000	$2,500,000	

Tournament Place Finished

First Floor

Lobby

RomanLobby	The first floor's lobby
RomanBouncer	The bouncer in front of the elevator
RomanBouncerText	The bouncer's text when accessing the elevator
RomanCashMO	Enter the Cashier's Cage mouse over
RomanElevUpMO	Access the elevator up mouse over (to second floor)
RomanExitMO	Exit the game (and save) mouse over
RomanGrandMaster	Enter the Grandmaster button (play Trevor). Only displayed when player has enough reputation points to access the "Special Floor" and has not played Trevor yet
RomanGrandMasterMO	Enter the Grandmaster button mouse over
RomanPokMO	Play the Nontournament Poker Room mouse over
RomanPrizeMO	Enter the Prize Vault mouse over
RomanSlotsMO	Enter the Slot Machine Room mouse over
RomanTournMO	Play in a Poker Tournament mouse over

Poker Room

Four Player
    Roman Table
    Roman Deal normal, mouse over, on click buttons
    Roman Lobby normal, mouse over, on click buttons
    Roman Stats Screen normal, mouse over, on click buttons
    Profiles Turn On and Turn Off buttons
    Profile Exit normal and mouse over button

Eight Player
    Roman Table
    Roman Deal normal, mouse over, on click buttons
    Roman Lobby normal, mouse over, on click buttons
    Roman Stats Screen normal, mouse over, on click buttons

Tournament Room

Four Player
    Roman Table
    Roman Deal normal, mouse over, on click buttons
    Roman Lobby normal, mouse over, on click buttons
    Roman Stats Screen normal, mouse over, on click buttons
    Profiles Turn On and Turn Off buttons
    Profile Exit normal and mouse over button

Second Floor

Lobby

OrientalLobby	The second floor's lobby
OrientalBouncer	The bouncer in front of the elevator
OrientalBouncerText	The bouncer's text when accessing the elevator
OrientalCashMO	Enter the Cashier's Cage mouse over
OrientalElevUpMO	Elevator up mouse over (to third floor, if able)
OrientalElevDownMO	Elevator down mouse over (to first floor)
OrientalExitMO	Exit the game (and save) mouse over
OrientalGrandMaster	Enter the Grandmaster button (play Trevor)
OrientalGrandMasterMO	Enter the Grandmaster button mouse over
OrientalPokMO	Play the Nontournament Poker Room mouse over
OrientalPrizeMO	Enter the Prize Vault mouse over
OrientalSlotsMO	Enter the Slot Machine Room mouse over
OrientalTournMO	Play in a Poker Tournament mouse over
LeftPot	Animation of fire spiraling out of the left pot
RightPot	Animation of fire spiraling out of the right pot

(Programming note: Offset the two pots' spiraling fire so they look more natural.)

Chapter 15

Poker Room

Four Player
    Oriental Table
    Oriental Deal normal, mouse over, on click buttons
    Oriental Lobby normal, mouse over, on click buttons
    Oriental Stats Screen normal, mouse over, on click buttons
    Profiles Turn On and Turn Off buttons
    Profile Exit normal and mouse over button

Eight Player
    Oriental Table
    Oriental Deal normal, mouse over, on click buttons
    Oriental Lobby normal, mouse over, on click buttons
    Oriental Stats Screen normal, mouse over, on click buttons

Tournament Room

Four Player
    Oriental Table
    Oriental Deal normal, mouse over, on click buttons
    Oriental Lobby normal, mouse over, on click buttons
    Oriental Stats Screen normal, mouse over, on click buttons
    Profiles Turn On and Turn Off buttons
    Profile Exit normal and mouse over button

Third Floor

Lobby

EgyptianLobby	The third floor's lobby
EgyptianBouncer	The bouncer in front of the elevator
EgyptianBouncerText	The bouncer's text when accessing the elevator
EgyptianCashMO	Enter the Cashier's Cage mouse over
EgyptianElevUpMO	Elevator up mouse over (to fourth floor, if able)
EgyptianElevDownMO	Elevator down mouse over (to first floor)
EgyptianExitMO	Exit the game (and save) mouse over
EgyptianGrandMaster	Enter the Grandmaster button (play Trevor)
EgyptianGrandMasterMO	Enter the Grandmaster button mouse over
EgyptianPokMO	Play the Nontournament Poker Room mouse over
EgyptianPrizeMO	Enter the Prize Vault mouse over
EgyptianSlotsMO	Enter the Slot Machine Room mouse over
EgyptianTournMO	Play in a Poker Tournament mouse over

| LeftTorch | Animation of fire flickering from the left torch |
| RightTorch | Animation of fire flickering from the right torch |

(Programming note: Offset the two torches' flickering fire so they look more natural.)

Poker Room

Four Player
    Egyptian Table
    Egyptian Deal normal, mouse over, on click buttons
    Egyptian Lobby normal, mouse over, on click buttons
    Egyptian Stats Screen normal, mouse over, on click buttons
    Profiles Turn On and Turn Off buttons
    Profile Exit normal and mouse over button

Eight Player
    Egyptian Table
    Egyptian Deal normal, mouse over, on click buttons
    Egyptian Lobby normal, mouse over, on click buttons
    Egyptian Stats Screen normal, mouse over, on click buttons

Tournament Room

Four Player
    Egyptian Table
    Egyptian Deal normal, mouse over, on click buttons
    Egyptian Lobby normal, mouse over, on click buttons
    Egyptian Stats Screen normal, mouse over, on click buttons
    Profiles Turn On and Turn Off buttons
    Profile Exit normal and mouse over button

Chapter 15

Special Floor

Boiler Room Table
Boiler Room Deal normal, mouse over, on click buttons
Boiler Room Lobby normal, mouse over, on click buttons
Boiler Room Stats Screen normal, mouse over, on click buttons
Profiles Turn On and Turn Off buttons
Profile Exit normal and mouse over button

It has long been rumored that there is a great and mysterious poker player who frequently visits the poker palace. Legend says he is a dedicated poker master who will only play against the best players and for the highest stakes. He doesn't play in the posh poker rooms of the poker palace, but rather in the humble boiler room deep in the basement of the palace.

The rumors are true and this is your chance. His name is Trevor and Your skilled play has earned you an invitation to sit at his table and play against him one on one in the ultimate showdown! The stakes are high as you compete for 2.5 Million dollars and the title of greatest poker player in the world. Just remember, in this game there is no set number of hands, you must play until someone wins.

Good luck.

Four-Player Poker Characters

First Floor: Roman Motif

Yvette

Profile

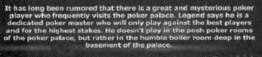

Yvette

Yvette works as a Showgirl at a nearby casino. She has recently taken up poker as a way to kill time between shows.
She's intelligent, with a bubbly personality, but hasn't been playing the game long enough yet to understand all of the intricacies.

Poses

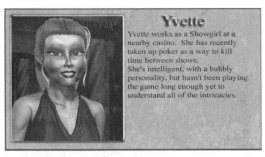

Mouth Animations

| AH | EE | EH | FV | MM | OH | OO | PB | UH | SMILE |

Phonemes for each of Yvette's poses ("ah," "ee," "eh," "fv," "mm," "oh," "oo," "pb," "uh," and a smile).

Animated Eyes

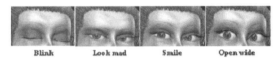

| Blink | Look mad | Smile | Open wide |

For each of Yvette's poses, the eyes should blink, look mad, smile, and open wide.

Sven

Profile

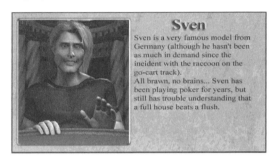

Poses

Mouth Animations

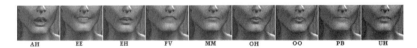

| AH | EE | EH | FV | MM | OH | OO | PB | UH |

Phonemes for each of Sven's poses ("ah," "ee," "eh," "fv," "mm," "oh," "oo," "pb," and "uh."

Animated Eyes

| Blink | Look mad | Open wide |

For each of Sven's poses, the eyes should blink, look mad, and open wide.

Hoyt

Profile

Hoyt

Hoyt has been frequenting our Poker Palace for several months. He's not much of a player, but our poker rooms are among the few places where people actually pay attention to him. He shows up every day in his best suit, orders his "Super Fruity Watermelon Schnapps Ka-Blammo", and loses a little more money.

Poses

Mouth Animations

Phonemes for each of Hoyt's poses ("ah," "ee," "eh," "fv," "mm," "oh," "oo," "pb," "uh," and a smile).

Animated Eyes

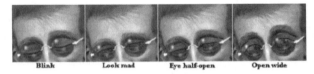

For each of Hoyt's poses, the eyes should blink, look mad, eye half-open, and open wide.

Second Floor: Oriental Motif

Melvis

Profile

Poses

Mouth Animations

Phonemes for each of Melvis' poses ("ah," "ee," "eh," "fv," "mm," "oh," "oo," "pb," "uh," a smile, and a sneer of course!).

Animated Eyes

For each of Melvis' poses, the eyes should blink, look mad, brow up, left brow up, and right brow up.

Chapter 15

Jacqueline

Profile

Poses

Mouth Animations

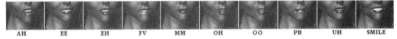

Phonemes for each of Jacqueline's poses ("ah," "ee," "eh," "fv," "mm," "oh," "oo," "pb," "uh," and a smile).

Animated Eyes

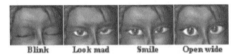

For each of Jacqueline's poses, the eyes should blink, look mad, smile, and open wide.

Mortimer

Profile

Poses

Mouth Animations

Phonemes for each of Mortimer's poses ("ah," "ee," "eh," "mm," "oh," "oo," "sah," "seh," "smm," "soh," and a smile).

Animated Eyes

Chapter 15

For each of Mortimer's poses, the eyes should blink, look mad, smile, and open wide.

Third Floor: Egyptian Motif

Lizzie

Profile

Poses

Mouth Animations

Phonemes for each of Lizzie's poses ("ah," "ee," "eh," "fv," "mm," "oh," "oo," "pb," "uh," and a smile).

Animated Eyes

For each of Lizzie's poses, the eyes should blink, look mad, and open wide.

Qiangsheng (aka "Q")

Profile

Poses

Mouth Animations

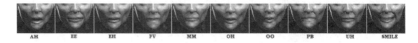

Phonemes for each of Qiangsheng's poses ("ah," "ee," "eh," "fv," "mm," "oh," "oo," "pb," "uh," and a smile).

Animated Eyes

For each of Qiangsheng's poses, the eyes should blink, look mad, and open wide.

Lou

Profile

Lou

If you were to ask Lou, he'd tell you that he runs a "family business." With his savvy play, guts, and money to spare, he's considered a "High Roller" by the biggest casinos in town... but he always visits the Poker Palace for high-stakes poker. (Several players who have beaten Lou in the past have requested Security Escorts for the remainder of their stay.)

Poses

Mouth Animations

Phonemes for each of Lou's poses ("ah," "ee," "eh," "fv," "mm," "oh," "oo," "pb," and "uh."

Animated Eyes

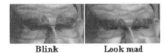

Blink   Look mad

For each of Lou's poses, the eyes should blink and look mad.

Special Floor: World Championship Poker Room

Trevor

Profile

Poses

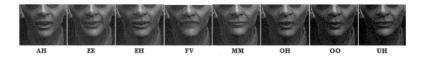

Mouth Animations

Phonemes for each of Trevor's poses ("ah," "ee," "eh," "fv," "mm," "oh," "oo," and "uh"). (The World's Best Poker Player doesn't smile!)

Animated Eyes

For each of Trevor's poses, the eyes should blink, look mad, and look up.

Trevor Has Been Beaten (Red Dress Dance)

TrevorEnd	Trevor dancing in a red dress animation (loops until Exit clicked)
Ending Background	Boiler Room background
Close	Ending Scene on click and mouse over

Eight-Player Poker Characters

Players (static 2D images)

Normal	Eyes Open/Closed	Mouth Open/Closed	Extra Animation
Beth	BethEC	BethMO	
Carol	CarolEC	CarolMO	CarolWink
Carver	CarverEC	CarverMO	
Cathy	CathyEC	CathyMO	
Curly	CurlyEC	CurlyMO	CurlyTiltHead
Gerald	GeraldEC	GeraldMC	
Harry	HarryEC	HarryMO	
Hazel	HazelEC	HazelMO	
Lakisha	LakishaEC	LakishaMO	
Mark	MarkEC	MarkMO	
Meredith	MeredithEC	MeredithMO	
Mitch	MitchEC	MitchMC	
Thomas	ThomasEC	ThomasMO	

Chapter 15

Cards

There are 52 cards (or one deck) in poker. There are four suits named clubs, diamonds, hearts, and spades ("alpha" order) with rankings from a two or deuce (low) to the ace (high). In a low game like Chicago Low, the ace can be the lowest card or the highest card or both.

All cards are placed in racks for the four- and eight-player poker games.

Most casinos use the "reverse alpha" order to break ties, meaning that the best suit is a spade, followed by the hearts, diamonds, and clubs.

Whole Cards

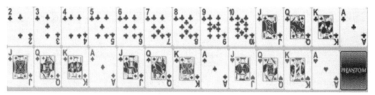

The 52 card faces and the decorated back of the card are used as "community cards," cards shown in the middle of the table and used by all of the players such as center cards in Texas Hold 'Em, Omaha, and other variations if there are not enough cards left to play. (Seven-Card Stud with eight players needs 56 cards, so the last card must be a "community card.")

Discarded Cards

In Draw Poker, the player may discard his unwanted cards in order to receive new replacement cards. The player clicks on the card (as a toggle On/Off) to turn the clicked-on card "gray," meaning "to discard." Since the game places the cards in a rack, the cards (all 52) need to be only half drawn.

No Alpha Round Cards

All 52 cards plus the back of the card, drawn half size since the cards are placed in a rack, are mainly used as the top right card without a shadow.

Fake Drop Round Cards

All 52 cards plus the back of the card, drawn half size since the cards are placed in a rack, are mainly used as the "discarded" cards beneath another card.

Fake Drop Shadow Cards

All 52 cards plus the back of the card, drawn half size since the cards are placed in a rack, are mainly used as the cards beneath another card (not a discarded card).

Cashier's Cage

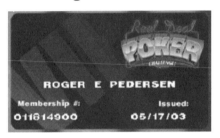

VIP Casino Card

Fonta numbers 0 through 9
Fonta letters capital A through Z and lowercase a through z

VIP Clipboard

VIP Clipboard (see Registration Screen)
Numbers 0 through 9
Letters capital A through Z and lowercase a through z
Symbols dash and slash
Back of First Name, back of Last Name, back of Address, back of City, back of State, back of Zip Code, back of Birthday, back of Birth Month, Cancel and Done on click buttons

Cashier's Cage

Cashier Screen	The Cashier's Cage screen
Player Name area	Up to 20 previous players who registered
Cash Prestige font	Numbers 0 through 9 for Cash and Reputation areas
Lobby	To return to the lobby (must be a registered player)

Credits	To honor those who have worked hard on this game
Register	To register to play in the casino
Additional Funds	An ATM in the casino, like calling your parents for money
Statistics	To view the playing statistics for each poker variation
Ambient Sound	To turn on or off the ambient music
Character Comments	To turn on or off the four-player verbal comments

Credits Screen

Credits	The staff that will produce the vision

Statistics Screen

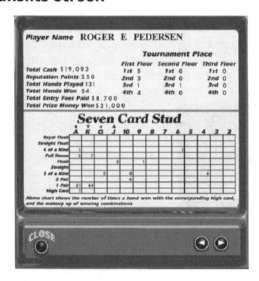

Note: On the chart, the Straight Flush (including a Royal Flush) and Flush will mark the high card in the winning hand. The Flush winning hands will be indicated in the columns marked spades, hearts, diamonds, and clubs ("reverse alpha" order). The chart numbers reflect their winning hands from the currently registered player's games (not just their winning hands) from all play in either the Poker Room or the Tournament Room.

- Bookman Demi10 font numbers 0 through 9 (for chart)
- Bookman Demi14 font numbers 0 through 9 plus the $ and , (for upper section)
- Bookman Demi24 font letters capital A through Z and lowercase a through z (for player's name)

The statistics are saved and can be cycled through for each of the poker variations such as Chicago High, Chicago Low, Five-Card Draw, Five-Card Draw Jacks or Better, Five-Card Stud, Texas Hold 'Em, Omaha, and Seven-Card Stud.

- Close normal, mouse over, and on click buttons
- Left arrow normal and mouse over to scroll back through the poker variations
- Right arrow normal and mouse over to scroll forward through the poker variations

The Prize Vault

- Lobby on click and Lobby mouse over to exit back to the Lobby
- Stat Screen on click and Stat Screen mouse over to view the Statistics screen

Chapter 15

Chips

Chips are to be displayed for betting (click on a chip to bet that amount) and placed on the table in three varying positions to look randomly thrown. Betting chips are valued from $1 to $5 million.

Table chips are valued from $1 to $5 million in three varying positions (one or two positions for the $50K to $5M chips).

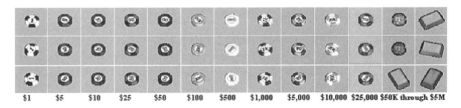

$1 $5 $10 $25 $50 $100 $500 $1,000 $5,000 $10,000 $25,000 $50K through $5M

Tournament First Prizes

Floor 1: $5,000 Tournament Prizes

In addition to the cash prize the casino is awarding the following prize to the winner:

COOKWARE

Cooking just got easier with this 3 piece cookware set. This sturdy set features the latest non-stick technology. Stainless steel bases, and beautiful wooden handles.

In addition to the cash prize the casino is awarding the following prize to the winner:

Cappuccino Machine

Enjoy the gourmet flavor of a real Cappuccino with this machine. Complete with drip tray, stainless filter, and frothing arm.

Floor 1: $25,000 Tournament Prizes

In addition to the cash prize the casino is awarding the following prize to the winner:

DVD PLAYER

Bring the theater experience home with this DVD player. Features include 5.1 surround sound, optical output, and remote control.

In addition to the cash prize the casino is awarding the following prize to the winner:

AQUARIUM

Experience the breathtaking beauty of the coral reef without ever leaving your home. This 75 Gallon saltwater aquarium comes fully stocked with beautiful sea life.

In addition to the cash prize the casino is awarding the following prize to the winner:

GUITAR

Enjoy the beautiful sound of this handmade acoustic guitar. Rosewood sides and Mother of Pearl inlay make this K.R. Blenius original a real collector's piece.

Floor 2: $25,000 Tournament Prizes

In addition to the cash prize the casino is awarding the following prize to the winner: **VASE**

Add beauty to your home with this beautiful ceramic vase. From the famous Edgegood factory comes this limited-edition piece, sure to increase in value.

In addition to the cash prize the casino is awarding the following prize to the winner: **COMPUTER**

The digital world is at your fingertips with this state of the art desktop PC. Powered by the new EFX Phantium 7 processor, it's super fast. What do you want to do today?

Floor 2: $100,000 Tournament Prizes

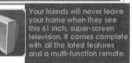

In addition to the cash prize the casino is awarding the following prize to the winner: **TELEVISION**

Your friends will never leave your home when they see this 61 inch, super-screen television. It comes complete with all the latest features and a multi-function remote.

In addition to the cash prize the casino is awarding the following prize to the winner: **HOT TUB**

Anything less then total relaxation is not an option with this deluxe hot tub. Over twenty high-pressure jets soothe your aches away and the wood design compliments any decor.

In addition to the cash prize the casino is awarding the following prize to the winner: **SCULPTURE**

A monument to your casino skill, this striking steel and marble sculpture adds class to any room.

Floor 3: $100,000 Tournament Prizes

In addition to the cash prize the casino is awarding the following prize to the winner:

SLOT MACHINE

Now you can enjoy the thrill of real slots action in the comfort of your own home. Fully functional, this %100 authentic, "Wheel of Cash" machine is the ultimate casino memento.

In addition to the cash prize the casino is awarding the following prize to the winner:

WATER CRAFT

Experience the thrill of the open water as you ride the waves in style on this personal watercraft. Unique styling and high performance make for an unbeatable ride.

Floor 3: $500,000 Tournament Prizes

In addition to the cash prize the casino is awarding the following prize to the winner:

VACATION

Tour Italy in style as you visit the wonders of ancient Rome on this deluxe tour package. Five-star acommodations on your trip make this the vacation of a lifetime.

In addition to the cash prize the casino is awarding the following prize to the winner:

FUR COAT

You'll be the toast of the town as you wear this gorgeous fur coat to all your social events. Made from only the most endangered species, this fur makes a statement.

In addition to the cash prize the casino is awarding the following prize to the winner:

STOCK CAR

Go ahead and sleep in, you'll get to work in record time now! This 650 horse-power custom race car is super-fast and ultra-cool!

Special Floor: $2,500,000 World Championship

Exit Game

"Yes" mouse over and on click buttons (save player's game settings) and "No" mouse over and on click buttons

Betting/Raising

Clicking the button for Open or Raise (shown at left) brings up the expanded box shown at right to enter the amount.

Check	On click and mouse over buttons
Fold	On click and mouse over buttons
Open	On click and mouse over buttons
Call	On click and mouse over buttons
Raise	On click and mouse over buttons
Cancel	On click and mouse over buttons
LED Font	Numbers 0 through 9
Right Arrow	On click and mouse over buttons
Left Arrow	On click and mouse over buttons
Chips	See artwork: Chips to set amount of open or raise chips values displayed are determined by the Min and Max betting amount set by the poker game amounts selected before entering the Poker Room.

Chapter 15

Scriptwriting

Note: For standard script formatting rules, see Chapter 11, "Game Narrative Scriptwriting."

```
[                   3         4                   6           ]
[12345678901234567890123456789012345678901234567890123456789012345678901234567890]
```

```
                              YVETTE
                    Wow! Good hand.
                              YVETTE
                    Oh, I like that.
                              YVETTE
                    Nice try.
                              YVETTE
                    Call.
                              YVETTE
                    I can't lose.
                              YVETTE
                    Check.
                              YVETTE
                    Now, that's a cute little card.
                              YVETTE
                    Did that feel good?
                              YVETTE
                    Fold.
                              YVETTE
                    I'm in, way in.
                              YVETTE
                    That's the card I'm looking for.
                              YVETTE
                    Not good for me.
                              YVETTE
                    Oh, baby.
                              YVETTE
                    Pass.
                              YVETTE
                    Where did you pull that out of?
                              YVETTE
                    Show me yours and umm... I'll show you mine.
                              YVETTE
                    I suppose.
                              YVETTE
                    Sweet!
                              YVETTE
                    That was too close for comfort.
                              YVETTE
                    I wouldn't pass this up for anything.
                              SVEN
                    (German stuff)
                              SVEN
                    I'll be back.
                              SVEN
                    I can't believe you don't play now.
                              SVEN
                    Better luck next time.
                              SVEN
                    Call.
                              SVEN
                    I can't believe it's not better.
```

```
            SVEN
Check.
            SVEN
My day will come.
            SVEN
Fold!
            SVEN
I fold now.
            SVEN
(German stuff) I'm in.
            SVEN
Look at you, little girlie cards.
            SVEN
Ha! Ha! Ha! (German stuff)
            SVEN
I am triumphant!
            SVEN
I'm in.
            SVEN
I'm out.
            SVEN
I'm liking these cards.
            SVEN
Your money will be mine now.
            SVEN
I must raise now.
            SVEN
Nice cards there.
            SVEN
Pass.
            SVEN
Raise.
            SVEN
Oh, (German stuff) enee guta.
            SVEN
(German stuff)
            SVEN
Sure, why not.
            HOYT
Bah.
            HOYT
Call.
            HOYT
Check.
            HOYT
Doh!
            HOYT
Fold.
            HOYT
You gotta know when to fold 'em.
            HOYT
Good job, buddy!
            HOYT
Hmmm!
            HOYT
I'm in the money! I'm in the money!
            HOYT
I'm in.
            HOYT
```

```
                              I'm there.
                                      HOYT
                      Later tator.
                                      HOYT
                      Not me.
                                      HOYT
                      On to you, pal.
                                      HOYT
                      Shazam!
                                      HOYT
                      Doh! I knew I should have run.
                                      HOYT
                      Well, spank my ass and call me
                      Shirley!
                                      HOYT
                      You stayed in with that?
                                      HOYT
                      This must be my lucky day.
                                      HOYT
                      This pot's mine!
                                      HOYT
                      Well, why not.
                                      MELVIS
                      Ahhh... Yah.
                                      MELVIS
                      Baby!
                                      MELVIS
                      Can't love these cards.
                                      MELVIS
                      Ah... You can't treat the King like
                      that.
                                      MELVIS
                      Ah... Check baby!
                                      MELVIS
                      Ah... That's a hell of a clambake!
                                      MELVIS
                      Foldin'.
                                      MELVIS
                      I'm gonna call.
                                      MELVIS
                      Ain't nothin' but a hound dog, baby.
                                      MELVIS
                      Melvis has left the building!
                                      MELVIS
                      Baby needs some blue suede shoes.
                                      MELVIS
                      Ohh... Nice hand there.
                                      MELVIS
                      Oh, mama!
                                      MELVIS
                      Ouch, man!
                                      MELVIS
                      Uh! hun huh!
                                      MELVIS
                      Uh thank ya. Thank ya very much!
                                      MELVIS
                      Oooh, yeah baby!
                                      MELVIS
                      You betcha!
                                      JACQUELINE
```

Oh, you'll do better next time.
> JACQUELINE

Check!
> JACQUELINE

That pot was only "chump change" anyways.
> JACQUELINE

Can we play yet?
> JACQUELINE

My daddy told me I can't lose.
> JACQUELINE

Daddy always said I could do it.
> JACQUELINE

Hmmmmp!
> JACQUELINE

I did it! I did it!
> JACQUELINE

Sure, I have plenty.
> JACQUELINE

Impressive!
> JACQUELINE

Why won't you let me win?
> JACQUELINE

Hmm... Pass.
> JACQUELINE

Daddy, I need more money.
> JACQUELINE

I must fold now.
> JACQUELINE

Never too rich for my blood.
> JACQUELINE

Oooo!
> JACQUELINE

I'll see that and raise you.
> JACQUELINE

You know what they say, the rich get richer.
> JACQUELINE

Simply divine.
> JACQUELINE

Sure, why not.
> JACQUELINE

I want to win.
> MORTIMER

Hee! Hee! Ain't missing this opportunity. Hee! Hee!
> MORTIMER

Chuckle
> MORTIMER

Eh... that's what Daddy's talking about.
> MORTIMER

Don't feel bad, it's only money.
> MORTIMER

In my day we ran from cards like this, but I'm feelin' frisky.
> MORTIMER

Now that's a good return on investment.
> MORTIMER

Yeah... sure. What have I got to lose?

```
                    MORTIMER
          Horse hockey!
                    MORTIMER
          This isn't worth a hill of beans.
                    MORTIMER
          I'm in.
                    MORTIMER
          I should've invested less.
                    MORTIMER
          There goes my kids' inheritance.
                    MORTIMER
          I'm in for the long haul.
                    MORTIMER
          Nice hand.
                    MORTIMER
          In my day, we played with nickels.
          And we were thankful for it.
                    MORTIMER
          In my day, we never saw cards like
          these.
                    MORTIMER
          Whoopee!
                    MORTIMER
          Call.
                    MORTIMER
          Check.
                    MORTIMER
          Fold.
                    MORTIMER
          Raise.
                    LOU
          I was actually nervous.
                    LOU
          Call.
                    LOU
          Hey. I can't win your money if we
          don't play.
                    LOU
          Fold.
                    LOU
          Get out while you still can.
                    LOU
          Oh, give it a shot.
                    LOU
          Good cards, pal-ie.
                    LOU
          Have fun spending my money.
                    LOU
          Hell yeah!
                    LOU
          I'm in.
                    LOU
          Bet on.
                    LOU
          No more for me.
                    LOU
          Not me.
                    LOU
          I'm out-ie.
                    LOU
```

Pass.

          LOU

I can't possibly lose.

          LOU

Raise.

          LOU

I'll raise ya.

          LOU

See ya!

          LOU

Suckers!

          LOU

Let's sweeten the pot.

          LOU

You talkin' to me?

          LOU

What were you thinkin'?

          LOU

Check.

          Q

Ha! Ha! Ha! I always win.

          Q

I cannot beat that hand! I could
beat a weaker hand.

          Q

Beginner's luck.

          Q

I do not believe in your bluff.

          Q

Call.

          Q

Ha! Ha! Ha! You cannot defeat me.

          Q

Check.

          Q

A cherry blossom knows when to fall.
I know when to get out.

          Q

I do not want it.

          Q

I will live to fight another day.

          Q

Fold.

          Q

Only a fool fights in a burning
house.

          Q

This pot is only half full.

          Q

I'm in.

          Q

Your cards are like sand, no
substance.

          Q

Observe the lotus blossom, it needs
no timekeeping.

          Q

Our money must experience more
togetherness.

          Q

Pass.
                Q
How long does it take one to learn
patience?
                Q
Raise.
                Q
For everything there is a season.
This is not mine.
                Q
I will see what happens.
                Q
This hand cannot help but spill gold.
                Q
Victory belongs to the honorable.
          LIZZIE
Bingo! Wait, wrong game.
          LIZZIE
How do you feel, taking my bus fare?
          LIZZIE
Guess I'll take the bus home.
          LIZZIE
Check.
          LIZZIE
That's okay sweetie, you deserve it.
          LIZZIE
Fold.
          LIZZIE
(hiccup)
          LIZZIE
See if you can keep up, sweetie.
          LIZZIE
I'm kicking butt and taking names.
          LIZZIE
How did you like that?
          LIZZIE
Macy's, here I come!
          LIZZIE
This is sweeter than a Mai Tai.
          LIZZIE
Maybe next time.
          LIZZIE
Nice win.
          LIZZIE
Oh, well.
          LIZZIE
Okay.
          LIZZIE
I'll stay for one more card.
          LIZZIE
Pass.
          LIZZIE
Raise.
          LIZZIE
Shame on you for pushing an old lady out.
          LIZZIE
Wow! Squeaked that one out.
          LIZZIE
How do you like that can of whup-ass?
          LIZZIE

Too rich for my blood.
            LIZZIE
Very nice.
            LIZZIE
There goes my Wayne Newton ticket
money.
            LIZZIE
Yeah! Why not?
            TREVOR
Ahhh!
            TREVOR
Hey, we don't have all day.
            TREVOR
Bad luck.
            TREVOR
Check.
            TREVOR
Count me in.
            TREVOR
That didn't turn out for me.
            TREVOR
Fold.
            TREVOR
Good deal.
            TREVOR
You gotta pay to play.
            TREVOR
Can you hang with me?
            TREVOR
Hmmm.
            TREVOR
How did I miss that?
            TREVOR
Sometimes, you need to know when to
hold 'em.
            TREVOR
Let's see what happens.
            TREVOR
Ah, maybe next time.
            TREVOR
Nice job!
            TREVOR
Nice play.
            TREVOR
Winning this hand is not my destiny.
            TREVOR
Pass.
            TREVOR
Raise.
            TREVOR
Today is a good day.
            TREVOR
Nice hand! But if you actually beat
me, I'll put on a dress.
            CASHIER
Your account balance is not low enough
to receive additional funds.
            BOUNCER
Uhhhm, excuse me.
            MANAGER

```
Welcome to Reel Deal Poker. Please
click the Register button to continue.
            MANAGER
Nice to have you back, Sir!
            MANAGER
Nice to have you back, Miss!
            MANAGER
Play well, Sir!
            MANAGER
Play well, Miss!
```

Programming

An animation for each character in four-player mode is a combination of the character's pose, the eye position, and the mouth position. A 0 (zero) for an eye or mouth animation means that the default pose for the eye or mouth is used; in other words, don't draw over the original eye or mouth if it's a zero.

YVETTE saying "Wow, good hand"
{{pose 1, eye 3, mouth 0},{1, 7, 0},{1, 7, 5},{1, 1, 5},{1, 1, 5},{1, 1, 5},
{1, 1, 5},{1, 1, 5},{1, 1, 5},{1, 6, 5},{1, 7, 5},{1, 7, 5},{1, 7, 0},{1, 3, 0},
{1, 3, 0},{1, 3, 0},{2, 10, 0},{2, 6, 5},{2, 6, 5},{2, 10, 5},{2, 3, 5},
{2, 10, 5},{2, 1, 5},{2, 1, 5},{2, 1, 5},{2, 1, 5}, {2, 3, 5},{2, 9, 4},{2, 9, 4},
{2, 9, 4},{2, 9, 4},{2, 9, 4},{2, 9, 4},{2, 9, 4},{2, 9, 4},{2, 9, 4},{2, 9, 4},
{2, 9, 4},{1, 5, 0},{1, 5, 0},{1, 5, 0},{1, 5, 0},{1, 5, 0}}}

For each character map (or associate) there are one to three phrases for actions such as checking, raising, folding, calling, when they win a pot, when they lose a pot (randomly select a character), when they are bluffing (betting on an average hand), and taunting the player when a minute has gone by without any input.

Basic Poker AI

The hand ranking is defined by a hand rank value plus the highest card value. The hand rank values are as follows: a royal flush is 180, a straight flush is 160, four of a kind is 140, a full house is 120, a flush is 100, a straight is 80, three of a kind is 60, two pair is 40, one pair is 20, and high card is 0.

All players are categorized as either "conservative" or "not conservative" and "strong," "average," or "weak."

The AI to Determine the Best Poker Hand Using Five to Seven Cards

1. Flush — Check to see if at least five cards are in the same suit.
2. Straight — Put cards in ascending order and check if there are five consecutive cards. (Reminder: Place the ace in the lowest and highest positions.)
3. If flush and straight came out positive, then we have a straight flush, check for ace high for royal flush.

4. If we have found a straight or a flush hand, set its value and return.

5. If nothing found so far, put the cards in rank order.

6. Check each rank from the ace (high) to the deuce (two, low card).

7. If one rank has four cards found, we have four of a kind; set its value and return.

8. If one rank has three cards found, we have at least found the highest three of a kind hand (set value to trip). (Remember we could be examining seven cards.) If another rank has at least two cards found, we have a full house (set value to full house).

     On three cards of same rank found, set value to a trip or full house and return.

9. If one rank has a pair (two of the same rank), we have at least found the highest pair (set value to a pair). If another rank has a pair, we have a two pair hand (set value to two pair). On a pair found, value a two pair or pair value and return.

10. We have only a high card, so set the value to the highest card and return.

Draw Poker (No Openers and Jacks or Better to Open)

All analysis assumes an eight-player game and the logic works for any number of players.

1. For strong players, don't open betting in position one through four without a pair of aces or two pair with queens or better.

     A pair of kings can open in positions five and six, while position seven needs a pair of queens or jacks with ace kicker. The dealer who goes last needs a pair of jacks or better to open betting.

2. In a high ante game, positions one through three need a pair of kings, positions four through six need a pair of queens, and the remaining positions need a pair of jacks to open betting.

3. Against strong players, don't "call" with less than two pair headed by at least a king. In last positions, seven, or dealer, you can call with two pair.

4. Against weak to average players, you can "raise" with a pair of aces or kings if you are alone with the opener and last in position.

5. Don't "raise" with opened straights or four flush cards and only call if the pot yields four times your bet.

6. "Raise" with trips (three of a kind) that are 10s or below. "Call" with jacks or better before the draw to force players out or keep them in for the kill with the higher hands. Against strong players, you need strong cards to raise when they open. Against weak players (players who open with jacks or queens under the gun), you can raise aggressively when holding aces or kings.

     Any player who checks during the first bet round can only call bets thereafter in the first round.

In Draw Poker Jacks or Better, the computer will check each hand to see if the hand passes the jacks or better test. If no player has this requirement, each player must check and the hand is redealt (the ante up will increase). If the player folds or tries to open and the requirement has not been met by any player, the computer assumes a check. If the player (non NPC), has a pair of kings and checks and no other player has met the requirements, a new hand is dealt (the computer must not force the player to make an opening bet). In Draw Poker, a minimum starting bet or "ante" is made by each player before the first card is dealt. All cards are dealt face down starting with the player to the left of the dealer. A player may discard up to three cards or four cards if they hold an ace (computer checks this situation) and receive replacement cards.

Discarded cards are immediately reshuffled into the remaining deck after that player has received cards so that a player will never get his discarded cards back. If a player opens by betting or raises a bet, he cannot raise again unless another player has raised.

In all poker games, a maximum of three raises is allowed per betting session.

Five-Card Stud

1. If hand value is a royal flush, straight flush, or four of a kind, "bet" or "raise" the maximum amount and return.

2. If hand value is a full house, flush, straight, or three of a kind (trip), "bet" or "raise" medium.

3. If the hand value is only a high card and seeing the others up cards shows that you have the highest single card (no one has a pair or better showing)…

    If asked to "check," then check.

    If you are to bet first and if it's the first round of betting and you have an ace (conservative) or a 10 (nonconservative), "bet" medium.

    If after betting round one, you have the highest card of at least a queen, "bet" medium (conservative) or maximum (nonconservative).

    If you are not the first to bet (a bet has been made) and you have an ace (conservative) or a queen (nonconservative), "bet" maximum.

    Otherwise, "call."

    If a raise has been made, conservative players always "fold."

    Strong players "call" on betting round one and afterward if they have the highest card showing or better, they "call."

    Otherwise, they "fold."

4. If you have no pair and not the highest hand showing and you are the first to bet…

    Conservative "folds."

Nonconservative...

> If betting round is three, then "fold."
>
> If betting round is one or two, then...
>
>> With ace, "bet" maximum
>>
>> With a queen or king, "bet" medium.
>
> Otherwise, "check."

5. If you have any pair on the opening bet round (first two cards) or any round a hand better than three of a kind...

> If the highest hand showing is better than your hand, on the last betting round "fold."
>
> If first to "bet" and pair is...
>
>> Less than a pair of queens, then "check."
>>
>> A pair of aces, then "bet" maximum.
>>
>> A pair of kings or queens, then "bet" medium.
>>
>> Two pair (remember the first pair may signal this code so check to see if there's a two pair hand), then "bet" maximum.
>
> Another player has bet and you have (a pair or better)...
>
>> A pair of aces or a better than a pair hand, then "bet" maximum.
>>
>> Otherwise, "check."
>
> Another player has raised and your pair is...
>
>> Less than the highest hand showing and you are a strong player...
>>
>>> With queens or better, then "call."
>>>
>>> Otherwise, "fold."
>>
>> Weak player, then "fold."

6. If you have a full house or better and raises made are less than three, then "raise" maximum.

> Otherwise, "call."

Seven-Card Stud, Chicago Low, and Chicago High

Special Case for Chicago High

One of your first two cards is a spade.

> You have the ace of spades and therefore you can't lose, so "bet" maximum.
>
> You have the highest spade since any higher ones are shown, so "bet" maximum.
>
> You have the king of spades, then "bet" medium.
>
> You have the next highest spade since any next higher ones are shown, so "bet" medium.
>
> If the spade you have is within three ranks of the highest spade not showing...
>
>> If no raises, then "call."
>>
>> If raise was made, then "check."

If you are to bet and…

> If the spade you have is within four ranks of the highest spade not showing, then "bet" minimum."
>
> If the spade you have is within nine ranks of the highest spade not showing, then "check."

Otherwise, follow steps one through six below.

Special Case for Chicago Low

One of your first two cards is a spade.

> You have the ace of spades and therefore you can't lose, so "bet" maximum.
>
> You have the lowest spade since any lower ones are shown, so "bet" maximum.
>
> You have the two (deuce) of spades, then "bet" medium.
>
> You have the next lowest spade since any next lower ones are shown, so "bet" medium.
>
> If the spade you have is within three ranks of the lowest spade not showing…
>
> > If no raises, then "call"
> >
> > If raise was made, then "check."
>
> If you are to bet and…
>
> > If the spade you have is within four ranks of the lowest spade not showing, then "bet" minimum.

Otherwise, follow steps one through six.

1. Hand value is better than three of a kind.

   Your hand beats any hand showing.

   > You are the first to bet, "bet" medium.
   >
   > Another player is the first to bet…
   >
   > > Round of betting is…
   > >
   > > > Conservative: Round one through three, then "check."
   > > >
   > > > > Rounds four through six, then "bet" maximum.
   > > >
   > > > Nonconservative: Round one, then "check."
   > > >
   > > > > After round one, "bet" maximum.

   Your hand is *not* better than anything showing…

   > Stay with it until the last (seventh) card and "call."
   >
   > If a raise is on the table, don't stay with a loser ("fold").

2. Hand value is at least a high pair.

   If hand is better than a pair or a pair of queens or better for conservative or eights or better for nonconservative, then…

   > Your hand is better than anything showing…
   >
   > > You are the first to bet, then "bet" maximum.

You are not the first to bet, then "raise" maximum.

Your hand is *not* the highest (a better one is showing)…

You are the first to bet, then "check."

"Call" bets until the fourth card is dealt, then "fold" if no improvement.

A "raise" is on the table, don't stay with a loser.

On the last card, your hand has not improved, so "fold."

3. Hand is at least a medium pair, which is a 10 or higher for a conservative player and a six or higher for a nonconservative player.

Your hand is better than anything showing…

You have a king or an ace in hand with the pair…

Betting rounds one to six…

You are the first to bet…

Betting rounds one to five, then "bet" medium.

Betting round six, then "check."

You are *not* the first to bet…

Betting round six, then "call."

Otherwise, "raise" maximum (if you can).

Last betting round (sixth)…

You are the first to bet, then "check."

Otherwise, "fold."

Your hand is *not* the highest (a better one is showing)…

You are the first to bet, then "check."

"Call" bets until the fourth card is dealt, then "fold" if no improvement.

4. Hand is at least a low pair.

Your hand is better than anything showing…

Betting rounds…

One and two for conservative and one through four for nonconservative…

Your hand is highest one showing…

You are the first to bet, then "bet" medium.

You are *not* the first to bet…

No player has raised, then "raise" medium.

Otherwise, "call."

Your hand is *not* the highest one showing…

You are the first to bet, then "check."

A bet has been made by another player…

Betting round two for conservative or betting round four for nonconservative, then "fold."

Otherwise, "call."

Three to six for conservative and five to six for nonconservative...

    You are the first to bet, then "check."

    Your hand is the highest one showing, then "call."

    Your hand is *not* the highest one showing...

        Betting round six, then "fold."

        Betting round six...

            If lucky, then "call."

            If unlucky, then "fold."

        Other betting rounds...

            If no raises yet, then "check."

            If raise then "fold."

  Your hand is *not* better than anything showing...

    Betting round six or conservative, then "fold."

    Otherwise...

        If lucky, then "call."

        If unlucky, then "fold."

5.   Hand possibly a flush or a straight.

    If your cards are of the same suit or rank within straight range.

    First bet round:

        You are first to bet, then "check."

        You are *not* first to bet, then "call."

    Second bet round:

        You are first to bet, then "bet" medium.

        You are *not* first to bet, then "call."

    Five and six betting rounds:

        If fifth betting round:

            King or better in hand...

                You are first to bet, then "check."

                Otherwise, "call."

        If sixth betting round:

            You are first to bet, then "check."

            You are *not* first to bet...

                Flush or straight, then "call."

                Otherwise, "fold."

    Three and four betting rounds:

        You are first to bet, then "check."

        You are *not* first to bet, then "call."

6.   If there's a raise and you have nothing in steps one through five, then "fold."

Texas Hold 'Em and Omaha

1. The player to the left of the dealer is forced to make a "blind bet" ("bet" minimum).

2. Determine if you should stay with the first two cards for Texas Hold 'Em (or first four cards for Omaha) in your hand.

   You have a pair (remember in Texas Hold 'Em you can use one, two, or none of your first two cards and in Omaha you must use two of your first four cards).

   If your pair for conservative is aces or for nonconservative is 10s or better, then "bet" or "raise" maximum.

   If your pair for conservative is queens or kings or for nonconservative is sixes or better, then "bet" or "raise" medium.

   If you have any pair, then "bet" minimum.

   Otherwise, "call" or "check."

3. For all remaining betting rounds, get the value of your hand.

   Your hand is only a high card...

   You are the first to bet, then "check."

   You are *not* the first to bet...

   Conservative players "fold."

   Nonconservative player "call" for the second and third betting rounds and "fold" after the last community card is turned over.

   Your hand is a pair...

   You are the first to bet, then "check."

   You are *not* the first to bet...

   A player has raised, then...

   If you have won the last two hands, then "call."

   Conservative players "fold."

   Nonconservative player "call" for the second and third betting rounds and "fold" after the last "community card" is turned over.

   A player has bet...

   For the second and third betting rounds, "call."

   "Fold" after the last community card is turned over.

   Players so far have checked, then you "check."

   Your hand is two pair...

   You are the first to bet...

   Conservative players "check."

   Nonconservative players "bet" medium.

   You are *not* the first to bet...

   No one has raised, then "call."

   A raise has been made...

You are in the first three players from the dealer, then "fold."

Otherwise, "call."

Only a call so far, so you then "call."

Your hand is three of a kind (a trip) or better...

You are the first to bet, then "bet" maximum.

You are *not* the first to bet...

Your hand is a straight or better, then "raise" maximum.

There are no raises yet, so "raise" maximum."

Another player has raised...

You are in the first three players from the dealer, then "call."

You are in the fourth player from the dealer, then "raise" medium.

You are more than four players from the dealer, then "raise" maximum.

Game Variations Order of Play

Draw Poker No Openers and Jacks or Better to Open

Players "ante" or place the minimum bet into the pot.

Five cards are dealt face down to each player.

Betting session or round.

Player to the left of the dealer bets first.

A player cannot bet and raise himself consecutively.

Only three raises per betting session allowed.

(In Draw Poker Jacks or Better, only a player meeting the requirements of a hand with at least a pair of jacks may bet. If a player doesn't select "check" and doesn't have the requirements, then a "check" is the default option. If all players "check," then the deck is reshuffled and another ante is made by all players. If a player "folds" before any bet is made, the default of a "check" is done instead. The computer never looks at anyone's hand to process the NPC AI except in this case of checking for the requirements of a hand of at least a pair of jacks.)

Players starting with the player to the left of the dealer may discard up to three cards (four cards if they hold an ace; computer checks for the ace).

(Immediately, the discarded cards are replaced and the discarded cards are shuffled into the end of the deck behind the original 52 cards so that the game doesn't run out of cards and a player will not receive his own discarded cards or someone else's discarded cards before the original deck has been dealt.)

Betting session or round.

> Player to the left of the dealer bets first.
>
> A player cannot bet and raise himself consecutively.
>
> Only three raises per betting session allowed.

Show all remaining players' cards.

Find the winning hand or hands if tied.

Pay the winner(s) from the pot.

Update statistics.

Five-Card Stud

Deal one card face down to each player (card one).

Deal one card face up to each player (card two).

Betting session or round…

> Best hand showing bets first.
>
> A player cannot bet and raise himself consecutively.
>
> Only three raises per betting session allowed.

If more than one player left…

> Deal one card face up to each player (card three).
>
> Betting session or round…
>
> > Best hand showing bets first.
> >
> > A player cannot bet and raise himself consecutively.
> >
> > Only three raises per betting session allowed.

If more than one player left…

> Deal one card face up to each player (card four).
>
> Betting session or round…
>
> > Best hand showing bets first.
> >
> > A player cannot bet and raise himself consecutively.
> >
> > Only three raises per betting session allowed.

If more than one player left…

> Deal one card face down to each player (card five).
>
> Betting session or round…
>
> > Best hand showing bets first.
> >
> > A player cannot bet and raise himself consecutively.
> >
> > Only three raises per betting session allowed.

Show all remaining players' cards.

Find the winning hand or hands if tied.

Pay the winner(s) from the pot.

Update statistics.

Seven-Card Stud, Chicago Low, and Chicago High

Deal two cards face down to each player (cards one and two, aka "the hole").

Deal one card face up to each player (card three, aka "door card").

Betting session or round...

The first round of betting starts either with a forced bet by the lowest up card by suit in alpha order (clubs is the lowest suit and spades is the highest suit) or by the highest up card.

Player cannot bet and raise himself consecutively.

Only three raises per betting session allowed.

If more than one player left...

Deal one card face up to each player (card four, aka "fourth street").

Betting session or round...

Best hand showing bets first.

A player cannot bet and raise himself consecutively.

Only three raises per betting session allowed.

If more than one player left...

Deal one card face up to each player (card five, aka "fifth street").

Betting session or round...

Best hand showing bets first.

A player cannot bet and raise himself consecutively.

Only three raises per betting session allowed.

If more than one player left...

Deal one card face up to each player (card six, aka "sixth street").

Betting session or round...

Best hand showing bets first.

A player cannot bet and raise himself consecutively.

Only three raises per betting session allowed.

If more than one player left...

Deal one card face down to each player (card seven, aka "the river"; also a "hole" card).

If more than 52 cards are needed (as when eight players need seven cards each, or 56 cards), the last card is a community card used by all players.

Betting session or round...

Best hand showing bets first.

A player cannot bet and raise himself consecutively.

Only three raises per betting session allowed.

Show all remaining players' cards starting with the last to bet.

(For Chicago High, the best hand and the highest spade in the hole shares the pot. For Chicago Low, the best hand and the lowest spade in the hole shares the pot. An ace may be used for high or low. If the seventh card is a community card, then it isn't a "hole" card. The winning "hole" card doesn't have to be part of the winning hand.)

Using five of the seven cards, find the winning hand or hands if tied.

Pay the winner(s) from the pot.

Update statistics.

Texas Hold 'Em

Deal two cards face down to each player (cards one and two, aka "the hole").

Betting session or round…

A "blind bet" is made by the player to the left of the dealer.

A player cannot bet and raise himself consecutively.

Only three raises per betting session allowed.

Community cards one, two, and three (the "flop") are dealt center table face up.

Betting session or round…

Player to the left of the dealer bets first.

A player cannot bet and raise himself consecutively.

Only three raises per betting session allowed.

Community card four (the "turn" card) is dealt center table face up.

Betting session or round…

Player to the left of the dealer bets first.

A player cannot bet and raise himself consecutively.

Only three raises per betting session allowed.

Community card five (the "river") is dealt center table face up.

Betting session or round…

Player to the left of the dealer bets first.

A player cannot bet and raise himself consecutively.

Only three raises per betting session allowed.

Find the winning hand or hands if tied using any combination of the player's own two down cards and the five community cards.

Pay the winner(s) from the pot.

Update statistics.

Chapter 15

Omaha

Deal four cards face down to each player (cards one, two, three, and four (aka "the hole").

Betting session or round…

> A "blind bet" is made by the player left of the dealer.
>
> A player cannot bet and raise himself consecutively.
>
> Only three raises per betting session allowed.

Community cards one, two, and three (the "flop") are dealt center table face up.

Betting session or round…

> Player to the left of the dealer bets first.
>
> A player cannot bet and raise himself consecutively.
>
> Only three raises per betting session allowed.

Community card four (the "turn" card) is dealt center table face up.

Betting session or round…

> Player to the left of the dealer bets first.
>
> A player cannot bet and raise himself consecutively.
>
> Only three raises per betting session allowed.

Community card five (the "river") is dealt center table face up.

Betting session or round…

> Player to the left of the dealer bets first.
>
> A player cannot bet and raise himself consecutively.
>
> Only three raises per betting session allowed.

Find the winning hand, or hands if tied, using a combination of two of the player's four down cards and three of the five community cards. Remember, "two from the hand, three from the board."

Pay the winner(s) from the pot.

Update statistics.

Workshop

Exercises

Exercise 1: Discuss how the Game Proposal or the Executive Summary helps in writing a Game Design Document.

Exercise 2: Write a page of VO narrative scripting and get feedback for how realistic it reads.

Exercise 3: Write a game script of a person looking for a place to eat.

Unguided Exercises

Unguided Exercise 1: Write a linear and a nonlinear story based on an original concept.

Unguided Exercise 2: Using a game scripting language or pseudo-language, define a few game entities and environments.

Internet Reading Assignment

"The Anatomy of a Design Document" by Tim Ryan
    http://www.gamasutra.com/features/19991019/ryan_01.htm
    http://www.gamasutra.com/features/19991217/ryan_05.htm

"I Have No Words & I Must Design" by Greg Costikyan
    http://www.costik.com/nowords.html

"Design Document: Play with Fire" by Chris Bateman
    http://gamasutra.com/features/20070220/bateman_01.shtml

"Guidelines for the Technical Specification" by Tim Ryan
    http://www.gamasutra.com/features/19991217/ryan_03.htm

Chris Taylor's excellent and humorous GDD template
    http://www.runawaystudios.com/articles/chris_taylor_gdd.asp

Suggested Activities

Activity 1: Describe the benefits to writing a Game Design Document before development begins.

Activity 2: Discuss the benefits and problems of developing a multiplatform game.

Activity 3: Discuss the difference in design and in the user interface between a console video game and the computer versions.

Activity 4: Discuss the differences between VO, narration scripting, and game scripting.

Chapter 15

Appendix A

Contact Information

Websites

Gaming News

www.gamasutra.com
www.gamedev.net
www.gignews.com
www.gdmag.com
www.mobygames.com
http://games.slashdot.org/
http://ve3d.ign.com/

www.gamespot.com
www.ign.com
www.edge-online.com
www.1up.com/do/news?ct=NEWS
http://www.bluesnews.com
www.shacknews.com

Gaming Conferences

Game Developers Conference   www.gdconf.com
Austin Game Developers   www.gdcaustin.com
Conference
America's Video Game Expo   www.videogame.net
E3 aka Electronic Entertainment   www.e3expo.com
Expo
Casual Connect   http://seattle.casualconnect.org/

Game Networking

www.linkedin.com
www.meetup.com

www.facebook.com
www.myspace.com

Game Job Sites

www.gamasutra.com
www.gamesjobnews.com
www.indiegamejobs.com
www.dice.com
www.gamesondeck.com/jobs/
http://gamerbytes.com/jobs/
http://indiegames.com/jobs/

www.gamedev.net
www.hotjobs.com
www.monster.com
www.gamesrecruit.co.uk/index.aspx
www.seriousgamessource.com/jobs/
www.gamesetwatch.com/jobs/

Game Job Agencies

Premier Search   www.premier-search.net/m_26.asp
Mary-Margaret Network   www.mary-margaret.com
TSC Management Services Group   www.tscsearch.com
Change (Europe)   www.change-job.com

Gaming Schools and Colleges

The most well-known gaming colleges are DigiPen Institute of Technology, Full Sail University, and The Guildhall at SMU.

I am personally familiar with Rochester Institute of Technology, DeVry University (which I attended for my undergraduate degree), and UAT (University of Advancing Technology) Online (for my graduate degree). Additionally, I have developed the curriculum and taught at Bloomfield College in New Jersey and interviewed at Westwood College as an adjunct professor.

Any prospective student should select a college based on its reputation, cost, on-campus vs. online learning, and the degree offered.

My philosophy in selecting a college and degree is to earn a degree that will get you a future job in the real world if the game world doesn't work out or has industry layoffs. For example, a game programming degree can transfer into any IT department, such as of a bank or brokerage firm. A graphics and animation degree can transfer into the advertising and website design world and film and television industries.

Following is a list of some well-known schools and their website pages. (Also check out www.gamecareerguide.com/schools/.)

The Art Institute of Pittsburgh
  www.aionline.edu/information/programs/animation/
  game_art_design/index.asp
Bloomfield College
  http://campus.bloomfield.edu/cat/gamedev.asp
Brown College
  www.browncollege.edu
Carnegie Mellon University
  www.etc.cmu.edu
Cornell University
  http://gdiac.cis.cornell.edu/
Daniel Webster College
  www.dwc.edu/admissions/programs/gsr/
DePaul University
  http://gamedev.depaul.edu
DeVry University
  www.devry.edu/programs/game_and_simulation_programming/
  about.jspDigiPen
DigiPen Institute of Technology
  www.digipen.edu

Full Sail University
    www.fullsail.com/game-development/overview.html
Game Institute
    www.gameinstitute.com
SMU (Southern Methodist University) Guildhall
    guildhall.smu.edu
Iowa State University (Ames, IA) College of Design
    www.design.iastate.edu/DMM/
The New School (Parsons) for Design
    http://cdt.parsons.edu/
Rochester Institute of Technology
    rit.edu/programs/program_listing.php?display=college
Savannah College of Art and Design
    www.scad.edu
University of Advancing Technology (UAT)
    www.uat.edu/majors/game_design.aspx
UAT (University of Advancing Technology) Online
    http://www.gamedegree.com/levelingUp_OnlineDegrees.asp
Westwood College/Westwood College Online
    http://www.westwood.edu/degree-programs/gaming/
    game-software-dev/degree.asp

Software Noted in
Chapter 10, "Knowing the Entire Team"

Graphic Systems

| DirectX | http://msdn.microsoft.com/en-us/directx/default.aspx |
| OpenGL | www.khronos.org/opengl/ |

Scripting Languages

Adobe ActionScript	http://www.adobe.com/devnet/actionscript/ #getting_started?promoid=DJGVP
Adobe Flash	www.adobe.com/products/flash/?promoid=DTEMA
Lua	www.lua.org/
MAXScript	http://usa.autodesk.com/adsk/servlet/ index?id=5659302&siteID=123112
MEL	http://usa.autodesk.com/adsk/servlet/ index?siteID=123112&id=7635018
Perl	www.perl.org/
Python	www.python.org/
Microsoft Silverlight	http://silverlight.net/
Unreal Editor (UnrealEd)	http://www.unrealtechnology.com/ features.php?ref=editor

Art/Graphics Tools

Adobe After Effects	www.adobe.com/products/aftereffects/?promoid=DTEMG
Adobe Illustrator	www.adobe.com/products/illustrator/?promoid=DTELU
Adobe Premiere Pro	www.adobe.com/products/premiere/?promoid=DTEMD
Autodesk Face Robot	http://usa.autodesk.com/adsk/servlet/index?id=12426041&siteID=123112
Character Studio	http://usa.autodesk.com/adsk/servlet/index?id=5659302&siteID=123112
CorelDRAW	http://www.corel.com/servlet/Satellite/us/en/Product/1191272117978#versionTabview=tab1&tabview=tab0
Corel Painter	www.corel.com/servlet/Satellite/us/en/Product/1166553885783#tabview=tab0
DeBabelizer	http://oldsite.equilibrium.com/Internet/Equil/Products/DeBabelizer/index
Houdini	www.sidefx.com/index.php?option=com_content&task=view&id=142&Itemid=55
LightWave 3D	www.newtek.com/
Maya	http://usa.autodesk.com/adsk/servlet/index?siteID=123112&id=7635018
mental ray Standalone	http://usa.autodesk.com/adsk/servlet/index?siteID=123112&id=
MotionBuilder	http://usa.autodesk.com/adsk/servlet/index?id=6837710&siteID=123112
Mudbox	http://usa.autodesk.com/adsk/servlet/index?id=10707763&siteID=123112
Photoshop	www.adobe.com/products/photoshop/?promoid=DTELR
Photoshop Elements	www.adobe.com/products/psprelements/?promoid=DTEMP
Softimage	http://usa.autodesk.com/adsk/servlet/index?id=12339670&siteID=123112
3ds Max	http://usa.autodesk.com/adsk/servlet/index?id=5659302&siteID=123112
3DVIA Virtools	http://a2.media.3ds.com/products/3dvia/3dvia-virtools/
ZBrush	www.pixologic.com/home.php

Physics and Performance Analyzer Tools

NVIDIA PhysX	www.nvidia.com/object/nvidia_physx.html
Havok Behavior/Havok Physics	www.havok.com/

PIX	http://msdn.microsoft.com/en-us/library/bb173085(VS.85).aspx
Intel VTune	www.intel.com/cd/software/products/asmo-na/eng/239144.htm

Asset Management, Source Control, and Software Configuration Management

Alienbrain	www.alienbrain.com/
CVS (Concurrent Versions System)	www.nongnu.org/cvs/
Darcs	http://darcs.net/
Microsoft Office Visio	http://office.microsoft.com/en-us/visio/default.aspx
Perforce	www.perforce.com/
Subversion (SVN)	http://subversion.tigris.org/
TACTIC 2.5	http://www.southpawtech.com/
Visual SourceSafe	http://msdn.microsoft.com/en-us/library/ms181038(VS.80).aspx

Sound and Audio Tools

Ableton Live	www.ableton.com/
Adobe Audition	www.adobe.com/products/audition/
cSounds	http://www.csounds.com/
Cubase Studio	www.steinberg.net/en/products/musicproduction/cubasestudio5_product0.html
FMOD	www.fmod.org/
Logic Studio Pro	www.apple.com/logicstudio/
Max 5 (Max/MSP/Jitter)	www.cycling74.com/products/max5
Nuendo	www.steinberg.net/en/products/audiopostproduction_product/nuendo4.html
Peak Pro	www.apple.com/downloads/macosx/audio/peakpro.html
Pro Tools M-Powered	www.m-audio.com/products/en_us/ProToolsMPowered8.html
PureData	http://puredata.info/
SCREAM	http://files.egrsoftware.com/site/research/whitepapers/scream_whitepaper.v1.1.1.pdf
Sound Forge	http://www.sonycreativesoftware.com/products/soundforgefamily.asp
Waves Tune	www.waves.com/Content.aspx?id=182
Wwise	www.audiokinetic.com/4105/wwise-solution-overview.asp
XACT	http://msdn.microsoft.com/en-us/library/cc308030(VS.85).aspx

Appendix B

An Interview with Roger E. Pedersen

How did you get interested in computers and gaming?

In the sixth grade we played Avalon Hill games and Diplomacy as part of our history lessons. I became addicted to war games and started subscribing to magazines like *Strategy & Tactics*. Later I designed several war games (Global Conquest, LunarCity, and The PentaLegions) and corresponded with other game designers like Gary Gygax (who developed D&D) and a fellow who had me game test Conquest, a chess-like game played by two to four players on a board or through the mail. I also became an avid chess player (eventually earning the rank of USCF Chess Master).

My high school was fortunate enough to hook up to a Texas Instruments mini-computer and started a computer class. Although I was too young to take the classes (you had to be in 10th grade), I hung out in the computer room and taught myself BASIC. I also attended computer lectures and fairs run monthly by David Ahl, editor of the number one PC magazine at the time called *Creative Computing*, and I prepared simulations and easy single-player games that ran via a paper terminal (there were no monitors back then).

My interest in computers led to an opportunity to teach a high school computer course while I was still a student. The computer teacher was also a math teacher and taught computers through math solving, so the principal asked me to teach real-world computing like searching, sorting, simulations, and creating games like tic-tac-toe.

Throughout college I studied AI, game theory, and database theory. I worked part-time for a mini company (Nova Computers) and was given a TI Silent 700 to use in my dorm room (a paper terminal that connected to the terminals at Nova). Most other students interested in computers at the time only had 1-4 K PCs that they had assembled from Heathkits.

What made you decide to work in the game industry, especially from its beginning?

In 1981 I bought myself an Apple 2 and Pascal and wrote a few simple eight-color 48 K graphic games. In 1983 I moved back to the New York

361

City area looking for a job. A headhunter called me and asked if I wanted to work at home (part-time) programming games for a book publisher who wanted adventure games for the Apple as a selling device (e.g., "buy 40 books and get a game that relates to the subject matter.") I agreed to do several games for Laidlaw, a division of Doubleday, where the student could travel throughout the U.S. visiting state capitals, throughout the world visiting famous cities and capitals, and visiting Indian reservations and learning their customs.

Then I got a contract with CBS to rewrite the series Success with Math, which included modules for addition, subtraction, multiplication, division, and long division, for the Commodore Vic-20 and 64. CBS bought me a Vic-20 and a Commodore 64 and gave me the Apple disks (no code).

In 1985 I met with a Florida game/toy company called Gametek who wanted to get into the computer game business. They had several hot TV show and board game licenses. As a result of that meeting I formed Pedersen Systems, Inc. and designed, produced, co-programmed, did the artwork and sound (music), and created the database for two games in a month for three SKUs (the Apple 2, Commodore 64/128, and IBM PC). The game Candyland took me four days to design and program for the three computers.

Also in 1985 I was introduced to Michael Hausman, who became my copartner and developed a toolbox consisting of code routines and a graphics converter for each machine. This allowed us to make games in IBM PC DOS and finish the code in Manx/Aztec C. We then ported the games to the Commodore 64 and Apple versions, which only required a new compile into their assembler code and running the graphics from the IBM PC through Michael's converter toolbox. Go To the Head of The Class took us five days for three versions (I had to type and update the 1,000 questions used in the game). From there we put on the store shelves Press Your Luck, based on a TV show; Chutes and Ladders, based on the Milton Bradley board game; Sorry, based on the Parker Brothers' board game; and Fisher Price games Perfect Fit, I Can Remember, and Fun Flyer (which never shipped). Also developed and never shipped were games based on the board games Trouble and Big Boggle.

In 1988 Michael and I ported a game for the company Hi-Tech Expressions from the IBM PC to the Apple. The game was called Swimwear, and was a swimsuit calendar program where you could customize calendars and select swimsuit-clad women to represent each month. The port and redesign of the printer graphics were done in four weeks.

In 1989 we designed, programmed, and did the sound and artwork for a project based on the Don Bluth film *All Dogs Go to Heaven*. The original film (unfinished, part color and part black and white) was provided and we created a storybook with 10 games that related to the film and its characters. The soundtrack was digitized and played back through the PC speaker and Sound Blaster card (this was the first game to use digital sound through these devices). Michael and I both programmed this title, and the magnificent artwork was done by an up-and-coming computer graphics artist named Juan Sanchez. The design, artwork, and programming took 10 weeks for the IBM version. The IBM PC code and graphics were then easily ported to the Amiga.

After making millions for Gametek, I published several games (Cyber Cop, Zombies: Undead or Alive!, Crazy Cola, and Dome of Champions) that won CES awards but sold poorly (proving that the creative techies should stay away from the business end of accounting, marketing, and sales).

After developing for Gametek, Hi-Tech Expressions, and Merit Software, all of which became huge publishers during and after your association with them, what did you do?

In 1992 at the CES show (pre-E3 days), I contracted with Dan Sejzer of Villa Crespo Software to do design, programming, artwork, and sound for a video poker game. Within four weeks, a prototype was finished and Dan showed it to several distributors who wanted it ASAP. I moved to Chicago to become director of development for Villa Crespo Software, initially a three-person company. Within a year, VCS had over 30 titles on the store shelves and over a dozen employees, and developers in Europe and throughout the U.S. were working with us to sell their titles. My job was to work with these developers, create internal projects, head up the QA group, and work with marketing and manual writers.

The titles that I developed and programmed for Villa Crespo Software were Stanford Wong's Video Poker, Flicks!: Film Review Library, Dr. Wong's Jacks+ (IBM DOS, Windows), Combination Lock (IBM DOS), Casino Girls Video Poker (IBM DOS), and Real Mother Goose (IBM DOS).

Titles that I managed were Amarillo Slim's Dealer's Choice, Rosemary West's House of Fortunes, Gold Sheet Pro Football Analyst, Games Magazine: Word Games, and the Coffee Break Series.

Titles that I managed and produced were The Coffee Break CD, Amarillo Slim 7 Card Stud (IBM DOS), Flicks!: Film Review Library (IBM DOS), Hearts (IBM DOS), and Casino Craps (IBM DOS).

I also designed the gameplay for Rosemary West's House of Fortunes and Games Magazine: Word Games, created the concept of great software at budget prices ($13) for the Coffee Break Series (abridged versions of VCS premium software and upgraded shareware titles), and designed the packaging for Failsafe and Flicks!

From 1994 to 1995 I worked for Merit Industries as manager of product development for their video game/arcade machine called MegaTouch. I designed and programmed numerous touch-screen games on the IBM PC for the Atari Jaguar (to be the brains and engine inside the arcade box) and redesigned the previous MegaTouch system and games written in 16-color mode to a 16/24-bit system with stereo sound. While developing new touch-screen games, we tested the games with non-technical players for addictiveness, ease of play, and understanding, which taught me the valuable lesson that in the arcade market if the product isn't fun or addictive, the player will quickly move on to a competitor's product.

From August 1996 to May 1997 I was senior producer for Acclaim Entertainment and later earned the role of executive producer and game designer for numerous titles on the PC and video game platforms.

As executive producer, I worked on titles with Ocean of America such as Cheesy (PSX), Break Point, Tennis (Saturn), Tunnel B1 (PSX, Saturn, IBM DOS, WIN 95), and Project X2 (PSX, Saturn); the Fox Interactive title Die Hard Trilogy (IBM DOS, Saturn); titles with Taito such as Psychic Force (PSX) and Puzzle Bobble/Bust-A-Move 3 (PSX); and titles with Acclaim such as Justice League of America (acting as licensing liaison with Warner Brothers and DC Comics) and Bloodshot (PSX, IBM DOS). I also designed an original script based on the Acclaim Comic character Bloodshot and his many enemies and prepared executive treatments as well as design and technical specifications.

As senior producer, I worked on the original Shadowman (PSX, IBM Win 95, N64), and managed over a dozen producers and associate producers, each with four to six titles for several SKUs that had budgets of $1-5 million.

For Psychic Force, I localized the storyline for the U.S. market, directed voice-over talent, and edited the VO DATs from a digital editor to Mac audio format. I also directed the motion capture studio for sample data for JLA and Shadowman

As executive producer I reviewed potential products for Acclaim distribution from outside developers and tested numerous products before turn-over (Turok, Forsaken, Space Jam, WWF Wrestling, and Magic: The Gathering); selected QA staff to head and work on various projects; met with licensors such as Warner Brothers, DC Comics, and Acclaim Comics to discuss game design and licensing matters regarding character descriptions, storylines, arch-enemies, three view artwork, and acceptable design issues (death or injury to a superhero); mentored and gave suggestions to producers and game analysts in their design efforts; and met as a technical expert with various "hot" development teams/groups (like offshoots of id Software, makers of Doom and Quake) for title/concept negotiations.

From 1994 to 2000, my pet project as director, producer, designer, and programmer was The Six Stones of Serena, an interactive fantasy-adventure, for PSI Productions. The project involved first writing the interactive adventure/role-playing game (500 pages with over 300 parts). I then used a Sony BetaCam and Hi-8 cameras to shoot script (100 actors) during a four-week period, worked on video editors (Toaster, Grass Valley, AVID) and various 3D art packages (such as Animated World Builder) for the virtual world, and designed and programmed an interactive scripting system (language) to create interactive characters and the storyline.

In 1997, I contracted with Sports Simulation to design and program Pro Soccer, a location-based simulation where a human player kicks a soccer ball at a virtual goalie. Designed as an "all-sports" system linking any sports module to a ball trajectory DLL (library) and a sensor DLL, the Pro Soccer module used actual kicked soccer ball trajectory data to move a virtual ball toward a virtual goalie. As producer I filmed various soccer players (male, female, teen, college, including the St. John's University soccer team, and pro) against an ultramat background and placed the "virtual" players in a 3D soccer world (goal and field) for varying soccer kick options including direct penalty, indirect penalty, and corner.

In 1998 Michael Hausman and I again teamed up by contracting with Hypnotix as game designer, producer, and programmer for General Mills' Big G All-Stars vs. Major League Baseball (IBM PC Windows '95, 3.1). The advertising for the game appeared from April to July 1998 on 60 million boxes of General Mills cereal, and the game CD sold over 1 million copies. The GM trademarked characters including the Trix Rabbit, Count Chocula, and the Lucky Charms Leprechaun vs. the MLB players (nine players on 30 teams).

What role do you typically play in the development of a game?

Ideally, the game designer and producer, then I oversee the programming and artwork. Usually the basic game design is provided and I help with redesigning the game, documenting, and programming. It's important to understand the original game design so when you make changes to it, both the investors and the original designers agree with your improvements and ideas. Many people think they can design a great game even though they've never done it, or designers in one genre think they can easily create great concepts without research in other areas (for example, an adventure game designer trying to make a sports game).

What advice can you offer to people who want to get started with game development, perhaps to turn it into a career?

Study. Learn to do. I studied filmmaking so I could understand an art form that has had a successful life. Games will eventually become interactive (where users can chat with their virtual world citizens). Actors (on-screen, voice-over, and motion capture) work better with knowledgeable and experienced directors and producers. Lighting, camera angles, and cut-scenes are proven methods in film that video/PC/interactive designers, directors, and producers need to understand. In designing The Six Stones of Serena, I had several binders full of research on mythology, ancient architecture, geographical topography, and sci-fi lore just to justify the ideas and gameplay. In baseball, you must understand the statistical data and its relevance and how they relate to the player and to the other data. If the user is shown believable scenarios, then the game experience is more enjoyable.

What in your opinion makes a good game?

I look at games from the user's point of view, often asking myself "Is this game worth $60?", "What features would help the user?", and "My goal is

X. How can I get there easier and faster?" For adventure games, the story must be good. Sports games must be realistic. Puzzle games should be addictive with the ability to play unlimited variations. As CPUs get faster and memory and storage becomes cheaper and more abundant, the stories can be more elaborate. More polygons, more actors on the CD, better sound, and perhaps orchestrated soundtracks.

Why do you enjoy making games?

I enjoy the creative process of making something that's never existed that is addictive, challenging, and fun to play. I enjoy watching people play my games. I enjoy hearing people say they loved a game I worked on. I enjoy reading reviews (all of them favorable so far… knock on wood or silicon) of games that I had a part of.

Lastly, with so many titles released each year, do you have any advice for what designers or programmers need to do to distinguish themselves from others to get a job in the industry? Or will demand be too low?

Unless I work for a company full-time (and I'm always looking), I contract one to two titles per year. When I started, a developer could be a "lone wolf." Fortunately, I have been teamed up with talented programmers, artists, and co-workers. Now it takes a dozen people to create a commercial game, which is fine as long as one person has a clear vision. "Newbies" should join a game company at any salary, design a game themselves, or use a standard development system to show potential employers that they can really program or design a game to completion. The Internet has opened up a venue for virtual gaming companies. You can design a game and look online (try gamasutra.com) for programmers and artists to help on the back-end work (work for free now and hopefully get a royalty later when the game is selling). Or if you have programming talent and need artwork, you could try to find artists willing to collaborate with you at sites like 3dcafe.com.

At a conference back in 2000, I heard that the film industry's 1998 box office revenues were way above those of the gaming industry and that in 1999, the two industries were close in revenues. But by 2000, the gaming industry had outproduced the revenues of both the film and music industry combined in the U.S.

Wow! That's the place to be and now's the time to be there!

Like creating film, books, and art, computer gaming is an art obtainable through talent and hard work as well as education.

Appendix C

Designing Great Games

In an interview with David Brake for Mindjack in 2002, game designer Sid Meier (Sim Golf, Gettysburg!, Sid Meier's Antietam!, Civilization, Sid Meier's Alpha Centuri, Pirates! Gold, Railroad Tycoon) explained, "We don't evaluate a game idea on how much learning is possible, we basically evaluate it on how much fun the game could be."

On his website (www.dperry.com) David Perry, founder of Shiny Entertainment (Earthworm Jim, Wild9, MDK, Messiah, Sacrifice, R/C Stunt Copter, Cool Spot, Aladdin, Global Gladiators, Enter the Matrix) and now an executive video game industry consultant, states that one of the key elements in good game design is fun. "[Fun] is the magic element in all designs. You've got to step back from your design and say, if everything goes as planned, would I like to play this game? Would anyone else?"

Currently, I am an adjunct professor at NYU teaching game design, an author, a freelance game designer, and a frequent speaker at game conferences. I also worked with NYU on their NYU Summer Game Camp for high school and college students.

Many students and professionals often ask questions like "What makes a great game?" and "Is this 'magical' element called 'fun' the key to designing a great game?"

What is "fun" and how do we define it? Fun can be defined as "enjoyable or amusing activities" or "a source of enjoyment, amusement, diversion." The Webster dictionary defines fun as "what provides amusement or enjoyment."

Does designing an addictive game mean it's a great game? Do designers and publishers want players to put their real lives on hold in order to play this game or play into the early morning hours? Publishers do want top-selling games, but they also want a working, healthy audience that has the money and time available to purchase and play their other games. There has been a lot discussion about "addictive" warnings due to several suicides involving avid gamers. Rather than addictive, which has a bad connotation, let's design compelling and intriguing games.

The word "funny" is derived from "fun." Does a funny or comedic game mean that it should be successful? A joke may be funny the first few times, but eventually it becomes stale and painful to listen to.

Great games are entertaining and give the player the feeling of personal achievement and accomplishing their goals. Solving puzzles, successfully navigating adventure games, and finding the answers to mysteries (like whodunits) gives players a feeling of accomplishment and success and validates their problem-solving skills.

In a game, I suggest rewards and personal interaction throughout the game ranging from nibbles to grandiose, spectacular endings for both the successful and the unsuccessful ("You're DEAD!").

In several games I designed, giving the player unexpected rewards or access to trophy rooms allows the player to add to his or her sense of accomplishment. For example, Reel Deal Poker Challenge, which I designed and programmed for Phantom EFX, had an empty trophy room that made players wonder about how and what items were placed in that space. By winning in each level's poker tournaments, the prizes that were won answered those trophy room questions. The game also had a few Easter egg hints such as a birthday cake and a $100 chip that could be won if the date of the win was close to the birth date entered when the player registered. Another trick was to forbid the players from entering the highly visible elevator until they had achieved an unknown number of "prestige points." Like the boys in *A Night at the Roxbury*, players hate to be excluded as not "cool" enough to enter an unauthorized area. This feature had players eagerly trying to win prestige points to access higher levels, gain more money, and compete against better opponents. The final plateau was to accumulate enough money and prestige to enter the "basement" to challenge the world champion in a $5 million winner-takes-all shootout. Upon the player's victory, the previous world champion would don a red dress and dance around the screen.

In my games for children, I constantly have the game address the child by name and play music that the child seemed to enjoy. I also provide lots of animations and feedback based on input, as well as animations during the pause time between input or mouse movement.

In a game I'm currently designing, I'm using astrological characteristics by having the player state his birth date to tailor the game for that player. The common astrological characteristics let the game appear to interact with the player. Using favorable characteristics, the game can entice the player and gain his or her trust. By setting up interactions with nonplayer characters defined with unfavorable characteristics or an astrological sign that's incompatible with that of the player, he or she will be placed on the defensive. The age data the player enters will allow the game to display age-appropriate room settings. The address information the player enters allows customizing the display of objects pertaining to the player's location, such as the state bird chirping outside the window on the state's tree, the state's flowers on the kitchen table, and the state's professional sports team poster on the wall.

When designing your game, think about your audience and the challenges and hoops you've put them through to reach the final plateau, the end where they now stand awaiting their reward.

Design an ending both worthy of winners and acceptable to non-winners who have just finished your game, such as fireworks, a ticker-tape parade, or the cheers of millions. These may seem overboard and silly, but to a traveler who has spent time journeying across the game you've designed, the spectacular ending is a marvelous reward and justly warranted. Think of your gamer as the conquering hero who is entering the city to pay homage to you the designer, or the parade for the sports team who has won the national championship, or the audience's excitement and atmosphere wanting an encore at a concert.

All games have two common characteristics: education and imagination. This means that games educate or train the players. The obvious lessons in games such as Civilization and Age of Empires are about historical events, even if they are not entirely accurate, and simulations that teach players the how-to's of a task. The less obvious lessons in games like adventure or action games (and even Pac-Man) are learning patterns and timing techniques so players can better their results (when Blinky is moving up, then move left to the blinking circle).

Imagination in gaming is evident in role-playing games where players assume various roles and skills, adventure games where players roam exotic locales and solve puzzles, and simulation games where players get to perform tasks in a safe environment. In games, players can assume the roles of superheroes, become Greek heroes and combat mythological monsters, or actively participate in guilt-free criminal acts such as killing, carefree sex romps, stealing, and corruption.

Games differentiate from other forms of entertainment in that they are interactive. Films are entertaining, but I've never heard anyone exclaim "Boy, that movie was fun!" The simplest and most basic form of interactivity is fighting, which is a normal part of both human and animal behavior. A more complex interaction is romance. In King Arthur's court there's a lot of interaction, such as the romance between Arthur and Guinevere and between Guinevere and Lancelot, as well as the court's rumor mill. Other complex interactions include training, politics, charitable work, writing, rumor spreading, corporate communication, and interviewing or researching.

Examples of nonviolent game designs could be a Gandhi game where the goal is to remain on a hunger strike until your demands are met, being a homeless street person who must survive each day, or living in an Amish community or on an Indian reservation (without casino gaming). In my game design example called "Survival of the Fittest," mankind must survive from the Neanderthal era to the Cro-Magnon era. In solo and multiplayer versions, each player controls the destiny and daily lives of a clan. In order to survive, the clan must hunt, fish, and make clothes and shelter. The goal is to survive through several generations and avoid extinction.

In Pedersen Principle 6, I suggest that one day's pay should equal a week's worth of fun. A game that can be finished in a few hours could disappoint players or make them feel ripped off. Let's be an industry known for designing and producing great entertainment and giving our customers their money's worth. Phenomenal graphics, immersive sounds, and foot stomping music is great, but without solid gameplay, it's going to waste. As an example of the opposite scenario, the game Deer Hunter didn't have great music or superb graphics, but it did have solid, entertaining, and easy-to-use gameplay. The game Myst, on the other hand, had solid gameplay combined with immersive music, sounds, and graphics, and was a huge hit.

If you're designing a horror or suspense game, having the player turn the corner to be scared by a zombie corpse lying in a casket may give the intended scary reaction only the first time or two it's seen. However, designing various triggers to make the zombie open the casket and jump out at the player at different points of action would prolong the scary effect (for example, the first time the zombie jumps out right away, the next time after the player walks around the casket, another time a few seconds after the player touches or knocks on the casket). This variety will keep the players on their toes and the effect will work beyond the first few encounters.

At NYU where I taught game design, there was an entire unit about famous game designers and another unit about famous characters such as Mario, Zelda, Sonic the Hedgehog, Mega Man, Max Payne, Lara Croft, and others. These gaming icons were not based on pre-existing licensed characters; each was original and launched many sequels (and prequels as in Super Mario World 2: Yoshi's Island, 1995). The Sonic and Mario characters even spun off educational and non-sequel games such as pinball and racing games. The characters helped the gameplay, and their images branded and marketed their product lines. Each of these characters needed a solid design and entertaining gameplay to become successful. Players can identify and fantasize about playing these characters and existing in (or escaping into) their worlds.

Games need to be designed in a manner that gives players the feeling that they are achieving something or progressing, making steps forward, and are just about to solve their gaming dilemma — that there's a ray of hope and success just around the corner. Players need to feel that they're learning a new skill, desiring to improve and become better, especially in competition were they can become the best.

Today's players have gaming as part of their culture. No longer are just the "geeks" and "nerds" reading gaming magazines, surfing the web to learn about gaming issues and cheats, and buying games to play alone at home. Players now carry portable gaming devices with them as well as cell phones and CD players. Arcades and computers are part of the player's everyday world. People on the streets are constantly chatting about games and anticipating what games are coming out.

All games contain an educational element and stimulate the fantasy world in the players' minds, but great games also have solid, entertaining, and amusing aspects in their design.

Appendix C

Appendix D

War Stories

The following stories are passed down to you as game industry folklore. The truths they reveal to future game designers are more important than their accuracy.

Lesson One

In the late 1990s, Acclaim Entertainment licensed the movie *Batman Forever* to be developed into a video game. The second Batman movie was expected to be a major hit, with hot stars like Michael Keaton as Batman, Jim Carrey as the Riddler, and Tommy Lee Jones as Two Face. At the time, Acclaim was among the top video game publishers in the world.

When I was hired at Acclaim as producer and then executive producer, many staff members including producers, assistant producers, and QA testers had protested the release of the current version of Batman Forever due to extremely poor gameplay.

Management wanted the game released to coincide with the movie's opening. They felt that the reputation of Acclaim and the anticipated success of the movie would be the selling point and that gameplay was least important.

The Batman Forever video game almost destroyed Acclaim Entertainment. Their stock plummeted, they lost millions of dollars, and a large percentage of employees (including the author) were laid off.

Lesson: Nothing is more important than gameplay.

Lesson Two

In March 1997, an experienced game designer named John Romero (from the team that created the FPS Doom) and his staff (equally famous and talented) began Daikatana (Japanese for "big sword").

Daikatana was touted as the next super game. John Romero is quoted as saying "Daikatana is a super-fast, Doom-style blast-a-thon. If people don't like it, they don't need to buy it."

Daikatana was a time-traveling FPS game that was marketed very early on by publisher Eidos Interactive. The ads that ran in magazines stated "John Romero's about to make you his bitch. Suck it down."

After numerous delays and two years late, reports of staff conflict and mass exodus of team members didn't help and the public's anticipation turned sour. Designer Romero's attitude of "Damn the lot of you" was not the way to turn the situation around.

A release of Daikatana in March 1997 would have put the game ahead of the pack in gameplay and technology (using the Quake 2 engine). Being released two years later when the Quake 3 engine was available, the game seemed simple and not what one would expect from the hype and its famous designer from id Software.

Lesson: The "dream team" can easily turn into a dictatorship nightmare. (See Pedersen Principle 2: No Designer or Producer Is an Island.) A designer must respect his team and audience. "Hard work and great gameplay — not hype" should be written on the designer's wall.

Lesson Three

First Row Software's game called The Honeymooners took a great license and produced a product with poor gameplay.

The game was designed with several mini-games featuring Ralph and Ed. One game had Ralph driving the streets of New York in his bus picking up various passengers throughout the city. For some reason, the designers had Groucho Marx as one of the random passengers. This gimmick not only added nothing to the game, but the publisher was in violation of copyright and trademark infringements since they had not received permission to use the name Groucho or his likeness.

Research and double-check your sources for storylines, artwork, and sound (especially sound bites).

Lesson: Research is critical and must be accurate. Don't take anything for granted.

Lesson Four

In Capstone/Intercorp's game Search for the Titanic, the player re-enacts the discovery of the *Titanic*.

One of the gimmick features of the game was that the first player to solve the adventure would win a valuable prize. Obviously, the designer didn't want players winning too soon, so the game was made with one extremely difficult level of play. Just before the game's release the licensor, upon learning of the "prize" gimmick, demanded that it be removed. The game was released as a tough, almost impossible to solve adventure. The reaction, as you can imagine, was poor.

Think of designing a Titanic game with multiple levels from novice (easy) to championship (prizeworthy tough). Perhaps the player can master the controls and map out the underwater terrain in the easier levels. In the harder levels, new areas of exploration open up and there are new objects to discover. This multi-level design approach would work whether the "prize" gimmick was offered or not.

For most players, purchasing and spending time playing an extremely tough game is just frustrating and wrong. Players who have conquered lower levels of play and then are elevated to an extremely tough level feel that they have earned the right to be frustrated. Design multiple levels and options of play in your game. For example, when heading toward an iceberg, allow multiple options well in advance. Having only one option, just a straight path through the iceberg, may leave you with a "sink or swim" result.

Lesson: Design multiple scenarios for playing and winning the game. Don't let gimmicks sell the game; let good gameplay sell it.

Lesson Five

Patton Strikes Back from Broderbund was designed by legendary game designer Chris Crawford. He reasoned that war games are fun, yet only a small percentage of game players were buying them. Perhaps that would change if there was a new type of war game designed for the non-wargaming audience. If the game was easier to use, different from the standard hex-based war games, it would reach a larger base of players.

This seemed reasonable; in fact, testers seemed to confirm these thoughts. So what could possibly go awry?

Well, first the sales and marketing people failed to express this new type of "war game for the rest of us" concept. Next, the magazines assigned their "war game" experts to review Patton. These experts were not the intended audience, so they knocked the game for lacking the standard controls, not having hexes, and lacking the NATO markings. Thus the expert war gamers shunned the novice players away from Patton.

Lesson: Sometimes the obvious isn't worth anything.

Lesson Six

In the late 1990s, Southpeak Entertainment had shown me a licensed game design involving the cartoon *The Jetsons*. The Jetsons game was to be a standard space racing game using the characters as drivers.

My response was "What a waste of a great license and a real disappointment for Jetsons fans."

I suggested a Jetsons space road rally game where each player as George Jetson, his wife Jane, daughter Judy, son Elroy, the dog Astro, or Rosie the robot housekeeper would navigate their space car throughout the Jetsons world looking for clues leading to various objects to collect.

Licenses attract an audience who know the property, its characters, venues, storylines, and interactions. Licenses are valuable assets that need to be exploited as an advantage in your game.

Lesson: Use to your advantage your license and its fans.

Index

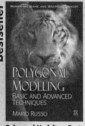

About the CD

The companion CD includes source code for the Tic-Tac-Toe game discussed in the book, a demo version of the game Reel Deal Poker, a chapter on game ideas, and a movie file titled *What Is Machinima?*

These are organized in the following folders:

- PhantomEFX — The Reel Deal Poker Demo is located in this folder. Simply double-click on the setup.exe file to install.

- Wordware — This folder includes the code and other files needed for the Tic-Tac-Toe game presented in Chapter 13, along with an expanded version of the game ideas information in Chapter 4, "Game Concepts and Ideas," in PDF format. You will need Adobe Acrobat Reader, which is available for download at http://www.adobe.com/products/acrobat/readermain.html, to read this file.

- WhatIsMachinima — This folder contains a movie that explains the cinematic art form called "machinima." You will need an application like Windows Media Player or Apple's Quicktime in order to view this file. Permission to reproduce this movie was kindly granted by Frank L. Fox.

The CD contents can be accessed using Windows Explorer.

✗ Caution: By opening the CD package, you accept the terms and conditions of the CD/Source Code Usage License Agreement. Additionally, opening the CD package makes this book nonreturnable.

CD/Source Code Usage License Agreement

Please read the following CD/Source Code usage license agreement before opening the CD and using the contents therein:

1. By opening the accompanying software package, you are indicating that you have read and agree to be bound by all terms and conditions of this CD/Source Code usage license agreement.

2. The compilation of code and utilities contained on the CD and in the book are copyrighted and protected by both U.S. copyright law and international copyright treaties, and is owned by Wordware Publishing, Inc. Individual source code, example programs, help files, freeware, shareware, utilities, and evaluation packages, including their copyrights, are owned by the respective authors.

3. No part of the enclosed CD or this book, including all source code, help files, shareware, freeware, utilities, example programs, or evaluation programs, may be made available on a public forum (such as a World Wide Web page, FTP site, bulletin board, or Internet news group) without the express written permission of Wordware Publishing, Inc. or the author of the respective source code, help files, shareware, freeware, utilities, example programs, or evaluation programs.

4. You may not decompile, reverse engineer, disassemble, create a derivative work, or otherwise use the enclosed programs, help files, freeware, shareware, utilities, or evaluation programs except as stated in this agreement.

5. The software, contained on the CD and/or as source code in this book, is sold without warranty of any kind. Wordware Publishing, Inc. and the authors specifically disclaim all other warranties, express or implied, including but not limited to implied warranties of merchantability and fitness for a particular purpose with respect to defects in the disk, the program, source code, sample files, help files, freeware, shareware, utilities, and evaluation programs contained therein, and/or the techniques described in the book and implemented in the example programs. In no event shall Wordware Publishing, Inc., its dealers, its distributors, or the authors be liable or held responsible for any loss of profit or any other alleged or actual private or commercial damage, including but not limited to special, incidental, consequential, or other damages.

6. One (1) copy of the CD or any source code therein may be created for backup purposes. The CD and all accompanying source code, sample files, help files, freeware, shareware, utilities, and evaluation programs may be copied to your hard drive. With the exception of freeware and shareware programs, at no time can any part of the contents of this CD reside on more than one computer at one time. The contents of the CD can be copied to another computer, as long as the contents of the CD contained on the original computer are deleted.

7. You may not include any part of the CD contents, including all source code, example programs, shareware, freeware, help files, utilities, or evaluation programs in any compilation of source code, utilities, help files, example programs, freeware, shareware, or evaluation programs on any media, including but not limited to CD, disk, or Internet distribution, without the express written permission of Wordware Publishing, Inc. or the owner of the individual source code, utilities, help files, example programs, freeware, shareware, or evaluation programs.

8. You may use the source code, techniques, and example programs in your own commercial or private applications unless otherwise noted by additional usage agreements as found on the CD.

✗ **Warning:** By opening the CD package, you accept the terms and conditions of the CD/Source Code Usage License Agreement. Additionally, opening the CD package makes this book nonreturnable.